Multimodal Transport Law

An accessible introduction to multimodal contracts of carriage, *Multimodal Transport Law* works from general principles toward specific, technical problems. Adopting an international approach, it addresses such key topics as:

- Contracts of carriage
- Transport documents
- The parties to a contract of carriage
- International conventions on the carriage of goods
- Multimodal situations covered by unimodal conventions
- Conflict of laws
- The rules applicable to the individual legs of multimodal contracts of carriage
- The Rotterdam Rules

Providing a close examination of the relevant rules, regulations and case law, this is essential reading for law students, useful for claims handlers and practitioners, and of interest for academics and legislators seeking a better appreciation of multimodal contracts of carriage.

Michiel Spanjaart is an advocate at the law firm Kneppelhout Korthals in Rotterdam, the Netherlands, and an assistant professor at the Erasmus School of Law in Rotterdam. He also teaches multimodal transport law at the National University of Singapore.

Multimodal Transport Law

Michiel Spanjaart

Routledge
Taylor & Francis Group
LONDON AND NEW YORK

First published 2018
by Routledge
2 Park Square, Milton Park, Abingdon, Oxon OX14 4RN

and by Routledge
711 Third Avenue, New York, NY 10017

Routledge is an imprint of the Taylor & Francis Group, an informa business

British Library Cataloguing-in-Publication Data
A catalogue record for this book is available from the British Library

Library of Congress Cataloging-in-Publication Data
Names: Spanjaart, Michiel, author.
Title: Multimodal transport law / Michiel Spanjaart.
Description: New York : Routledge, 2017.
Identifiers: LCCN 2017015286| ISBN 9780415789813 (pbk) | ISBN 9780415789820 (hbk)
Subjects: LCSH: Transportation—Law and legislation. | Shipment of goods—Law and legislation. | Contracts, Maritime. | Transportation, Automotive—Law and legislation. | Rotterdam Rules (2008)
Classification: LCC K4025 .S63 2017 | DDC 343.09/32—dc23
LC record available at https://lccn.loc.gov/2017015286

ISBN: 978-0-415-78982-0 (hbk)
ISBN: 978-0-415-78981-3 (pbk)
ISBN: 978-1-315-21369-9 (ebk)

Typeset in ITC Galliard Std
by Swales & Willis Ltd, Exeter, Devon, UK

Contents

Preface

The idea for this book came up in 2013 when I was asked to teach multimodal transport law at the National University of Singapore. The course did not yet exist at that time, and I was more or less free to devise the structure and select suitable reading materials for the students. In this process I read several books (and many articles) on multimodal transportation, but it seemed that a recent entry-level textbook was missing. Hence the idea behind this book: an introduction to multimodal contracts of carriage, suitable (and affordable) for advanced law students, useful for claims handlers and practitioners, and of interest for academics and legislators.

As so often happens, the project was never entirely mine alone, and I have received a lot of help. Herman Boonk, Stephan Geense, Paul Myburgh, Susan Niessen, Marc Padberg and Jan Teunissen have all read one or two chapters of the manuscript and provided me with valuable recommendations. I have furthermore learned a lot from my discussions with Tobias Eckardt, Stephen Girvin, Olaf Hartenstein and Frank Smeele. Obviously, any remaining mistakes or inadequacies are my own.

1 Introduction

A unimodal contract of carriage requires only one single means of transportation to carry the goods to their destination. This means of transportation will often be a ship, a train, a truck or an airplane. A multimodal contract of carriage requires the use of more than one means of transportation to carry the goods to their destination, for instance one leg by truck from the factory to the port, followed by a sea leg to the port of discharge, and completed by a rail leg to the final destination.

The added value of multimodal transport

The added value of multimodal contracts of carriage can perhaps best be illustrated with an example. A Dutch seller and an American buyer agree on the sale of a shipment of ham. The seller operates from a refrigerated warehouse in the port of Rotterdam; the buyer has adequate storage facilities in the port of Baltimore. The seller loads the shipment of ham in a 20-foot reefer container, and instructs a carrier to carry the goods by sea from Rotterdam to Baltimore for delivery to his buyer.

This contract for the carriage of the shipment of ham by sea is a unimodal contract of carriage. The carrier receives the goods for transportation in the port of loading (Rotterdam) and he only needs one single means of transportation (namely, a sea-going ship) to carry them across the Atlantic for delivery to the buyer/consignee in the port of discharge (Baltimore).

A unimodal contract of carriage of goods by sea works very well in these specific circumstances. In reality, however, only a few buyers and sellers have access to such facilities in the ports of Rotterdam and Baltimore. The average buyer has no facilities in Baltimore at all, and only a production plant in, say, Denver. Besides, it is very likely that the shipment of ham is not even in Rotterdam at the time of the conclusion of the sale, but still needs to be brought in from Parma (Italy). Under these circumstances, a single unimodal contract of carriage by sea only solves part of the logistic puzzle; it does not deal with the transportation to the port of Rotterdam and from the port of Baltimore to the final destination.[1]

The seller could then of course decide to instruct two extra carriers, one to carry the goods by road from Parma to Rotterdam, and another one to carry the goods by rail from Baltimore to Denver. Clearly, this is first of all not very convenient.[2] The seller now not only has to negotiate three separate contracts with three different carriers, but he also has to ensure that the movements of these carriers are aligned. Then there is the additional paperwork. Each carrier will issue a different transport document to evidence his contract of carriage, and these transport documents will in turn very likely refer to different terms and conditions. Moreover, these three different contracts of carriage will probably be governed by different international conventions and/or domestic legislation.

Apart from the inconvenience, however, the three different contracts of carriage will not always provide 100 per cent coverage of the entire voyage. This problem surfaces, for instance, when the goods are stolen in the course of their transhipment from the truck into the ship. The road carrier has already delivered the goods into the custody of the sea carrier, and his liability under the contract of carriage has therewith ended. The sea carrier has indeed received the goods for transportation, but he has validly excluded his liability for the loss of the goods prior to their loading on-board the ship. Under these circumstances, neither of the two carriers would then be liable for the loss.

Another potential risk relates to unlocalized losses, namely when the shipment of ham is stolen somewhere between Parma and Denver, but it cannot be established afterwards when and where this has happened. Each carrier could point to the carelessness, misconduct or even involvement of the other carriers, and at the end of the day they would all escape liability as the seller cannot prove that the loss occurred in one of the respective periods of responsibility.

This is where the multimodal contract of carriage comes in. The seller could also decide to instruct just one carrier to carry the goods by road to Rotterdam, by sea to Baltimore and then by train to Denver. Such a multimodal contract of carriage makes the seller's life a lot easier. Instead of three different contracts of carriage, he now only needs to conclude one contract of carriage. At the same time, his recourse position also improves. Admittedly, the individual legs of this multimodal contract of carriage are still likely to be subject to different rules, but the carrier will not be able to avoid liability for unlocalized losses as he is responsible for the entire voyage.

The structure of the book

In line with its objective to provide an accessible introduction to multimodal transport law, this book works its way up from general principles to very

1 In theory, the shipment of ham could also be flown from Parma to Denver, but that would be a very costly affair.

2 Inconvenience can be overcome in practice. A seller who lacks either the necessary time or the necessary contacts can engage a specialized freight forwarder to arrange for the contract of carriage on his behalf.

specific, multimodal problems.[3] The book does not have a specific civil or common law signature, but instead adopts an international approach. This makes considerable sense as cross-border contracts for the carriage of goods are often governed by international conventions,[4] and only supplemented by domestic legislation.

Still, some conventional rules are applied differently in different countries; see for instance article 2 of the Convention relative au contrat de transport international des Marchandises par Route (CMR). Sometimes principles are simply not universally shared, like the position of the consignee. Some rules have territorial limits (Rome I), and sometimes one specific problem has two fundamentally different solutions, for instance whether the CMR applies directly to an international road leg within a multimodal contract of carriage. The different solutions and interpretations are then clarified with references to literature and case law from both civil law and common law jurisdictions.[5]

The book has nine chapters, the first of which is this introduction. Chapter 2 covers the contract of carriage in general, and the multimodal contract of carriage in particular. This chapter also highlights the differences between contracts of carriage and forwarding contracts. The third chapter discusses the different transport documents, such as charter parties, (through) bills of lading, waybills, consignment notes and their multimodal equivalents. Chapter 4 deals with the parties to a (multimodal) contract of carriage, the right of disposal, the right of suit and the position of the carrier's agents, servants and subcontractors.

The five (most important) international conventions on carriage of goods are discussed in Chapter 5, i.e. the Uniform Rules Concerning the Contract of International Carriage of Goods by Rail (CIM 1999), the Hague Rules as Amended by the Brussels Protocol 1968 (HVR), the Convention for the Unification of Certain Rules for International Carriage by Air (MC), CMR and the Budapest Convention on the Contract for the Carriage of Goods by Inland Waterway (CMNI). Some of these conventions regulate (potentially) multimodal situations, and these situations are dealt with in Chapter 6. Chapter 7 is then dedicated to the law that applies in the absence of an international convention. It covers the common law conflict rules, Rome I and the general Paramount clause in (bill of lading) contracts of carriage.

The different issues discussed in these last three chapters come together in Chapter 8. This chapter deals with the question of which rules apply to the

3 As an introduction to multimodal transport law, the book is obviously far from exhaustive. The carriage of goods by sea under the United Nations Convention on the Carriage of Goods by Sea of 31 March 1978 (Hamburg Rules), the carriage of dangerous goods and the shipper's liability are hardly discussed. Several carriage-related issues, such as salvage, casualties, the position of passengers, the arrest of ships and global limitation of liability, have in fact been left completely untouched.

4 For convenience's sake, all references are straight to the provisions of the conventions, for instance article 1 (b) HVR or 17 (4) CMR, even though they require incorporation in jurisdictions with a dualist system.

5 Obviously, this required a lot of translation work. The translations in the book are the author's, except when an English version was already available, for instance of the provisions of the German Commercial Code (GCC) and the Dutch Forwarding Conditions.

individual legs of a multimodal contract of carriage. These legs are sometimes governed by one of the international conventions, sometimes by mandatory domestic law and sometimes by contractual provisions.

Finally, Chapter 9 covers the Rotterdam Rules (RR). These rules have not yet entered into force, but they are meant to replace the HVR in due course. However, the RR do not just relate to contracts for the carriage of goods by sea (under a bill of lading); they also cover multimodal contracts of carriage, provided that a sea leg is involved.

2 Contracts of carriage

This chapter introduces the contract of carriage in general and the multimodal contract of carriage in particular, and it distinguishes contracts of carriage from forwarding contracts.

2.1. The contract of carriage

A contract for the carriage goods encompasses more than just their physical carriage between two points. The contract indeed requires the carrier to carry the goods from one place to another, but in addition requires the carrier to deliver them to the consignee.[1] A contract of carriage could therefore be defined as a contract whereby the carrier agrees with the shipper to carry certain goods from the place of receipt and to deliver them to the consignee at the place of their destination.

Receipt and delivery

The receipt of the goods by the carrier and their delivery to the consignee mark the start and finish of each contract of carriage. The carrier only assumes his responsibilities upon receipt of the goods for transportation, and he is only discharged from these responsibilities once he delivers the goods to the consignee. Lord Diplock described the nature of the contract of carriage (by sea) in *Barclays Bank v. Commissioners of Customs and Excise*:[2]

> The contract for the carriage of goods by sea ... is a combined contract of bailment and transportation under which the shipowner undertakes to accept possession of the goods from the shipper, to carry them to their contractual destination and there to surrender possession of them to the person who, under the terms of the contract, is entitled to obtain possession of them

1 See also § 407 (1) GCC: 'By virtue of the contract of carriage the carrier is obliged to carry the goods to their destination and there to deliver them to the consignee.'

2 *Barclays Bank v. Commissioners of Customs and Excise* (1963) 1 Lloyd's Rep. 81.

> from the shipowners. Such a contract is not discharged by performance until the shipowner has actually surrendered possession (that is, has divested himself of all powers to control any physical dealing in the goods) to the person entitled under the terms of the contract to obtain possession of them.[3]

The receipt and delivery of the goods is different to the loading and discharge of the goods. The process of bringing goods into a means of transportation (loading) and taking them out again (discharging) is factual. The process of receipt and delivery, however, is consensual. The carrier on the one hand and consignor/consignee of the goods on the other must have the intention to abandon or accept the actual control over the goods. The Dutch Supreme Court held in *Tele Tegelen v. Stain Alloys*:[4]

> For the delivery of goods by a carrier, an agreement thereto between the carrier and the consignee is required: the carrier cannot just 'leave the goods on the doorstep' (unless the consignee has asked for delivery in this way, but then there is an agreement thereto). The consignee will often receive the goods after discharge. In cases whereby it is agreed that the consignee arranges for discharge himself, it can be sufficient for a valid delivery that the carrier transfers the actual control over the goods to the consignee, e.g. by release of the keys to the container or by opening the doors in the presence of the consignee and allow him access to his truck, after which the consignee then discharges the goods.

Within these boundaries, the parties are perfectly free to agree how the delivery under the contract of carriage should take place.[5] The delivery under a contract of carriage will often be achieved by the physical handover of the goods to the consignee, but may just as well be achieved by their delivery to one of his agents, a warehouse of his choice or a subsequent carrier.[6]

3 Bailment is a common law concept whereby a bailor gives property in possession (goods in the case of a contract of carriage) to the bailee for safekeeping, storage, carriage or another reason, and this bailee is held to return these goods to the bailor or a third party. If the bailee fails to return the goods he is liable in bailment. Bailment 'represents a conveyance of personal property created by contract and enforceable in tort'; see N.E. Palmer, *Palmer on bailment* (Thomson Reuters, 2009), 1.

4 HR 17 February 2012, S&S 2012/60 (*Tele Tegelen v. Stain Alloys*).

5 There is an exception to this rule, namely when the goods are carried under a bill of lading. The delivery is then still consensual, but requires the presentation of an original bill of lading.

6 The Dutch Supreme Court held in the *Sriwijaya* (HR 5 September 1997, NJ 1998, 63, S&S 1997/121) that the carrier may also have delivered the goods even though they are still in his care, yet under a different agreement: 'Delivery can take place because the carried goods are brought under the actual control of the one entitled thereto or in that of a third party representing the one entitled thereto. It can furthermore not be excluded that carried goods upon arrival at the destination, pursuant to a different agreement with the one entitled thereto, either remain in the care of the carrier, or in the care of the one that held the goods pursuant to an agreement with the carrier, and that in those cases the contract of carriage ends once this other agreement commences.'

Receptum nautarum

This obligation to deliver the goods to the consignee at their destination can be traced back to Roman times. The carrier (together with the stable holder and the innkeeper) apparently enjoyed a rather dubious reputation in those days. It was therefore necessary to ensure that the goods (or horses, luggage/personal belongings) were indeed either returned to their owner or delivered to the consignee at their destination. To achieve this objective, the owner was given an action against the carrier if his goods were somehow 'lost' on the way and could not be returned.

This action was known as the 'receptum nautarum',[7] and it is safe to say that the concept has stood the test of time. Both the rule and the ratio behind the 'receptum nautarum' were for instance unambiguously affirmed in early English case law. The carrier was liable for damage to the goods in his care unless he could rely on one of the few exemptions recognized at common law.[8] This meant that the carrier would have to prove that the damage was indeed the result of an exempted cause, and the decision in *Forward v. Pittard* shows that this was far from an easy task.[9]

Pittard ran a public road wagon service between London and Shaftsbury, and Forward engaged him for the carriage of '12 pockets of hops'.[10] The wagon made a scheduled stop at Andover where the goods were stored for the night in a warehouse. That night a fierce fire broke out in another warehouse, so fierce in fact that the fire leapt over to the warehouse where Forward's goods were stored. The cause of the fire remained unknown and negligence on the part of Pittard could not be established, but the court held the carrier liable for the damage all the same:[11]

> The question is, whether this common carrier is liable in this case of fire? It appears from all the cases from 100 years back, that there are events for which the carrier is liable independent of his contract. By the nature of his contract, he is liable for all due care and diligence; and for any negligence he is suable under his contract. But there is a further degree of responsibility by the custom of the realm, that is, by the common law; a carrier is in the nature of an insurer. It is laid down that he is liable for every accident, except by the act of God, or the King's enemies.

7 'Nautae caupones stabularii quod cuiusque salvum fore receperint nisi restituent in eos iudicium dabo.' In a (rather) free translation from Latin to English: I give an action against carriers, inn keepers and stable holders who receive goods in their care but do not return these.

8 In civil law jurisdictions, these exemptions were codified in domestic legislation a few years later; see for instance article 345 (2) of the Dutch Commercial Code of 1838 stipulating that the carrier was liable for all damages to the goods, unless these damages were caused by an inherent vice of the goods, force majeure or the fault or negligence of the shipper.

9 *Forward v. Pittard* (1785) 99 ER 953.

10 These pockets were in fact large jute sacks with 64 kg of hop each.

11 *Forward v. Pittard* (1785) 99 ER 953.

The common law at that time recognized only two exemptions: an act of God or an act of the King's enemies. All other causes (including the unknown causes) remained for the account of the carrier since he was liable for the goods in his care as if he were an insurer. The ratio behind this division of the onus of proof was painfully stressed in *Riley v. Horne*.[12] Dealing with the disappearance of a shipment of silk in the course of its voyage from London to Kettering by coach, Best CJ said:

> If they should be lost or injured by the grossest negligence of the carrier or his servants, or stolen by them, or by thieves in collusion with them, the owner would be unable to prove either of these causes of loss; his witnesses must be the carrier's servants, and they, knowing that they could not be contradicted, would excuse their masters and themselves. To give due security to property, the law has added the responsibility of a carrier, which immediately rises out of his contract to carry for a reward, namely, that of taking all reasonable care of it, the responsibility of an insurer. From his liability as an insurer, the carrier is only relieved by two things, ..., the act of God and the King's enemies.

The carrier's '*liability as an insurer*' meant that he had to do better than his best endeavours during the voyage. The obligation to deliver the goods to the consignee implied that the carrier had to achieve a certain result: he had to ensure that the goods were delivered at their destination in the same (sound) condition as in which they were received for transportation. The carrier would only be exempted from liability in the case of an act of God or an act of the King's enemies, and he was liable for the damage resulting from all other causes. These other causes would include the unknown causes as the carrier could clearly not be trusted.[13]

Contractual exemptions of liability

The two common law exemptions – an act of God and an act of the King's enemies – applied to every contract of carriage, but the decision in *Riley v. Horne* suggested that they could be extended with additional exemptions in individual contracts of carriage.

Horne had put up a notice in the Blue Boar, a public house and the starting point of the coach service. The notice said that he would not be responsible for shipments with a value of more than 5*l*.[14] Ultimately, this particular notice was held to be ineffective as it was unlikely to have reached the owner of the silk, but its consideration in *Riley v. Horne* shows that the court was not principally opposed to such a contractual exemption of liability, provided that sufficient

12 *Riley v. Horne* (1828) 130 ER 1044.

13 *Forward v. Pittard* (1785) 99 ER 953; *Riley v. Horne* (1828) 130 ER 1044.

14 The silk in question was allegedly worth 46*l*.

notice was given and the carrier had not caused the loss through his gross negligence.[15]

By the second half of the nineteenth century, the use of contractual exemptions of liability had become widespread, especially when the goods were carried by sea under a bill of lading. The British supremacy at sea was at its peak at that time. In the absence of any serious competition the British ship owners could more or less dictate their terms and conditions, and obviously they did. A typical negligence clause in those days would exclude liability for:[16]

> The act of God, the Queen's enemies, pirates, restraint of princes and rulers, perils of the sea, rivers, navigation and land transit, of whatever nature or kind, restrictions at port of discharge, loss or damage from delays, collisions, straining, explosion, heat, fire, steam boilers and machinery or defects therein, transhipment, escape, accidents, suffocation, mortality, disease or deterioration in value, negligence, default or error in judgment of pilots, master, mariners, engineers, stevedores, or any other person in the employ of the steamship or of the owners or their agents.

Whereas the 'liability as an insurer' might have been a little harsh on the carriers, the balance had now completely shifted to other side. The carriers excluded their liability for just about every conceivable event, including the unseaworthiness of the ship and their own negligence, leaving the cargo-interested parties without any serious prospect of recovery.

The need for rules

This was an unsustainable situation, and at the end of the nineteenth century the merchants and ship owners met on several occasions to discuss a solution.[17] The delegates were actually able to agree on a standard bill of lading form without the catch all negligence clauses, but its use was not mandatorily imposed. Given their unchallenged position in the market, the ship owners really did not have any incentive to part with their negligence clauses and this 'common form' was therefore never generally adopted.[18]

As the matter could apparently not be resolved amicably, Ohio Congressman Harter then successfully introduced national legislation to restrict the use of contractual exemptions of liability within the US.[19] The Harter Act of 1893 applied

15 Best CJ held: 'Although a carrier may prove that the owner of goods knew that the carrier had limited his responsibility by a sufficient notice, yet, if a loss be occasioned by gross negligence, the notice will not protect him.'

16 This is the negligence clause in The *Caledonia* (1895) 157 U.S. 124.

17 The delegations met in Liverpool in 1882, and later in Hamburg in 1885 and in London in 1887 to try and agree on a standard bill of lading form.

18 See F. Berlingieri (ed.) *The Travaux Préparatoires of the Hague Rules and the Hague-Visby Rules* (CMI: Antwerp, 1997) 16.

19 Act of 13 February 1893, Chap. 105, 27 Stat. 445–6, 46 U.S. Code Appendix 190–6.

to all incoming and outgoing carriage by sea, and specifically targeted the infamous negligence clauses in the bill of lading.[20] All clauses excluding or limiting the carrier's liability for either the unseaworthiness of the ship or the negligence of the crew were rendered null and void.[21]

The Harter Act proved to be very successful.[22] Several other countries such as Australia, New Zealand, Fiji and Canada adopted similar rules in the first decade of the twentieth century, and the ship owners soon found themselves more often than not confronted with mandatory, merchant-friendly legislation. When the discussions on a balanced regime were resumed after the First World War, the ship owners were this time genuinely eager to participate.[23]

The delegates representing ship owners, merchants and bankers met in The Hague for the first time in 1921. Initially, the objective was to try and agree on a 'code', but the delegates eventually produced an international convention.[24] The Hague Rules were signed in 1924,[25] and were later amended with the Visby Protocol in 1968 (HVR).[26] The rules govern contracts of carriage by sea covered by a bill of lading or similar document of title.[27]

International conventions on carriage of goods

Meanwhile, in continental Europe, the first international transport convention had by then already entered into force. The uniform rules 'Concernant le transport

20 The *Delaware* (1896) 161 U.S. 459.

21 Sections 190 and 191 of the Harter Act read: 'It shall not be lawful for the manager, agent, master, or owner of any vessel transporting merchandise or property from or between ports of the United States and foreign ports to insert in any bill of lading or shipping document any clause, covenant, or agreement whereby it, he, or they shall be relieved from liability for loss or damage arising from negligence, fault, or failure in proper loading, stowage, custody, care, or proper delivery of any and all lawful merchandise or property committed to its or their charge. Any and all words or clauses of such import inserted in bills of lading or shipping receipts shall be null and void and of no effect.'

'It shall not be lawful for any vessel transporting merchandise or property from or between ports of the United States of America and foreign ports, her owner, master, agent, or manager, to insert in any bill of lading or shipping document any covenant or agreement whereby the obligations of the owner or owners of said vessel to exercise due diligence to properly equip, man, provision, and outfit said vessel, and to make said vessel seaworthy and capable of performing her intended voyage, or whereby the obligations of the master, officers, agents, or servants to carefully handle and stow her cargo and to care for and properly deliver same, shall in any wise be lessened, weakened, or avoided.'

22 P. Myburgh, *Uniformity or unilateralism in the law of carriage of goods by sea?* (2000) 31 VUWLR 359.

23 F. Berlingieri (ed.) *The Travaux Préparatoires of the Hague Rules and the Hague-Visby Rules* (CMI: Antwerp, 1997) 35.

24 A draft code was circulated in advance. This initial draft covered all contracts of carriage by sea (just like the Harter Act), but the Hague Rules only relate to contracts of carriage under a bill of lading.

25 The Brussels Convention for the Unification of Certain Rules of Law relating to Bills of Lading of 25 August 1924.

26 The Brussels Convention for the Unification of Certain Rules of Law relating to Bills of Lading of 25 August 1924 as amended by the Visby Protocol of 23 February 1968.

27 Article I (b) HR/HVR.

international ferroviaire des marchandises' (CIM) were signed in 1890 in Bern (Switzerland).[28] Whereas the CIM initially started off as a European convention, it now has a geographical reach as far east as Pakistan. The convention governs the rights and obligations of the parties under a contract of carriage of goods by rail.[29] It has seen several amendments over the years; the most recent of these amendments was agreed upon in Vilnius (Latvia) in 1999.[30]

For obvious reasons, there was no immediate need for the regulation of international carriage by air at the turn of the century.[31] Still, the Convention for the Unification of Certain Rules Relating to International Carriage by Air is only a few years younger than the Hague Rules.[32] The Warsaw Convention was signed in 1929 and has been amended several times.[33] By the end of the twentieth century, however, the initial text of the convention had been amended so often with additional protocols that it was eventually replaced by an entirely new convention, the Montreal Convention of 1999 (MC).[34]

The international carriage of goods by road was regulated in 1956 in the Convention relative au contrat de transport international de Marchandises par Route (CMR). The territorial reach of the CMR, other than the more global reach of the HVR and the MC, has remained limited to Europe and several Eurasian and North African countries. The convention has not been amended over the years.

The youngest of the conventions covered in this book is the Convention relative au contrat de transport de Marchandises en Navigation Intérieure (CMNI). This convention was signed in Budapest (Hungary) in 2001; it governs the international carriage of goods by inland waterways. The CMNI is (as yet) a strictly European affair; the Ukraine forms the outer boundary in the east.

Although some of these international conventions also cater for certain multimodal situations,[35] they are basically designed to cover cross-border carriage by one specific means of transportation. Their system of liability still follows the Roman concept of the receptum nautarum. The carrier is liable for the loss of or

28 The Act of Mainz (1831) and the Act of Mannheim (1868, and still in force) are even older, but they provide rules of public law for inland vessels sailing on the river Rhine.

29 The uniform rules 'Concernant le transport international ferroviaire des voyageurs et des bagages' (CIV) regulates the transportation of luggage and passengers.

30 The amended Convention of Bern is sometimes referred to as Cotif-CIM. The amendments over the years were brought together under the auspices of the Organisation intergouvernementale pour les Transport Internationaux Ferroviaire (OTIF) in Cotif 1980. The CIM forms appendix B to this convention, hence the reference to Cotif-CIM.

31 In fact, the convention is surprisingly old considering that the Wright brothers were the first to fly an airplane in 1903 and Charles Lindbergh only crossed the Atlantic in 1927.

32 Although the timing might suggest otherwise, the Warsaw convention was not modelled on the Hague Rules, but instead on the Convention of Bern of 1890 on international rail carriage.

33 The Hague Protocol of 1955, the Guadalajara Convention of 1961, the Guatemala City protocol of 1971 and the four Montreal Protocols of 1975. The Warsaw Convention in fact still applies in some trades.

34 The Convention for the Unification of Certain Rules for International Carriage by Air, signed at Montreal on 28 May 1999 (Montreal Convention).

35 These situations are discussed in Chapter 6.

damage to the goods in his care, unless he can invoke one of the conventional exemptions, immunities and limitations of liability. The carrier cannot circumvent this system of liability as all these conventions provide for mandatory law.[36]

2.2. Multimodal contracts of carriage

In the spring of 1956 a modified tanker by the name of Ideal X carried 58 containers from Newark (US) to Houston (US). Only one year later the Gateway City completed the same voyage, but this time with 226 containers stacked on top of each other. By 1970 the container had already become more or less indispensable for the (door-to-door) carriage of general cargo.

A container is a steel box with a length of either 20 or 40 foot, a width of 8 foot and a height of 8 foot.[37] Differently sized containers circulate as well, but they are exceptions to the rule.[38] The standard 20 by 8 by 8-foot container equals one TEU,[39] the standard unit to indicate the capacity of a container ship.[40] The container not only fits most means of transportation; its rectangular shape also allows for an economic use of the available space on the ship, truck or train.[41]

Besides, the use of containers has several very practical advantages. Containers are made of steel. They are not very expensive, but they are all the same very strong. They will easily last for years and they are (usually) watertight. As such, they provide excellent protection for the goods inside, not only against the elements but also against rough handling in the course of the voyage.

It is difficult to underestimate the impact of the use of containers on the development of multimodal transport. The carriage of goods by more than one means of transportation was obviously possible (and practised) well before 1970, but the recurring problem was the goods always had to be transhipped at least once in the course of the voyage. This meant that the goods needed to be discharged from one means of transportation, sometimes stored for a short period of time,

36 Articles 5 CIM 1999, III (8) HVR, 49 MC, 41 CMR and 25 (1) CMNI.

37 Article 2.1 of the International Convention for Safe Containers 1972 allows for more flexibility in its definition of the container, though: 'Container means an article of transport equipment: (a) of a permanent character and accordingly strong enough to be suitable for repeated use; (b) specially designed to facilitate the transport of goods, by one or more modes of transport, without intermediate reloading; (c) designed to be secured and/or readily handled, having corner fittings for these purposes; (d) of a size such that the area enclosed by the four outer bottom corners is either: (i) at least 14 sq. m. (150 sq. ft.) or (ii) at least 7 sq. m. (75 sq. ft.) if it is fitted with top corner fittings; the term "container" includes neither vehicles nor packaging; however, containers when carried on chassis are included.'

38 The height of the container will sometimes, for instance, be 8.5 foot. Smaller-sized containers are often used for carriage of goods by air. The bigger aircraft can, however, also accommodate standard size air containers; see the AGA 20-ft box container for Boeing 747 and 777.

39 Twenty-foot Equivalent Unit.

40 The capacity of modern container ships, such as the Emma Maersk and her sister ships, easily exceeds 10,000 TUE.

41 The rectangular shape also allows for an economic use of the available space within the containers itself, especially when the container is stuffed with (again rectangular) boxes, cartons or palletized goods.

and then loaded onto another means of transportation for the continuation of the voyage. The transhipment of the goods during the voyage thus implied additional costs, additional delays and additional risks.

The containerization of goods has brought these costs, delays and risks back to a minimum. The standard size makes it very easy to discharge containers from one means of transportation and to load them onto the next means of transportation in one and the same movement. The use of containers is therefore particularly attractive in multimodal contracts of carriage as it reduces the chances of damage to the goods during the voyage in general, and during the transhipment operations in particular.

The definition of a multimodal contract of carriage

A multimodal contract of carriage is obviously a contract of carriage, and its definition therefore closely resembles the definition of a contract of carriage in general. A multimodal contract of carriage is a contract whereby the carrier agrees with the shipper to carry certain goods from the place of receipt using more than one means of transportation and to deliver them to the consignee at the place of their destination.[42]

Similar definitions of a multimodal contract of carriage are found in the different domestic legislations on multimodal transport law, but these definitions may impose additional requirements. § 452 of the German Commercial Code (GCC), for instance, demands that 'at least two of these contracts would have been subject to different legal rules.'[43]

Article 102 of the Maritime Code of the People's Republic of China (CMC), for instance, requires a sea leg, and defines the multimodal contract of carriage as 'a contract under which the multimodal transport operator undertakes to transport the goods, against the payment of freight for the entire transport, from the place where the goods were received in his charge to the destination and to deliver them to the consignee by two or more different modes of transport, one of which being sea carriage'.

The Indian Multimodal Transportation of Goods Act (IMTGA) requires cross-border carriage. Article 2 (k) IMTGA defines multimodal transport as 'carriage of goods, by at least two different modes of transport under a multimodal transport contract, from the place of acceptance of the goods in India to a place of delivery of the goods outside India'.

The reference to 'multimodal contracts of carriage' is widely adopted, but certainly not exclusive.[44] Contracts of carriage within this definition are sometimes

42 See also article 103 CMC: 'The responsibility of the multimodal transport operator with respect to the goods under multimodal transport contract covers the period from the time he takes the goods in his charge to the time of their delivery.'

43 A contract of carriage under German law, partly by rail and partly by road, is therefore not a multimodal contract of carriage as both legs are subject to the regime of § 407 GCC and further.

44 The term 'multimodal transport' seems to be widely accepted, but the Dutch Civil Code, for instance, refers to combined transport ('gecombineerd vervoer').

also referred to as 'intermodal' or 'combined' contracts of carriage. It is submitted that there is no material difference between multimodal, intermodal and combined transport. They are just different names for the same concept.[45]

The different requirements for multimodal transport

A means of transportation includes ships, trucks, trains, barges, airplanes or any other means by which the goods can be carried.[46] Warehouses, terminals or tanks are obviously not means of transportation, and the storage of the goods prior to, in the course of or following the actual carriage does not convert a unimodal contract of carriage into a multimodal contract of carriage.

A multimodal contract of carriage needs to involve two or more of these different means of transportation. A contract of carriage by road, whereby the goods are transhipped into a different truck halfway, and then carried to the final destination for their delivery to the consignee, is therefore still a unimodal contract of carriage of goods by road as the two different trucks are one and the same means of transportation.

The carriage by a certain means of transportation must be able to stand on its own feet. This implies that the carriage of the goods with a specific means of transportation must constitute a separate leg within a multimodal contract of carriage. A contract for the carriage of goods by sea, whereby the goods are discharged from the sea-going vessel into small barges for their delivery to the terminal,[47] is therefore still a unimodal contract of carriage. Indeed, two different means of transportation are necessary to complete the voyage, but the barge service within the port area is ancillary to the contract of carriage by sea. The barge service facilitates the carriage of goods by sea, and as such it is absorbed by the unimodal contract of carriage by sea.[48]

Conversely, a contract for the carriage of goods, whereby the goods are first carried on-board a sea-going vessel, and then discharged into barges for their further transportation by river to an inland terminal, is a multimodal contract of carriage. Once again, two different means of transportation are necessary to complete the voyage, but this time the carriage by inland waterways stands on

45 R. de Wit, *Multimodal transport* (LLP: London, 1995) 4; M. Clarke, *Contracts of carriage by air* (Lloyd's List: London, 2010) 192: 'Combined carriage (also called multimodal or intermodal carriage)'.

46 A means of transportation is not exactly the same as a 'modality' or a 'mode of transport'; see, for instance, article 2 (j) IMTGA: '"mode of transport" means carriage of goods by road, air, rail, inland waterways, or sea.' Strictly speaking, a ship is then a means of transportation that could be used for the carriage of goods by two modalities or modes of transport, but confusion in this respect is unlikely to occur. In fact, in the case of carriage of goods under the CMNI, the reference to a means instead of a mode is probably more accurate as the international carriage of goods with a single ship, mainly on inland waterways, but also in waters to which maritime regulations apply, is a unimodal contract of carriage.

47 The bigger sea-going vessels are sometimes simply too big to reach the terminal, for instance because they are too long for the quay or because the port area is not deep enough.

48 HR 28 November 1997, S&S 1998/33 (*General Vargas*).

its own feet. It is not an ancillary service, it is not absorbed by the contract of carriage by sea and it constitutes a separate leg within the multimodal contract of carriage.[49]

Transhipment in the course of a multimodal contact of carriage

The discharge of the goods from one means of transportation and their subsequent reloading into the next are obviously transport-related operations, but they do not qualify as individual transport legs. All the same, the transhipment of the goods occasionally requires their transportation in the process. This raises the question of whether the transportation of the goods in the course of transhipment constitutes a separate leg within a multimodal contract of carriage.

In principle, the transportation of the goods in the course of transhipment will not qualify as an individual leg.[50] In the *Salar*, for instance, a trailer with deep-frozen chicken was pulled by a so-called 'tugmaster' to cover the few hundred metres between the sea terminal in Vlissingen (the Netherlands) and the ship. The idea was to follow the same procedure later upon arrival in Sheerness (UK), but both the trailer and the goods went overboard during the sea passage. The cargo-interested parties argued that the transportation at the terminal qualified as carriage by road,[51] but the Court of Appeal in The Hague disagreed:[52]

> Decisive for the question at hand is whether the parties intended to perform part of the carriage by road. There is no support for an affirmative answer to that question in the circumstances of the case. ... The mere fact that the trailer was carried on own premises from Olau Line Vlissingen to the ship by means of a tugmaster and the same modus operandi would have been followed in Sheerness does not imply that the parties intended to perform part of the carriage by road.

A similar case was brought before the German Supreme Court in 2007, and a similar conclusion was reached. In this case a box with printing machinery fell off a so-called 'Mafi-trailer' in the course of transportation over a distance of 300 metres from the ship to a truck. The Hamburg Court of Appeal had earlier qualified this transportation as a separate leg within the multimodal contract of carriage,[53] but the Supreme Court held that the transhipment operation formed part of the upcoming road leg:[54]

49 This discussion is also relevant for an understanding of article 18 (4) MC; see Chapter 6.

50 BGH 3 November 2005, TranspR 2006, 35; I. Koller *Die Rechtsnatur des Umschlagvertages und ihre Bedeutung fur die Teilstrecke* TranspR 2008, 333.

51 If that were correct, the Dutch courts would have had jurisdiction on the basis of article 31 CMR. If not, the case would have to be referred to London arbitrators.

52 Hof's-Gravenhage 17 October 1995, S&S 1996/54 (*Salar*).

53 OLG Hamburg 19 August 2004 TranspR 2004, 402, discussed (amongst others) by R. Herber, *Nochmals: Multimodalvertrag, Güterumschlag und anwendbares Recht* TranspR (2005) 59.

54 BGH 18 October 2007, TranspR 2007, 472.

> Still, the transportation of the goods after their discharge from the ship within the port area to the truck with which the on-carriage had to be performed, contrary to the opinion of the court of appeal, cannot be seen as an individual (land) leg. ... The circumstances of the case – transportation of the goods on a Mafi-trailer within the port area over a distance of 300 metres – do not suggest a different assessment.

It is submitted that the qualification ultimately depends on the underlying reason for the transportation. If the goods are carried (for a few hundred metres within a confined area) to facilitate their transhipment, then clearly the transportation will not constitute a separate leg within a multimodal contract of carriage. This may be different, though, if the goods are transhipped to be carried onwards, for instance into a truck (instead of a tugmaster or Mafi-trailer) and to a destination beyond the terminal premises, or when there are other 'special circumstances' to support its qualification as a separate leg within a multimodal contract of carriage.[55]

Implied multimodal contracts of carriage

It is easy enough to recognize a multimodal contract of carriage if the contract prescribes that the goods must first be carried by train to the airport, then by air for the second leg and finally by road for delivery to the consignee. In practice, however, the contracting parties often fail to specify the means of transportation in their contract. The qualification of the contract of carriage as either unimodal or multimodal then depends on the circumstances of the case at hand.[56]

The value and the size of the goods will often give a first indication. A contract for the carriage of a box of jewellery from Alice Springs (Australia) to Singapore may remain silent on the means of transportation, and yet it is surely a unimodal contract of carriage by air. The box of jewellery is light and very valuable, and its carriage by air, albeit certainly more expensive than by any other means of transportation, is the safest, quickest and in fact only viable option in the given circumstances.

The exact same contract of carriage between Alice Springs and Singapore, however, would surely be multimodal if the box of jewellery were exchanged for a large industrial crane. The crane is too big and too heavy to be carried by air, and since Alice Springs lies in the middle of Australia and the Indian Ocean and Java Sea need to be crossed to reach Singapore, multimodal transportation is the

55 BGH 3 November 2005, TranspR 2006, 35: 'The question whether the transhipment within the sea terminal qualifies as a separate leg ... must in any case be answered with no when – as in this case – there are no special circumstances in this respect.' I. Koller, *Die Rechtsnatur des Umschlagvertages und ihre Bedeutung fur die Teilstrecke* TranspR (2008) 333 says at 339 that transhipment will only constitute a separate leg in 'Extremfällen', i.e. exceptional circumstances.

56 Verheyen gives an example whereby goods are carried from the US to a destination in Europe, neither at a port nor at an airport and also refers to OLG Karlsruhe 18 May 2011, 18 U 23/10 (otherwise unpublished). W. Verheyen, *Contractuele aansprakelijkheid van vervoersintegratoren* (Diss.: Leuven, 2013) 365.

only available option. The crane will have to be carried by road or rail from Alice Springs to Darwin (or another Australian port), and will subsequently have to be carried by sea to Singapore. Even if the contract of carriage fails to specify the use of more than one means of transportation, the circumstances of the case really leave no other choice.

Optional contracts of carriage

Whereas some contracts of carriage remain silent on the means of transportation, others explicitly give the carrier the freedom to choose the means of transportation. These optional contracts of carriage are common practice in the case of parcel delivery services, provided by companies such as DHL, UPS, TNT and FedEx. The DHL Express standard terms and conditions for instance contain the following provision:[57]

> 'Shipment' means all documents or parcels that travel under one waybill and which may be carried by any means DHL chooses, including air, road or any other carrier.

The carrier will obviously want to select the most cost-efficient routing, and this may vary per package. Under normal circumstances, for instance, the easiest, cheapest and fastest way to carry a package from Zurich (Switzerland) to Luxemburg is probably by road. All the same, if the package can easily be consolidated with another shipment bound for the airport of Liege (Belgium), it may very well be more cost-efficient, albeit perhaps not faster, to carry the package by air to Liege, and then by either truck or van to Luxembourg.

An optional contract of carriage can therefore not immediately be qualified as either unimodal or multimodal. Instead, the qualification remains open until the actual transportation of the goods. The contract of carriage only loses its optional character once the carrier has selected the means of transportation.[58] If the carrier decides to carry the goods by just one means of transportation, the contract of carriage is unimodal. If the goods are carried by more than one means of transportation, however, it is a multimodal contract of carriage.

Fleximodal contracts of carriage

The approach of optional contracts of carriage as described above is followed in the UK, Germany and the Netherlands, but it is not followed in Belgium. A contract for the carriage of a package from one place to another whereby the means of transportation has not been agreed beforehand, and whereby the carrier

57 This provision comes from the terms and conditions of DHL Express, given in fact under the heading: 'Important notice'.

58 See, for instance, in the UK, Germany and the Netherlands respectively, *Datec v. UPS* (2007) 2 Lloyd's Rep. 114; BGH 29 June 2006, TranspR 2006, 466; Hof's-Gravenhage, 28 November 2007, S&S 2008/28 (*DHL v. Landis*).

is instead free to choose the most efficient means of transportation, qualifies as a fleximodal contract under Belgian law.[59]

In *TNT v. Mitsui* the carrier/contractor had negotiated the freedom to choose any means of transportation. TNT ultimately decided to carry the package by road, but that decision did not affect the qualification of the contract afterwards. The Belgian Supreme Court held that the agreement to carry the goods by road should have been reached at the time of the conclusion of the contract to qualify as a contract for the carriage of goods by road in the sense of article 1 CMR:[60]

> Considering that, the application of the CMR requires the existence of an agreement with respect to the carriage of goods by road; That this condition is not met when the agreement fails to determine the manner of transportation and it does not follow from the circumstances of the case either that the parties had intended the carriage by road.

The Belgian Supreme Court therewith upheld the decision of the lower court that the prior consensus to carry the goods by road was a *condition sine qua non* for the application of the CMR,[61] this notwithstanding the fact that the carrier had in fact carried the package in question by road from Londerzeel (Belgium) to Belm (Germany).[62] Instead, the Belgian Supreme Court qualified the contract as a *sui generis* package delivery contract.[63]

This is a controversial decision, and one with serious consequences as *sui generis* package delivery contracts are not governed by any international convention on the carriage of goods.[64] It is submitted that the decision in *TNT v. Mitsui* is far too formalistic. The carrier can obviously negotiate the freedom to choose the most efficient means of transportation, but that freedom cannot affect the general nature of the agreement, i.e. a contract of carriage. The negotiated freedom only relates to the means of transportation, and once the carrier has made his choice, that initial freedom is spent. The contract is then either a unimodal or a multimodal contract of carriage depending on the (one or more) chosen means of transportation, but certainly not a *sui generis* package delivery contract.[65]

59 W. Verheyen, *Fleximodal contracts and CMR: The Belgian approach* (2012) 18 JIML 364.

60 Hof van Cassatie 8 November 2004, *TNT v. Mitsui* (2006) ETL 228.

61 The Supreme Court's reference to the circumstances of the case has had little effect in practice. The circumstances that a package had to be delivered that same day in combination with the fact that a distance of approximately 100 kilometers had to be covered were not enough as the court held that the possibility of carriage by train could not be discarded. Hof van Beroep Brussels, 2 September 2011, 2008/AR/1077 (*DPD Belgium v. Timmermans*).

62 In fact, the lower court (Vredegerecht Overijse-Zaventem) had said that the manner in which the carrier performed the instruction to deliver the goods at their destination was 'completely irrelevant'.

63 Hof van Cassatie 8 November 2004, *TNT v. Mitsui* (2006) ETL 228.

64 See, for instance, K.F. Haak at the SVA 50 years CMR seminar: 'Optional carriage may not lead to outlaw carriage.'

65 See in great depth on fleximodal contracts of carriage, freight integration and the consequences for the liability: W. Verheyen, *Contractuele aansprakelijkheid van vervoersintegratoren* (Diss.: Leuven, 2013).

International conventions on multimodal carriage of goods

Whereas unimodal contracts of carriage are often governed by international conventions, there is at present no such convention to govern multimodal contracts of carriage. It has been tried in the past, though, and it is in fact currently being tried again.

The United Nations Convention on International Multimodal Transport of Goods was signed in Geneva in 1980 (MMTL 1980), but the convention never entered into force. Only 11 countries have ratified the convention to date. A minimum of 30 ratifications, however, was required for its entry into force.[66]

The United Nations Convention on Contracts for the International Carriage of Goods Wholly or Partly by Sea was signed in Rotterdam in 2009. This convention does not just relate to carriage by sea (under a bill of lading), but also covers multimodal contracts of carriage, provided that a sea leg is involved. The rules have not entered into force (yet). Only three countries have now ratified the convention;[67] this time a minimum of 20 ratifications is required for its entry into force.[68]

In the absence of a dedicated international convention on multimodal contracts of carriage, the provisions of the different unimodal conventions may apply to certain multimodal situations.[69] Besides, a unimodal convention may also govern an individual (unimodal) leg within a multimodal contract of carriage. Article 38 MC, for instance, ensures the application of the MC to international air legs within multimodal contracts of carriage:

> In the case of combined carriage performed partly by air and partly by any other mode of carriage, the provisions of this Convention shall, subject to paragraph 4 of Article 18, apply only to the carriage by air, provided that the carriage by air falls within the terms of Article 1.

In fact, a unimodal convention may even apply to an individual leg within a multimodal contract of carriage without such a specific provision. The CMR does not

66 Article 36 (1) MMTL 1980 reads: 'This Convention shall enter into force 12 months after the Governments of 30 States have either signed it not subject to ratification, acceptance or approval or have deposited instruments of ratification, acceptance or approval or accession with the depositary.'

67 The current status can be found at https://treaties.un.org.

68 Article 94 (1) RR reads: 'This Convention enters into force on the first day of the month following the expiration of one year after the date of deposit of the twentieth instrument of ratification, acceptance, approval or accession.'

69 Article 2 CMR stipulates that the convention covers piggy back and ro/ro legs in the course of a contract of carriage by road, articles 1 § 3 and 4 CIM 1999 prescribes the application of the convention to certain 'supplemental services', and article 18 (4) MC extends the scope of the convention to certain 'ancillary services', provided that it cannot be established that the loss occurred during these ancillary services. All these examples are discussed in far more detail in Chapter 6.

contain such a provision,[70] but in the UK the convention still applies to international road legs within a multimodal contract of carriage.[71]

2.3. Forwarding contracts

A forwarding contract is different to a contract of carriage. A forwarding contract is a contract whereby the forwarder agrees with his principal to arrange for the carriage of goods.[72] This definition shows that forwarding contracts and contracts of carriage share certain superficial similarities, but that there is (at least) also one crucial difference. The forwarder merely arranges for transportation; he does not assume the carrier's obligation to achieve a certain result, i.e. the delivery of the goods to the consignee at their destination.[73]

Freedom of contract

Forwarding contracts are not regulated by an international convention, and they are therefore not subject to conventional mandatory rules either. The forwarder is therewith in principle free to limit or exclude any liability in his contract with the principal, and that is of course exactly what he will do. Freight forwarders generally work under general terms and conditions drafted by dedicated branch organizations, such as the FENEX and the BIFA.[74] These general terms and conditions are very forwarder friendly; see, for instance, article 11 of the Dutch Forwarding Conditions:

1 All operations and activities shall be at the principal's expense and risk.
2 Without prejudice to the provisions of Article 16, the forwarder shall not be liable for any damage whatsoever, unless the principal shall prove that the damage has been caused by fault or negligence on the part of the forwarder or the latter's servants.

70 Mutatis mutandis the same applies to an international rail leg within a multimodal contract of carriage under the CIM 1999. The HVR is also silent on this point, but here its drafters clearly contemplated their application to sea legs within multimodal contracts of carriage. See the discussion in Chapter 8 and F. Berlingieri (ed.) *The Travaux Préparatoires of the Hague Rules and the Hague-Visby Rules* (CMI: Antwerp, 1997) 90.

71 *Quantum Corp. v. Plane Trucking* (2002) 2 Lloyd's Rep. 24, affirmed in *Datec v. UPS* (2007) 2 Lloyd's Rep. 114.

72 The discussion in this section covers the forwarder acting within the scope of this definition, but related (yet ultimately not necessarily always different) figures exist as well, such as the commissionaire-expediteur, freight integrator, freight consolidator and so on. In fact, forwarders are in practice sometimes disguised as digital platforms where shippers and carriers meet to agree on a contract of carriage. The operator of the platform essentially brokers this agreement and acts as a forwarder in relation to the shipper.

73 § 453 (1) GCC reads: 'By virtue of the forwarding contract the forwarder is obliged to arrange for the dispatch of the goods.'

74 The Dutch Federation of Forwarders and the British International Freight Association.

3 The forwarder's liability shall in all cases be limited to 10,000 SDR per occurrence or series of occurrences with one and the same cause of damage, on the understanding that in the event of damaging, loss of value or loss of the goods comprised in the order, the liability shall be limited to 4 SDR per kilogram damaged or lost gross weight, the maximum being 4,000 SDR per consignment.

Clause 23 of the BIFA Standard Trading Conditions stipulates that the forwarder '*shall perform its duties with a reasonable degree of care, diligence, skill and judgment*'. A reasonable degree of care is clearly different to the obligation to achieve a certain result. Besides, even when the forwarder should act in breach of this reasonable degree of care, article 26 BIFA Standard Terms of Contract ensures that the forwarder's exposure remains limited as it provides that:[75]

> the Company's liability howsoever arising and, notwithstanding that the cause of loss or damage be unexplained, shall not exceed (i) in the case of claims for loss or damage to Goods: (a) the value of any loss or damage, or (b) a sum at the rate of 2 SDR per kilo of the gross weight of any Goods lost or damaged whichever shall be the lower. (ii) subject to (iii) below, in the case of all other claims: (a) the value of the subject Goods of the relevant transaction between the Company and its Customer, or (b) where the weight can be defined, a sum calculated at the rate of two SDR per kilo of the gross weight of the subject Goods of the said transaction, or (c) 75,000 SDR in respect of any one transaction, whichever shall be the least.

The forwarder acting in his own name

The classic forwarder acts as an agent.[76] He brings the shipper and the carrier together, takes a commission for his work, and his involvement ends then and there. He does not become a party to the contract of carriage. This is a comfortable position as far as his liability is concerned, but it is not without commercial disadvantages. Once the shipper and the carrier have established contact with the help of a forwarder, what is preventing them from liaising directly with each other next time?

Besides, the forwarder may very well be able to make more money if he presents himself to his principal as a carrier instead of a forwarder. He can then use his contacts to delegate the actual transport to a (sub) carrier at a favourable rate, and he will then simply invoice his principal for a higher amount. The forwarder then

75 See in great detail on the BIFA Standard Terms of Contract, D.A. Glass, *Freight forwarding and multimodal transport contracts* (Informa: London, 2012) 40 and further.

76 The commissionaire de transport under French law is not a carrier, but not exactly a forwarder either. He arranges the transportation of the goods in his own name, ensures the due performance of that contract and his responsibility for the goods equals the responsibility of a carrier in his care. F.G.M. Smeele, *Legal conceptualizations of the freight forwarder: Some comparative reflections on the disunified law of forwarding*, JIML (2015) 452. See also article 1432 Code de Transports.

takes the difference between the freight invoiced and the freight due (instead of commission for a fixed percentage).

Despite the obvious risk from a liability perspective, these commercial upsides are apparently very tempting, and forwarders in practice often assume a sort of hybrid position. The forwarder does not unambiguously present himself as a forwarding agent (acting for a principal) when the contract is concluded. Instead, he acts in his own name, but assumes the position of a forwarding agent in the proceedings afterwards.

In *Coli v. Merzario* both the claimant and the defendant were forwarders.[77] Samsung had instructed Merzario to arrange for the transportation of its goods between the UK and Russia. Merzario in turn approached Coli because of its good contacts with the intended carrier, Transfennica. Merzario and Coli thus both acted as middlemen in arranging for the carriage of these Samsung goods. In fact, Coli's invoices mentioned that the services concerned 'accounts effected for and on behalf of the Owner/Charter of the undermentioned vessel'.

Still, in the conclusion of their contract Merzario and Coli had both acted in their own name, and not in the name of Samsung or Transfennica. When Coli later initiated proceedings against Merzario for the payment of an outstanding demurrage claim for one of the Transfennica trucks, Merzario played the agency card. Merzario argued that Coli had no right of suit as that rested with its principal Transfennica, and furthermore argued that it was not the debtor of the claim as it had acted as a forwarder for its principal Samsung. Both arguments were rejected in court:

> The whole tenor of negotiations was that terms were being agreed between Coli and Merzario, irrespective of what may or may not have been operative between Coli and Transfennica and between Merzario and Samsung respectively. Moreover, there were clear arrangements between Coli and Merzario, whereby it was established that Coli would look to Merzario for payment and, for their part, Merzario accepted liability for payment: see the invoices raised directly to Merzario and the way in which Merzario sought to dispute them. In that regard, I attach no weight to the formal wording of Coli's invoices. The true position, supported indeed by the evidence of Merzario's own witnesses, was that insofar as money was due, Merzario considered themselves obliged to meet any invoice which was presented, subject of course to the credit terms to which I have just referred.

Hybrid contracts with different responsibilities

In the *Maheno* 'freight consolidator' Holyman arranged for the carriage of radio parts from Sydney to Wellington.[78] EMI was the buyer of the goods, and it instructed Holyman to consolidate the shipment, pack the (7-ft) container, bring it to the port in Sydney and arrange for transportation to Wellington. Holyman

77 *Coli v. Merzario* (2002) 1 Lloyd's Rep. 608.

78 The *Maheno* (1977) 1 Lloyd's Rep. 81.

did not own any ships and instructed the owners of the Maheno for the sea leg. In fact, Holyman hardly had any choice in that matter since that was the only available service across the Tasman Sea. The owners of the Maheno issued a bill of lading for the carriage by sea to Holyman, and Holyman in turn issued a consignment note to EMI.

When the goods were lost during the sea leg to Wellington, EMI initiated proceedings against Holyman. EMI argued that Holyman had acted as a carrier, and therefore that it was also liable as a carrier, but the court differentiated between Holyman's responsibilities towards EMI. Beattie J held that Holyman had indeed been a carrier for the land leg, but at the same time only a forwarding agent for the sea leg:

> I infer from these matters that it was the intention of the parties that the role of the defendant was to pack the goods in the seafreighter and then get them on the ship. ... Neither the plaintiff nor its agents nor the defendant envisaged that the defendant would carry by sea as there is only one service to New Zealand. The contract itself envisaged that the defendant would enter into a contract of sea carriage as agent for the consignor and upon the terms of the bills of lading issued by the sea carrier. ... In my view, therefore, Mr. Bryers was right when he submitted that the liability of the defendant is restricted to its position, first, as a carrier and bailee for reward for the land segments of the journey, and secondly, that its liability for the sea leg is simply that of a ship forwarder or shipper's agent.

Criteria to distinguish between forwarding and carriage

As the circumstances obviously differ per case, there is no hard and fast rule to establish whether parties have agreed on a forwarding contract or a contract of carriage. The literature and case law on this question have produced several criteria to assess the position of the forwarder/carrier though.[79] In *Aqualon v. Vallaja*, Mance J listed the following five relevant factors to qualify the contract:[80]

(a) the terms of the particular contract including the nature of the instructions given, for example whether they were to carry or for carriage or were to arrange carriage . . . ; in this connection the nature and terms of any governing conditions also arise for consideration;
(b) any description used or adopted by the parties in relation to the contracting party's role;
(c) the course of any dealings . . . ;
(d) the nature and basis of charging (in particular whether an all-in fee was charged, leaving the contracting party to make such profit as he could from the margin between it and costs incurred);
(e) the nature and terms of any CMR note issued.

79 P.M. Bugden/S. Lamont-Black, *Goods in transit* (Sweet & Maxwell: London, 2013) 374.
80 *Aqualon v. Vallana* (1994) 1 Lloyd's Rep. 669.

Arguably, the reference to 'any CMR note issued' can be read as 'any transport document issued', as the terms of a bill of lading, waybill or any other document may be equally important. Other circumstances that could be instrumental are, for instance, the description of the company's activities in the Chamber of Commerce and the (lack of) possession of any means of transportation.[81]

Not all of these factors weigh evenly heavy. Logistic service providers will not always clearly discriminate between 'carrying' and 'arranging for carriage' in their contracts and correspondence. Besides, they will in practice often offer a full package of services, including but not limited to forwarding and carriage, and they may even refer to different sets of terms and conditions for these different services.

It is submitted that the intention of the parties to the contract is ultimately decisive,[82] and that the wording of the contract (and/or correspondence between the parties) provides the best possible evidence of that intention. When the contract is ambiguous, though, and the intention of the parties is difficult or even impossible to establish, the invoice mentioning either commission for a certain percentage or an (all-in) amount for freight is then probably the most reliable and objective factor. In fact, the invoice for an all-in fee is in some jurisdictions already decisive in itself. § 459 GCC prescribes:

> If a fixed sum is agreed as remuneration which includes the costs of carriage, the forwarder has, as far as the carriage is concerned, the rights and duties of a carrier or sea carrier. In this case, he may claim compensation for his outlays only to the extent that this is customary.

German law thus adopts a straightforward and very strict approach in dealing with such situations. When a carrier/forwarder charges an all-in sum for his services, instead of a commission for a certain percentage of the freight, he assumes the duties of a carrier by law.

81 The *Maheno* (1977) 1 Lloyd's Rep. 81.
82 *Coli v. Merzario* (2002) 1 Lloyd's Rep. 608.

3 Transport documents

A contract of carriage is form free: its existence does not depend on formal requirements such as signatures, stamps or the issuance of specific transport documents.[1] The parties must reach an agreement on the essentials of their contract,[2] and the corresponding intention of the contracting parties constitutes the contract of carriage.[3]

In practice, however, the contracting parties will not just want to rely on their inevitably subjective recollections afterwards. Whenever possible, they will instead want to avoid any discussion as to the contents of their arrangements. Accordingly, most contracts of carriage are evidenced in writing, usually by a transport document 'which evidences a contract of carriage and the taking over or loading of goods by a carrier, made out in the form of a bill of lading or consignment note or of any other document used in trade'.[4]

Such a transport document will often be a bill of lading, a sea waybill, an air waybill, a consignment note, or a multimodal version of such a document.[5] At a certain point, however, these 'traditional' documents will surely be replaced by electronic versions thereof or yet to be devised instruments.[6] In fact, the drafters

1 M. Clarke & D. Yates, *Contracts of carriage by land and air* (Informa: London, 2008) 1.

2 *Anglo Overseas v. Titan Industrial* (1959) 2 Lloyd's Rep. 152 per Berry J: 'As to the first of those questions, there can, I think, be no doubt concerning the answer. As I have already indicated, it is quite clear, and indeed no longer disputed by the defendants, that, in transactions of this kind, a binding contract is effected when shipping space is offered at a certain freight rate and is accepted by the forwarding agents or by the company, such as the plaintiff company, which is carrying out the transaction.'

3 The contract of carriage can thus also be concluded verbally; see *Mayhew v. Overseas Container Lines* (1984) 1 Lloyd's Rep. 317, in (e-mail) correspondence or in a booking or shipping note, see *George Kallis v. Success Insurance* (1985) 2 Lloyd's Rep. 8.

4 This is the definition of article 1 (6) CMNI.

5 There are many other documents, e.g. booking notes, delivery orders, mate's receipts and bulletins de remise, but these are the ones most often used.

6 See in this respect already *Glencore International v. MSC* (2015) 2 Lloyd's Rep 508, discussed by M. Goldby (2015) 21 JIML 339, but also for instance T. Eckardt, *The Bolero Bill of Lading under German and English Law* (Sellier: European Law Publisher, 2004).

of the RR have already anticipated this development. Article 1 (18) RR gives the following definition of an electronic transport record:[7]

> information in one or more messages issued by electronic communication under a contract of carriage by a carrier, including information logically associated with the electronic transport record by attachments or otherwise linked to the electronic transport record contemporaneously with or subsequent to its issue by the carrier, so as to become part of the electronic transport record, that: (a) Evidences the carrier's or a performing party's receipt of goods under a contract of carriage; and (b) Evidences or contains a contract of carriage.

Still, it is safe to say that the traditional paper transport documents will continue to be around for quite some time.[8] The shipping community is rather conservative and slow to change its habits.[9] Besides, not all countries are equally ready yet, not all systems have been aligned, and not all governments have adapted their legislation to these changes.[10]

3.1. Charter parties

The charter party has taken its name from the Roman concept of a 'charta partita', i.e. a divided or split document. The document would evidence a sale contract, the ownership of property or the use of a ship to carry goods by sea. The document was signed by the parties, and then torn in two so that the contracting parties both availed of an original part.

7 The electronic transport record comes in a negotiable and non-negotiable version; see article 1 (19) and (20) RR: '"Negotiable electronic transport record" means an electronic transport record: (a) That indicates, by wording such as "to order", or "negotiable", or other appropriate wording recognized as having the same effect by the law applicable to the record, that the goods have been consigned to the order of the shipper or to the order of the consignee, and is not explicitly stated as being "non-negotiable" or "not negotiable"; and (b) The use of which meets the requirements of article 9, paragraph 1. "Non-negotiable electronic transport record" means an electronic transport record that is not a negotiable electronic transport record.'

8 N. Gaskill, 'Bills of lading in an electronic age' *LMCLQ* (2010) 283: 'There is a fear of the unknown among some lawyers when they consider the impact of technology on legal provisions; ... It may be comforting, therefore, that the life of the traditional paper bill of lading is being prolonged by technological advances which have been rather taken for granted by those more interested in radical developments, such as the introduction of full electronic bills of lading.'

9 Lord Blackburn said as early as 1882 with regard to the practice to issue bills of lading in three originals that 'because, as I suspect, merchants dislike to depart from an old custom for fear that novelty may produce some unforeseen effect, bills of lading are still made out in parts, and probably will continue to be so made out'. *Glyn Mills & Co v. East and West India Dock* (1882) 7 App Cas 591.

10 S.D. Girvin, *Carriage of goods by sea* (OUP: Oxford, 2011) 196 and further.

The nature of the contract

Following the definition of the transport document given above, a charter party is really not a transport document at all.[11] A charter party does not evidence the receipt of the goods by the carrier. In fact, the charter party often does not even evidence a contract of carriage.[12] It evidences a contract for the use of a ship.[13]

Charter parties are in practice often negotiated between specialized brokers acting for the owners and the charterers. The contract is in place – the ship is fixed – when they reach an agreement on the essentials. This agreement is then often summarized in a so-called fixture recap,[14] and the signed charter party forms the ultimate tangible result.

A charter party involves an owner and a charterer. The owner agrees to make the ship available to the charterer for a fixed period or a certain voyage. The owner does not really need to own the ship, though; he can also be a disponent or chartered owner.[15] A registered owner can charter a ship to a charterer, who in turn may act as an owner to charter the ship to a sub-charterer, who in turn acts as an owner and so on. The owner in the context of a charter party is a contractual figure, i.e. the one who agrees to make the ship available to the charterer.

Bareboat charters, time charters and voyage charters

Three different types of charter parties are generally distinguished.[16] These are bareboat charters, time charters and voyage charters.[17]

A bareboat charter relates to just the ship and nothing else.[18] The charterer will need to appoint his own master and crew. He will have to insure the ship and he assumes both the operational and commercial risks. A bareboat charter is thus in fact a rental contract, and it does not come close to a contract of carriage. The owner makes the ship available, and the charterer is free to use it

11 Still, this is probably the best place to discuss the charter party.

12 See in more detail e.g. J. Wilson, *Carriage of goods by sea* (Longman: Harlow, 2010) 47; S.D. Girvin, *Carriage of goods by sea* (OUP: Oxford, 2011) 535; J. Cooke, T. Young, M. Ashcroft, A. Taylor, J. Kimball, D. Martowski, L. Lambert, M. Sturley, *Voyage charters* (Informa: London, 2014) 1.

13 An airplane or a set of train wagons can of course also be chartered; see e.g. *ICF v. Balkenende* (2010) 2 Lloyd's Rep. 400.

14 Y. Baatz (ed.) *Maritime law* (Routledge: London, 2014) 119.

15 Sir Bernard Eder, D. Foxton, A Burrows, S. Berry, S. Boyd, *Scrutton on charterparties and bills of lading* (Sweet & Maxwell: London, 2011) 84.

16 As so often, hybrid options are available as well. A consecutive voyage charter will in practice for instance closely resemble a time charter.

17 Slot charters do not really relate to the use of the ship, but instead to availability of a (certain number of) container slot(s) on board of a ship. The owner then makes one or more places for a container available for a voyage or period of time. J. Cooke, T. Young, M. Ashcroft, A. Taylor, J. Kimball, D. Martowski, L. Lambert, M. Sturley, *Voyage charters* (Informa: London, 2014) 70.

18 This type of charter is also known as a charter by demise.

as he sees fit, provided he stays within the contractual boundaries agreed upon in the charter party.[19]

In the case of a time charter, the ship is made available to the charterer for a specific period of time, sometimes three months, sometimes a year, but it can also be a longer period.[20] The owner has his own crew on board, insures the ship and has the operational control. The charterer runs the commercial risks in the exploitation of the ship. The charterer also pays for the variable costs, such as the bunkers of the ship.

A voyage charter governs just one specific trip, almost always for the carriage of goods between the place of receipt and the place of destination.[21] The owner of the ship runs the operational and commercial risks. The charterer only pays the freight and disbursements. A voyage charter, agreed upon with the objective to carry goods from the port of loading to the port of discharge for delivery to the consignee, fits the definition of a contract of carriage.[22]

3.2. Bills of lading

The bill of lading is a commercial document with three closely connected, yet different functions. The bill of lading serves as a receipt, it is a document of title and it evidences the contract of carriage. The bill of lading comes in three different forms; there are order, bearer and straight bills of lading.

The bill of lading as a receipt

The receipt function is the oldest function of the bill of lading. This function can be traced back to the fourteenth century.[23] As charter parties did not evidence the number, quality and condition of the goods, this information was initially recorded in the port of shipment by a local registrar in the Book of Loading. The registrar would make copies of the entry available to interested parties, and these copies later evolved into bills of lading issued directly by the carrier. The charter party then evidenced the contract between the carrier and the shipper, and the bill of lading evidenced the receipt of the goods and their condition.[24] The bill of lading has kept this function over the years. Article III (3) HVR stipulates:

19 See in great detail M. Davis, *Bareboat charters: A practical guide to the legal and insurance implications* (Informa: London, 2005).

20 A contract for the use of a ship with the objective to carry goods for a certain period of time may qualify as a contract of carriage.

21 Although a marine biologist could also charter a ship to conduct scientific experiments at sea during the voyage from Guayaquil (Ecuador) to the Galapagos.

22 J. Cooke, T. Young, M. Ashcroft, A. Taylor, J. Kimball, D. Martowski, L. Lambert, M. Sturley, *Voyage charters* (Informa: London, 2014) 20.

23 W.P. Bennett, *The history and present position of the bill of lading as a document of title* (Cambridge University Press, 1914) 5–6.

24 The goods carried by sea were in those days often commodities, such as grain, corn and cattle. The merchant would typically charter an entire sailing vessel for their transport, and then formalize the agreement in a charter party.

> After receiving the goods into his charge the carrier or the master or agent of the carrier shall, on demand of the shipper, issue to the shipper a bill of lading showing among other things:
>
> (a) The leading marks necessary for identification of the goods as the same are furnished in writing by the shipper before the loading of such goods starts, provided such marks are stamped or otherwise shown clearly upon the goods if uncovered, or on the cases or coverings in which such goods are contained, in such a manner as should ordinarily remain legible until the end of the voyage.
> (b) Either the number of packages or pieces, or the quantity, or weight, as the case may be, as furnished in writing by the shipper.
> (c) The apparent order and condition of the goods.

A bill of lading will typically contain a pre-printed statement that the goods were received on board 'in apparent good order and condition'.[25] If the goods are indeed in apparent good order and condition, the bill of lading is signed by either the master of the ship, an agent on his behalf or an agent for the carrier without any further remarks. Such a bill of lading is a so-called clean bill of lading. It provides evidence of the description and number of the goods and their apparent good order and condition. The evidence remains rebuttable between the original contracting parties, but it becomes conclusive evidence once the bill of lading is transferred to a third party acting in good faith:[26]

> Such a bill of lading shall be prima facie evidence of the receipt by the carrier of the goods as therein described in accordance with paragraphs 3(a), (b) and (c). However, proof to the contrary shall not be admissible when the bill of lading has been transferred to a third party acting in good faith.

A (clean) bill of lading plays an important role in international sale contracts. When the seller and the buyer have their seats in different countries, the delivery of the goods under the sale contract will often require their carriage from one country to another. In the absence of mandatory law on this point, the seller and the buyer are free to agree on the exact manner and moment of delivery. In practice, they will then often choose one of the Incoterms, standardized delivery conditions for international sale contracts.[27]

When the delivery requires the carriage of the goods by sea, the Incoterms Free on Board (FOB) or Cost Insurance Freight (CIF) are commonly agreed upon. Under both of these Incoterms, the risk in the goods transfers from the

25 A 'received for shipment' bill of lading will only evidence the apparent order and condition of the goods at the time of their receipt by the carrier. Such a bill of lading provides less comfort as the carrier may exonerate his liability for the period between receipt and loading; see article VII HVR and Chapter 5.

26 Article III (4) HVR.

27 The International Commercial Terms 2010, published by the International Chamber of Commerce.

seller to the buyer at the time that the goods are brought on board of the ship in the port of loading.[28]

This means that the buyer is already at risk well before the arrival of the goods in the port of discharge. All the same, he is held under the sale contract to pay the purchase price. The buyer of the goods will therefore want to secure his position as much as possible, and this is where the bill of lading comes in. A clean bill of lading gives him the assurance that the goods were in any case in apparent good order and condition at the time they were received on board. Since payment against the physical delivery of the goods is not possible, the buyer will settle for the next best thing, i.e. payment of the purchase price against a clean on board bill of lading.[29]

A document of title

The bill of lading is furthermore a document of title, a function that can be split into two different sub-functions. The bill of lading is a document of title as its presentation is required for the release of the goods in the port of discharge. The bill of lading is furthermore a document of title (at common law) as it symbolizes the goods carried thereunder.[30]

Whereas the merchants would generally accompany their goods during the voyage throughout the Middle Ages, they abandoned that practice around 1500 AD. Instead, they would instruct a local agent or factor to deal with the goods at their final destination. This required additional flexibility, for instance to allow an as yet unknown buyer to take delivery of the goods in the port of discharge. Hence, the bill of lading would not just be made out to a named consignee, but instead to a named consignee 'or his assigns', to the consignee 'or his order or assigns' or simply 'to order'. The right to the release of the goods in the port of discharge could therefore be transferred with the transfer of the bill of lading.

Since the bill of lading was usually issued in three originals, a carrier would occasionally find himself confronted with more than one person claiming the release of the goods in the port of discharge. To protect themselves against claims for misdelivery, the carriers introduced attestation clauses in their bills of lading.[31]

28 On this point, the Incoterms 2010 deviate from its predecessors. Under earlier versions (of 2000 for instance), the risk would shift from the seller to the buyer upon the passing of the ship's rail in the port of loading. *International Chamber of Commerce Incoterms 2010* (ICC Services Paris, 2010) 9.

29 This is the system of a documentary sale; the parties agree on cash against documents. These documents (often listed in a letter of credit) will in any case include a clean bill of lading, but often also a health certificate, insurance papers, certificate of origin etc.

30 In a more lenient approach, order, bearer and straight bills of lading are all document of title as they are subject to the presentation rule (see the discussion in the *Rafaela S.* (2005) 1 Lloyd's Rep. 347). In a stricter approach, only order and bearer bills of lading have this symbolic function, and are recognized as documents of title at common law. See *The Law Commission and The Scottish Law Commission Rights of suit in respect of carriage of goods by sea* (HMSO: London, 1991) 20.

31 These clauses are nowadays present on the face of every bill of lading; see N.J.J. Gaskill, R. Asariotis, Y. Baatz, *Bills of lading: Law and contracts* (LLP: London, 2000) 420.

The carrier could therefore safely release the goods against the presentation of one original as the remaining two originals would become void in the process:

> In wytness of the truythe I the sayde master or the purser for me have firmyd iij bylls of the one tenor the one complyed with and fulfilled the other to stand voyd. [32]

Since the bill of lading effectively ensured the right to the release of the goods, merchants started to use the bill of lading as a symbol of those goods. This 'custom of merchants' was recognized near the end of the eighteenth century in *Lickbarrow v. Mason*.[33]

Turing had sold a shipment of corn to Freeman and he instructed Holmes to carry the goods from Middelburg (the Netherlands) to Liverpool (UK). Holmes issued four original bills of lading;[34] he gave three originals to Turing and kept one himself. Turing then sent two of these original bills of lading to Freeman, who in turn sold the corn and transferred the same two original bills of lading to Lickbarrow. The purchase price was paid to Freeman by Lickbarrow, but Freeman went bankrupt and never paid Turing. At that time, Turing still held one of the original bills of lading. He sent this original to Mason with the instructions to present the bill of lading to Holmes, and to sell the goods on his behalf. When Lickbarrow found out what had happened, he initiated proceedings against Mason, and with success. The court held, over a series of trials and appeals,[35] that Lickbarrow had acquired the property in the goods since:[36]

> by the custom of merchants, bills of lading, expressing goods or merchandise to have been shipped by any person or persons to be delivered to order or assigns, have been, and are at any time after such goods have been shipped, and before the voyage performed, for which they have been or are shipped, negotiable and transferable by the shipper or shippers endorsing such bills of lading with his, her or their name or names, and delivering or transmitting the same so indorsed, or causing the same to be so delivered or transmitted to such other person or persons; and that by such indorsement and delivery, or transmission, the property in such goods hath been, and is transferred and passed to such other person or persons.

32 This is the wording of the bill of lading in the *Mary Martyn* (1539); see R.G. Marsden, *Select pleas in the Court of Admiralty* (Bernard Quaritch, 1894, Vol. I) 88–9. Remarkably, the wording of the attestation has hardly changed over the years; see for instance the wording of the clause in the *Rafaela S.* (2005) 1 Lloyd's Rep. 347.

33 *Lickbarrow v. Mason* (1794) 5 TR 683; *Barber v. Meyerstein* (1870) LR 4 HL 317; *Sanders Brothers v. Maclean* (1883) 11 QBD 327.

34 The issuance of four originals was not uncommon in those days. In fact, it was later prescribed by the Dutch Commercial Code of 1838.

35 The entire trial is discussed by M. Bools, *The bill of lading: A document of title to goods – An Anglo-American Comparison* (LLP: London, 1997) 8–19.

36 *Lickbarrow v. Mason* (1794) 5 TR 683.

The bill of lading symbolizes the goods carried under that bill of lading. As long as the goods are in the care of the carrier, they can be delivered from a seller to a buyer by the transfer of the bill of lading. After that, the bill of lading is 'spent' as a document of title.[37]

The transfer of a bill of lading

The transfer formalities are different for order, bearer and straight bills of lading. An order bill of lading is made out to someone's order (usually the buyer of the goods or a bank), or just 'to order' in which case the bill of lading is held to have been issued to the order of the shipper. Order bills of lading are easily transferable by endorsement and delivery;[38] they are in fact meant to be transferred regularly in the course of the voyage. The shipper (or the person to whose order the bill of lading has been made out) then endorses the bill of lading to the transferee,[39] and completes the endorsement with the delivery.[40]

The shipper (or the person to whose order the bill of lading has been made out) does not have to endorse the bill of lading to a specific transferee. He can also endorse the bill of lading in blank, and he does so by simply signing the bill of lading on the reverse without the mention of any endorsee.[41] The initial order bill of lading thus becomes a bearer bill of lading. A bearer bill of lading is even easier to transfer, i.e. by its mere delivery just as any other item in possession.[42]

The straight bill of lading already mentions the intended consignee on its face. The straight bill of lading is thus clearly not meant to be transferred in the course of the voyage on a regular basis.[43] Nonetheless, the straight bill of lading is certainly transferable, but only once, and only between the shipper and the consignee mentioned on the bill of lading.[44] This transfer does not require further formalities: its delivery by the shipper to the named consignee is sufficient.[45]

37 R. Aikens, M. Bools, R. Lord, *Bills of lading* (LLP: London, 2006) 30; S.D. Girvin, *Carriage of goods by sea* (OUP: Oxford, 2011) 109.

38 An endorsement is in fact a written instruction on the reverse ('en dos' is French for on the back) of the bill of lading, e.g. 'from me (A) to the order of (B)' or similar words.

39 The transfer from the shipper to the person to whose order the bill of lading has been made out is, however, form free as the bill of lading is meant to be endorsed by the party to whose order it was issued, and not by the shipper. C. Debattista, *Bills of lading in export trade* (Tottel Publishing: Haywards Heath, 2009) 100; M. Bridge (ed.) *Benjamin's Sale of Goods* (Sweet & Maxwell: London, 2010) 114; S.D. Girvin, *Carriage of goods by sea* (OUP: Oxford, 2011) 65–6; G.H. Treitel and F.M.B. Reynolds, *Carver on bills of lading* (Sweet & Maxwell: London, 2011) 11–12; *UCO Bank v. Golden Shore* (2005) SGCA 42.

40 See the Court of Appeal judgment in the *Erin Schulte* (2014) EWCA Civ 1382 for the meaning of 'completion of the endorsement with the delivery', and M. Spanjaart (2015) 21 JIML (1) 18 for an analysis of the decision in the *Erin Schulte.*

41 The bill of lading is usually also stamped for good measure.

42 G.H. Treitel and F.M.B. Reynolds, *Carver on bills of lading* (Sweet & Maxwell: London, 2011) 11.

43 See also Rix LJ in the *Rafaela S.* (2003) 2 Lloyd's Rep. 113.

44 W. Tetley, *Marine cargo claims* (ISPB: Montreal, 1988) 184, C. Murray, D. Holloway, D. Timson-Hunt, *Schmitthoff's Export Trade* (Sweet & Maxwell: London, 2007) 310 and S.D. Girvin, *Carriage of goods by sea* (OUP: Oxford, 2011) 43.

45 M. Spanjaart, *The surrender of the bill of lading 'duly endorsed'* (2014) 20 JIML 327.

The final transferee must present an original bill of lading to the carrier for delivery of the goods in the port of discharge.[46] This 'presentation rule' equally applies to order, bearer and straight bills of lading.[47] The presentation of the bill of lading creates both rights and obligations for the carrier. On the one hand the carrier has to release the goods to the lawful holder of the bill of lading, but on the other hand he is discharged from further obligations under the contract of carriage once he releases the goods to that lawful holder.[48]

Whereas the payment of the purchase price against the receipt of a (clean) bill of lading secures the position of the buyer in a documentary sale, the presentation rule secures the position of the seller in a documentary sale.[49] As the purchase price is paid against certain documents, including a clean bill of lading, the seller will either have received payment for the goods or he will still be able to prevent the release of the goods by the carrier to the buyer.[50]

Evidence of the contract of carriage

Finally, the bill of lading evidences the contract of carriage. The bill of lading acquired this third function in the course of the nineteenth century. As a result of the industrial revolution, new products became available, and instead of just trading commodities in bulk, merchants were more and more often trading general cargo. As the transportation of these goods did not require the use of an entire ship, there was no need for a charter party either. Under these circumstances the practice developed to just issue (and accept) a bill of lading as the evidence of the

46 The presentation rule has been codified in the CMNI. Article 13 (2) reads: 'At the place of destination, the goods shall be delivered only in exchange for the original of the bill of lading submitted initially; thereafter, further delivery cannot be claimed against other originals.'

47 See for instance *Voss v. APL* (2002) 2 Lloyd's Rep. 707; The *Rafaela S.* (2005) 1 Lloyd's Rep. 347; *Carewins v. Bright Fortune* (2007) 3 HKLRD 396. All the same, USCA 80110 (b) stipulates that the carrier may deliver the goods to '(1) a person entitled to their possession; (2) the consignee named in a nonnegotiable bill; or (3) a person in possession of a negotiable bill if (A) the goods are deliverable to the order of that person; or (B) the bill has been indorsed to that person or in blank by the consignee or another indorsee'.

48 The *Stettin* (1889) Lloyd's Rep 14 PD 142; *Carlberg v. Wemyss* (1915) SC 616; *Sze Hai Tong bank v. Rambler Cycle Co* (1959) AC 576; *Barclays Bank v. Commissioners of Customs and Excise* (1963) 1 Lloyd's Rep 81; The *Sormovsky 3068* (1994) 2 Lloyd's Rep 266; The *Houda* (1994) 2 Lloyd's Rep 541; *Motis v. Dampskibsselskabet* (2000) 1 Lloyd's Rep 211; *Erin Schulte* (2014) EWCA Civ 1382.

49 *Scottish & Newcastle v. Othon Ghalanos* (2008) 2 ALL ER 768 per Lord Rodger: 'A term under which the seller is to retain the bills of lading until payment is, of course, common in both CIF and FOB contracts. Since the bill of lading is the symbol of the goods, under such an arrangement the seller or his agent not only retains the bill of lading but also, thereby, retains the right to possession of the goods until the price is paid. Often, the property in the goods will also be intended to pass only on payment. In such a case, even though the seller ships the goods on board a vessel nominated by the buyer, by doing so he does not intend to transfer possession of the goods to the buyer.'

50 See S. 19 (2) UK Sale of Goods Act: 'Where goods are shipped, and by the bill of lading the goods are deliverable to the order of the seller or his agent, the seller is prima facie to be taken to reserve the right of disposal.'

contract of carriage, especially in those trades where ship owners were offering regular liner services.[51]

The contract of carriage is evidenced by both the face and the reverse of the bill of lading. The face of the bill of lading will already provide certain essential information on the terms of the contract, such as the port of loading, the port of discharge, the name of the ship and sometimes the identity of the carrier. The reverse of the bill of lading then stipulates the carrier's terms and conditions.[52]

Not every bill of lading will evidence the contract of carriage, though. A bill of lading may also have been issued pursuant to a charter party, and its function as evidence of the contract of carriage is then considerably watered down. The bill of lading in the hands of the charterer is a 'mere receipt',[53] and it does not regulate the relation between the charterer and the carrier.[54]

3.3. Through bills of lading

A through bill of lading is rather difficult to define.[55] A through bill of lading is sometimes seen as a port-to-port bill of lading that allows for substitution and transhipment,[56] sometimes as a document evidencing a contract of carriage with at least one sea leg,[57] and sometimes as a bill of lading whereby the carrier arranges the pre- and/or on-carriage as a forwarder.[58] Adding to this confusion, the reference to a through bill of lading is (in American case law) often effectively a reference to a multimodal bill of lading.[59]

The through bill of lading and the multimodal bill of lading are not interchangeable documents.[60] A multimodal bill of lading evidences a contract of

51 W.L.P.A. Molengraaff, *Kort begrip van het nieuwe Nederlandse zeerecht* (Erven F. Bohn: Haarlem, 1928) 1.

52 A bill of lading that is issued pursuant to a charter party will often incorporate the provisions of that charter party so that they become part of the bill of lading contract (as well). See for the requirements for a successful incorporation for instance article 8:415 DCC and S.D. Girvin, *Carriage of goods by sea* (OUP: Oxford, 2011) 186 and further.

53 *Rodocanachi v. Milburn* (1886) 18 QBD 67; *President of India v. Metcalfe Shipping* (1969) 2 Lloyd's Rep. 476 (*Dunelmia*).

54 See also article I (b) HVR, and the discussion in section 3.6.

55 S.D. Girvin, *Carriage of goods by sea* (OUP: Oxford, 2011) 48.

56 P. Todd, *Bills of lading and bankers' documentary credits* (Informa: London, 2007) 67; D. Rhidian Thomas, *Multimodalism and through transport: Language, concepts, and categories* Tul. Mar. L.J. (2012) 762.

57 Sir Bernard Eder, D. Foxton, A Burrows, S. Berry, S. Boyd, *Scrutton on charterparties and bills of lading* (Sweet & Maxwell: London, 2011) 367. R. de Wit, *Multimodal transport* (LLP: London, 1995) 296 labelled this type whereby the carrier assumes the responsibility for the entire voyage as a 'pure through bill of lading'.

58 R. Aikens, M. Bools, R. Lord, *Bills of lading* (LLP: London, 2006) 27.

59 *Kirby v. Norfolk* (2004) AMC 2705; *KKK v. Regal-Beloit* (2010) AMC 1521, and see also the discussion in Chapter 8 on the application of the HVR to sea legs in multimodal contracts of carriage under a bill of lading.

60 See also *The Law Commission and The Scottish Law Commission Rights of suit in respect of carriage of goods by sea* (HMSO: London, 1991) 24: 'A "through" bill of lading, or "through" transport

carriage that requires more than one means of transportation;[61] a through bill of lading is a port-to-port bill of lading that allows for substitution and transhipment, and that may furthermore reckon with pre- and on-carriage in addition to the sea leg.[62] Nevertheless, the actual transhipment of the goods into another means of transportation may cause the through bill of lading to evidence a multimodal contract of carriage after all.

Substitution and transhipment

The traditional port-to-port bill of lading only evidences a contract of carriage by sea from one port to another. The face of the bill of lading reveals the port of loading and the port of discharge, but makes no mention of any different place of receipt or delivery, let alone any different means of transportation.

Contracts of carriage under a traditional port-to-port bill of lading are always unimodal; just the vessel is required to bridge the distance between the port of loading and the port of discharge. As the contract of carriage runs from receipt to delivery,[63] it may also encompass additional handling or barge operations. These activities do not constitute separate legs, though. They are instead absorbed by the unimodal contract of carriage by sea.[64]

All the same, some port-to-port bills of lading are more flexible than others. The bill of lading may for instance allow the carrier the freedom to substitute the nominated vessel and/or tranship the goods during the voyage. Instead of using just the one nominated vessel to complete the voyage, the carrier then

document, generally refers to a document containing a contract for the carriage of goods in separate stages, one stage of which involves a conventional sea transit, but in circumstances where the carrier issuing the document acts as a principal only when he has control of the goods (usually the sea transit) and as an agent at all other times, during which the merchant will be subject to the terms and conditions of, say, the rail, road or air carrier. A combined transport bill of lading, or combined transport document, generally refers to a document issued by a combined transport operator who acts as principal throughout all the stages of the transit, so the shipper has complete cover on a door-to-door basis and need concern himself with no person other than the combined transport operator.'

61 M. Rogert, *Einheitsrecht und Kollisionrecht im internationalen multimodalen Gütertransport* (Diss.: Hamburg, 2005) 45.

62 German law distinguishes between simple ('einfache'), false ('unechte') and shared ('gemeinschaftliche') through bills of lading. A simple through bill of lading allows for transhipment, but does not restrict the carrier's liability. A carrier under a false through bill of lading is bound to perform the sea leg that he has taken on himself, but with regard to any pre- or on-carriage he has only assumed the responsibilities of a forwarder. A shared through bill of lading binds the participating carriers only for their respective parts in the joint performance of the carriage. H. Prüssmann/D. Rabe, *Seehandelsrecht* (C.H. Beck: München, 2000) 764–6.

63 The HVR will mandatorily govern the contract of carriage in the tackle-to-tackle period but articles I (e) and VII HVR do allow the carrier to exonerate his liability for the period between the receipt and loading of the goods and discharge and delivery of the goods. Obviously, sea carriers invariably do so; see for instance article 2 (last paragraph) of the Congenbill 2007: 'The Carrier shall in no case be responsible for loss of or damage to cargo arising prior to loading, after discharging, or with respect to deck cargo and live animals.'

64 See the discussion in Chapter 2.

either deploys two (or more) vessels from his fleet or instructs a sub-carrier to complete the voyage.[65] Articles 6 and 7 of the Conline 2000 bill of lading for instance read:

> The Carrier shall be at liberty to carry the cargo or part thereof to the Port of discharge by the said or other vessel or vessels either belonging to the Carrier or others, or by other means of transport, proceeding either directly or indirectly to such port.
>
> The Carrier shall be at liberty to tranship, lighter, land and store the cargo either on shore or afloat and reship and forward the same to the Port of discharge.

These liberties upgrade the traditional port-to-port bill of lading to a through bill of lading. The through bill of lading contract then 'comes into existence when the carrier contracts to carry on a port-to-port basis and issues a transport document that covers the entire carriage. The carrier thereafter exercises a contractual right of transhipment coupled with a right to subcontract out any part of the contractual undertaking'.[66]

This means that the through bill of lading does not necessarily evidence a multimodal contract of carriage. The contract of carriage may indeed have two or more separate legs, but that is first of all left to the discretion of the carrier. Besides, the mere transhipment of the goods from one sea-going vessel into another does not convert the unimodal contract of carriage into a multimodal contract of carriage. A through bill of lading only evidences a multimodal contract of carriage if these different legs are performed by two or more different means of transportation, for instance when the goods are carried by sea under a through bill of lading from Buenos Aires (Argentina) to Hamburg (Germany), and instead of sailing straight for Hamburg, the carrier discharges the goods in Bremen (Germany) to have them carried by road to Hamburg.[67]

Optional pre-carriage and on-carriage

The through bill of lading will allow for substitution and transhipment, but may also regulate any pre-carriage and on-carriage. In fact, this optional pre-carriage and on-carriage is sometimes seen as one of the trademarks of a through bill of lading:[68]

> Under a typical through bill of lading the principal carrier undertakes to perform a portion of the carriage, for example, the sea leg, and also undertakes to arrange, as agent, an additional leg, for example, acting as forwarding

65 The rationale is purely commercial. The freedom to substitute and/or to tranship allows the carrier to optimize the use of the ships at his disposal.

66 D. Rhidian Thomas, *Multimodalism and through transport: Language, concepts, and categories* Tul. Mar. L.J. (2012) 769.

67 If the goods are just transhipped in Bremen from one sea-going vessel into another, the performance of the contract of carriage still only requires one single means of transportation. The through bill of lading then evidences a unimodal contract of carriage.

68 R. Aikens, M. Bools, R. Lord, *Bills of lading* (LLP: London, 2006) 314.

> agent on behalf of C (the cargo owner, ms) for the onwards road carriage, by a different carrier, from the discharge port.

The face of the Conlinebill 2000 contains the usual boxes to fill out the port of loading and the port of discharge, but in addition thereto boxes to identify the pre-carrier, the place of receipt by the pre-carrier and the place of delivery by the on-carrier. These last boxes are marked with two asterisks to indicate that they apply 'only when pre-/on-carriage is arranged in accordance with Clause 8'. This clause 8 on the reverse of the bill of lading then reads:

> When the Carrier arranges pre-carriage … or on-carriage of the cargo … the Carrier shall contract as Merchant's agent only and the Carrier shall not be liable for any loss or damage arising during any part of the carriage other between the port of loading and the port of discharge even though the freight for the whole carriage has been collected by him.

Such a bill of lading indeed allows for pre-carriage and on-carriage by another means of transportation, but it does not evidence a multimodal contract of carriage as the sea carrier in principle only acts as a forwarding agent. The sea carrier does not agree to carry the goods other than by sea; he only agrees to arrange for any other carriage as an agent of the shipper, and for risk and account of the shipper.[69] The actual contract of pre- or on-carriage is then between the shipper and the carrier instructed on his behalf.[70]

So far, so good for the theory; but this may work out differently in practice. The carrier will not always just arrange for the pre-carriage and on-carriage; he will occasionally assume the responsibility for the pre-carriage from the place of receipt or on-carriage to the final destination himself. Again, this does not necessarily mean that the bill of lading then evidences a multimodal contract of carriage, not even if the pre-carriage or on-carriage is performed by a different means of transportation. The contract of pre- or on-carriage is in that case simply not governed by the initial contract of carriage evidenced by the through bill of lading, but instead by a new contractual arrangement between the shipper and the carrier.

One contract or two contracts

It is not always easy to distinguish the two (or more) sea legs under one single through bill of lading from two (or more) consecutive contracts of carriage by sea. As so often, it depends on the intention of the parties to the contract(s).

In *Mayhew v. OCL* a shipment of chicken/turkey meat was carried from Uckfield to Shoreham (both in the UK), and then by sea to Jeddah (Saudi Arabia).[71] The meat was deep frozen and had to be kept that way during the voyage. OCL issued a bill of lading for the entire voyage, specifically mentioning that

69 See the discussion in Chapter 2.

70 *Stafford Allen & Sons v. Pacific Steam Navigation* (1956) 1 Lloyd's Rep. 104.

71 *Mayhew Foods v. Overseas Containers* (1984) 1 Lloyd's Rep. 317.

the goods were to be carried by sea from Southampton (and thus not Shoreham) to Jeddah on board of the Benalder. The bill of lading allowed for both transhipment and substitution of the nominated vessel.

The meat was carried from Shoreham to Le Havre (France) on the Voline, and subsequently discharged there for transhipment. The meat was only then brought on board of the Benalder for the remainder of the voyage to Jeddah. Whereas the required temperature setting was minus 18 degrees C, the temperature setting was changed to plus 2 to 4 degrees C in the course of the transhipment in Le Havre, and the meat arrived in Jeddah in a damaged condition.

The carrier argued that the contract of carriage had only taken effect upon transhipment in Le Havre. The carrier submitted that the bill of lading just mentioned the Benalder as the nominated vessel, that the bill of lading was actually issued a few days after the arrival of the goods in Le Havre, and that the contract of carriage under that bill of lading had therefore only started when the damage had already been done. Bingham J disagreed and held that:

> the contract here clearly provided for shipment at a United Kingdom port, intended to be Southampton but in the event Shoreham .... It does not matter that the vessel on which the container left this country was not Benalder, because OCL had liberty to substitute vessels or tranship and Benalder was only the intended vessel. Nor does it matter that the bill of lading was issued some days after the goods had arrived in Le Havre showing Benalder and Southampton as the intended vessel and port of shipment. The parties clearly expected and intended a bill of lading to be issued and when issued it duly evidenced the parties' earlier contract.

Since the carrier had negotiated the freedom to carry the goods on board of another vessel than the Benalder, the transhipment and substitution clause now actually worked against OCL. The entire contract of carriage from Shoreham to Jeddah, including the period of transhipment in Le Havre where the damage was caused, was covered by one single bill of lading.

In the Rafaela S, on the other hand, the voyage following the transhipment was held to be governed by a second contract.[72] MSC had agreed to the carriage of a shipment of printing machinery from the port of loading Durban (South Africa) to the port of discharge Felixstowe (UK). This was not the final destination, though; the goods eventually had to be carried to Boston (US). MSC issued a bill of lading in Durban mentioning the Rosemary as the vessel, Durban as the port of loading, Felixstowe as the port of discharge and Boston as the final destination. The bill of lading furthermore provided in article 3:

> The Carrier agrees to carry the goods from the Port of Loading to the Port of Discharge, and shall have the right at its sole discretion to substitute other vessels, feederships, lighters or other modes of transport for the vessel named

72 The *Rafaela S.* (2003) 2 Lloyd's Rep. 113.

> herein (Box 6). If boxes 5 and/or 9 are filled out, the Carrier will, acting as shipper's agent, only arrange for transport of the cargo by other carriers from the place of origin to Port of Loading and/or from Port of Discharge to destination.

The goods were discharged in Felixstowe, subsequently brought on board of the Rafaela S. and carried to Boston by (again) MSC. The printing machinery was damaged during the voyage from Felixstowe to Boston, and the cargo-interested parties pursued payment of the damage from MSC in London.[73] MSC argued that it had issued a through bill of lading covering the entire voyage from Durban to Boston. The cargo-interested parties argued that the parties had agreed on a second contract of carriage for the voyage for Felixstowe to Boston.[74] The UK Court of Appeal decided the issue in favour of the cargo-interested parties.[75] Rix LJ held:[76]

> I conclude that although MSC was contracted to arrange on-carriage to Boston, it was not contracted to carry the machinery to Boston until it entered into a new arrangement at some stage, the details of which are not reported, to on-carry the goods from Felixstowe. That was a separate contract of carriage.

3.4. Multimodal bills of lading

A multimodal bill of lading has all the features of any other (ocean) bill of lading. The difference is that a multimodal bill of lading will typically evidence a multimodal contract of carriage,[77] and that the place of receipt of the goods and the place of their delivery are then identified on the face of the bill of lading in addition to the port of loading and the port of discharge.

The multimodal bill of lading as a document of title

It is submitted that a multimodal bill of lading shares all three functions with an ocean bill of lading, including therefore the document of title function. Multimodal bills of lading will need to be presented for delivery, and multimodal

73 First in arbitration, and later all the way to the House of Lords.

74 If MSC was right, the COGSA 1936 limitation of US$ 500 per package would apply. The cargo-interested parties argued that a second bill of lading for the voyage from Felixstowe to Boston had perhaps not been issued, but its issuance in Felixstowe had certainly been contemplated. If the cargo-interested parties were right, the HVR would apply in accordance with article I (b) and X (b) limiting the carrier's liability to either SDR 667 per collo or 2 SDR per kilo. See also Chapter 5.

75 This issue was no longer pursued before the House of Lords. Chapter 5 discusses the House of Lords judgment on the question of whether a straight bill of lading was in fact a bill of lading in the sense of article I (b) HVR.

76 The *Rafaela S.* (2003) 2 Lloyd's Rep. 113.

77 There is of course nothing wrong with a multimodal bill of lading or waybill evidencing a unimodal contract of carriage (by sea), just as an air waybill or consignment note can effectively evidence a multimodal contract of carriage.

order and bearer bills of lading may symbolize the goods carried thereunder. The authors of Carver (although still carefully) say in this respect:[78]

> It is also arguable that the now common use of multimodal transport documents, and the increasing degree of their standardisation may support the view that a mercantile custom, similar to that established in *Lickbarrow v. Mason*, exists in relation to such documents, at least where they are issued by, or on behalf of sea carriers; but for the present it awaits judicial recognition.

The Bimco Multimodal Transport Bill of Lading (Multidoc 95) may very well be one of these standardized documents referred to. The consignee box mentions 'Consigned to order of', the bill of lading is furthermore explicitly labelled as 'Negotiable',[79] and the attestation clause prescribes that 'One of the MT Bills of lading must be surrendered duly endorsed in exchange for the goods or delivery order.'

The Multidoc 95 is transferable by endorsement and delivery;[80] this transferability is in fact affirmed by the clear reference to its negotiability,[81] and its presentation in the port of discharge is required for the delivery of the goods.[82] The judicial recognition may indeed have yet to follow, but it is in view of the above submitted that multimodal bills of lading such as the Multidoc 95 are documents of title to the goods carried thereunder.

Dual purpose bills of lading

Standard liner bills of lading can often be used as either port-to port-bills of lading or as multimodal bills of lading. The MSC bill of lading forms a good example. The face of the MSC bill of lading provides boxes to identify the port of loading and the port of discharge, but also boxes for the place of receipt and the place of delivery.[83] If only the boxes for the port of loading and port of discharge are filled out, it is a port-to-port bill of lading. If, however, the boxes for the place of receipt and the place of delivery are filled out as well, it becomes a multimodal bill of lading.

Obviously, this goes wrong once every while. In the *Antwerpen* a shipment of 13 containers with whisky was carried from Felixstowe (UK) to Sydney (Australia)

78 G.H. Treitel & F.M.B. Reynolds, *Carver on bills of lading* (Sweet & Maxwell: London, 2011) 577.
79 *Kum v. Wah Tat Bank* (1971) 1 Lloyd's Rep. 439
80 Or just delivery of curse when it is endorsed in blank.
81 *Kum v. Wah Tat Bank* (1971) 1 Lloyd's Rep. 439 and G.H. Treitel & F.M.B. Reynolds, *Carver on bills of lading* (Sweet & Maxwell: London, 2011) 578.
82 D.A. Glass, *Freight forwarding and multimodal transport contracts* (Informa: London, 2012) 249, is slightly more cautious: 'Further, if the bill or other document in negotiable form is issued, the expectation might be that delivery will be taken on its presentation.'
83 These latter boxes designated for the place of receipt and the place of delivery specifically mention that they are for '(Combined Transport ONLY – see Clauses 1 & 5.2)'.

under a similar multipurpose bill of lading.[84] Article 1 of the terms and conditions on the reverse stipulated:

> 'Combined transport' arises when the place of acceptance and/or place of delivery are indicated on the face hereof in the relevant spaces and 'Port to port shipment' arises where the carriage called for by this bill of lading is not combined transport.

The face of the bill of lading mentioned Felixstowe as the port of loading and Sydney as the port of discharge. The box designated for the place of acceptance also mentioned Felixstowe, but the place of delivery was left open. The vessel arrived in Sydney without any incidents, but two of the containers were later stolen from the terminal. The cargo-interested parties argued that the bill of lading evidenced a multimodal contract of carriage, but the New South Wales Court of Appeal disagreed:

> There is nothing to indicate that any carriage other than sea carriage by Antwerpen was contemplated. The specification speaks only of the port of loading and the port of discharge. The absence of an address for the place of acceptance was probably not an oversight but rather the consequence of the fact that no inland carriage was contemplated. It is also significant that 'Felixstowe' has been inserted in the box for 'Port of Loading (Ocean Vessel)' and that 'Sydney' has been nominated as the 'Port of Discharge (Ocean Vessel)'. As, in my view the insertion of 'Felixstowe' in the box 'Place of Acceptance' was a patent error, it should be ignored. ... Thus I hold that the bill of lading is for port to port shipment.

The court concluded that the mention of Felixstowe as the place of acceptance was only a clerical error, and it let the intention of the parties prevail over the information listed on the face of the bill of lading.

3.5. Waybills and consignment notes

Waybills and consignment notes serve as a receipt and they evidence the contract of carriage. They do not symbolize the goods, however, and they do not have to be presented in the port of discharge.

Sea waybills

A sea waybill may resemble a bill of lading at first sight, but the two documents are certainly not the same. The crucial difference is that a sea waybill is not a document of title. The Singapore Court of Appeal made this very clear in *Voss v. APL*:[85]

84 The *Antwerpen* (1994) 1 Lloyd's Rep. 213.
85 *Voss v. APL* (2002) 2 Lloyd's Rep. 707.

> A sea waybill is the maritime version of a document that has long been in use in the context of land and air carriage. It operates as a receipt for goods received for shipment and evidences the contract of carriage. One significant difference between it and a bill of lading is that it is never ever a negotiable instrument and is therefore usually used on short sea routes and where neither the shipper nor the cargo receiver needs to pledge shipping documents in order to raise finance. It is not issued in sets and the receiver is able to take delivery of the goods merely by establishing his identity. The original sea waybill need not be produced.

Sea waybills are in practice often used in short sea shipping. The distance covered is then relatively short; so short in fact that the bill of lading will not always be able to keep up with the goods. Given its function in a documentary sale, the original bill of lading is often still held by the buyer's bank (or his buyer's bank when the bill of lading is transferred more than once) by the time the ship enters the port of discharge. Obviously, the bill of lading is in that case not available for presentation.[86] The advantage of a sea waybill over a bill of lading is then that its presentation is not required, and that the goods can be released to the consignee without further delays or complications. The face of the MSC sea waybill for instance reads:

> Unless instructed otherwise in writing by the Shipper delivery of the Goods will be made only to the Consignee or his authorised representatives. This Sea Waybill is not a document of title to the Goods and delivery will be made, after payment of any outstanding Freight and charges, only on provision of proper proof of identity and of authorisation at the Port of Discharge or Place of Delivery, as appropriate, without the need to produce or surrender a copy of this Sea Waybill.

Air waybills

The Montreal Convention discusses the air waybill in articles 4, 5, 6, 7 and 8 MC. The air waybill needs to mention the place of departure and destination, the stopping place (or places) if the place of departure and destination are in the same country and the weight of the shipment. The conditions of carriage are then printed on the reverse. The air waybill is issued in three originals, one for the carrier, one for the consignee and one for the consignor upon receipt of the cargo.[87] Article 11 (1) MC deals with the evidentiary value of the air waybill:[88]

86 The goods then still need to be released of course, and to avoid any delays in this process, the goods are then instead released against a letter of indemnity to hold the carrier harmless against later claims (by the bill of lading holder) for misdelivery.

87 Non-compliance with these provisions does not affect the existence of the contract; see article 9 MC.

88 Article 11 (2) MC covers the evidentiary value of the air waybill with regard to the goods: 'Any statements in the air waybill or the cargo receipt relating to the weight, dimensions and packing

> The air waybill or the cargo receipt is prima facie evidence of the conclusion of the contract, of the acceptance of the cargo and of the conditions of carriage mentioned therein.

The air waybill thus functions as a receipt and evidences the contract of carriage, but it is not a document of title.[89] The consignee is not required to present an original air waybill to obtain the release of the goods. In fact, article 13 MC gives the consignee the right 'to require the carrier to hand over to him the air waybill and to deliver the cargo to him'.

Multimodal waybills

The multimodal waybill is not regulated by any international convention, but the general idea is the same as for sea and air waybills. Again, the multimodal waybill is not transferable, it does not symbolize the goods and it does not have to be presented in the port of discharge. In fact, the Bimco Multimodal Waybill (Multiwaybill 95) stipulates in article 8 of its terms and conditions:

> The MTO undertakes to perform or procure the performance of all acts necessary to ensure Delivery of the Goods, upon proof of his identity, to the person named as Consignee.

The multimodal waybill functions as a receipt of the goods by the carrier, it evidences a multimodal contract of carriage, but it is not a document of title.

Consignment notes

At this point, it would make sense to discuss the 'rail waybill' and the 'road waybill', but these terms are not in use. Instead, contracts for the carriage of goods

of the cargo, as well as those relating to the number of packages, are prima facie evidence of the facts stated; those relating to the quantity, volume and condition of the cargo do not constitute evidence against the carrier except so far as they both have been, and are stated in the air waybill or the cargo receipt to have been, checked by it in the presence of the consignor, or relate to the apparent condition of the cargo.'

89 Nevertheless, article 12 (3) MC links the right of disposal to the consignor's presentation of his original air waybill: 'If the carrier carries out the instructions of the consignor for the disposition of the cargo without requiring the production of the part of the air waybill or the cargo receipt delivered to the latter, the carrier will be liable, without prejudice to its right of recovery from the consignor, for any damage which may be caused thereby to any person who is lawfully in possession of that part of the air waybill or the cargo receipt.' Admittedly, this provision brings the air waybill closer to a document of title than the sea waybill, but not much more than that. The presentation of the air waybill only relates to the exercise of the right of disposal by the consignor. The carrier is liable for the damage if he has complied with the consignor's instructions in the course of the voyage, but cannot produce the (third) original afterwards. The rule thus ensures efficiency and protects third-party holders of the original (other than the consignee mentioned in the air waybill); see M. Clarke & D. Yates, *Contracts of carriage by land and air* (Informa: London, 2008), first at 445, and then at 346.

by either rail or road are evidenced by so-called consignment notes, transport documents with essentially the same functions as a waybill. As such, the consignment note is not a document of title,[90] but it serves as a receipt, it evidences the contract of carriage and it may stipulate the carrier's conditions of carriage. Article 4 CMR reads:

> The contract of carriage shall be confirmed by the making out of a consignment note. The absence, irregularity or loss of the consignment note shall not affect the existence or the validity of the contract of carriage which shall remain subject to the provisions of this Convention.

Article 6 § 2 CIM 1999 prescribes that the contract of carriage by rail is confirmed by a consignment note.[91] The consignment note needs to follow a uniform model;[92] it needs to be signed by the consignor and the carrier, and the latter needs to confirm the receipt of the goods.[93] Article 7 § 1 CIM 1999 then lists the particulars that any consignment note should contain, such as the date, the place of delivery, the name of the consignee and a description of the goods.[94]

The evidentiary value of the consignment note then follows from article 12 § 1 CIM 1999 and article 9 (1) CMR. These two provisions are almost identical (to article 11 (1) MC). Article 9 (1) CMR stipulates that the consignment note 'shall be prima facie evidence of the making of the contract of carriage, the conditions of the contract and the receipt of the goods by the carrier'.[95] Articles 12 §§ 2 and 3 CIM 1999 and 9 (2) CMR ensure that the description of the goods in the consignment note gives prima facie evidence of their condition and number at the time of receipt.[96]

90 In fact, article 6 § 5 CIM 1999 explicitly stipulates that the consignment note is not a bill of lading. Again, and in line with article 12 (3) MC, the right of disposal under the CIM is linked to the presentation of the consignment note; see article 19 § 1 CIM 1999: 'If the consignor or, in the case referred to in Article 18 § 3, the consignee wishes to modify the contract of carriage by giving subsequent orders, he must produce to the carrier the duplicate of the consignment note on which the modifications have to be entered.'

91 The second sentence of article 6 § 2 CIM 1999 equals the second sentence of article 4 CMR: 'However, the absence, irregularity or loss of the consignment note shall not affect the existence or validity of the contract which shall remain subject to these Uniform Rules.'

92 This uniform model consignment note is drafted by the international associations of carriers; see article 6 § 8 CIM.

93 Article 6 § 2, § 3 and § 4 CIM 1999.

94 Articles 4, 5 and 6 CMR more or less follow the same pattern, except for the requirement of a uniform model consignment note.

95 See the discussion of article 11 MC above. Article 12 § 1 CIM 1999 reads: 'The consignment note shall be prima facie evidence of the conclusion and the conditions of the contract of carriage and the taking over of the goods by the carrier.'

96 Provided that the carrier made no reservations (see articles 12 § 4 CIM 1999 and 9 (2) CMR) and that the rail carrier either loaded the goods or examined their loading; see 12 § 2 and 3 CIM 1999.

3.6. The relation between the contract of carriage and the transport document

A bill of lading, a waybill, a consignment note or any other transport document will often be issued pursuant to a contract of carriage, i.e. once the parties have already agreed on the contract of carriage.[97] This raises the question of whether the issuance of a transport document affects the contract of carriage as earlier agreed upon between the parties.

As a general rule, the issuance of a bill of lading, waybill or consignment note cannot affect the contract of carriage pursuant to which it is issued since 'it would be absurd to suppose that the parties intend the terms of the contract to be changed when the bill of lading is issued: for the issue of the bill of lading does not necessarily mark any stage in the development of the contract.'[98]

The contract of carriage thus in principle takes precedence over the transport document.[99] The contract of carriage governs the relationship of the parties, and the issuance of a bill of lading, waybill, consignment note or any other document does not change the relationship between the contracting parties.[100] The transport document may then still evidence the existence of the contract of carriage, but it essentially only functions as a receipt.[101]

The third-party consignee acting in good faith

The initial parties to the contract of carriage are obviously well aware of the contents of their agreement, but that cannot always be said about third parties, more in particular the consignee to whom the goods must be delivered. The consignee

97 Article III (3) HVR stipulates that the bill of lading of lading is issued on demand of the shipper. For there to be a shipper, there must first be a contract of carriage.

98 *Pyrene v. Scindia* (1954) 2 ALL ER 158, per Devlin J.

99 In principle, because parties can agree otherwise, see for instance the (double) superseding clause in the booking note in the *Pembroke* (1995) 2 Lloyd's Rep. 290: 'It is hereby agreed that this Contract shall be performed subject to the terms contained on pp. 1 and 2 hereof which shall prevail over any previous arrangements and which shall in turn be superseded ... by the terms of the Bill of Lading, the terms of which (in full or in extract) are found on the reverse side hereof.'

100 Arguably, this is perhaps not entirely true as the issuance of a bill of lading pursuant to a contract of carriage other than a charter party may trigger the application of the HVR; see *The Happy Ranger* (2002) 2 Lloyd's Rep. 357. This is less likely to happen under Dutch law; see article 8:410 DCC: 'If a contract of carriage is concluded and furthermore a bill of lading is issued, ... the relation between the carrier and the shipper is governed by the provisions of the contract of carriage, and not by those of the bill of lading.'

101 *Rodocanachi v. Milburn Brothers* (1886) 17 Q.B.D. 316, and especially *President of India v. Metcalfe Shipping* (1969) 2 Lloyd's Rep. 476 (*Dunelmia*): 'The bill of lading here was not separate or severable from the charter-party. It was issued in pursuance of it. The Italian sellers A.N.I.C. had already contracted to sell the fertilizer to the Government of India: and the Government had chartered the ship to carry it. The bill of lading was a mere instrument to carry out those contracts. It did not evidence any separate contract at all. As between charterers and shipowners, it was only a receipt for the goods.'

may not be aware of the arrangements in the initial contract of carriage, and he may only have seen the bill of lading issued pursuant to that contract. In that case, the terms of the contract of carriage cannot be held against a consignee acting in good faith. This consignee may rely on the terms as he finds them in the bill of lading.[102]

In *Leduc v. Ward* a shipment of rapeseed had to be carried by sea from Fiume (nowadays Rijeka, Croatia) to Dunkerque (Belgium).[103] The contract of carriage itself was concluded orally, but Ward had also issued a bill of lading to the shipper. The shipper/seller of the goods then in turn transferred this bill of lading to Leduc, the consignee/buyer of the goods.

Unfortunately, the ship did not sail straight for Dunkerque. Instead, it sailed via Glasgow (Scotland). This detour seriously extended the duration of the voyage, but more importantly also exposed the cargo to additional risks that indeed materialized: the ship and its cargo perished in the waves off the Scottish coast. When Leduc initiated proceedings against the carrier for the loss of his rapeseed, Ward argued that he was at liberty to sail via Glasgow as he had agreed this with the shipper. All the same, the bill of lading did not reflect such an agreement. The court therefore held that Ward could not invoke the liberty to sail via Glasgow against Leduc as their relation was governed by the provisions of the bill of lading:[104]

> Although the bill of lading is only a receipt as between the charterer and the shipowner, it is more than a receipt between the endorsee and the shipowner; it contains the contract between them.

This rule of *Leduc v. Ward* is far from absolute. In fact, the rule first of all only applies to the relation between the carrier and a third-party holder of the bill of lading. The transfer of the bill of lading to a charterer does not qualify as a transfer to a third party.[105] In fact, the transfer of the bill of lading to a forwarding agent acting on behalf of the charterer does not qualify as a transfer to a third party either.[106] The rule furthermore only applies if the third-party holder of the bill of lading acts in good faith. Leduc could therefore not have relied on the bill of lading if he had (tacitly) agreed to the course via Glasgow.

102 S.D. Girvin, *Carriage of goods by sea* (OUP: Oxford, 2011) 194: 'When a bill of lading is endorsed by a charterer to a third party bona fide purchaser, the terms of the bill of lading supplant the charter party and become conclusive evidence of the contract of carriage.' See also article 8:441 (2) DCC: 'Against the holder of the bill of lading, who was not the shipper, the carrier under bill of lading is bound to and may rely on the stipulations of this bill of lading.'

103 *Leduc v. Ward* (1888) 20 Q.B.D. 475.

104 *Leduc v. Ward* (1888) 20 Q.B.D. 475.

105 *President of India v. Metcalfe Shipping* (1969) 2 Lloyd's Rep. 476 (*Dunelmia*).

106 HR 16 January 1998, NJ 1999, 284 (ann. M.H. Claringbould), S&S 1998/53 (*Enarxis*).

The application of the rule to other transport documents

The decision in *Leduc v. Ward* specifically relates to a bill of lading, but it is submitted that the scope of the rule is not just limited to bills of lading (or similar documents of title). In fact, it is submitted that the rule also extends to waybills, consignment notes and other transport documents.

The justification for this submission follows from the rationale behind the rule. The objective of the rule is to protect a third party that relied, and could in fact have relied, on the bill of lading to evidence his relation with the carrier. This is the bill of lading assuming its contractual role; it functions as the evidence of the contract of carriage. The protection of a third party acting in good faith should then arguably not be reserved for third-party holders of a document of title,[107] but should instead be extended to all third parties that in good faith relied on a transport document that evidences the contract of carriage.[108]

An example may be helpful, and the facts and circumstances in *Leduc v. Ward* only need a few amendments to make the point. A Croatian merchant sells a shipment of rapeseed to a Belgian buyer, Leduc. The seller and the buyer agree that the purchase price is paid against the receipt of an original consignment note (confirming that the rapeseed was received by the carrier in apparent good order and condition).

The seller instructs Ward to carry the goods by truck from Rijeka to Dunkerque. Ward accepts the instructions, loads the shipment of rapeseed in his truck and signs the consignment note for good receipt. The seller then instructs a courier to bring the original consignment note to Leduc. The consignment note indeed confirms the good receipt of the shipment by Ward, contains no further anomalies and Leduc pays the purchase price.

Ward is meanwhile on his way to Belgium when one of his Spanish customers calls with a request to carry a shipment of meat from San Sebastian (Spain) to Antwerp (Belgium). Ward is tempted. There is still room in his truck and he calls the Croatian merchant to see whether he has any objections. Ward promises him a discount on the initially agreed freight to sweeten the deal, and the merchant agrees to the detour via San Sebastian. Neither party to the contract, however, feels the need to inform Leduc of the change of plans.

In the end, the detour adds a week to the duration of the voyage. This extra week in the truck has not benefited the quality of the rapeseed. In fact, when Ward finally arrives in Dunkerque the quality of the rapeseed has seriously

107 The *Carso* (1930) 38 Lloyd's Rep. 22.

108 See also J. von Werder, *Zum Wirksamkeit von Gerichtsstandklauseln in Seefrachtbriefen gegenüber dem Empfänger* TranspR (2005) 112. Von Werder discusses the effect of forum choices in sea waybills against the consignee, and writes at 113: 'The custom of trade established for bills of lading can therefore – since it does not concern the quality of a bill of lading as a document of title – equally be applied to sea waybills.'

deteriorated, and its value has decreased accordingly. Leduc sues Ward for the damage, but Ward relies on his agreement with the seller.

Clearly, this defence will not hold, and it makes no difference that the consignment note is not a document of title. Ward will be able to rely on the terms of the varied contract of carriage in his relation to the Croatian merchant, but this defence will not be successful against Leduc who in good faith relied on the consignment note to evidence the contract of carriage.[109]

109 See on this point also article 41 (c) RR that prescribes that proof to the contrary by the carrier of certain contract particulars 'shall not be admissible against a consignee that in good faith has acted in reliance on any of the following contract particulars included in a non-negotiable transport document or a non negotiable electronic transport record' and Y. Baatz in Y. Baatz, C. Debattista, F. Lorenzon, A. Serdy, H. Staniland, M. Tsimplis, *The Rotterdam Rules: A practical annotation* (Informa: London, 2009) 120, saying with regard to the 'contract particulars' in this provision: 'It may be argued … that – as statements of fact – they may have given rise to an estoppel against the carrier anyway.' See on the other hand, however, article 25 (4) RR: 'The carrier is not entitled to invoke subparagraph 1 (c) of this article against a third party that has acquired a negotiable transport document or a negotiable electronic transport record in good faith, unless the contract particulars state that the goods may be carried on deck.' Apparently, the consignee in good faith is then still unprotected when any other document evidences the contract of carriage.

4 The parties to the contract of carriage

The effect of a contract of carriage often goes beyond the two contracting parties. In fact, the provisions of a contract of carriage will also affect the third-party consignee, and may even affect the rights and obligations of third parties that were instrumental in the performance of the contract. This chapter identifies the initial parties to the contract, deals with the position of the consignee, discusses the right of disposal and the right of suit, and covers the liability of the carrier's servants, agents and subcontractors under a contract of carriage.

4.1. The initial parties to the contract of carriage

Every contract of carriage has at least two parties. One of these parties is the carrier; the other is the shipper, the consignor or the sender, depending on the means of transportation and the applicable convention. They are the initial parties to the contract.

The carrier

The carrier is a contractual figure.[1] Article 3 (a) CIM 1999 for instance defines the carrier as 'the contractual carrier with whom the consignor has concluded the contract of carriage'. Article I (a) HVR stipulates that the carrier 'includes the owner or the charterer who enters into a contract of carriage with a shipper'.[2]

1 Article 102 CMC defines the multimodal transport operator as 'the person who has entered into a multimodal transport contract with the shipper either by himself or by another person acting on his behalf'.

2 Bill of lading contracts will often contain a so-called 'Identity of carrier clause'. Such a clause identifies the (sole) carrier under the bill of lading contract, and channels the liability, for instance: 'The Contract evidenced by this Bill of Lading is between the Merchant and the Owner of the vessel named herein (or substitute) and it is therefore agreed that said Shipowner only shall be liable for any damage of loss due to any breach or non-performance of any obligation arising out of the contract of carriage, whether or not relating to the vessel's seaworthiness.' See *The Starsin* (2003) 1 Lloyd's Rep. 571, F.G.M. Smeele, *Passieve legitimatie uit cognossement* (Diss.: Rotterdam, 1998), and article 37 RR.

This implies that the carrier is contractually bound to the proper performance of the contract, and (unless of course sub-carriage has been excluded in the contract) that he does not actually have to carry the goods himself.[3]

A carrier will in practice very often instruct a sub-carrier,[4] who may in turn again instruct another sub-carrier and so on.[5] A contract of sub-carriage is a contract of carriage as any other. In the relation between a carrier and a sub-carrier, the carrier then assumes the role of the shipper, and the sub-carrier assumes the role of the carrier, and this equally applies to all the other contracts in the chain.[6] The last carrier in such a chain of contracts of carriage is the actual carrier, the one physically carrying the goods (to their destination).[7]

The contractual carrier is liable for the proper performance of the contract of carriage, irrespective of the number of sub-carriers in the chain. The instruction of a sub-carrier, or in fact any other agent or servant instrumental in the performance of his obligations under the contract,[8] simply does not affect the liability position of the contractual carrier. Article 3 CMR is very clear in that respect:[9]

> For the purposes of this Convention the carrier shall be responsible for the acts and omissions of his agents and servants and of any other persons of whose services he makes use for the performance of the carriage, when such

3 In fact, he does not even need to have any means of transportation at his disposal. This is relevant for the position of a NVO(C)C, a non-vessel operating (common) carrier. The NVO(C)C has no ships yet presents himself as a carrier (and issues bills of lading in the process). The NVO(C)C therefore also assumes the liabilities of a carrier.

4 Article 3 (b) CIM 1999 defines the substitute carrier as 'a carrier, who has not concluded the contract of carriage with the consignor, but to whom the carrier referred to in letter a) has entrusted, in whole or in part, the performance of the carriage by rail'.

5 Chains of three, four or even five carriers in the international carriage by road, and an exploitation chain with an owner, a bare boat charterer, a time charterer and a voyage charterer in the international carriage by sea are in fact not uncommon.

6 See the second sentence of article 4 (1) CMNI: 'For the purpose of such contract, all the provisions of this Convention concerning the shipper shall apply to the carrier and those concerning the carrier to the actual carrier.'

7 See article 39 MC; the actual carrier is someone who 'performs, by virtue of authority from the contracting carrier, the whole or part of the carriage'. Article 1 (3) CMNI defines the actual carrier as 'any person, other than a servant or an agent of the carrier, to whom the performance of the carriage or of part of such carriage has been entrusted by the carrier'. This is a rather unfortunate definition as such an 'actual carrier' could then in turn still entrust the performance to another sub-carrier, which would imply that he is therefore not an actual carrier. The last sentence of article 4 (4) CMNI provides the actual carrier with an extra line of defence: 'The actual carrier may avail himself of all the objections invocable by the carrier under the contract of carriage.'

8 Article 18 RR reads: 'The carrier is liable for the breach of its obligations under this Convention caused by the acts or omissions of: (a) Any performing party; (b) The master or crew of the ship; (c) Employees of the carrier or a performing party; or (d) Any other person that performs or undertakes to perform any of the carrier's obligations under the contract of carriage, to the extent that the person acts, either directly or indirectly, at the carrier's request or under the carrier's supervision or control.'

9 See also article 27 § 1 CIM 1999 and article 4 (2) CMNI.

agents, servants or other persons are acting within the scope of their employment, as if such acts or omissions were his own.

The recourse gap

A contractual carrier is responsible for the acts and omissions of (any one of) his sub-carriers. If the carrier is liable for loss or damage under the contract of carriage, he can take recourse under the contract of sub-carriage. Since the contract of carriage and the contract of sub-carriage are separate contracts, however, his liability position under the contract of carriage and his recourse position under the contract of sub-carriage are not necessarily aligned.

A contractual carrier may for instance need the resources of several unimodal sub-carriers to perform a multimodal contract of carriage. He has contractually assumed the responsibility to deliver the goods to their consignee at the final destination, but he has delegated the domestic road leg to sub-carrier A, the international sea leg to sub-carrier B and the final train leg to sub-carrier C. If the goods are lost or damaged during the voyage, the contractual carrier is liable for this damage under the multimodal contract of carriage.

The multimodal carrier will then turn to the sub-carrier responsible for the loss or damage. Their relation is governed by the contract of sub-carriage, a contract of carriage as any other. For his recourse action to succeed, the multimodal carrier must therefore prove that the sub-carrier in question received the goods in a sound condition, but failed to deliver the goods in that same sound condition.

This will often be easy enough. The goods were, for instance, stolen from an unguarded parking place, contaminated with sea water or damaged when the train derailed, and the circumstances of the case then identify the responsible sub-carrier. If, however, the goods arrive in a damaged condition, and the cause of the damage cannot be localized, the multimodal carrier has a recourse problem. He cannot prove which one of his sub-carriers received the goods in a sound condition, but failed to deliver the goods in that same sound condition, and his recourse claim is likely to fail.

Mutatis mutandis the same applies if the damage can be localized, but the contract of carriage and the contract of sub-carriage are governed by different liability rules.[10] The liability of the multimodal carrier in the example may be limited to 8,33 SDR/Kg under the multimodal contract of carriage.[11] At the same time, however, the liability of the sub-carrier for the domestic road leg may be limited

10 See for instance Rechtbank Arnhem 18 July 1996, S&S 1997/33, a case wherein live animals were carried from Herwijnen (the Netherlands) to Dundalk (Ireland). The multimodal carrier had subcontracted the passage of the Channel to a sea carrier, and a large number of animals died during the sea leg. The multimodal carrier's liability was limited to SDR 8.33 per kilo, but when he turned to the sea carrier in the recourse proceedings, the court denied his claim. The sea carrier was not liable at all since he had validly excluded his liability for the carriage of live animals.

11 8,33 SDR is approximately 10 EUR.

to 3,40 EUR/Kg under the contract of sub-carriage by road.[12] If the loss or damage occurred during the domestic road leg, the multimodal carrier will only be able to recover EUR 3,40 per kilo lost. The difference between 8,33 SDR/Kg and 3,40 EUR/Kg is his recourse gap.[13]

The successive carrier

The CIM 1999, MC and CMR also regulate the 'successive carrier'. The concept of successive carriage is closely linked to the early days of the carriage of goods by rail. The domestic railroad networks were expanding rapidly in nineteenth-century Europe, but there were still quite a few challenges for the international carriage of goods by rail.

One problem was that the different domestic railways were not compatible, for one thing because they used a different gauge,[14] but also because they used different technical standards for the system of the brakes,[15] the couplings and the locks of the wagons.[16] Besides, all these railroads, engines and wagons were state-owed and state-operated in those days, and most countries had restricted the access of foreign carriers to their local markets.[17] Finally, the notion of a TIR Carnet did

12 The limitation of liability of article 8:1105 DCC for domestic carriage by road.

13 Multimodal contracts of carriage will therefore sometimes stipulate that the multimodal carrier's liability (in the absence of mandatory rules of course) is governed by the terms and conditions of the contract of sub-carriage to avoid such a gap. Article 5.2.2. (b) of the multipurpose MSC bill of lading stipulates that 'where no international convention, national law or regulation would have been compulsorily applicable, by the contract of carriage issued by the Subcontractor carrier for that stage of transport, including any limitations and exceptions contained therein, which contract the Merchant and the Carrier adopt and incorporate by reference, it being agreed that the Carrier's rights and liabilities shall be the same as those of the Subcontractor carrier, but in no event whatsoever shall the Carrier's liability exceed GBP 100 sterling legal tender per package'.

14 This changed after the British inventor/engineer George Stephenson had introduced his 1435-mm gauge in 1830. This 1435-mm gauge became the standard in UK, and, once it had been adopted by the German, Belgian and Italian railways, later became the 'standard international railway gauge'. I. Anastasiadou, *In search of a railway Europe: Transnational railway developments in interwar Europe* (Eindhoven: Technische Universiteit Eindhoven, 2009) 18. Not every country followed the standard, though. In fact, it is these days still not possible to enter Russia without switching trains. See for instance Rechtbank Midden-Nederland 16 December 2015, S&S 2016/43.

15 The railroads in the nineteenth century were notoriously unsafe. One of the problems was that the couplings and the brakes needed to be operated manually, and casualties and injuries were very common in that process. See e.g. M. Aldrich, *Death Rode the Rails: American Railroad Accidents and Safety, 1828–1965* (Baltimore, MD: Johns Hopkins University Press, 2006).

16 These technical issues were discussed at several international conferences in Berne (Switzerland) at the end of the century. A conference on the 'technical standards' was held in 1882, and the problem of the gauge was discussed at the conference of 1886. Article 1 of the Convention of Berne of 1886 prescribed a minimum gauge of 1435 mm and a maximum gauge of 1463 mm. The delegates also agreed on a standard master key, the so-called 'Berne key', that could open the locks of all the different wagons in use; see S. Lommers, 'The Berne Key: The key to railway harmony', *Inventing Europe*, http://www.inventingeurope.eu/story/the-berne-key-the-key-to-railway-harmony.

17 In fact, some still do. Sec. 27 of the Jones Act (46 App. U.S.C. 883 (2002) reads: 'No merchandise . . . shall be transported by water, or by land and water, on penalty of forfeiture of the merchandise . . . between points in the United States, including Districts, Territories, and possessions thereof embraced within the coastwise laws, either directly or via a foreign port, or for any

not exist yet,[18] and this meant that the goods had to be discharged, inspected and cleared with customs with the crossing of each border.

In practice, a contract for the carriage of goods of goods by rail from Berlin to Madrid would therefore require three different, successive carriers. A German carrier would receive the goods from the consignor for their carriage to the French border. He would hand the goods together with the consignment note to a French carrier who would then take over until he reached the Spanish border, and there the exact same process would be repeated.

To ensure that the individual, domestic carriers could not hide behind their foreign colleagues if the goods arrived in a damaged condition, the CIM 1890 regulated the position of the successive carrier. Article 26 § 1 CIM 1890 ensured that the first carrier was liable until the delivery of the goods at their final destination,[19] and article 26 § 2 CIM 1890 provided that 'each successive carrier, just by taking over the goods together with the initial consignment note, accedes to the contract of carriage evidenced by the consignment note and accepts the obligations following therefrom.'[20]

These provisions on the successive carrier were adopted by the Warsaw Convention in 1929,[21] and later found their way into the CMR in 1956.[22] The wording of article 34 CMR closely resembles the original wording of article 26 § 2 CIM 1890:[23]

part of the transportation, in any other vessel than a vessel built in and documented under the laws of the United States and owned by persons who are citizens of the United States.'

18 A TIR Carnet allows for easy access of goods in transit between the contracting states. The Customs Convention on the International Transport of Goods under Cover of TIR Carnets (TIR Convention) was signed in Geneva in 1959, and has meanwhile been replaced by the TIR Convention 1975. Instead of dealing with the customs formalities at each different border, these formalities are then dealt with only once, i.e. when the goods arrive at their destination.

19 As the CIM 1890 was originally drafted in French and German only, this is not the authentic wording of the provision, but a translation.

20 The wording has been amended over the years, but not very much. Article 26 CIM 1999 for instance stipulates: 'If carriage governed by a single contract is performed by several successive carriers, each carrier, by the very act of taking over the goods with the consignment note, shall become a party to the contract of carriage in accordance with the terms of that document and shall assume the obligations arising there from. In such a case each carrier shall be responsible in respect of carriage over the entire route up to delivery.'

21 Article 30 (1) Warsaw Convention; article 36 MC.

22 Y. Boon/D. Dokter in M.L Hendrikse/Ph.H.J.G. van Huizen (eds), *CMR: Internationaal vervoer van goederen over de weg* (Paris: Zutphen, 2005) 282; Rechtbank Rotterdam (in summary proceedings) 26 September 2006, S&S 2007/90.

23 Clearly, article 34 CMR does not cover straightforward contracts of sub-carriage. Loewe has been very specific in that respect, saying that 'where a person concludes a contract of carriage as a carrier but does not himself perform any part of the carriage, the provisions of articles 34 et seq. cannot be applied'. R. Loewe, *Commentary on the Convention of 19 May 1956 on the Contract for the International Carriage of Goods by Road (CMR)* ETL 1976, at 397. The (probably) original German text is even more specific; see *Erläuterungen zum Übereinkommen vom 19. Mai 1956 über den Beförderungsvertrag im internationalen Strassengüterverkehr (CMR)* ETL 1976, at 589: 'Schliesst jemand als Frachtführer einen Beförderungsvertrag, befördert er aber selbst nicht einmal auf einer Teilstrecke, sondern lässt er die gesamte Beförderung von einem oder mehreren Frachtführern durchführen, so kommen Artikel 34 ff. nicht zur Anwendung.'

> If carriage governed by a single contract is performed by successive road carriers, each of them shall be responsible for the performance of the whole operation, the second carrier and each succeeding carrier becoming a party to the contract of carriage, under the terms of the consignment note, by reason of his acceptance of the goods and the consignment note.

It is submitted that the successive carrier is a relic from the past.[24] It may indeed have been necessary to regulate the position of the successive carrier at the end of the nineteenth century, but nowadays this has little added value. In fact, the provisions on successive carriage in the CMR do more harm than good as they are in practice applied differently in the different contracting states.[25]

The maritime performing party

Article 1 (7) RR introduces the maritime performing party,[26] i.e. a person other than the carrier that 'performs or undertakes to perform any of the carrier's obligations under a contract of carriage during the period between the arrival of the goods at the port of loading of a ship and their departure from the port of discharge of a ship. An inland carrier is a maritime performing party only if it performs or undertakes to perform its services exclusively within a port area'.[27]

The liability of the maritime performing party is regulated by the rules.[28] Article 19 RR prescribes that his obligations and liabilities equal those of the carrier under the convention if:

24 M. Spanjaart, *The successive carrier: A relic from the past* (Unif. L. Rev., 2016) 1–12.

25 The Belgium, Italian and Spanish courts stay close to the wording of article 34 CMR; see for Belgium Hof van Cassatie 30 June 1995 ETL 1996, 545 (with a critical note by S. Geeroms) and L. Keijser Ondervervoer – opvolgend vervoer (artikel 3 – 34 e.v. CMR) ETL (2007) 331; for Italy Corte di Cassazione, Cass. civ. Sez. III, 17-04-1992, n. 4728; for Spain Tribunal Supremo 14 July 1987, RJ\1987\5489; Tribunal Supremo 29 June 1998, RJ\1998\5282, Audencia Provencial 24 July 2012, JUR\2014\155768, and also F. Sanchez-Gamborino/A. Cabrera Cavonas E; Covenio CMR (Marge Books: Valencia, 2012) 159. The German and Austrian courts in any case require the (initial) consignment to pass through the chain of carriers, BGH 19 April 2007, TranspR 2007, 416; OLG Stuttgart 20 April 2011, TranspR 2011, 340; OGH 9 January 2002, TranspR 2003, 463. The English, French and Dutch courts, however, will apply the provisions on successive carriage to contracts of sub-carriage, *Ulster-Swift v. Taunton* (1977) 1 Lloyd's Rep. 346, *Coggins v. LKW* (1998) 1 Lloyd's Rep. 255; Cour de Cassation 11 December 1990, BTL 1990, 223; Cour d'Appel Paris 4 June 2008, BTL 2008, 433. Cour d'Appel Paris 10 October 2012, 11/06530 and HR 11 September 2015, NJ 2016, 219 (ann. K.F. Haak), S&S 2016/1.

26 A dissertation on the position of the maritime performing party (S. Niessen, Erasmus Rotterdam) is expected in the course of 2017.

27 Article 1 (6) RR defines the 'performing party'. Upon instruction of the carrier (only), 'he performs or undertakes to perform any of the carrier's obligations under a contract of carriage with respect to the receipt, loading, handling, stowage, carriage, keeping, care, unloading or delivery of the goods, to the extent that such person acts, either directly or indirectly, at the carrier's request or under the carrier's supervision or control'.

28 Conversely, the liability of the performing party is not regulated by the RR.

(a) The maritime performing party received the goods for carriage in a Contracting State, or delivered them in a Contracting State, or performed its activities with respect to the goods in a port in a Contracting State; and (b) The occurrence that caused the loss, damage or delay took place: (i) during the period between the arrival of the goods at the port of loading of the ship and their departure from the port of discharge from the ship and either (ii) while the maritime performing party had custody of the goods or (iii) at any other time to the extent that it was participating in the performance of any of the activities contemplated by the contract of carriage.

If the carrier and the maritime performing party are both liable for the loss, damage or delay, their liability is joint and several.[29] Their aggregate liability, however, cannot exceed the overall limitation of liability under the rules.[30]

The shipper/consignor/sender

Whereas all the conventions use the unambiguous term 'carrier', they at the same time use three different terms for his (contractual) counterpart. The CIM 1999 and MC refer to the 'consignor', the HVR and CMNI refer to the 'shipper' and the CMR refers to the 'sender'.[31]

The consignor under the CIM 1999 is clearly a contractual figure. This follows from the wording of article 3 (a) CIM 1999. This article defines the carrier as 'the contractual carrier with whom the consignor has concluded the contract of carriage pursuant to these Uniform Rules, or a successive carrier who is liable on the basis of this contract'. In the process of defining the carrier, article 3 (a) CIM 1999 therefore defines the consignor as the carrier's contractual counterpart.

Besides, article 6 § 2 CIM 1999 prescribes that the contract of carriage is confirmed by a consignment note, and article 6 § 3 CIM 1999 requires this consignment note to be signed by the consignor and the carrier. Again, this confirms that the consignor is the contractual counterpart of the carrier.

The MC does not define the consignor. In fact, the consignor only surfaces in article 7 MC,[32] and then not so much as the carrier's contractual counterpart, but

29 Article 20 (1) RR.

30 Article 20 (2) RR.

31 This is unfortunate, but perhaps even more unfortunate is that 'shipper' and 'consignor' have a slightly different meaning in contracts of carriage by sea or inland waterways. R. Aikens, M. Bools & R. Lord, *Bills of lading* (LLP: London, 2006) give the following description of the shipper respectively consignor (Preface, p. vii): 'Shipper. This is generally the person who consigns the cargo for shipment, who contracts with the carrier, and is named the shipper in the bill of lading. . . . Consignor. The party who has possession of the goods prior to shipment or delivery to the carrier or his agents.'

32 The full text of article 7 MC reads: '1. The air waybill shall be made out by the consignor in three original parts. 2. The first part shall be marked "for the carrier"; it shall be signed by the consignor. The second part shall be marked "for the consignee"; it shall be signed by the consignor and by

instead as his physical counterpart, i.e. the party actually handing the goods to the carrier for transportation.[33] Article 7 MC stipulates that the air waybill 'shall be made out by the consignor in three original parts', and that the third part 'shall be signed by the carrier who shall hand it to the consignor after the cargo has been accepted'. This suggests that the air waybill is issued upon receipt of the cargo, and that the consignor hands the goods to the carrier (and is mentioned as such on the air waybill).

In *Western Digital v. British Airways*, however, Mance LJ held that the underlying contractual relation should not be set aside as 'the Convention's references to consignor and consignee should not . . . be read in an exclusive sense'. This in turn implies that the consignor under the (at that time Warsaw) convention is not per definition the party mentioned as such on the waybill,[34] but that he may also be the carrier's contractual counterpart:[35]

> I adopt the view, taken by other Courts which have considered this problem, that there are, in this respect, strong considerations of commercial sense in favour of an interpretation which recognizes and gives effect to the underlying contractual structure, save in so far this is positively inconsistent with the Warsaw and Guadalajara Conventions.

The HVR do not explicitly define the shipper. The rules do define the carrier, though, and the definition of article I (a) HVR identifies the shipper as a contractual figure (as well).[36] Since the carrier 'enters into a contract of carriage with a shipper', the contractual relation is decisive, and not any involvement in the physical handover of the goods to the carrier for transportation or any reference in the shipper's box on the face of the bill of lading.[37] The German Supreme Court held in the *Dithmarschen*:[38]

the carrier. The third part shall be signed by the carrier who shall hand it to the consignor after the cargo has been accepted. 3. The signature of the carrier and that of the consignor may be printed or stamped. 4. If, at the request of the consignor, the carrier makes out the air waybill, the carrier shall be deemed, subject to proof to the contrary, to have done so on behalf of the consignor.'

33 The consignor in this sense may of course at the same time be the shipper, but he will in practice often be a FOB or FCA seller or a freight forwarder, and thus not a party to the contract of carriage between the shipper and the carrier.

34 The Multiduc 95 defines the consignor as 'the person who concludes the Multimodal Transport Contract'.

35 *Western Digital v. British Airways* (2000) 2 Lloyd's Rep. 142.

36 All the same, § 513 (1) HGB, the German incorporation of article III (3) HVR, prescribes that the bill of lading is issued to the 'Ablader', i.e. the one physically handing the goods to the carrier. The objective is to protect the fob seller: 'Unless otherwise agreed in the contract for the carriage of general cargo, the carrier must issue to the Ablader, at the latter's request, an order bill of lading that – at the choice of the Ablader – is made out "To Order" of the Ablader, "To Order" of the consignee, or simply "To Order" (blank); in the last case, this shall be deemed to mean "To Order" of the Ablader.'

37 *The Roseline* (1987) 1 Lloyd's Rep. 18, but see also *The Athanasia Comninos* (1990) 1 Lloyd's Rep. 277.

38 The *Dithmarschen*, OLG Hamburg 11 September 1986, TranspR 1987, 67; affirmed in BGH 25 April 1988, TranspR 1988, 288.

> The FOB buyer was not the shipper; he was just mentioned as such on the bill of lading for the sake of convenience. . . . The three original bills of lading were clearly issued to the plaintiff as he, exporter and owner of the goods still not paid for by the FOB buyer, wanted to and had to in compliance with the CAD arrangement present these three original bills of lading to the bank in order to receive the payment of the purchase price. [39]

The shipper may only have been defined implicitly in the HVR, but article 1 (2) CMNI comes straight to the point. The shipper is a contractual figure as he is 'any person by whom or in whose name or on whose behalf a contract of carriage has been concluded with a carrier'.

The CMR does not offer a definition of the 'sender'. In fact, the convention just mentions the sender in article 5 CMR.[40] The sender under the CMR will often (also) be the party actually handing the goods to the carrier,[41] and the wording of some of the provisions of the convention confirms this,[42] but again it is quite clear that the sender is the contractual counterpart of the carrier. Article 4 CMR stipulates that the 'contract of carriage shall be confirmed by the making out of a consignment note' and article 5 CMR then requires the carrier and the sender to sign the consignment note.[43]

4.2. The consignee

The consignee is the person to whom the goods must be delivered at their destination.[44] At the same time, however, he is not an initial party to the contract, unless he is also the shipper. This raises the question of whether the third-party consignee is entitled to exercise any rights under the contract of carriage against the carrier.

39 The RR have introduced the documentary shipper. Article 1 (9) RR defines the documentary shipper as 'a person, other than the shipper, that accepts to be named as "shipper" in the transport document or electronic transport record'.

40 'The consignment note shall be made out in three original copies signed by the sender and by the carrier. These signatures may be printed or replaced by the stamps of the sender and the carrier if the law of the country in which the consignment note has been made out so permits. The first copy shall be handed to the sender, the second shall accompany the goods and the third shall be retained by the carrier.'

41 It is obviously easier for trucks to access the premises of the 'contractual' sender than it is for ships and airplanes, and the sender thus really has no need to instruct a stevedore or forwarder.

42 See for instance article 22 CMR: 'When the sender hands goods of a dangerous nature to the carrier'.

43 In the further course of this book, it will for convenience's sake be assumed that the shipper/consignor/sender and the carrier have agreed on the contract of carriage together, and only the term 'shipper' shall hereinafter be used to avoid an endless reference to the 'shipper/consignor/sender', provided of course that this is not inappropriate.

44 The face of a bill of lading will often also mention a 'notify party'. The notify party is usually a freight forwarder, instructed to collect the goods in the port of discharge as an agent of the shipper or the consignee, but he may also be the consignee himself. In any case, the mere identification of someone on the bill of lading as the notify party does not bind him to the bill of lading contract.

The universal answer to that question is yes, but there are several ways to reach this answer. The position of the consignee can be regulated in a convention, which is what the drafters of the CIM 1999, MC, CMR and (in a way) CMNI have done. When the position of the consignee is not addressed in the convention, though, as in the case of bill of lading contracts under the HVR or multimodal contracts of carriage to the extent that they are not governed by a unimodal convention, that position is governed by the applicable domestic law.[45]

The regulation of the position of the consignee in the convention

Perhaps the easiest way to deal with the position of the consignee is to regulate it in an international convention. This is a very attractive option as potential dogmatic difficulties are simply avoided.

With the exception of the HVR, all other transport conventions discussed in this book have adopted this solution. They ensure by way of conventional provisions that the consignee acquires rights under the contract of carriage. Article 17 § 1 CIM 1999 requires the carrier to deliver the goods to the consignee at the place of destination against a receipt and payment of the amounts payable under the contract of carriage. The first sentence of article 17 § 3 CIM 1999 then explicitly stipulates that 'the consignee may ask the carrier to hand over the consignment note and deliver the goods to him' when the goods arrive at their destination.

Articles 13 (1) MC and 13 (1) CMR contain more or less similar provisions. Both articles give the consignee the right to demand the delivery of the goods upon their arrival at the place of destination. Article 13 (1) MC for instance provides that 'the consignee is entitled, on arrival of the cargo at the place of destination, to require the carrier to deliver the cargo to it, on payment of the charges due and on complying with the conditions of carriage.'[46]

Article 1 (5) CMNI defines the consignee as 'the person entitled to take delivery of the goods', and article 3 (1) CMNI requires the carrier to 'carry the goods to the place of delivery within the specified time and deliver them to the consignee'. The CMNI does not contain an explicit provision similar to article 13 (1) MC/CMR, but the wording of article 10 (1) CMNI certainly implies that the consignee is entitled to delivery as 'the consignee who, following the arrival of the goods at the place of delivery, requests their delivery, shall, in accordance with the contract of carriage, be liable for the freight and other charges due on the goods, as well as for his contribution to any general average.'

45 Obviously, this applies to all unregulated contracts of carriage, such as carriage of goods by sea under a waybill or carriage of goods by air between two non-contracting states.

46 Article 13 (1) CMR stipulates: 'After arrival of the goods at the place designated for delivery, the consignee shall be entitled to require the carrier to deliver to him, against a receipt, the second copy of the consignment note and the goods. If the loss of the goods is established or if the goods have not arrived after the expiry of the period provided for in article 19, the consignee shall be entitled to enforce in his own name against the carrier any rights arising from the contract of carriage.'

A third-party stipulation

The HVR do not regulate the position of the consignee. Apart from a brief reference in article X HVR, the rules do not even mention the consignee, and instead focus on the holder of the bill of lading.[47] In the absence of a conventional provision, the position of the consignee therefore follows from the applicable domestic law, and this is where common and civil law systems have adopted two different dogmatic approaches.

Civil law jurisdictions will generally accept that a third party may acquire rights under a contract through the working of a third-party stipulation. In fact, the third-party stipulation has meanwhile been recognized as one of the Principles of European Contract Law (PECL). A contract obviously binds the (two) contracting parties, but it may at the same time benefit a third party.[48] Article 6:110 PECL reads:[49]

> A third party may require performance of a contractual obligation when its right to do so has been expressly agreed upon between the promisor and the promisee, or when such agreement is to be inferred from the purpose of the contract or the circumstances of the case. The third party need not be identified at the time the agreement is concluded.
>
> If the third party renounces the right to performance the right is treated as never having accrued to it.
>
> The promisee may by notice to the promisor deprive the third party of the right to performance unless: (a) the third party has received notice from the promisee that the right has been made irrevocable, or (b) the promisor or the promisee has received notice from the third party that the latter accepts the right.

The exact working of a third-party stipulation may be different in the different jurisdictions though.[50] Under German law a third-party stipulation has an

47 Article I (b) HVR.

48 Apart from a contract of carriage, a contract of life insurance also forms a good example: the insurer and the assured agree on the life insurance yet the assured sum is ultimately paid to the surviving beneficiary.

49 See for German law § 328 BGB: 'A performance to a third party can contractually be agreed upon so that the third party acquires an own right to claim the performance.' For Dutch law see article 6:253 BW: 'An agreement creates the right for a third party to claim a certain performance from one of the parties or to otherwise rely on the agreement against one of them, if the agreement contains a stipulation to that effect and the third party accepts this stipulation.' And for French law, see article 1121 CC: 'One may likewise stipulate for the benefit of a third party, where it is the condition of a stipulation which one makes for oneself or of a gift which one makes to another. He who made that stipulation may no longer revoke it, where the third party declares that he wishes to take advantage of it.'

50 F. Smeele, 'The bill of lading contracts under European national laws: Civil law approaches to explaining the legal position of the consignee under bills of lading' in D. Rhidian Thomas (ed.) *The Evolving Law and Practice of Voyage Charterparties* (Informa: London, 2009) 269.

immediate effect on the beneficiary. This immediate effect obviously invades the principle of party autonomy, and the third party can accordingly reject the stipulation pursuant to § 333 BGB. Under Dutch law the third party needs to accept the stipulation made to his benefit to accede to the contract. The initial two-party contract then becomes a three-party contract upon the acceptance of the third-party stipulation by the beneficiary.[51]

The acquisition of rights through the working of a third-party stipulation is, just as the conclusion of the contract itself, in principle form free. The carrier arrives at the place of destination, delivers the goods to the consignee or someone authorized to take delivery on his behalf, and further paperwork is not required.[52] The consignee (tacitly) accepts the third-party stipulation in the contract of carriage when he either takes or demands the delivery of the goods or when he claims the loss or damage in the absence of a delivery.

The third-party stipulation in bill of lading contracts

Mutatis mutandis the same system applies to bill of lading contracts, but this time there is a form requirement for the acquisition of rights through the working of a third-party stipulation. Given the easy transferability of a bill of lading, the property in the goods may very well have been transferred during the voyage without the carrier's knowledge. In light of this possibility, the consignee cannot simply take delivery of the goods. The consignee first needs to identify himself as the person entitled thereto, and he does so by presenting the carrier with an original bill of lading.[53] This requirement applies to all bills of lading, including therefore straight bills of lading. As the presentation of the bill of lading is required for the release of the goods, the presentation of the bill of lading is also required for the acquisition of rights on the basis of a third-party stipulation.[54] The Dutch Supreme Court held in the *Ladoga 15* that:[55]

> the idea that the mere fact that a straight bill of lading mentions someone else than the shipper as the consignee implies that this bill of lading contains a third party stipulation for the benefit of that consignee that may in principle be accepted at any time – hence for instance also before the bill of lading

51 See article 6:254 DCC: 'When the third party has accepted the stipulation, he counts as a party to the agreement.'

52 The carrier will obviously require the recipient's signature in the designated box on the waybill or consignment note, but that 'formality' only evidences the delivery of the goods by the carrier.

53 The presentation rule; see in more detail Chapter 3.

54 The Dutch Supreme Court has allowed one exception to this rule, namely when all parties involved, i.e. the shipper, the carrier and the consignee, agree in the course of the voyage that the named consignee may accede to the contract of carriage without presentation. HR 22 September 2000, NJ 2001, 44 (ann. K.F. Haak), S&S 2001/37 (*Eendracht*). This exception is unlikely to apply to order and bearer bills of lading, unless all originals are still in the hands of the shipper.

55 HR 29 November 2002, NJ 2003, 373 (ann. K.F. Haak), S&S 2003/62 (*Ladoga 15*).

> was handed to him – and in any form with the result that he accedes to the contract of carriage, cannot be accepted as correct.

The rationale behind the rule is obvious: the shipper/seller will only want to part with an original bill of lading once the purchase price has been paid in accordance with the underlying sale contract, and the required presentation protects the interests of the seller. The consignee/buyer can only exercise any rights under the bill of lading when he pays the purchase price, acquires the bill of lading in return and presents it to the carrier.[56]

Common law complications

The civil law notion of a third-party stipulation does not work in common law jurisdictions. Instead, the common law doctrine of privity of contract ensures that a contract only affects the parties to that contract.[57] Third parties can therefore neither be held to nor rely on the provisions of the contract: [58]

> My Lords, in the law of England certain principles are fundamental. One is that only a person who is a party to a contract can sue on it. Our law knows nothing of a jus quaesitum tertio arising by way of contract. Such a right may be conferred by way of property, as, for example, under a trust, but it cannot be conferred on a stranger to a contract as a right to enforce the contract in personam.

The application of this 'fundamental principle' has complicated contracts for the carriage of goods by sea under a bill of lading.[59] The symbolic function of the bill of lading only related to the transfer of the property in the goods.[60] The transfer of the bill of lading did not establish the transfer of any contractual rights under the contract of carriage. Parke B. unambiguously said in *Thompson v. Dominy* that the bill of lading 'transfers no more than the property in the goods; it does not transfer the contract'.[61]

As a result, all rights under the bill of lading contract remained with the shipper even though the property in the goods had already passed to the buyer/holder of the bill of lading. This caused a problem when the goods arrived at their destination in a damaged condition or were lost on the way. The buyer/bill of lading holder had suffered the loss, but he would nevertheless be unable to

56 *Scottish & Newcastle v. Othon Ghalanos* (2008) 2 ALL ER 768.

57 *Tweddle v. Atkinson* (1861) 121 ER 762.

58 *Dunlop v. Selfridge* (1915) AC 847.

59 The reference to 'fundamental' suggests that it is an ancient principle that goes back as far as the law merchant, but that is very doubtful. Lord Denning said in *Midland Silicones v. Scruttons* (1961) 1 Lloyd's Rep. 365: 'First of all let me remind your Lordships that this "fundamental principle" was a discovery of the 19th century. Lord Mansfield and Mr. Justice Buller knew nothing of it.'

60 *Lickbarrow v. Mason* (1794) 5 TR 683.

61 *Thompson v. Dominy* (1845) 14 M. & W. 403.

exercise any rights against the carrier as he had not been a party to the contract,[62] and had not become a party to the contract either.[63]

The Bills of Lading Act 1855

The problem was addressed in the Bills of Lading Act 1855. The preamble of the act immediately states its intentions, i.e. to remedy the *Thompson v. Dominy* problem. The objective of the act was to have the contractual rights pass together with the property rights:

> Whereas by the custom of merchants a bill of lading of goods being transferable by endorsement the property in the goods may thereby pass to the endorsee but nevertheless all rights in respect of the contract contained in the bill of lading continue in the original shipper or owner, and it is expedient that such rights should pass with the property.

S. 1 of the Bills of Lading Act then ensured that this objective was reached as 'every consignee of goods named in a bill of lading and every endorsee of a bill of lading to whom the property in the goods therein mentioned shall pass, upon or by reason of such consignment or endorsement, shall have transferred and vested in him all rights of suit, and be subject to the same liabilities in respect of such goods, as if the contract contained in the bill of lading had been made with himself.'

Still, the effect of the act proved to be limited in practice.[64] In *Sewell v. Burdick*, for instance, the bill of lading was transferred to a bank to establish a right of

62 The seller/shipper was a party to the contract, but he could not sue the carrier either as he had already sold the goods to the consignee and was no longer their owner. As the seller/shipper had not suffered any damages, he would not be allowed in his claim against the carrier as damages are compensatory at common law; see for instance *The Albazero* (1976) 3 ALL ER 129, at 470: 'Their function is to put the person whose right has been invaded in the same position as if it had been respected so far as the award of a sum of money can do so.'

63 In light of the obvious inequity of this result, creative ways were found to circumvent the privity of contract doctrine. The House of Lords introduced the notion of a 'special contract' between the shipper and the carrier in *Dunlop v. Lambert.* It allowed the shipper to claim the damages on the consignee's behalf 'if the consignor made a special contract with the carrier, and the carrier agreed to take the goods from him, and to deliver them to any particular person at any particular place, the special contract supersedes the necessity of showing ownership in the goods; and . . . the person making the contract with the carrier, may maintain the action, though the goods may be the goods of the consignee.' *Dunlop v. Lambert* (1839) 6 Cl & F 600.

64 Again, creative solutions were found. The damages in *Brandt v. Liverpool* were suffered by an agent (Brandt). He had paid the freight, costs and other expenses incurred in the course of a contract of carriage under a bill of lading between Buenos Aires (Argentina) and Liverpool (UK). Brandt had no privity of contract since he had acted for Vogel, his principal and the shipper under the contract. Still, Brandt had presented the bill of lading to the carrier in the port of discharge to secure the release of the goods, and he had also offered to pay the freight. The House of Lords held: 'The bill of lading holder offered the freight before the goods were delivered, and in fact paid it, and in those circumstances it seems to me that the subsequent delivery by the shipowner is an acceptance of an offer to accept the goods as described upon the terms of the bill of lading.' The offer by the bill of lading holder and the subsequent acceptance thereof by the carrier constituted an implied contract that was governed by the provisions of the bill of lading. Given the existence of this implied contract between Brandt and Liverpool, the privity of contract issue was resolved and Brandt was allowed in his claim for damages. *Brandt v. Liverpool* (1924) 1 K.B. 575.

pledge on the goods. The court held that the establishment of a right of pledge did not qualify as a transfer of property, and the bank was therefore not exposed to the liabilities under the bill of lading contract.[65]

The requirement that the property had to be transferred 'upon or by reason of such consignment or endorsement' caused difficulties as well. It was (and still is) not uncommon for commodities to be sold more than once during the voyage. As the documents need to be checked on their compliance in each individual transaction, this effectively means that the goods will sometimes arrive at the port of discharge well before the bill of lading. Obviously, the ship needs to move on, and the goods are then released against a letter of indemnification instead of an original bill of lading.

This practice formed a problem under the Bills of Lading Act 1855. When the goods were physically delivered to the buyer against a letter of indemnity, the contractual rights under the contract of carriage remained where they were as the bill of lading had not played any role in the transfer of the property.[66]

The COGSA 1992

Given these issues over the years, the Bills of Lading Act 1855 was repealed and replaced by the Carriage of Goods by Sea Act 1992 (COGSA 1992).[67] The Law Commission was quite clear on its intentions with the new act: the number of changes should be kept at a minimum, but the shortcomings of the 1855 Act needed to be addressed so that 'there would no longer be a link between the transfer of contractual rights and the passing of property. Instead, any lawful holder of a bill of lading would be entitled to assert contractual rights against the carrier.'[68]

The COGSA 1992 has a wider scope of application than its predecessor. The act obviously covers the statutory transfer of rights under bill of lading contracts, but furthermore provides for a statutory transfer of rights under contracts of carriage covered by 'any sea waybill' or 'any ship's delivery order'.[69] S. 2 (1) COGSA 1992 stipulates:

> Subject to the following provisions of this section, a person who becomes – (a) the lawful holder of a bill of lading; (b) the person who (without being an original party to the contract of carriage) is the person to whom delivery of the goods to which a sea waybill relates is to be made by the carrier in accordance with that contract; or (c) the person to whom delivery of the goods to which a ship's delivery order relates is to be made in accordance with the

65 *Sewell v. Burdick* (1884) 10 App Cas 74.

66 *The Delfini* (1990) 1 Lloyd's Rep. 252.

67 In Singapore this is the Bills of Lading Act 1994.

68 *The Law Commission and The Scottish Law Commission Rights of suit in respect of carriage of goods by sea* (HMSO: London, 1991) 15.

69 See S. 1 (1) COGSA 1992. The act does not regulate the transfer of contractual rights under charter parties, consignment notes or other documents evidencing the contract of carriage. In the absence of a statutory provision such contracts of carriage thus remain subject to the general rule: a contract only affects the parties to that contract.

> undertaking contained in the order, shall (by virtue of becoming the holder of the bill or, as the case may be, the person to whom delivery is to be made) have transferred to and vested in him all rights of suit under the contract of carriage as if he had been a party to that contract.

The act thus ensures that all rights under the contract of carriage are statutorily transferred to the lawful holder of the bill of lading and the consignee mentioned on the sea waybill or delivery order. Such a statutory transfer of rights obviously benefits the transferee, but comes at a price. S. 3 (1) COGSA 1992 links the transfer of contractual rights to the transfer of contractual obligations. When the transferee exercises his rights under the contract of carriage, he becomes 'subject to the same liabilities under that contract as if he had been a party to that contract'.

The transferee is then liable for any obligations under the contract, for instance payment of the freight or claims for demurrage. The transferor, on the other hand, provided he is not the shipper under the contract of carriage,[70] may have lost his contractual rights under the contract of carriage, but he is no longer liable for any claims under the contract of carriage either.[71]

The definition of a bill of lading under the COGSA 1992

A bill of lading in the sense of the COGSA 1992 is either an order bill of lading or a bearer bill of lading. S. 1 (2) COGSA 1992 stipulates that a bill of lading does not include 'a document which is incapable of transfer either by indorsement or, as a bearer bill, by delivery without indorsement'. This requirement implies that straight bills of lading do not qualify as bills of lading under the act. The Law Commission explained the distinction in its report by saying that:[72]

> clause 1(2) of the Bill stipulates that a bill of lading must be transferable, thus following the preamble to the 1855 Act. A 'straight' consigned bill of lading, such as one made out 'to X' without any such words as 'to order', is not a document of title at common law.

It is submitted that this distinction between order/bearer and straight bills of lading is unfortunate. Whereas the 1855 act indeed had the objective to transfer the contractual rights together with the property rights, it never excluded the straight bill of lading from its application. In fact, S. 1 of the Bills of Lading Act specifically refers to 'every consignee of goods named in a bill of lading'. Besides, this

70 S. 3 (3) COGSA 1992: 'This section, so far as it imposes liabilities under any contract on any person, shall be without prejudice to the liabilities under the contract of any person as an original party to the contract.'

71 *The Berge Sisar* (1998) 2 Lloyd's Rep. 475.

72 *The Law Commission and The Scottish Law Commission Rights of suit in respect of carriage of goods by sea* (HMSO: London, 1991) 20.

distinction between order/bearer and straight bills of lading may have the undesirable side effect that the named consignee/buyer of the goods would already be able to exercise rights under the contract of carriage even though he has not paid the purchase price yet.[73]

The definition of a bill of lading under the COGSA 1992 includes the multimodal bill of lading.[74] First of all, the wording of S. 1 (1) (a) COGSA 1992 specifically refers to any bill of lading, and therefore not just to ocean bills of lading. Second, the Law Commission explicitly addressed the issue in its report saying that 'since implementing legislation is expressed to cover any bill of lading, including "received for shipment" bills, multimodal documents are capable of falling within its ambit.'[75]

The Contracts (Rights of Third Parties) Act

This act entered into force in the UK in 1999; it is thus only a few years younger than the COGSA 1992. The (Contracts) Rights of Third Parties Act forms another statutory infringement of the privity of contract doctrine. S. 1 (1) of the act gives the main rule:

> Subject to the provisions of this Act, a person who is not a party to a contract (a 'third party') may in his own right enforce a term of the contract if – (a) the contract expressly provides that he may, or (b) subject to subsection (2), the term purports to confer a benefit on him.

To avoid any interference with the provisions on the position of the consignee in the COGSA 1992, CIM (1980), WC/MC and CMR, the Rights of Third Parties Act only has a limited scope of application. In fact, S. 6 (5) of the act precludes '(a) a contract for the carriage of goods by sea, or (b) a contract for the carriage of goods by rail or road, or for the carriage of cargo by air, which is subject to the rules of the appropriate international transport convention' from the application

73 The question should therefore not be whether the straight bill of lading is a 'document of title at common law', but really whether it is transferable. The House of Lords touched upon the matter in the Rafaela S: 'In the hands of the named consignee the straight bill of lading is his document of title. . . .Except for the fact that a straight bill of lading is only transferable to a named consignee and not generally, a straight bill of lading shares all the principal characteristics of a bill of lading as already described.' *The Rafaela S.* (2005) 1 Lloyd's Rep. 347.

74 See specifically with regard to this question D. Rhidian Thomas in B. Soyer/A. Tettenborn (eds) *Carriage of goods by sea, land and air: Unimodal and multimodal transport in 21st century* (Informa: London, 2014) 152 and further.

75 *The Law Commission and The Scottish Law Commission Rights of suit in respect of carriage of goods by sea* (HMSO: London, 1991) 25. Given the wording of S. 1 (1) (a) COGSA 1992, however, the act may not cover straight multimodal bills of lading. The straight bill of lading equals a waybill under the act, but S. 1 (1) (a) COGSA 1992 specifically refers to 'any sea waybill', and therefore not to any waybill in general. In fact, the Law Commission defines the sea waybill as 'a receipt which contains or evidences a contract for the carriage of goods by sea'.

of the act.[76] Accordingly, the act does not affect the position of the consignee in contracts of carriage by sea or internationally regulated contracts of carriage by rail, by road or by air.[77]

Still, there is no international convention on multimodal contracts of carriage, and the scope of application of the COGSA 1992 does not seem to include multimodal contracts of carriage evidenced by a waybill. Whereas the COGSA 1992 refers to 'any bill of lading', it also refers to 'any sea waybill', and therefore not to any waybill in general.[78] This implies that the (Contracts) Rights of Third Parties Act may govern the position of the consignee in multimodal contracts of carriage under a waybill,[79] a consequence the Law Commission is clearly at ease with:[80]

> Although there are some provisions dealing with carriage of goods by more than one mode of transport (see, e.g., Art 2(1) of CMR and Art 31 of the Warsaw Convention) we are aware that there can be difficulties in deciding on the extent to which, if at all, the international conventions (and the Carriage of Goods by Sea Act 1992) apply to the 'multimodal' carriage of goods. Insofar as none of the relevant international conventions applies to the contract of carriage in question, and nor does the Carriage of Goods by Sea Act 1992, we see no objection to a third party who can satisfy the test of enforceability being given rights under our proposed Act.

The Law Commission explicitly contemplated the possibility that certain contracts of carriage may not be covered by either an international convention or by the COGSA 1992, and the position of the consignee under those contracts of carriage may then indeed be regulated by the (Contracts) Rights of Third Parties Act.[81]

4.3. The right of disposal

The right of disposal is the right to instruct the carrier both prior to and during the voyage. These instructions can relate to the scope of the voyage, the place of destination, but also to the identity of the consignee.

As the carrier's principal under the contract of carriage, the shipper is entitled to give instructions to the carrier, and most of the conventions contain specific

76 The last part of this sentence reads: 'except that a third party may in reliance on that section avail himself of an exclusion or limitation of liability in such a contract'. This exception to the exception does not touch the position of the consignee, but it does enhance the position of the carrier's servants, agents and subcontractors.

77 The CMNI did not yet exist at that time, but the UK is still not a contracting state either.

78 S. Baughen, *Shipping law* (Routledge: London, 2015) 169.

79 And again, since the COGSA 1992 sees the straight bill of lading as a waybill, mutatis mutandis the same would then apply to a straight multimodal bill of lading.

80 *Law Commission Report 242* (HMSO: London, 1996) 143.

81 Arguably, this then also applies to the position of the consignee in international contracts for the carriage of goods by inland waterways subject to English law.

and similar provisions to that extent; see articles 18 § 1 CIM 1999, 14 (1) CMNI, 12 (1) MC and 12 (1) CMR:

> The sender has the right to dispose of the goods, in particular by asking the carrier to stop the goods in transit, to change the place at which delivery is to take place or to deliver the goods to a consignee other than the consignee indicated in the consignment note.

The right of disposal passes from the shipper to the consignee when the carrier arrives at the place of destination and the consignee takes delivery of the goods. This implies that the right of disposal rests with only one party at the time, i.e. either the shipper or the consignee, and not both. Articles 18 § 2 and 3 CIM 1999, 14 (2) CMNI, 12 (4) MC and 12 (2) CMR ensure there is no overlap:

> This right shall cease to exist when the second copy of the consignment note is handed to the consignee or when the consignee exercises his right under article 13, paragraph 1; from that time onwards the carrier shall obey the orders of the consignee.

An air waybill or a consignment note is not a document of title, but the exercise of the right of disposal may still be subject to its presentation.[82] Article 12 (3) MC stipulates that the carrier is liable for any damage if he follows the consignor's instructions other than against presentation of his part of the air waybill. Article 19 § 1 CIM 1999 in fact imposes an obligation to present the duplicate consignment note:

> If the consignor or, in the case referred to in Article 18 § 3, the consignee wishes to modify the contract of carriage by giving subsequent orders, he must produce to the carrier the duplicate of the consignment note on which the modifications have to be entered.

The right of disposal in bill of lading contracts

A bill of lading evidences the contract of carriage, but it has two other functions as well, and one of these is the document of title function.[83] To secure the unaffected working of the bill of lading as a document of title, the right of disposal in a bill of lading contract attaches to that bill of lading. The shipper/transferor

82 Article 18 § 3 CIM 1999 prescribes: 'The consignee shall have the right to modify the contract of carriage from the time when the consignment note is drawn up, unless the consignor indicates to the contrary on the consignment note.'

83 The goods travelling under a bill of lading may easily be transferred during the voyage by the transfer of that bill of lading. When a third-party transferee indeed acquires proprietary rights to these goods in the course of the voyage, provided always that he is acting in good faith (*Snee v. Prescott* (1743) 26 ER 157), these rights may then not be infringed by any action of the shipper; see *Ellis v. Hunt* (1789) 100 ER 679.

loses his right of disposal upon the transfer of the bill of lading and the transferee then acquires the right of disposal. The HVR do not contain any provisions on the right of disposal, but article 14 (2) CMNI stipulates:

> The shipper's right of disposal shall cease to exist once the consignee, following the arrival of the goods at the scheduled place of delivery, has requested delivery of the goods and, ... where carriage is under a bill of lading, once the shipper has relinquished all the originals in his possession by handing them over to another person.

In light of the document of title function of the bill of lading, its presentation is also required for the exercise of the right of disposal. Article 15 CMNI prescribes that a shipper or consignee 'must, if he wishes to exercise his right of disposal . . . submit all originals prior to the arrival of the goods at the scheduled place of delivery'.[84]

The right of disposal is thus always an exclusive right, irrespective of the means of transportation, the applicable convention or even the nature of the transport document issued. If the contract of carriage is evidenced by a multimodal bill of lading, however, the right of disposal attaches to the bill of lading. The right of disposal rests either with the shipper/bill of lading holder or with a transferee/lawful bill of lading holder, but never with two parties at the same time.

The right of control

The RR do not refer to the right of disposal, but instead to the right of control.[85] This right is defined in article 1 (12) RR as 'the right under the contract of carriage to give the carrier instructions in respect of the goods in accordance with chapter 10'.

Article 50 RR regulates the extent of the right of control. The right exists throughout the entire contract of carriage, may only be exercised by the controlling party and is limited to:

> (a) The right to give or modify instructions in respect of the goods that do not constitute a variation of the contract of carriage;
> (b) The right to obtain delivery of the goods at a scheduled port of call or, in respect of inland carriage, any place en route; and
> (c) The right to replace the consignee by any other person including the controlling party.

The right of control is an exclusive right. Article 51 (1) (a) RR identifies the shipper as the initial controlling party, but the shipper can designate someone else as the

84 Whereas the release of the goods only requires one original bill of lading, the exercise of the right of disposal requires all (3/3) originals; see for instance article 8:440 DCC.

85 See in more detail L. Zhao, *The right of control in carriage of goods by sea* (2014) LMCLQ 393.

controlling party.[86] The controlling party can transfer the right of control pursuant to article 51 (1) (b) RR, and then the transferee becomes the controlling party. When a negotiable document or record is issued, the right of control attaches to that document or record, and its holder is then the controlling party.[87]

Stoppage in transitu

The shipper's right of disposal (or control) is something different than the seller's right of stoppage in transitu, i.e. the right of the unpaid seller to either stop or redirect the goods underway to their bankrupt buyer.[88] The right of stoppage in transitu was originally an equitable right, 'founded on principles of natural justice and equity',[89] and thus not a contractual right under the sale contract, let alone a contractual right under the contract of carriage. The seller's right to stop the goods in transit and the shipper's right to give the carrier instructions during the voyage are to some extent connected, though, especially when the goods are carried under a bill of lading.

The first reports on the right of stoppage in transitu go back as far as the seventeenth century. Two Italian sellers had sold two cases of silk to Bonnell, a London-based merchant. After the sale, but before the ship carrying the silk had left Italy, the sellers learned that Bonnell had gone bankrupt. They quickly changed their initial instructions to the carrier, this time consigning the goods to Vandeputt. Wiseman, Bonnell's assignee under the Bankruptcy Statute, started proceedings against Vandeputt claiming that the initial consignment of the goods had already transferred the property to Bonnell's. The Chancery Court disagreed, and was reported to have said that: [90]

> the silks were the proper goods of the two Florentines, and not of the Bonnells, nor the produce of their effects; and therefore they having paid no money for the goods, if the Italians could by any means get their goods again into their hands, or prevent their coming into the hands of the bankrupts, it was but lawful for them so to do, and very allowable in equity.

The seller's right of stoppage in transit was affirmed in several later cases over the years,[91] and it was ultimately codified in S. 44 of the Sale of Goods Act 1979 (SGA 1979):

86 This can be the consignee or documentary shipper, but also a bank that has financed the underlying transaction. M.F. Sturley, T. Fulita, G. van der Ziel, *The Rotterdam Rules* (Sweet & Maxwell: London, 2010) 275.

87 Article 51 (3) and (4) RR.

88 M. Bridge (ed.), *Benjamin's sale of goods* (Sweet & Maxwell: London, 2010) 908.

89 C. Abbott, *A treatise of the law relative to merchant ships and seamen* (Brooke, Rider & Butterworth: London, 1802, compiled and edited by C. MacKenzie in 2011) 298.

90 *Wiseman v. Vandeputt* (1690) 2 Vern 203, 23 ER 732.

91 *Snee v. Prescott* (1743) 1 Akt 245, 26 ER 157, *Ellis v. Hunt* (1789) 3 TR 464, 100 ER 679, *Lickbarrow v. Mason* (1794) 5 TR 683, *Bothlingk v. Inglis* (1803) 3 East 381, 102 ER 643.

> Subject to this Act, when the buyer of goods becomes insolvent the unpaid seller who has parted with the possession of the goods has the right of stopping them in transit, that is to say, he may resume possession of the goods as long as they are in course of transit, and may retain them until payment or tender of the price.

When the goods travel under a bill of lading, its function as a document of title affects the seller's right of stoppage in transitu. The property rights of a third-party transferee of the bill of lading, provided of course that he acts in good faith, prevail over the unpaid seller's right of stoppage in transitu.[92] S. 47 (2) SGA 1979 stipulates:

> Where a document of title to goods has been lawfully transferred to any person as buyer or owner of the goods, and that person transfers the document to a person who takes it in good faith and for valuable consideration, then – (a) if the last-mentioned transfer was by way of sale the unpaid seller's right of lien or retention or stoppage in transit is defeated; and (b) if the last-mentioned transfer was made by way of pledge or other disposition for value, the unpaid seller's right of lien or retention or stoppage in transit can only be exercised subject to the rights of the transferee.

4.4. The right of suit

The right of suit is the right to sue the carrier for the loss of or damage to the goods in the course of the voyage. Obviously, the shipper will (generally) be entitled to sue the carrier as his contractual counterpart, but that still leaves a number of questions, namely whether the consignee has a right of suit, whether the right of suit is an exclusive right (in line with the right of disposal) and whether the actual suffering of the loss or damage is conditional for the exercise of the right of suit.

Again, the easiest way to deal with the right of suit is to regulate it in the international transport conventions. The CIM 1999, MC and CMR indeed contain provisions on the right of suit, but there is a significant difference between the approach of the CIM 1999 on the one hand and the approach of the MC and CMR on the other. The HVR and CMNI do not contain any provisions on the right of suit, and this effectively means that the right of suit is governed by domestic law.[93]

The right of suit under the CIM 1999

The CIM 1999 explicitly links the right of suit to the right of disposal. Article 44 § 1 CIM 1999 stipulates that the consignor is entitled to sue the carrier under the

92 *Lickbarrow v. Mason* (1794) 5 TR 683; *Nippon Yusen Kaisha v. Ramjiban Serowgee* (1938) AC 429.

93 This domestic law is not per definition the lex fori or lex causae; article 10:162 DCC for instance prescribes that the right of suit in a bill of lading contract is governed by the law of the port of discharge.

contract of carriage,[94] but only 'until such time as the consignee has 1. taken possession of the consignment note, 2. accepted the goods, or 3. asserted his rights pursuant to Article 17 § 3 or Article 18 § 3', and from that moment on, only the consignee has a right of suit. To exercise this right of suit, article 44 §§ 5 and 6 CIM 1999 requires the production of the duplicate of the consignment note by the consignor respectively consignee.[95]

The consignor in the sense of article 44 § 1 CIM is the party with whom the carrier has concluded the contract of carriage by rail.[96] The consignee in the sense of article 44 § 1 CIM is the consignee mentioned as such on the consignment note.[97] Other parties, such the owner of the goods or the principal of the consignee mentioned on the consignment note, are not entitled to claim the damage from the carrier, irrespective of whether their claim is contractual or extra-contractual.[98]

Obviously, the goods must have been damaged during the voyage, but the provisions of article 44 CIM 1999 do not require the consignor or consignee to have suffered the damage himself. The consignor or the consignee identified by article 44 CIM 1999 is entitled to sue the carrier for the damage, irrespective of whether he suffered this damage in his own account.

The right of suit under the CIM 1999 this follows the right of disposal. It is an exclusive right that rests with either the consignor or the consignee and it cannot be exercised simultaneously.[99] The rationale behind this rule lies in the protection of the position of the carrier: he should only be confronted with one claimant entitled to sue him for the damage to the goods.[100]

The right of suit under the MC/CMR

Articles 13 (3) MC and 13 (1) CMR contain almost identical provisions on the right of suit. In the case of the loss of or damage to the goods, both articles

94 Article 44 § 3 CIM 1999 gives the person who made the payment an exclusive right of suit for the recovery of those sums paid. Article 44 § 4 CIM 1999 gives the consignor an exclusive right of suit for an action in respect of a cash on delivery payment.

95 Failing such a presentation, article 44 § 5 CIM 1999 requires the consignor to either show an authorization from the consignee or to prove that the consignee refused the goods, and if necessary to prove the absence or the loss of the consignment note.

96 See article 3 (a) CIM referring to the carrier 'with whom the consignor has concluded the contract of carriage'.

97 The carrier obviously knows the identity of the consignor, but it is not always easy to identity the 'real' consignee. Hence, only the nominal consignee has the right of suit; see M. Clarke & D. Yates, *Contracts of carriage by land and air* (Informa: London, 2008) 226–7.

98 M. Clarke & D. Yates, *Contracts of carriage by land and air* (Informa: London, 2008) 227.

99 J.H.P. Boudewijnse, *De aansprakelijkheid van de vervoerder volgens het internationale verdrag betreffende het goederenvervoer per spoorweg (CIM)* (diss.: Rotterdam, 1982) 370.

100 B. de Nánássy, *Le droit international des transports par chemins de fer: Commentaire à la convention internationale concernant le transport des marchandises par chemins de fer (C.I.M.) du 23 novembre 1933* (Rittmann/Bauer: London, 1946) 649.

provide that the consignee is entitled to enforce (in his own name) the rights arising from the contract of carriage.[101]

Other than under the CIM 1999, however, this enforcement of rights by the consignee does not affect the shipper's right of suit under the contract of carriage. Whereas article 12 (2) CMR explicitly stipulates that the consignee acquires his right of disposal at the expense of the sender, the CMR remains completely silent on any loss of the sender's right of suit. The sender therefore retains his right of suit under the contract of carriage in the absence of such an explicit provision.[102]

The MC does not make any connection between the right of disposal and the right of suit either. On the contrary, in fact; article 14 MC positively ensures that both the consignor and the consignee can exercise their rights (of suit) under the convention in their own name:[103]

> The consignor and the consignee can respectively enforce all the rights given to them by Articles 12 and 13, each in its own name, whether it is acting in its own interest or in the interest of another, provided that it carries out the obligations imposed by the contract of carriage.

Furthermore, since neither convention contains any restrictions on the right of suit of third parties, such as the owner of the goods or a bank with a right of pledge on the goods, these third parties are also entitled to sue the carrier for damages.[104] This is perhaps best illustrated by the judgment in *Gatewhite v. Iberia*. This case related to a contract of carriage by air (under the WC), but its reasoning equally applies to contracts of carriage by road under the CMR:[105]

> In my view the owner of goods damaged or lost by the carrier is entitled to sue in his own name and there is nothing in the Convention which deprives him of that right. As the Convention does not expressly deal with the position by excluding the owner's right of action (though it could so easily have done so) the lex fori, as it seems to me, can fill the gap.... The fact is that

101 This consignee does not necessarily need to be mentioned as such on the consignment note; see the French Cour de cassation, 12 May 1980, BTL 1980, 370.

102 The non-exclusivity of the right of suit has never really been an issue in CMR cases; see in The Netherlands HR 7 December 1973, S&S 1974/20 and Hof's-Gravenhage 20 June 1999, S&S 1999/125. In Germany, the non-exclusivity of the right of suit ('Doppellegitimation') has been codified in § 421 (1) HGB.

103 Nevertheless, the Dutch Supreme Court held in *KLM v. Sainath* that the right of suit follows the right of disposal, HR 19 April 2002, NJ 2002, 412 (ann. K.F. Haak); S&S 2003/13 (*KLM v. Sainath*). The Supreme Court referred in its judgment to article 44 § 1 CIM 1999 which indeed connects the right of suit to the right of disposal, but the MC does not contain a similar provision. It is therefore submitted that this decision is not correct; see also K.F. Haak in his comment under HR 19 April 2002, NJ 2002, 412, I. Koning, *Aansprakelijkheid in het luchtvervoer: Goederenvervoer onder de verdragen van Warschau en Montreal* (Paris: Zutphen, 2007) 328, M. Spanjaart, *Vorderingsrechten uit cognossement* (Paris: Zutphen, 2012) 50–1.

104 Hof's-Gravenhage 20 June 1999, S&S 1999/125.

105 *Gatewhite v. Iberia* (1989) 1 Lloyd's Rep. 160, M. Clarke, *Contracts of carriage by air* (Lloyd's List: London, 2010) 190.

> the Convention is silent where it could easily have made simple and clear provision excluding the rights of the 'real party in interest', had that been the framers' intention.

In the absence of conventional restrictions, this approach then also applies to multimodal contracts of carriage unless the applicable domestic law prescribes otherwise. The consignee can acquire a right of suit, but not at the expense of the shipper. The shipper retains his right of suit. Third parties may have an extra-contractual right of suit, provided that they have in fact suffered the damage.[106]

An accumulative right of suit

The existence of multiple rights of suit makes a lot of sense from a practical point of view, especially since it avoids all sorts of formal discussions on the admissibility of the claim. Still, it also raises certain questions, particularly since it is not very likely that all these different parties with a right of suit have actually suffered the damage to the goods. The party suffering the damage should of course have a right of suit, but what then justifies the right of suit of an unharmed party? Furthermore, what happens if the carrier pays an unharmed party, but is later sued by the party that actually suffered the damage?

As to the first question, the justification follows from the contract itself. For any contract to have effect, a party to that contract must be allowed to enforce his rights under that contract, and according to the Dutch Supreme Court 'it makes no difference whether this party suffers the damages in its own account or claims this damage solely or also on behalf of its principal with the objective to obtain compensation of its damage.'[107]

As to the second question, the solution follows from a legal presumption.[108] The carrier is discharged from his obligations under the contract of carriage once he in good faith pays one of the parties with a right of suit, irrespective of the question of whether that party actually suffered the damage.[109] The German Supreme Court accepted in that respect that the carrier only has to pay once:[110]

> If the consignee makes a justified claim for damage to the goods, then the carrier, when he is then again sued for the damage by his contractual counterpart – the shipper – can argue that he has already fulfilled his obligation to pay the damage against one of the parties with a right of suit and that he is therewith discharged.

106 *The Aliakmon* (1986) 2 ALL ER 145.

107 HR 11 March 1997, NJ 1977, 521 (*Kribbebijter*).

108 The issue is to some extent only of academic interest as the goods in transit will in practice always be insured. When they are indeed damaged in the course of the voyage, the cargo insurers (having reimbursed the shipper, the consignee or another party with an interest in the goods under the policy) will take the lead in any recourse actions. Conflicts of interest between the shipper, consignee or other parties are not likely to occur in that case.

109 See also article 6:34 DCC.

110 BGH 6 July 1979, VersR. 1979, 1106.

The right of suit in bill of lading contracts

Since the HVR and CMNI fail to regulate the issue, and since multimodal bill of lading contracts are not internationally regulated at all,[111] the right to sue the carrier under a (multimodal) bill of lading contract is governed by the applicable domestic law. Again, as with the position of the consignee, there is a dogmatic difference in approach between civil law and common law jurisdictions.

A bill of lading contract is essentially a contract of carriage, and as such it contains a third-party stipulation for the benefit of the consignee from a civil law perspective. As the bill of lading furthermore functions as a document of title, its presentation in the port of discharge identifies the holder of the bill of lading as the consignee, and the carrier must release the goods to this bill of lading holder/consignee. The shipper is then still a party to the contract of carriage, and in the absence of any provision to the contrary in the HVR or CMNI, the shipper should therefore in principle (also) be entitled to sue the carrier for loss or damage.

This general civil law approach of the right of suit does not apply to contracts of carriage under a bill of lading, though. In Germany and the Netherlands, for instance, the document of title function of the bill of lading overrides its contractual function. The right of suit then passes with the transfer of the bill of lading, and only its lawful holder is then entitled to sue the carrier. § 519 GCC stipulates:

> claims by virtue of a contract for the carriage of goods by sea as confirmed in a bill of lading may be asserted only by the person entitled by virtue of the bill of lading. The presumption shall be that the rightful holder of a bill of lading is also the person entitled by virtue of the bill of lading.[112]

The Dutch Supreme Court held in the *Brouwersgracht* that 'only the lawful holder of a bill of lading is entitled to exercise the rights under that bill of lading against the carrier.' This implies that claims by any other party than the lawful holder are inadmissible.[113]

Admittedly, it makes a lot of sense to give the lawful holder of the bill of lading an exclusive right to the release of the goods against the presentation of the bill of lading in the port of discharge. The carrier is in a hurry, he will want to discharge the goods without delay and the presentation of the bill of lading immediately identifies the person to whom he can safely release the goods.

111 Certain multimodal situations and/or contracts of carriage are regulated by unimodal conventions, though; see Chapter 6 in this respect. However, these situations and/or contracts of carriage are not likely to involve bills of lading.

112 The lawful holder's exclusive right of suit under to the bill of lading contract under German law does not bar an extra-contractual right of suit; see O. Hartenstein/F. Reuschle, *Handbuch des Fachanwalts Transport- und Speditionsrecht* (Karl Heymanns Verlag: Köln, 2012) 213.

113 HR 8 November 1991, NJ 1993, 609 (ann. J.C. Schultsz), S&S 1992/37 (*Brouwersgracht*). The right of suit is under Dutch law in fact so exclusive that claims under a charter party and claims in tort are only allowed if they are brought by the lawful holder of the bill of lading; see Hof's-Gravenhage 8 November 2005, S&S 2006/53 (*Maipo*).

All the same, that still does not explain why the shipper would then lose his right to sue the carrier for the damage.[114] In fact, an exclusive right of suit of the lawful holder of the bill of lading is rather difficult to reconcile with the concept of a third-party stipulation. Besides, the bill of lading no longer operates as a document of title once it has been presented to the carrier.[115] It is therefore submitted that the shipper should keep his right of suit as it follows directly from the contract of carriage as evidenced by the bill of lading, and not from the bill of lading as a document of title.[116]

The statutory transfer of the right of suit

Although the underlying dogmatism is different, the end result is basically the same in common law jurisdictions. The right to sue the carrier in contracts for the carriage of goods by sea under a bill of lading is then regulated by the COGSA 1992 or the local implementation thereof. When the contract of carriage is covered by a bill of lading, S. 2 (1) (a) COGSA 1992 links the right of suit to the lawful holdership of that bill of lading and stipulates that 'a person who becomes . . . the lawful holder of a bill of lading . . . shall . . . have transferred to and vested in him all rights of suit under the contract of carriage as if he had been a party to that contract.'[117]

The statutory right of suit is in principle an exclusive right.[118] As the right of suit passes together with the transfer of the bill of lading, the transferee/lawful holder acquires his right of suit at the expense of the transferor/former lawful holder. S. 2 (5) COGSA 1992 ensures this exclusivity:

> Where rights are transferred by virtue of the operation of subsection (1) above in relation to any document, the transfer for which that subsection provides shall extinguish any entitlement to those rights which derives – (a) where that

114 The identity of the shipper may in any case not be the problem. The carrier knows the shipper quite well as he is his contractual counterpart.

115 The bill of lading is then 'spent'; see Chapter 3.

116 M. Spanjaart, *Vorderingsrechten uit cognossement* (Paris: Zutphen, 2012) 345.

117 Since S. 1 (2) COGSA 1992 requires a bill of lading to be transferable by endorsement and delivery (or just delivery), the transfer of the right of suit in contracts of carriage evidenced by a straight bill of lading is then governed by S. 2 (1) (b) COGSA 1992. The named consignee of a straight bill of lading does not have to become the lawful holder; he only has to be the person 'to whom delivery of the goods to which a sea waybill relates is to be made by the carrier in accordance with that contract', and that is enough to ensure that he shall 'have transferred to and vested in him all rights of suit under the contract of carriage as if he had been a party to that contract'. Since the named consignee is not required to be the lawful holder of the bill of lading, he could in theory acquire a right of suit even though he has left the purchase price unpaid. The shipper can frustrate this, though, as he can return his (3/3) bill of lading, and subsequently instruct the carrier to issue a new (3/3) set. See *AP Moller-Maersk v. Soneac Villas* (2011) 1 Lloyd's Rep. 1 and article 8:440 DCC.

118 The working of the COGSA 1992 remains limited to the contractual rights under the contract evidenced by the bill of lading, sea waybill or delivery order. Other claims, in tort, bailment or under the charter party, are not affected by the act. *The Law Commission and The Scottish Law Commission Rights of suit in respect of carriage of goods by sea* (HMSO: London, 1991) 21.

> document is a bill of lading, from a person's having been an original party to the contract of carriage; or (b) in the case of any document to which this Act applies, from the previous operation of that subsection in relation to that document.

There is one exception to this rule, though. The operation of S. 2 COGSA 1992 is 'without prejudice to any rights which derive from a person's having been an original party to the contract contained in, or evidenced by, a sea waybill'. This means that the shipper under a sea waybill or a delivery order retains his right of suit even though the consignee has acquired a right of suit. Clearly, given the definition of a bill of lading under the COGSA 1992,[119] the same applies to the shipper under a straight bill of lading contract.

The right of suit of an agent

The lawful holder of the bill of lading or the consignee mentioned on the sea waybill will not always be the party suffering the damage. In fact, he will often be a forwarder instructed to accept the delivery of the goods for his principal. This forwarder, and not his principal, is then entitled to sue the carrier for the damage even though he did not suffer this damage himself. S. 2 (4) of the COGSA 1992 expressly provides that the forwarder (or any other party with the right of suit) 'shall be entitled to exercise those rights for the benefit of the person who sustained the loss or damage to the same extent as they could have been exercised if they had been vested in the person for whose benefit they are exercised'.[120]

This raises the question of whether the forwarder's principal is (next to his agent) also entitled to sue the carrier for the damage, or whether the forwarder has an exclusive right of suit.[121] In *East West v. DKBS* the bills of lading had been transferred by East West to the order of several Chilean banks; not as a security for a loan, but to keep them safe pending further instructions. When East West later initiated proceedings under the contract of carriage, the carrier successfully contested its right of suit. The Court of Appeal held:[122]

119 *The Law Commission and The Scottish Law Commission Rights of suit in respect of carriage of goods by sea* (HMSO: London, 1991) 20.

120 Such an express provision was necessary to trump the authority of the Albazero (1976) 3 ALL ER 129. *The Law Commission and The Scottish Law Commission Rights of suit in respect of carriage of goods by sea* (HMSO: London, 1991) 13.

121 G.H. Treitel & F.M.B. Reynolds, *Carver on bills of lading* (Sweet & Maxwell: London, 2011) 230: 'Where, indeed, the bill names the agent as consignee or bears a personal indorsement to, and is in the possession of, the agent, then the principal could not be a "holder" of it for the purposes of the Act; . . . It is less clear whether rights of suit are similarly transferred to the agent where he is not named either in the indorsement or in the bill: i.e. where the bill is a bearer bill or an order bill that has been indorsed in blank.'

122 *East West v. DKBS* (2003) 2 All ER 700.

> There is nothing in the ... Act to lend any support to the idea that, after a statutory transfer of contractual rights ... to its agent, the principal can still sue in contract in its own name.

As the transfer of the bills of lading to the banks qualified as a transfer in the sense of the COGSA 1992, the banks were also the lawful holders of these bills of lading in the sense of the COGSA 1992. As such, they were also the only ones with a right to sue the carrier under the bill of lading contract.[123]

4.5. Servants, agents and subcontractors

The issues with regard to the position of the consignee to some extent also surface with regard to the position of the carrier's servants, agents and subcontractors. They are obviously not a party to the contract of carriage, but their services are required in the performance of that contract of carriage. The question then arises whether, and if so to what extent, these servants, agents and subcontractors may benefit from the protection offered by the contract of carriage.

The protection of the carrier's servants, agents and subcontractors

The protection of the carrier's servants, agents and subcontractors was hardly an issue at the beginning of the twentieth century. They were not a party to the contract of carriage, and their mere negligence or carelessness would not result in liability.[124] This comfortable liability position may explain why the delegates in The Hague did not discuss the position of third parties in 1921, and why the Hague Rules of 1924 fail to offer any protection to the carrier's servants, agents and subcontractors. There was at that time simply no need to regulate their position.

123 See for a different outcome the Singapore case of *The Cherry* (2003) 1 SLR(R) 471; (2002) SGCA 49. In the first instance the court held: 'The law was changed to empower the agent who hitherto cannot sue to sue. The change did not confer the right to sue on the agent in substitution for the principal's right. The agent's new right runs with the principal's, not in its place.' On appeal, the Court of Appeal noted with regard to an endorsement in blank and subsequent forwarding of the bill to Glencore UK: 'The judge found that Glencore UK was holding the bill simply as the agent of the respondents for the transmission of documents and therefore the respondents were the holders of the bill for the purposes of the Bills of Lading Act (Cap 384). On appeal the appellants did not contest this finding.'

124 The textbook example follows from the infamous Dutch Supreme Court decision in HR 10 June 1910, W 9038. In this case water was leaking from a tap in the top apartment into the lower apartment. The owner of the lower apartment warned the owner of the top apartment and asked her to close the tap. She bluntly refused, however, and the furniture in the lower apartment was damaged as a result of the leakage. The owner of the lower apartment claimed the damage in tort, but his claim was denied. The Supreme Court held that her actions were certainly uncalled for, but that the defendant was nevertheless not liable for the damage as she had not violated any obligation under the law. The Dutch Supreme Court corrected its course shortly afterwards in HR 31 January 1919, NJ 1919, 161 (*Lindebaum v. Cohen*).

This all changed only a decade later.[125] Lord Atkin said in *Donoghue v. Stevenson* that one 'must take reasonable care to avoid acts and omissions which you can reasonably foresee would be likely to injure your neighbour' who he went on the describe as 'persons who are so closely and directly affected by my act that I ought reasonably to have them in contemplation as being so affected'. The House of Lords accepted that a breach in the duty of care could lead to liability,[126] and this new approach obviously affected the position of the carrier's servants, agents and subcontractors.

By the time that the CMR entered into force in 1956, the protection of the carrier's servants, agents and subcontractors was addressed in the convention. Article 28 (1) CMR prevents the circumvention of the convention by means of an extra-contractual claim, and article 28 (2) CMR explicitly allows the carrier's servants, agents and subcontractors (or in fact anyone within the scope of article 3 CMR) to rely on the provisions of the convention:[127]

> In cases where the extra-contractual liability for loss, damage or delay of one of the persons for whom the carrier is responsible under the terms of article 3 is in issue, such person may also avail himself of the provisions of this Convention which exclude the liability of the carrier or which fix or limit the compensation due.

When the Hague Rules underwent their revision in 1968, the position of the carrier's servants and agents was regulated, but the position of the carrier's subcontractors remained untouched.[128] Article IV bis HVR thus has the same objective as article 28 (2) CMR, but a more limited scope:

> If such an action is brought against a servant or agent of the carrier (such servant or agent not being an independent contractor), such servant or agent shall be entitled to avail himself of the defences and limits of liability which the carrier is entitled to invoke under this Convention.

125 *Donoghue v. Stevenson* (1932) A.C. 562.

126 See also Lord Macmillan at 619: 'The grounds of action may be as various and manifold as human errancy; and the conception of legal responsibility may develop in adaptation to altering social conditions and standards. The criterion of judgment must adjust and adapt itself to the changing circumstances of life. The categories of negligence are never closed. . . . Where there is room for diversity of view, it is in determining what circumstances will establish such a relationship between the parties as to give rise, on the one side, to a duty to take care, and on the other side to a right to have care taken.'

127 Article 30 (1) MC closely resembles this provision, and so does article 17 (3) CMNI.

128 Article 4 (1) RR stipulates: '1. Any provision of this Convention that may provide a defense for, or limit the liability of, the carrier applies in any judicial or arbitral proceeding, whether founded in contract, in tort, or otherwise, that is instituted in respect of loss of, damage to, or delay in delivery of goods covered by a contract of carriage or for the breach of any other obligation under this Convention against: (a) The carrier or a maritime performing party; (b) The master, crew or any other person that performs services on board the ship; or (c) Employees of the carrier or a maritime performing party.'

The cargo-interested parties will not be able to profit from cumulative actions against the carrier and his servants or agents (or subcontractors). The rule of article 20 (5) CMNI prevents this as the 'aggregate of the amounts of compensation recoverable from the carrier, the actual carrier and their servants and agents for the same loss shall not exceed overall the limits of liability provided for in this article'.[129]

Himalaya clauses

A Himalaya clause is a clause in the contract between the shipper and the carrier, yet for the benefit of the carrier's agents, servants and subcontractors. The clause allows them to rely on all of the carrier's defences, exemptions and immunities under the contract.

The Himalaya clause is named after the cruise ship in *Adler v. Dickson.*[130] This case had nothing to do with the carriage of goods, but in fact related to the carriage of passengers on a cruise vessel. Ms Adler had booked a cruise on the Mediterranean Sea with the Himalaya. The itinerary allowed for several stops, and one of them was in the city of Trieste. When she returned from her visit to the city, Ms Adler fell off the gangway when it was suddenly lifted by the wind. She suffered injuries as a result of the incident, but decided against a claim on the (owners of the) Himalaya since the company had excluded all liability for personal injuries and other damage in the ticket:

> Passengers and their baggage are carried at passengers' entire risk. ... The company will not be responsible for and shall be exempt from all liability in respect of any ... damage or injury whatsoever of or to the person of any passenger.

Instead, she initiated proceedings against the master (Dickson) and another crew member, alleging that they had breached their duty to safely secure the gangway. The defendants then relied on the exemptions listed in the ticket, and argued that they could benefit from their protection. The House of Lords rejected the defence as the exemptions in the ticket were not meant to protect the master and crew members, but Lord Denning did suggest that an adequately worded clause might have achieved this objective:

> My conclusion therefore is that, in the carriage of passengers as well as of goods, the law permits a carrier to stipulate for exemption from liability not only for himself but also for those whom he engages to carry out the contract; and this can be done by necessary implication as well as by express words. When such a stipulation is made, it is effective to protect those who

129 See also article 30 (2) MC and article IV bis (3) HVR.
130 *Adler v. Dickson* (1954) 2 Lloyd's Rep. 267 (*Himalaya*).

> render services under the contract, although they were not parties to it, subject however to this important qualification: The injured party must assent to the exemption of those persons.

This specific clause did not work, but *Adler v. Dickson* paved the way. Lord Reid accepted in *Midland Silicones v. Scruttons* that the carrier, acting as an agent of his subcontractors, could agree on an exemption for their benefit provided that four conditions were met:[131]

> I can see a possibility of success of the agency argument if (first) the bill of lading makes it clear that the stevedore is intended to be protected by the provisions in it which limit liability, (secondly) the bill of lading makes it clear that the carrier, in addition to contracting for these provisions on his own behalf, is also contracting as agent for the stevedore that these provisions should apply to the stevedore, (thirdly) the carrier has authority from the stevedore to do that, or perhaps later ratification by the stevedore would suffice, and (fourthly) that any difficulties about consideration moving from the stevedore were overcome.

The first two requirements could easily be tackled in the Himalaya clause itself, and the subcontractor was generally more than happy to confirm (or ratify) the carrier's authority. The fourth requirement remained difficult, but the consideration hurdle was eventually taken in the *Eurymedon*. Lord Wilberforce recognized the added value of (in this case again) a stevedore in a contract for the carriage of goods for the benefit of the shipper, and accepted that they were bound to one another when the stevedore discharged the goods:[132]

> The performance of these services for the benefit of the shipper was the consideration for the agreement by the shipper that the appellant should have the benefit of the exemptions and limitations contained in the bill of lading.

Whereas the Law Commission did not want to interfere with the position of the consignee,[133] it had no such reservations with regard to the position of the carrier's servants, agents and subcontractors. S. 6 (5) of the (Contracts) Rights of Third Parties Act 1999 indeed precludes contracts of carriage from the application of the act, but the final sentence of that provision provides for an exception to the exception, namely that 'a third party may in reliance on that section avail himself of an exclusion or limitation of liability in such a contract.'

The (Contracts) Rights of Third Parties Act 1999 does not require agency, authority or consideration.[134] Instead, S. 1 (1) of the act allows a third party to

131 *Midland Silicones v. Scruttons* (1961) 1 Lloyd's Rep. 365.

132 *The Eurymedon* (1974) 1 Lloyd's Rep. 534.

133 See the discussion in section 4.2.

134 J. Chuah, 'The port terminal operators' case' in D. Rhidian Thomas (ed.) *The carriage of goods by sea under Rotterdam Rules* (Informa: London, 2010) 225.

enforce a term of the contract if 'the contract expressly provides that he may, or . . . the term purports to confer a benefit on him'.[135]

Himalaya clauses in other contracts in the chain

The carriage of goods from one place to another is often governed by more than one contract, especially when more than one means of transportation is involved. A shipper instructs a forwarder, the forwarder instructs a carrier and the carrier instructs one or more sub-carriers, and all these contracts may in fact contain Himalaya clauses for the benefit of servants, agents or subcontractors. This raises the question of whether such a servant, agent or subcontractor may rely on the favourable provisions in all of these contracts in the chain.

The answer follows from the US Supreme Court judgment in *Kirby v. Norfolk*.[136] Kirby had instructed ICC for the carriage of a shipment of machinery from Sydney (Australia) to Huntsville (US). This was a multimodal contract of carriage; the first leg was by sea from Sydney to Savannah (US), and the second leg completed the voyage by rail to Huntsville. ICC issued a bill of lading for the entire voyage. This ICC bill of lading contained a limitation of liability for inland carriage of 667 SDR per package or 2 SDR per kilo. The ICC bill of lading also contained the following Himalaya clause:

> These conditions ... apply whenever claims relating to the performance of the contract evidenced by this (B/L) are made against any servant, agent or other person (including any independent contractor) whose services have been used in order to perform the contract.

ICC then instructed Hamburg Sud as its sub-carrier. Hamburg Sud also issued a bill of lading. This bill of lading limited the liability for inland carriage to 500 US$ per package,[137] and also contained a Himalaya clause, extending the benefit of the limitation of liability to 'all agents . . . (including inland) carriers . . . and all independent contractors whatsoever'.

Hamburg Sud performed the sea leg with one of its own vessels, yet instructed Norfolk for the inland rail leg. Unfortunately, the train derailed during the voyage to Huntsville and Kirby sued Norfolk for the damage. Norfolk obviously relied on the Himalaya clause in the ICC bill of lading, but he also relied on

135 Three out of the four requirements of Lord Reid had already been abandoned (to leave just the first requirement) in New Zealand in 1982 with the entry into force of its Contracts (Privity) Act. P.A. Myburgh in A.N. Yiannopoulos, *Ocean bills of lading: Traditional forms, substitutes, and EDI systems* (Kluwer International: The Hague, 1995) 250. See also the (similar) test applied by the US Supreme Court in *Kirby v. Norfolk* (2004) AMC 2705: 'It is clear to us that a railroad like Norfolk was an intended beneficiary of the ICC bill's broadly written Himalaya Clause. Accordingly, Norfolk's liability is limited by the terms of that clause.'

136 *Kirby v. Norfolk* (2004) AMC 2705.

137 The Hamburg Sud bill of lading in fact contractually extended the US COGSA limitation to inland carriage.

the Himalaya clause in the Hamburg Sud bill of lading to benefit from the very friendly 500 US$ per package limitation for inland (rail) carriage.

The Himalaya clause was drafted widely enough to cover Norfolk,[138] but the key hurdle was that Kirby had not been a party to the Hamburg Sud bill of lading, and therefore had not agreed to the 500 US$ per package limitation either. The Supreme Court nevertheless allowed the defence and held that Norfolk could rely on the limitation in the Hamburg Sud bill of lading:[139]

> When an intermediary contracts with a carrier to transport goods, the cargo owner's recovery against the carrier is limited by the liability limitation to which the intermediary and the carrier agreed. The intermediary is certainly not automatically empowered to be the cargo owner's agent in every sense. That would be unsustainable. But when it comes to liability limitations for negligence resulting in damages, an intermediary can negotiate reliable and enforceable agreements with the carrier it engages.

Kirby argued that this would be 'disastrous' for the shipping industry, but the Supreme Court was not impressed. It stressed that this 'limited agency rule' followed industry practices, that it also had an upside for shippers in the form of lower freights rates and that Kirby was of course still free to sue his contractual counterpart ICC for the difference between the 500 US$ per package and 2 SDR per kilo limitation.

Jurisdiction clauses

The next question is whether the protection of the Himalaya clause only extends to material exemptions and immunities or also extends to jurisdiction clauses. As the judgments in the *Mahkutai* and the *Berane* show,[140] there are convincing arguments for both possible answers.

The owners of the *Mahkutai* had given their ship in time charter to Sentosa, who in turn had given the ship in voyage charter to PT Jabarwood. Sentosa issued a bill of lading to PT Jabarwood for the carriage of a shipment of plywood from Jakarta (Indonesia) to Shantou (China). This bill of lading contained a Himalaya clause as well as a jurisdiction clause for the courts of Indonesia. Upon arrival in Shantou the wood had suffered damage by seawater. The next port of call was Hong Kong, and there the ship was arrested and proceedings were initiated.

The owners of the *Mahkutai* filed for a stay of these proceedings. They argued that the Himalaya clause worked to their benefit, and that they could rely on 'all exceptions, limitations, provisions, conditions and liberties herein benefiting the Carrier as if such provisions were expressly made for their benefit', therefore including the exclusive choice of jurisdiction Indonesia.

138 See also *Herd v. Krawill* (1959) AMC 879 and *Fruit of the Loom v. Arawak* (2000) AMC 387.
139 *Kirby v. Norfolk* (2004) AMC 2705.
140 *The Mahkutai* (1996) 2 Lloyd's Rep. 1; *Acciai v. M/V Berane et al.* (2002) AMC 528.

The Privy Council disagreed and refused the stay of proceedings.[141] It held that the objective of the Himalaya clause was to protect the carrier's subcontractors and that it 'cannot therefore extend to include a mutual agreement, such as an exclusive jurisdiction clause, which is not of that character'. The Privy Council furthermore considered that a jurisdiction clause would certainly not be beneficial to all subcontractors. A stevedore, for instance, would probably prefer to defend the claim before his home court, instead of the court agreed upon by his principals.

The outcome in the *Berane* was the opposite.[142] Acciai had instructed the owners of the *Berane* to carry a shipment of steel from Civitavecchia (Italy) to Baltimore (US). Again, the bill of lading contained both a Himalaya clause and a jurisdiction clause, this time for the courts of Valetta (Malta). The goods were damaged during the discharge operations and Acciai initiated proceedings against the stevedores in Maryland (US).

The stevedores argued that the Maryland court had no jurisdiction, and this time with success. The court held that it was not unreasonable to expect that the stevedore would want to benefit from the jurisdiction clause. In fact, it held that 'it would be grossly inefficient for an action against the carrier to be brought in one jurisdiction and another action, arising out of the same shipment, to be brought against the carrier's local agent in a different jurisdiction.'[143]

This may in general be true, but the efficiency argument is not very convincing in this particular case. This time the stevedores relied on the jurisdiction clause in the bill of lading, but the stevedores were not in any way held to rely on the bill of lading. It is very likely that they would have challenged the court's jurisdiction, this time conveniently discarding both the jurisdiction clause and the Himalaya clause, if the merchant had brought proceedings against them in Valetta.

Still, it is submitted that the Himalaya clause should also extend to jurisdiction clauses as the distinction between defences and immunities on the one hand and mutual agreements on the other is too artificial.[144] First of all, an exception or a limitation of liability is also a 'mutual agreement', and second, a jurisdiction clause is in practice one of the carrier's most powerful defences. The jurisdiction clauses in the bills of lading of major shipping lines, such as Maersk and MSC with their seats in Denmark and Switzerland, refer all disputes to the High Court in London. Surely this is in part because of the court's vast experience in shipping cases, but mostly because the prospect of the serious expenses and costs in London forms an extremely effective threshold against proceedings. If this 'defence' is available to the carrier, it should equally be available to the carrier's servants, agents and subcontractors.

141 *The Mahkutai* (1996) 2 Lloyd's Rep. 1.

142 *Acciai v. M/V Berane et al.* (2002) AMC 528.

143 In the end the Maryland court indeed declared itself incompetent, but in the same judgment it barred the stevedores from challenging the jurisdiction of the Valetta court.

144 This was the distinction made by the Privy Council in the *Mahkutai* (1996) 2 Lloyd's Rep. 1.

Circular clauses

At first sight, the objective of the Himalaya clause is to have the carrier's servants, agents and subcontractors benefit from the contract of carriage. In reality, however, the clause ultimately benefits the carrier himself. The carrier's servants, agents and subcontractors will work under general terms and conditions, and these will commonly stipulate an obligation for their principal to indemnify them against third-party claims.[145] When the carrier's servants, agents and subcontractors avail themselves of the same defences and immunities as the carrier himself, third parties are discouraged from bringing proceedings against them, and the carrier is less likely to be exposed to the indemnification clause.

Obviously, the carrier could also take this one step further. Whereas the classic (wording of the) Himalaya clause only covered the relation between the merchant and the carrier's servants, agents and subcontractors, a more elaborate Himalaya clause may furthermore contain a provision to ensure that no claims are made against them at all, for instance:[146]

> The Merchant undertakes that no claim or allegation shall be made against any servant, agent or sub-contractor of the Carrier which imposes or attempts to impose upon any of them or any vessel owned by any of them any liability whatsoever in connection with the Goods and, if any such claim or allegation should nevertheless be made, to indemnify the Carrier against all consequences thereof.

This is a so-called circular clause.[147] Such a clause effectively prevents any litigation against the carrier's servants, agents and subcontractors. If the merchant sues the carrier's servants, agents and subcontractors for the damage, and they in turn take recourse on the carrier, the merchant would have to indemnify the carrier for the consequences thereof.

145 See for instance clause 20 of the BIFA Standard Trading Conditions: 'The Customer shall save harmless and keep the Company indemnified from and against:- (A) all liability, loss, damage, costs and expenses whatsoever (including, without prejudice to the generality of the foregoing, all duties, taxes, imposts, levies, deposits and outlays of whatsoever nature levied by any authority in relation to the Goods) arising out of the Company acting in accordance with the Customer's instructions, or arising from any breach by the Customer of any warranty contained in these conditions, or from the negligence of the Customer, and (B) without derogation from sub-clause (A) above, any liability assumed, or incurred by the Company when, by reason of carrying out the Customer's instructions, the Company has become liable to any other party, and (C) all claims, costs and demands whatsoever and by whomsoever made or preferred, in excess of the liability of the Company under the terms of these conditions, regardless of whether such claims, costs, and/or demands arise from, or in connection with, the breach of contract, negligence or breach of duty of the Company, its servants, sub-contractors or agents, and (D) any claims of a general average nature which may be made on the Company.'

146 See also Article 15 (c) Conline 2000: 'The Merchant undertakes that no claim shall be made against any servant or agent of the Carrier and, if any claim should nevertheless be made, to indemnify the Carrier against all consequences thereof.'

147 In fact, this is the circular clause in the *Elbe Maru* (1978) 1 Lloyd's Rep. 206.

Besides, if the merchant initiates proceedings against them in spite of the clause, the carrier himself can also rely on the clause to achieve a stay of such proceedings. The cargo-interested parties in the *Elbe Maru* had initiated proceedings against a sub-carrier in violation of the circular clause. The carrier successfully pursued an indefinite stay of these proceedings as Ackner J held that:[148]

> the suggestion that the Court should … allow the action to proceed, then to be followed by a claim against the applicants and then to be followed by the applicants claiming against the respondent seems to me to ignore the well-established proposition … that there should be an end of useless litigation. If the action ought not to be brought, then the Court should intervene and stop it rather than allow a series of circuitous actions which ultimately end up achieving exactly what the stay sought would achieve, apart from the disbursement of a quite unnecessary amount of costs.

148 The *Elbe Maru* (1978) 1 Lloyd's Rep. 206.

5 International conventions on the carriage of goods

The parties to a contract of carriage are in principle free to define their rights and obligations in the contract, unless that freedom is restricted by either domestic law or an international convention. This chapter deals with the five most important conventions on carriage of goods, i.e. the CIM, HVR, MC, CMR and CMNI.[1] These conventions are at basis unimodal conventions.[2] They regulate contracts for the cross-border carriage of goods by respectively rail, sea (under a bill of lading), air, road and inland waterways. These five conventions have a lot in common.[3]

Mandatory systems of liability

The liability system adopted by all these conventions is generally the same, and still closely observes the Roman law concept of the receptum nautarum. The carrier is liable for loss of or damage to the goods in his care, but he avails of a

1 If a contract of carriage is not governed by one of the conventions, e.g. a contract of carriage by sea under a charter party, it is governed by the domestic law applicable to the contract. See Chapter 7 for the rules on private international law in this respect.

2 Some of these conventions also contain rules on multimodal situations, though. These situations are discussed in Chapter 6.

3 Unfortunately, the provisions in international conventions on carriage of goods are not always crystal clear. Whereas the meaning of contractual provisions may be construed on the basis of the reasonable expectations of the contracting parties in the given circumstances, see, for instance, *Investors Compensation Scheme v. West Bromwich Building Society* (1998) 1 WLR 896, HR 13 March 1981, NJ 1981, 635 (Haviltex) and HR 25 September 1998, NJ 1998, 892 (*Haefner v. ABN Amro*). The United Nations Convention on the Law of Treaties of 23 May 1969 (Vienna Convention) provides the necessary guidance for the interpretation of ambiguous provisions in a convention. Article 31 of the Vienna Convention gives the general rule of interpretation. A (provision in the) convention 'shall be interpreted in good faith in accordance with the ordinary meaning to be given to the terms of the treaty in their context and in the light of its object and purpose'. If its meaning then remains ambiguous or if the interpretation in accordance with article 31 of the Vienna Convention produces a 'manifestly absurd or unreasonable' result, article 32 of the Vienna Convention identifies the supplementary means of interpretation. The meaning of the provision may then be determined in accordance with the travaux préparatoires of the convention and the circumstances at the time of its conclusion.

number of conventional exemptions, immunities and limitations of liability. The carrier cannot exclude or mitigate his liability beyond these conventional defences as all five conventions provide for mandatory law.

Still, some conventions are more mandatory than others. The HVR allow for some contractual flexibility, but only at the expense of the carrier. Article III (8) HVR merely targets carrier-friendly provisions in the contract of carriage; contractual provisions to the detriment of the carrier are therefore perfectly valid under the convention:[4]

> Any clause, covenant, or agreement in a contract of carriage relieving the carrier or the ship from liability for loss or damage to, or in connection with, goods arising, from negligence, fault, or failure in the duties and obligations provided in this Article or lessening such liability otherwise than as provided in this Convention, shall be null and void and of no effect.

The mandatory character of the CIM, MC, CMR and CMNI works both ways. Neither party to the contract of carriage is allowed to depart from the conventional provisions,[5] irrespective of whether the contractual arrangement benefits the carrier or the cargo-interested parties, as 'any stipulation which would directly or indirectly derogate from the provisions of this Convention shall be null and void'.[6]

Obviously, a mandatory liability regime only works if the contracting parties cannot avoid the provisions of the convention. In that respect, all five conventions prescribe that an action for damages 'whether under this Convention or in contract or in tort or otherwise, can only be brought subject to the conditions and such limits of liability as are set out in this Convention'.[7] The system of liability thus applies to all claims within the conventional scope of application,[8] irrespective of whether they are presented under the contract of carriage, in tort[9] or otherwise.[10]

The mandatory character of these conventions affects the role of any domestic law applicable to the contract. If a mandatory convention regulates a certain issue,

4 Article III (8) HVR furthermore reads that 'a benefit of insurance in favour of the carrier or similar clause shall be deemed to be a clause relieving the carrier from liability'.

5 A convention may of course explicitly allow certain contractual exclusions. Article 25 (2) CMNI, for instance, authorizes exclusions of liability of errors in navigation, fire and hidden defects and article 20 (4 (b)) CMNI allows parties to agree on a higher limitation of liability.

6 This is the wording of article 41 CMR, but the content of article 5 CIM, article 49 MC and article 25 (1) CMNI is very much alike.

7 Article 29 MC, but see in a more or less similar wording also article 41 § 1 CIM, article IV bis HVR, article 28 CMR and article 22 CMNI.

8 The conventional system of liability also applies to claims against servants and agents (and subcontractors). These claims are discussed in more detail in Chapter 4.

9 Clearly, this rule does not apply only to real (third-party) extra-contractual claims for damages. When a road carrier hits a fence in the course of the voyage, its owner's claim for damages in tort is not governed by the CMR as there is no contract of carriage between them.

10 For instance in bailment, see the *Pioneer Container* (1994) 2 AC 324.

such as the liability of the carrier (or the exemption or limitation of that liability), that issue is solely governed by the provisions of the convention. The House of Lords held unanimously in *Sidhu v. British Airways*:[11]

> The Convention does not purport to deal with all matters relating to contracts of international carriage by air. But in those areas with which it deals -and the liability of the carrier is one of them – the code is intended to be uniform and to be exclusive also of any resort to the rules of domestic law. ... The domestic Courts are not free to provide a remedy according to their own law, because to do this would be to undermine the Convention. It would lead to the setting alongside the Convention of an entirely different set of rules which would distort the operation of the whole scheme.

This decision related to the carriage of goods by air under the Warsaw Convention, but it is submitted that its underlying reasoning applies to the other conventions as well.[12] All five conventions primarily deal with the carrier's liability, and when this liability is at stake, there is no room for the application of domestic law as the provisions of the international conventions on carriage of goods are meant to apply exhaustively.[13]

All the same, if a convention fails to regulate a certain issue, such as the right of retention, the payment of the freight or the termination of the contract, its provisions cannot be undermined either.[14] The unregulated issues are then supplemented by the domestic law applicable to the contract.[15] Obviously, a specific issue is also governed by domestic law when the convention explicitly says so,

11 *Sidhu v. British Airways* (1997) 2 Lloyd's Rp. 76, per Lord Hope of Craighead.

12 See for instance with regard to the application of *Sidhu v. British Airways* to carriage by road under the CMR: I. Koning *Aansprakelijkheid in het luchtvervoer* (Paris Zutphen, 2007) 245, F. Stevens in his annotation of the Belgian Supreme Court judgment of 16 January 2009, Rechtskundig Weekblad (2009) 739, M. Spanjaart, *Transfennica v. Schenker, the system of articles 17 and 23 CMR*, TranspR. 2016, 383, and, albeit with slightly more caution, A. Messent & D.A. Glass, *CMR: Contracts for the International Carriage of Goods by Road* (LLP: London, 2000) 13.

13 See also M. Clarke & D. Yates, *Contracts of carriage by land and air* (Informa: London, 2008), saying at 123 that 'CIM ... is intended to provide a self-sufficient regime, and thus, in principle, national law is irrelevant.'

14 Article 29 (1) and (2) CMNI explicitly stipulates: 'In cases not provided for in this Convention, the contract of carriage is governed by the law of the State agreed by the Parties. In the absence of such agreement, the law of the State with which the contract of carriage is most closely connected is to be applied.' This is arguably a rather harmless, if not redundant provision in view of the (current) list of contracting states to the CMNI in combination with articles 3 and 4 Rome I. However, it is also a rather strange provision as article 29 CMNI gives conflict rules on issues that the convention has willingly failed to regulate.

15 Still, it is sometimes difficult to draw the boundary between regulated and unregulated issues. Where a convention gives general rules, these rules may still apply to unregulated issues. See for the scope of the CMR limitation period for instance HR 11 February 2000, NJ 2000, 420, HR 18 December 2009, S&S 2010, 25, but also BGH 19 April 2009, I ZR 90/04 in which the German Supreme Court held: 'In accordance with standard Senate case law the time bar provision of article 32 CMR not only applies to claims under the CMR, but also to all claims in connection with CMR transportation that follow from domestic law.'

for instance with regard to the interruption of the limitation period in articles 48 CIM 1999 and 24 (3) CMNI.[16]

Short limitation periods

All these conventions furthermore prescribe (very) short limitation periods, but their exact duration varies between one and three years.[17] Not just the available amount of time varies, though; the consequences of any lapse of the limitation period and the available remedies to avoid this may also be different.

Article 48 § 1 CIM 1999 stipulates a general one-year limitation period, and a two-year limitation period if the loss or damage follows 'from an act or omission done with intent to cause such loss or damage, or recklessly and with knowledge that such loss or damage would probably result'.[18] The claimant can no longer exercise his right of suit when the limitation period has expired.[19]

Article III (6) HVR prescribes a one-year limitation period for claims against the carrier.[20] The carrier is 'discharged from all liability whatsoever in respect of the goods, unless suit is brought within one year of their delivery or of the date when they should have been delivered'.[21] This period cannot one-sidedly be interrupted; it can only be extended in mutual agreement.[22]

Article 35 (1) MC provides for a two-year limitation period.[23] Again, this period cannot be interrupted. Once the two years have lapsed, and if proceedings

16 The notorious article 29 CMR refers for the equivalent of wilful misconduct to the law of the court seized. This is of course also domestic law, yet not the lex causae, but instead the lex fori. The provision, including the trouble it has caused, is discussed later in this chapter.

17 And sometimes an extra three months in the case of recourse claims; see, for instance, article III (6bis) HVR.

18 Article 48 § 1 (c) CIM 1999. The article also prescribes a two-year period for an action a) to recover a cash on delivery payment collected by the carrier from the consignee; b) to recover the proceeds of a sale effected by the carrier; d) based on one of the contracts of carriage prior to the reconsignment in the case provided for in Article 28.

19 Article 48 § 4 CIM 1999.

20 The limitation for claims against the shipper, for instance for the freight, but see also articles IV (3) and IV (6) HVR, is therefore governed by the law applicable to the contract of carriage (as discussed in Chapter 7).

21 The reference to 'suit' encompasses both court proceedings and arbitration; see *The Merak* (1965) P 233.

22 Article III (6) HVR furthermore requires the claimant to complain within three days. If the claimant fails to comply with this requirement, the penalty is that the goods are deemed to have been delivered in accordance with their description in the bill of lading. This provision does not really have any added value as the claimant would need to prove the occurrence of the damages in the tackle-to-tackle period anyhow.

23 The MC does not just provide for a limitation period; it also prescribes an extremely short period (of 14 days in the case of goods) within which the claimant must have complained. Article 31 (2) MC stipulates: 'In the case of damage, the person entitled to delivery must complain to the carrier forthwith after the discovery of the damage, and, at the latest, within seven days from the date of receipt in the case of checked baggage and fourteen days from the date of receipt in the case of cargo. In the case of delay, the complaint must be made at the latest within twenty-one days from the date on which the baggage or cargo have been placed at his or her disposal.'

are still not pending by then, the right of suit expires. The claimant will then no longer be allowed in his claim as his 'right to damages shall be extinguished if an action is not brought within a period of two years, reckoned from the date of arrival at the destination, or from the date on which the aircraft ought to have arrived, or from the date on which the carriage stopped'.[24]

Article 32 (1) CMR in principle gives a one-year limitation period,[25] and the right of suit expires by lapse of that time.[26] Article 32 (1) CMR increases the one-year period to a three-year period, however, if the damages were caused by 'wilful misconduct, or such default as in accordance with the law of the court or tribunal seized of the case, is considered as equivalent to wilful misconduct'. Apart from the interruption in accordance with the law of the court where the proceedings are bought, the CMR limitation period can also be suspended by means of a written claim.[27]

Finally, article 24 (1) CMNI ensures that all 'actions arising out of a contract governed by this Convention shall be time-barred after one year'.[28] This one-year period may be extended by agreement,[29] suspended or interrupted.[30] The claimant loses his right of suit when the claim becomes time-barred, and the claim can then no longer be exercised by way of counter-claim or set-off either.[31]

Jurisdiction

Some of these conventions, i.e. the CIM 1999, the MC and the CMR, contain specific provisions on jurisdiction. These three conventions give the claimant a number of competent courts to choose from, but the available options differ per convention.[32]

24 Arguably, in the absence of a specific provision to that effect, this implies that the two-year limitation period cannot be extended at all, not even in mutual agreement. In OLG Frankfurt am Main 15 September 1999, TranspR 2000, 183, however, the court of appeal held that the carrier could not in good faith rely on the two-year period, since he had agreed to an extension thereof.

25 The one-year period also applies to recourse claims between successive carriers, but article 39 (4) CMR prescribes that this period only begins to run 'either on the date of the final judicial decision fixing the amount of compensation payable under the provisions of this Convention, or, if there is no such judicial decision, from the actual date of payment'.

26 Article 32 (4) CMR.

27 See article 32 (2) and (3) CMR, but there is a catch. The Dutch Supreme Court held in *Brinky v. Hazeleger* that a limitation period that had been suspended, yet started running again as the carrier had lifted the suspension, could then no longer be interrupted. HR 20 December 2013, NJ 2014, 295 (ann. L. Strikwerda), S&S 2014/62.

28 In line with the first sentence of article III (6) HVR, article 23 (4) CMNI prescribes a notice period of (this time) seven days. Again, the penalty is that the claimant must 'show that the damage was caused while the goods were in the charge of the carrier'. Again, however, it is submitted that this provision does not have any added value as the claimant has to prove the occurrence of the damages in this period anyhow.

29 Article 24 (2) CMNI.

30 The suspension and interruption are governed by the law applicable to the contract in accordance with article 24 (3) CMNI.

31 See article 24 (5) CMNI, in line with article 32 (4) CMR.

32 The MC and the CMR also allow for arbitration. The parties to the contract of carriage are free to agree on arbitration instead of the regular courts of law in accordance with articles 34 MC and 33

Article 46 § 1 CIM 1999 confers jurisdiction to 'the courts or tribunals of Member States designated by agreement between the parties or before the courts or tribunals of a State on whose territory a) the defendant has his domicile or habitual residence, his principal place of business or the branch or agency which concluded the contract of carriage, or b) the place where the goods were taken over by the carrier or the place designated for delivery is situated'.[33] The jurisdiction of these courts (or tribunals) is exclusive; the claim cannot be brought before any other court.

Article 33 (1) MC stipulates that 'an action for damages must be brought, at the option of the plaintiff, in the territory of one of the States Parties, either before the court of the domicile of the carrier or of its principal place of business, or where it has a place of business through which the contract has been made or before the court at the place of destination'. The provision remains silent on forum choices. Since the convention gives mandatory rules on jurisdiction, though, and the regulation of the jurisdiction is arguably intended to be exclusive,[34] the choice for any other court than the ones identified by article 33 MC is null and void.[35]

Article 31 (1) CMR allows for proceedings in 'any court or tribunal of a contracting country designated by agreement between the parties and, in addition, in the courts or tribunals of a country within whose territory: (a) The defendant is ordinarily resident, or has his principal place of business, or the branch or agency through which the contract of carriage was made, or (b) The place where the goods were taken over by the carrier or the place designated for delivery is situated'. The absence of any reference to 'a contracting country' under (a) and (b) implies that the courts of non-contracting countries may also have jurisdiction in CMR cases.[36] The specific reference to 'and, in addition' furthermore implies that a jurisdiction clause in the contract of carriage is not exclusive, but merely gives the contracting parties an extra option.[37]

CMR. A valid arbitration clause strips the regular courts from their competence; see for instance Rechtbank Amsterdam 25 March 2016, S&S 2016/111.

33 The reference to 'or' suggests that the choice of jurisdiction is not exclusive, and that the options a) and b) therefore remain open as well.

34 *Sidhu v. British Airways* (1997) 2 Lloyd's Rep. 76.

35 Article 34 (1) MC reads: 'Subject to the provisions of this Article, the parties to the contract of carriage for cargo may stipulate that any dispute relating to the liability of the carrier under this Convention shall be settled by arbitration. Such agreement shall be in writing.' Pursuant to article 34 (2) MC, 'the arbitration proceedings shall, at the option of the claimant, take place within one of the jurisdictions referred to in Article 33.'

36 Article 33 CMR stipulates: 'The contract of carriage may contain a clause conferring competence on an arbitration tribunal if the clause conferring competence on the tribunal provides that the tribunal shall apply this Convention.' Arguably, the result would have been the same if article 33 CMR had been left out. The parties to the contract of carriage are in the absence of such a provision, as for instance under the HVR or CMNI, equally free to agree on arbitration (within the framework of the New York Convention).

37 See, for instance, the UK Supreme Court decision in British American *Tobacco v. Exel Europe* (2016) 1 Lloyd's Rep. 463, but also M. Clarke & D. Yates, *Contracts of carriage by land and air* (Informa: London, 2008) 67.

These specific provisions on jurisdiction may sometimes collide with the provisions of Regulation (EU) No. 1215/2012 (recast), also known as Brussels I.[38] This regulation deals with the recognition and enforcement of judgments within the European Union,[39] but also provides rules on jurisdiction. Article 25 Brussels I allows the contracting parties to agree on the jurisdiction of a Member State,[40] and if they do, Brussels I dictates that 'such jurisdiction shall be exclusive unless the parties have agreed otherwise.'

Such an exclusive forum choice under Brussels I sits uncomfortably with the merely additional forum choices under the CIM 1999 and CMR, but potential collision problems are solved by article 71 Brussels I. In the case of a conflict between Brussels I on the one hand and the CIM 1999, MC or CMR on the other, article 71 (1) Brussels I ensures that 'this Regulation shall not affect any conventions to which the Member States are parties and which, in relation to particular matters, govern jurisdiction or the recognition or enforcement of judgments.' The specific provisions on jurisdiction in the CIM 1999, MC and CMR therefore prevail over the provisions on jurisdiction in Brussels I.[41]

Since the HVR and CMNI do not give any rules on jurisdiction at all, the competence of the courts is determined in accordance with the provisions of Brussels I (within the European Union) or the provisions of the domestic legislation of the country of the court seized. In practice, the competence of the court then simply follows from the jurisdiction clause in the bill of lading, (sea) waybill or other transport document.[42]

5.1. The CIM 1999

The first railroads can be traced back to the early seventeenth century.[43] These railroads were without exception local railroads in mining areas in the UK. The

38 Regulation (EU) No. 1215/2012 of the European Parliament and the Council of 12 December 2012 on jurisdiction and the recognition and enforcement of judgments in civil and commercial matters (recast).

39 With the exception of Denmark.

40 A contractual provision that identifies the competent court qualifies as a separate agreement, J. Eckoldt, *De forumkeuze in het zeevervoer* (Paris: Zutphen, 2014) 20.

41 W. Verheyen, *Afbakening toepassingsgebied vervoerverdragen door nationale wetgever: aanleiding tot parallelle procedures onder Brussel I (bis)?* NTHR 2016, at 51. See specifically for the relation between article 31 CMR and the provisions of Brussels I the decisions of the European Court of Justice of 4 May 2010 in *TNT v. AXA*, S&S 2010/95, of 19 December 2013 in *Nipponkoa v. Inter-Zuid*, S&S 2014/24 and of 4 September 2014 in *Nickel & Goeldner v. Kintra*, S&S 2015/26.

42 Article 23 (1) of the Fenex Conditions refers all disputes under the contract to arbitration: 'All disputes which may arise between the forwarder and the other party shall be decided by three arbitrators to the exclusion of the ordinary courts of law, and their decision shall be final. A dispute shall exist whenever any of the parties declares this to be so.' Even though this arbitration clause forms part of standard forwarding conditions, it may still be effective if the contract qualifies as a contract of carriage by road (and not as a forwarding contract) if the contracting parties failed to agree on the jurisdiction in the transport document. HR 25 January 2008, S&S 2008/45 (*GMS v. Peterson*).

43 The Wollaton Wagonway of 1604 was arguably the first. The rails were made of wood, and the track covered approximately 3 kilometres between Strelley and Wollaton (near Nottingham).

wooden tracks only covered the few kilometres from the coal mine to a warehouse, production plant or distribution centre, and the wagons were pulled by horses. Clearly, this all changed with the invention of the steam engine. The first 'modern' railroad opened to the public in 1825. The track ran between Stockton and Darlington and the steam engine could pull 21 coal wagons at a speed of almost 15 kilometres per hour.

By 1840 most European countries operated their own national railroads. The UK still enjoyed its early start; its network covered 2,390 kilometres, roughly twice as much as the railroads of Germany, France, Belgium and the Netherlands combined. By 1860, however, Germany (33,838 kilometres) had already overtaken the UK (25,060 kilometres) and France was closing in (23,089 kilometres).[44]

The first conference on the international carriage of goods by rail was held in Berne (Switzerland) in 1878.[45] The Convention concernant le transport International ferroviaire des Marchandises (CIM) was signed only a few years later, again in Berne in 1890. The convention regulated international contracts of carriage of goods by rail. It was amended quite a few times over the years, most recently in 1999 in Vilnius (Latvia).

The scope of application

Article 1 § 1 CIM 1999 stipulates that the convention applies to 'every contract of carriage of goods by rail for reward'.[46] In the absence of any form requirement,[47] the convention therefore applies to 'every' written, verbal or tacit contract of carriage by rail.[48] Article 1 §§ 3 and 4 CIM 1999 extends the scope of application to domestic carriage by road and inland waterways as well as carriage by sea or inland waterway on listed services, provided that this carriage by another means of transportation is performed as a supplement to carriage by rail.[49]

Article 1 § 1 CIM 1999 also gives the formal scope of application. The convention applies 'when the place of taking over of the goods and the place designated for delivery are situated in two different Member States, irrespective of the place of business and the nationality of the parties to the contract of carriage'.[50]

44 Paul Halsall, *Modern History Sourcebook: Spread of Railways in 19th Century* (1997), available at http://legacy.fordham.edu/halsall/mod/INDREV6.asp.

45 Attended by Germany, France, Hungary, Switzerland, Belgium, Italy, Russia and the Netherlands.

46 Gratuitous carriage by rail is therefore not governed by the convention. For obvious reasons, this does not occur very often.

47 The material scope of application was amended in Vilnius. Article 1 CIM 1980 still required the issuance of a consignment note.

48 The conclusion of the contract of carriage may be form free, but article 6 § 2 CIM 1999 still requires the contract to 'be confirmed by a consignment note'. The contracting parties' failure to comply with this requirement, however, does 'not affect the existence or validity of the contract which shall remain subject to these Uniform Rules'. In addition, article 6 § 6 CIM 1999 reads: 'A consignment note must be made out for each consignment. In the absence of a contrary agreement between the consignor and the carrier, a consignment note may not relate to more than one wagon load.'

49 This supplemental carriage is discussed in more detail in Chapter 6.

50 The reference to 'the place of taking over' on the one hand and 'the place designated for delivery' on the other suggests a distinction between an actual place and a contractual place. A contract of

The convention does not apply to domestic carriage by rail, and the convention does not apply to international carriage by rail if only one of the two countries is a party to the convention either. Article 1 § 2 CIM 1999 provides an escape, though. The convention still applies if at least one of the countries is a contracting state and the parties agree that their contract is subject to convention.[51]

In a way, article 1 § 1 CIM 1999 even provides the temporal scope of the convention as the Uniform Rules apply to a 'contract of carriage of goods by rail'. Article 6 § 1 CIM 1999 then prescribes that by such a contract 'the carrier shall undertake to carry the goods for reward to the place of destination and to deliver them there to the consignee.' The entire contract of carriage of goods by rail is therefore regulated by the provisions of the convention.

The system of liability

Article 23 § 1 CIM 1999 confirms the carrier's obligation to achieve a certain result, i.e. the delivery of the goods at their destination in the same sound condition as in which they were received for transport, and on time:

> The carrier shall be liable for loss or damage resulting from the total or partial loss of, or damage to, the goods between the time of taking over of the goods and the time of delivery and for the loss or damage resulting from the transit period being exceeded, whatever the railway infrastructure used.

Still, the carrier will not be liable if the loss or damage was caused by the fault of the consignor or consignee, an inherent defect in the goods or force majeure.[52] Both the existence of (one or more of) these exempted causes and the causal link between the cause and the loss or damage need to be proved by the carrier.[53]

The carrier will furthermore escape liability if the loss or damage was caused by 'special risks' inherent to certain circumstances listed in article 23 § 3 CIM 1999. These circumstances include:

carriage by rail between Basel (Switzerland, but very close to the German border) and Hamburg (Germany) would then be governed by domestic German law (instead of the convention) if it were somehow more convenient for the carrier to accept the goods for transportation at the first German train station just across the border. Conversely, the return transport from Hamburg to Basel would still be governed by the convention if it were more convenient for the consignee to have the goods delivered at the last German train station just before the border.

51 These two requirements of article 1 § 2 CIM 1999 are cumulative, and the mere reference to provisions of the CIM in the contract is insufficient for an agreement in the sense of article 1 § 2 CIM 1999; see Hof's-Hertogenbosch 21 June 2016, S&S 2016/114 and Rechtbank Midden-Nederland 16 December 2015, S&S 2016/43. All the same, Rome I seems to restrict choices of law to choices for the domestic law of a country. See Chapter 7 for this discussion.

52 Article 23 § 2 CIM 1999.

53 Article 25 § 1 CIM 1999.

(a) carriage in open wagons;
(b) absence or inadequacy of packaging);
(c) loading of the goods by the consignor or unloading by the consignee;
(d) the nature of certain goods which particularly exposes them to total or partial loss or damage, especially through breakage, rust, interior and spontaneous decay, desiccation or wastage;
(e) irregular, incorrect or incomplete description or numbering of packages;
(f) carriage of live animals;
(g) carriage which, pursuant to applicable provisions or agreements made between the consignor and the carrier and entered on the consignment note, must be accompanied by an attendant, if the loss or damage results from a risk which the attendant was intended to avert.

These 'special risks' affect the onus of proof. Article 25 § 2 CIM 1999 prescribes that the carrier will still have to prove that the loss or damage could have been the result of one of these circumstances, but if he succeeds, the causal link between the exempted cause and the loss or damage is presumed.[54] This presumption is rebuttable, though; the cargo-interested parties are still allowed to prove that the loss or damage (partly) resulted from another cause than any of these listed circumstances.[55]

The limitation of liability

The carrier's exposure under the convention is limited, first of all by article 30 § 1 CIM 1999. In the case of a (partial) loss of the goods, the carrier is only liable for their value on the day and at the place where he received the goods for transportation.[56]

Article 30 § 2 CIM 1999 furthermore limits the carrier's liability to 17 SDR/Kg gross weight of the goods lost, but any 'carriage charge, customs duties already paid and other sums paid in relation to the carriage of the goods lost' must be paid by the carrier as well.[57]

Whereas article 30 CIM 1999 deals with the compensation of loss, article 32 CIM 1999 deals with the compensation of damage. The general approach remains the same, though. The limitation of article 30 CIM 1999 still applies, but then pro rata. Article 32 § 1 CIM 1999 prescribes that the 'amount shall be

54 This regulation of the division of the burden of proof is identical to the rule of article 17 (4) jo 18 (2) CMR.

55 Article 25 § 3 CIM 1999 furthermore stipulates that the presumption does not apply to carriage in open wagons in the case of an 'abnormally large loss'. See also article 18 (3) CMR.

56 Article 30 § 1 CIM 1999 prescribes a sequence to establish this value, i.e. first the 'commodity exchange quotation', and in the absence thereof the 'current market price', or in the absence thereof the 'usual value of goods'.

57 See also article 23 (4) CMR.

calculated by applying to the value of the goods defined in accordance with article 30 the percentage of loss in value noted at the place of destination'.[58]

Finally, article 33 § 1 CIM 1999 limits the carrier's liability for delay to four times the freight. This limitation only applies to loss or damage as a result of the delay, not to loss of or damage to the goods.[59] If a shipment of fresh flowers arrives three weeks later than agreed, the flowers will have lost their value over time. The carrier's liability is then not limited to four times the freight, but instead limited by the provisions of articles 30/32 CIM 1999.[60]

Breaking the limitation of liability

The limitation of liability under the CIM 1999 is not absolute. Article 36 CIM 1999 stipulates that the carrier cannot rely on any limitation of liability 'if it is proved that the loss or damage results from an act or omission, which the carrier has committed either with intent to cause such loss or damage, or recklessly and with knowledge that such loss or damage would probably result'.

This is in practice an uphill battle for the cargo-interested parties. First of all, the provision requires an act or omission of the carrier himself, and therefore not an act or omission of his personnel, servants, agents or subcarriers. In fact, since the carrier will often be a corporation, the provision requires an act or omission of its management.

Second, the carrier's mere recklessness is not enough to break through the limits of liability. Article 36 CIM 1999 requires the carrier's 'knowledge that such loss or damage would probably result' from his recklessness. The carrier's knowledge is subjective knowledge;[61] this particular carrier must have been aware of the risks, and the probability of this loss or damage as a result thereof.

5.2. The Hague–Visby Rules

The original Hague Rules were signed in the Netherlands in 1924.[62] They are still in force in a number of countries, including most notably the US.[63] The Hague

58 The reference to loss of value being 'noted at the place of destination' does not change the method of calculation. The value, and the diminished value as a result of the damage to the goods, must still be established at the time and place of their acceptance. M. Clarke & D. Yates, *Contracts of carriage by land and air* (Informa: London, 2008) 207–8.

59 Article 33 §§ 2, 3 and 4 CIM 1999.

60 The carrier's liability is then limited to difference between their value at the time and the place of receipt for transportation minus their value established at the place of destination (or 17 SDR/Kg if that is less, of course).

61 The CIM 1980 still required 'wilful misconduct' instead of 'knowledge that such loss or damage would probably result' under the CIM 1999. M. Clarke & D. Yates, *Contracts of carriage by land and air* (Informa: London, 2008) 264.

62 The Brussels Convention for the Unification of Certain Rules of Law relating to Bills of Lading of 25 August 1924.

63 The Hague Rules have been incorporated in the US COGSA 1936.

Rules were amended by the Visby Protocol in 1968,[64] and several sea-going countries including France, Italy, Japan, the UK (and its former dominions) and the Scandinavian countries are currently contracting states to the Hague-Visby Rules (HVR).

The material scope of application

The HVR do not govern each and every contract for the carriage of goods by sea. The rules only apply to 'contracts of carriage covered by a bill of lading or any similar document of title'. Article I (b) HVR defines the contract of carriage under a bill of lading, and in the process defines the material scope of application of the convention:[65]

> 'Contract of carriage' applies only to contracts of carriage covered by a bill of lading or any similar document of title, in so far as such document relates to the carriage of goods by sea, including any bill of lading or any similar document as aforesaid issued under or pursuant to a charter party from the moment at which such bill of lading or similar document of title regulates the relations between a carrier and a holder of the same.

The reference to 'a bill of lading or any similar document of title' implies that a bill of lading in the sense of article I (b) HVR functions as a document of title. This requirement is easily met in the case of an order or bearer bill of lading, the archetypical 'fully negotiable, i.e. repeatedly transferable, bill of lading'.[66] It is less obvious, though, whether the straight bill of lading qualifies as a bill of lading (or a similar document of title) in the sense of article I (b) HVR.[67]

The question surfaced in the *Rafaela S.*[68] MSC carried 4 (rather heavy) packages with machinery from Felixstowe to Boston under a straight bill of lading, and the machinery was damaged underway. The bill of lading limited the carrier's liability to only 100 Pounds Sterling per package, but this provision would be null and void in accordance with article III (8) HVR. Instead, the carrier's liability under the HVR would be limited to 2 SDR/Kg. The key question therefore was whether the straight bill of lading qualified as a bill of lading or similar

64 The Visby Protocol of 23 February 1968. They were in fact amended again on 21 December 1979 with the SDR Protocol.

65 Article I (b) HVR requires the bill of lading to regulate the contract; it does not require its actual issuance. The intention of the contracting parties to have a bill of lading govern their relation is sufficient to make it a contract of a carriage 'covered by a bill of lading'. See *Pyrene v. Scindia* (1954) 2 QB 402, and *The Happy Ranger* (2002) 2 Lloyd's Rep. 357.

66 In the words of Rix LJ in the *Rafaela S.* (2003) 2 Lloyd's Rep. 113.

67 The straight bill of lading identifies the (intended) consignee in advance, is transferable only once, and then only to this named consignee. These characteristics caused the Law Commission to label the straight bill of lading as a sea waybill under the COGSA 1992.

68 The *Rafaela S.* (2005) 1 Lloyd's Rep. 347.

document of title in the sense of article I (b) HVR, and the House of Lords unanimously held that it did:[69]

> There is simply no sensible commercial reason why the draftsmen would have wished to deny the CIF buyer named in a straight bill of lading the minimum standard of protection afforded to the CIF buyer named in an order bill of lading. The importance of this consideration is heightened by the fact that straight bills of lading fulfil a useful role in international trade provided that they are governed by the Hague-Visby Rules, since they are sometimes preferred to order bills of lading on the basis that there is a lesser risk of falsification of documentation. On a broader footing it is apparent that the interpretation advanced by the carrier depends on fine and technical distinctions and arguments. Traders, bankers and insurers would be inclined to take a more commercial view of straight bills of lading.

The straight bill of lading may (just) be a sea waybill under the COGSA 1992, but a straight bill of lading contract is governed by the HVR as any other bill of lading contract.[70] In fact, the key difference between a (straight) bill of lading and a sea waybill is that the latter is not a document of title.[71] Consequently, the HVR do not apply to contracts of carriage evidenced by a sea waybill.[72]

Charter parties

The HVR do not apply to charter parties either. The wording of article I (b) HVR already implies as much, but the second sentence of article V HVR very explicitly stipulates that the 'provisions of these Rules shall not be applicable to charter parties.'[73]

69 The *Rafaela S.* (2005) 1 Lloyd's Rep. 347, per Lord Steyn at 360.

70 Lord Steyn also said in the *Rafaela S.*: 'The suggested comparison is plainly unrealistic. In the hands of the named consignee the straight bill of lading is his document of title. On the other hand, a sea waybill is never a document of title. No trader, insurer or banker would assimilate the two. The differences between the documents include the fact that a straight bill of lading contains the standard terms of the carrier on the reverse side of the document but a sea waybill is blank and straight bills of lading are invariably issued in sets of three and waybills not. Except for the fact that a straight bill of lading is only transferable to a named consignee and not generally, a straight bill of lading shares all the principal characteristics of a bill of lading as already described.'

71 The English text of article I (b) HVR leaves little room for discussion. The French text of article I (b) HVR, however, refers to a 'document similaire formant titre pour le transport' which does not exactly mean the same thing. It translates as 'a similar document that forms the cause for the transport'.

72 See also *Voss v. APL* (2002) 2 Lloyd's Rep. 707: 'Further, since it is not a bill of lading the Hague Rules and the Hague-Visby Rules do not apply to it', and C. Debattista, *LMCLQ* (1989) 403: 'Received wisdom has it that sea waybills are not documents of title and that consequently the Carriage of Goods by Sea Act 1971 does not apply to them, the Act requiring a contract which "expressly or by implication provides for the issue of a bill of lading or any similar document of title".'

73 Article V HVR then continues 'but if bills of lading are issued in the case of a ship under a charter party they shall comply with the terms of these Rules.' This last requirement was added at the

In fact, the HVR do not immediately apply between the contracting parties when the carrier issues the bill of lading pursuant to a charter party. The mere issuance of a bill of lading does not change the relationship between the owner/carrier and the charterer/shipper.[74] The charter party still evidences the contract of carriage,[75] and the bill of lading is in that relationship just a receipt:[76]

> The bill of lading here was not separate or severable from the charter-party. It was issued in pursuance of it. The Italian sellers A.N.I.C. had already contracted to sell the fertilizer to the Government of India: and the Government had chartered the ship to carry it. The bill of lading was a mere instrument to carry out those contracts. It did not evidence any separate contract at all. As between charterers and shipowners, it was only a receipt for the goods.

This changes once the bill of lading finds its way to a third-party holder acting in good faith. The last part of article I (b) HVR ensures that the rules apply as soon as the bill of lading 'regulates the relations between a carrier and a holder of the same'.[77] The owner/carrier may in one single voyage therefore face two different liability regimes: the provisions of the charter party in his relation to the charterer and the mandatory provisions of the HVR (supplemented by the provisions of the bill of lading contract) in his relation to the bill of lading holder.[78]

request of delegate Paine, representing the bankers in the discussions on the Rules: 'From the Bankers' point of view the essential thing is that the document which passes from hand to hand as representing the title to goods should be of a uniform character. We are not concerned as Bankers with the terms of charter parties which are entered into between individuals who, so far as we are concerned, can make their own bargain. But we become at once concerned and considerably interested as soon as a bill of lading, which may be negotiated with us, or may pass from hand to hand, is issued. Therefore very strongly I say that, if and so far as bills of lading are issued under Charter parties, they must conform to the Hague Rules.'

74 Under English law, this rule does not apply to bills of lading issued pursuant to any other contract of carriage (not being a charter party); see Tuckey LJ in *The Happy Ranger* (2002) 2 Lloyd's Rep. 357: 'It does not seem to me that the rules are concerned with whether the bill of lading contains terms which have been previously agreed or not. It is the fact that it is issued or that it is contemplated which matters. If a bill of lading is or is to be issued the contract is "covered" by it or "provides for its issue" within the definition of art. 1(b) and s. 1(4) of the 1971 Act. The rules make special provisions for charter parties and bills issued under them.' The wording of article I (b) HVR suggests otherwise, though; see also Tomlinson J in *The Happy Ranger* (2001) 2 Lloyd's Rep. 530.

75 *Rodocanachi v. Milburn* (1886) 18 QBD 67.

76 *President of India v. Metcalfe Shipping* (1969) 2 Lloyd's Rep. 476 (Dunelmia).

77 *Leduc v. Ward* (1888) 20 Q.B.D. 475: 'Although the bill of lading is only a receipt as between the charterer and the shipowner, it is more than a receipt between the endorsee and the shipowner; it contains the contract between them.'

78 The charter-party therefore often incorporates the (provisions of the) HVR and the bill of lading often incorporates the provisions of the charter party, so that the two regimes are aligned as much as possible.

Live animals and deck cargo

The HVR apply to the carriage of all sorts of goods, but not to the carriage of live animals and deck cargo.[79] Goods in the sense of article I (c) HVR include 'goods, wares, merchandise, and articles of every kind whatsoever except live animals and cargo which by the contract of carriage is stated as being carried on deck and is so carried'. A bill of lading contract for the carriage of cattle is therefore not subject to the rules. The shipper and (especially) the carrier enjoy full freedom of contract.[80]

Article I (c) HVR requires the contract of carriage to state that the goods are carried on deck. This is a strict requirement. Pilcher J. held in *Svenska Traktor v. Maritime Agencies* that 'a mere general liberty to carry goods on deck is not in my view a statement in the contract of carriage that the goods are in fact being carried on deck. To hold otherwise would in my view do violence to the ordinary meaning of the words of Art. I (c) of the Act.'[81] A contractual liberty to carry the goods on deck is not enough.[82]

This still leaves the question whether article I (c) HVR specifically requires a statement in the bill of lading or whether a statement in any contractual arrangement between the shipper and the carrier will suffice. It is submitted that both the statement and the contract of carriage in the sense of article I (c) HVR are form free.[83] This means that the shipper and the carrier can validly state the carriage on deck in the bill of lading, but also in a separate contract, a booking note, an e-mail or even verbally. A prudent carrier, however, will be sure to state the carriage on deck on the bill of lading as it 'regulates the relations between a carrier and a holder of the same' upon its transfer to a third party acting in good faith.[84]

79 The rationale behind the provision is to protect the carrier against risks beyond his control. Live animals can die during the voyage, deck cargo is often difficult to lash and more exposed to the elements, and the carrier can then exclude his liability in the absence of mandatory rules. The drafters of the CMR have also recognized these increased risks, but their solution is different. The CMR applies to these risks, but the carrier is exempted from liability if the risks materialize.

80 The Dutch Supreme Court held in the *Atlantic Frigo* that a valid contractual exclusion of liability then covers the entire contract of carriage, and not just the time that the goods are actually exposed to the additional risks on deck. The contractual provision thus excluded the carrier's liability during the loading and discharging operations. HR 27 September 2009, NJ 2003,139 (*Atlantic Frigo*).

81 *Svenska Traktor v. Maritime Agencies* (1953) 2 Lloyd's Rep. 124.

82 See for such a liberty clause for instance article 18.1 of the MSC bill of lading: 'Goods, whether packed in Containers or not, may be carried on deck or under deck without notice to the Merchant unless it is specifically stipulated on the front hereof that the Containers or Goods will be carried under deck.'

83 Admittedly, article I (b) HVR requires a contract of carriage covered by a bill of lading, but this bill of lading does not necessarily need to contain all the contractual arrangements of the parties. The key (preliminary) question is whether the HVR apply (see also *The Happy Ranger* (2002) 2 Lloyd's Rep. 357).

84 S.D. Girvin, *Carriage of goods by sea* (OUP: Oxford, 2011) 269: 'If the carrier wishes to avoid the applicability of the Rules, it would be essential to state on the bill of lading that the goods are being carried on deck.'

The formal scope of application

Article X HVR gives the formal scope of application of the convention. This provision was added at the time of the Visby amendment to ensure that the convention takes direct effect[85]. Article X HVR ensures that the provisions of this Convention shall apply to every bill of lading relating to the carriage of goods between ports in two different States if:

(a) the bill of lading is issued in a Contracting State, or
(b) the carriage is from a port in a Contracting State, or
(c) the Contract contained in or evidenced by the bill of lading provides that the rules of this Convention or legislation of any State giving effect to them are to govern the contract, whatever may be the nationality of the ship, the carrier, the shipper, the consignee, or any other interested person.

The reference to 'ports of two different states' implies that the HVR do not apply to national contracts of carriage. Whether a certain voyage is national or international depends on the agreement of the parties, and not on the execution of the agreement.[86]

The first of the three options (a) is then rather straightforward; the HVR apply to every international contract of carriage under a bill of lading issued in a contracting state. Since the reference to 'Contracting' is omitted in the first sentence of the article, the HVR also govern contracts of carriage between two non-contracting states as long as the bill of lading is issued in a contracting state.

The HVR furthermore apply to any bill of lading contract whereby the ship departs from a contracting state. This second option (b) seems to be rather straightforward as well, but it may cause some difficulties when the goods are transhipped in the course of the voyage. These difficulties usually surface when the port of loading is in a contracting state to the HVR and the port of transhipment is in a contracting state to the Hague Rules (or vice versa, of course).[87]

In the *Anders Maersk* two heavy steam boilers were carried under a bill of lading from Baltimore (US) to Shanghai (China). The two boilers were transhipped in Hong Kong, and damaged during the passage from Hong Kong to Shanghai. The carrier relied on the US$500 per package limitation under the

85 The Hague Rules do not have direct effect and the party states need to ensure their entry into force in national legislation. The Protocol of Signature of the Hague Rules reads: 'The High Contracting Parties may give effect to this Convention either by giving it the force of law or by including in their national legislation in a form appropriate to that legislation the rules adopted under this Convention.' See also the discussion in Chapter 7, especially on *Vita Food v. Unus Shipping* (1939) AC 277.

86 R. Aikens, M. Bools & R. Lord, *Bills of lading* (LLP: London, 2006) 218.

87 The Hague Rules only give a modest package limitation; the HVR give a package (collo) and a kilo limitation of which the highest one applies. These cases therefore often relate to the carriage of heavy (single pieces of) machinery.

US COGSA 1936,[88] but the cargo-interested parties argued that Hong Kong was 'a port in a Contracting State' in the sense of article X (b) HVR,[89] and this would mean that they were entitled to 2 SDR per kilo instead. The Hong Kong High Court found for the carrier:[90]

> All the references to shipment in the rules are consistent with shipment being confined to the initial shipment referred to in the bill of lading. The result of this is that the plaintiffs cannot establish that the Hague Visby Rules are applicable to the shipment of these boilers. The COGSA provisions incorporated in the bill of lading are applicable to the contract with the consequence that the limitation I have referred to is operative.[91]

Article X (c) HVR then relates to the general Paramount clause, a provision in the bill of lading whereby the parties agree on the application of the HVR to their contract of carriage. The existence and effect of the Paramount clause are only flagged here for good measure; the Paramount clause is discussed in full in Chapter 7.

The temporal scope of application

Article 1 (e) HVR gives the temporal scope of application. The mandatory period of liability under the contract of carriage 'covers the period from the time when the goods are loaded on to the time they are discharged from the ship'. This means that the HVR do not cover the entire contract of carriage from receipt to delivery. Instead, the rules only apply to the tackle-to-tackle period. Any liability before loading and after discharge may therefore validly be excluded and article VII HVR almost encourages carriers to do so:[92]

> Nothing herein contained shall prevent a carrier or a shipper from entering into any agreement, stipulation, condition, reservation or exemption as to the responsibility and liability of the carrier or the ship for the loss or damage to, or in connection with, the custody and care and handling of goods prior to the loading on, and subsequent to the discharge from, the ship on which the goods are carried by sea.

88 The US were (and still are) not a contracting party to the HVR; they have incorporated the Hague Rules in the US COGSA 1936.

89 The Hong Kong Carriage of Goods by Sea Order 1508 of 1980 incorporated the Carriage of Goods by Sea Act of 1971, and this act then ensured the application of the HVR.

90 *The Anders Maersk* (1986) 1 Lloyd's Rep. 483.

91 The outcome may be different, though, if the circumstances are different. On the basis of the wording of the through bill of lading in the Rafaela S, Rix LJ held in the *Rafaela S.* (2003) 2 Lloyd's Rep. 113 that the on-carriage after transhipment was subject to a new contract of carriage 'which entitled the shipper to demand a bill of lading and … meant that the contract was "covered by a bill of lading" for the purposes of art. I of the Hague or Hague-Visby Rules'. The *Rafaela S.* (2003) 2 Lloyd's Rep. 113.

92 If the carrier's liability is not excluded, the period between receipt and loading and discharge and delivery is simply governed by the terms of the contract of carriage.

Since it is (so very explicitly) allowed, the contractual exclusion of liability before loading or after discharge is common practice. These so-called 'before and after clauses' are found in each and every bill of lading. They ensure that 'the Carrier shall have no liability whatsoever for any loss or damage to the Goods, howsoever caused, if such loss or damage arises before acceptance by the Carrier of custody of the Goods or after the Carrier tendering the cargo for delivery.'[93]

The exclusion of liability only relates to the period before the initial loading and the period after the final discharge. A before and after clause does not protect the carrier in the period after discharge and before (re)loading in the course of any transhipment of the goods during the voyage.[94] Bingham J. held in *Mayhew Foods v. Overseas Containers*:[95]

> It would, I think, be surprising if OCL could, by carrying the goods to Le Havre and there storing the goods before transhipment, rid themselves of liabilities to which they would have been subject had they, as contemplated, shipped the goods at Southampton and carried them direct to Jeddah, the more so since Mayhew had no knowledge of any voyage to Le Havre. My conclusion is that the rules, having applied on shipment at Shoreham, remained continuously in force until discharge at Jeddah.

FIOS clauses

Even though the provisions of the convention are mandatory pursuant to article III (8) HVR, it is to some extent still possible to mitigate the carrier's exposure within the tackle-to-tackle period. This possibility is not explicitly mentioned in any of the provisions of the HVR, but must be read between the lines of article II HVR:

> Subject to the provisions of Article VI, under every contract of carriage of goods by sea the carrier, in relation to the loading, handling, stowage, carriage, custody, care and discharge of such goods, shall be subject to the responsibilities and liabilities and entitled to the rights and immunities hereinafter set forth.

In the *Jordan II* the carrier and the shipper had agreed on a so-called 'FIOS' (free in and out stowed) clause.[96] This effectively meant that the shipper had to arrange for the loading and stowage of the goods on board of the ship. When the cargo was damaged during the voyage, the carrier refused to pay the claim as the damages has resulted from inadequate stowage, precisely the job that the shipper had agreed to take on.

93 Article 5.2 of the Maersk bill of lading.

94 Article III (8) HVR.

95 *Mayhew Foods v. Overseas Containers* (1984) 1 Lloyd's Rep. 317.

96 This clause can also be limited to just the loading and discharging operation (FIO) or extended with the trimming operations (FIOST).

The shipper argued that the arrangement violated article III (8) HVR, but the House of Lords denied his claim as 'the whole contract of carriage is subject to the rules, but the extent to which loading and discharging are brought within the carrier's obligations is left to the parties themselves to decide.'[97] Affirming the authority of *Pyrene v. Scindia* and *Renton v. Palmyra*,[98] the House of Lords acknowledged in the *Jordan II* that the obligations of the carrier were subject to the mandatory regime of the HVR, but at the same time accepted that the parties to the contract were at liberty to define the extent of these obligations in their contract.[99]

The seaworthiness of the ship

The HVR do not specifically stipulate that the goods received in apparent good order and condition must be delivered at their destination in that same (sound) condition.[100] Instead, the HVR require the carrier to provide a seaworthy ship, properly equipped and for carriage at the beginning of the voyage:[101]

> The carrier shall be bound before and at the beginning of the voyage to exercise due diligence to:
>
> (a) Make the ship seaworthy;
> (b) Properly man, equip and supply the ship;
> (c) Make the holds, refrigerating and cool chambers, and all other parts of the ship in which goods are carried, fit and safe for their reception, carriage and preservation.[102]

Article III (1) HVR imposes an overriding obligation on the carrier. The obligation to provide a seaworthy ship cannot be delegated to subcontractors,[103] and

97 The Jordan II (2005) 1 Lloyd's Rep. 57.
98 *Pyrene v. Scindia* (1954) 2 QB 402; *Renton v. Palmyra* (1957) AC 149.
99 The approach in *Renton* and *The Jordan II* is not universally accepted, though. Lord Steyn specifically referred to dissenting US and South African case law, namely *Associated Metals and Minerals Corporation v. M/V The Arktis Sky*, 978 F.2d 47 (2nd Cir. 1992), *Tubacex Inc. v. M/V Risan*, 45 F. 3rd 951 (5th Cir. 1995) and *The Sea Joy* (1998) (1) S.A. 487, saying at 65: 'Internationally there is no dominant view.' See also N.J. Margetson, *The system of liability of Articles III and IV of the Hague (Visby) Rules* (Paris: Zutphen, 2008) 79–80 and I.N. Djadjev, *Law and practice of the obligations of the carrier over the cargo* (Diss.: Groningen, 2016) 89.
100 The obligation is certainly there, but must be read between the lines, more in particular in the system of articles III (1), III (2), IV (1) and IV (2) HVR.
101 The ship does not have to be seaworthy in an absolute sense; it must be sufficiently fit to complete the voyage at hand, see e.g. *McFadden v. Blue Star Line* (1905) 1 K.B. 697 and N.J. Margetson, *The system of liability of Articles III and IV of the Hague (Visby) Rules* (Paris: Zutphen, 2008) 52.
102 Articles 14 and 17 (5) (a) RR extends this obligation to 'any containers supplied by the carrier in or upon which the goods are carried'. Already anticipating on the entry into force of the RR, the Dutch Supreme Court held in the *NDS Provider*, HR 1 February 2008, NJ 2008, 505 (ann. K.F. Haak), that the duty also relates to the carrier-provided containers.
103 *The Muncaster Castle* (1961) 1 Lloyd's Rep. 57.

takes precedence over the exemptions of liability listed in article IV (2) HVR.[104] In *Maxime Footwear v. Canadian Government Merchant Marine* the damage to the cargo was caused by a fire in combination with the ship's unseaworthiness. The carrier relied on the fire exception of article IV (2) (b) HVR, but the Privy Council held:[105]

> Art. III, Rule 1, is an overriding obligation. If it is not fulfilled and the non-fulfilment causes the damages, the immunities of Art. IV cannot be relied on. This is the natural construction apart from the opening words of Art. IV, Rule 2. The fact that that Rule is made subject to the provision of Rule IV and Rule 1 is not so conditioned makes the point clear beyond argument.

An overriding obligation is not an absolute warranty, though, and the doctrine only governs those cases where the combined working of an exception and the ship's unseaworthiness actually caused the damage.[106] If a fire for instance causes damage to the cargo (an exempted cause under article IV (2) HVR), but this damage would have been less if the ship had carried a sufficient number of fire extinguishers on board (unseaworthiness in the sense of article III (1) (b) HVR), the overriding obligation doctrine only applies to the extra damage. The carrier is in that case not liable for the damage that also would have occurred if the ship had in fact been equipped with an adequate number of extinguishers.[107]

Article III (1) HVR/Hague Rules is applied slightly differently in the US. Under the Vallescura rule, the carrier may still rely on a conventional exception of liability if he proves the extent of its contribution to the damage. If he cannot provide this evidence, the carrier 'remains liable for the whole amount of the damage because it is unable to show that sea peril was a cause of the loss, it must equally remain so if it cannot show which part of the loss is due to that cause'.[108]

Unseaworthiness in spite of due diligence

In view of the hard obligation to exercise due diligence for the seaworthiness of the ship under article III (1) HVR, the wording of article IV (1) HVR is then at

104 The overriding obligation has not been maintained in the RR. Article 17 (6) RR stipulates: 'The carrier is liable for damages as a result of the ship's unseaworthiness When the carrier is relieved of part of its liability pursuant to this article, the carrier is liable only for that part of the loss, damage or delay that is attributable to the event or circumstance for which it is liable pursuant to this article.'

105 *Maxine Footwear v. Canadian Government Merchant Marine* (1959) 2 Lloyd's Rep. 105, later followed in HR 11 June 1993, NJ 1995, 235 (ann. E. Japikse), S&S 1993/123 (*Quo Vadis*).

106 R. Aikens, M. Bools & R. Lord, *Bills of lading* (LLP: London, 2006) 250.

107 Hof's-Gravenhage 20 December 2007, S&S 2010/107 (Theano).

108 *The Vallescura* 293 U.S. 296, later confirmed on this point by Frankel DJ in *The Irish Spruce* (1976) 1 Lloyd's Rep. 63 at 75: 'The law under the Carriage of Goods by Sea Act is clear that if both an excepted peril … and unseaworthiness …concur in causing cargo damage, the shipowner is liable for the entire loss unless he can exonerate himself from part of the liability by showing that some portion is attributable solely to the excepted peril.'

first sight somewhat puzzling. Article IV (1) HVR also deals with the seaworthiness of the ship and stipulates:

> Neither the carrier nor the ship shall be liable for loss or damage arising or resulting from unseaworthiness unless caused by want of due diligence on the part of the carrier to make the ship seaworthy, and to secure that the ship is properly manned, equipped and supplied, and to make the holds, refrigerating and cool chambers and all other parts of the ship in which goods are carried fit and safe for their reception, carriage and preservation in accordance with the provisions of paragraph 1 of Article III. Whenever loss or damage has resulted from unseaworthiness the burden of proving the exercise of due diligence shall be on the carrier or other person claiming exemption under this article.

The drafting of article IV (1) HVR is perhaps unfortunate, but its meaning follows from the discussions between the delegates.[109] The carrier may rely on article IV (1) HVR if he had in fact exercised due diligence to make the ship seaworthy at the beginning of the voyage, but to no avail. In those circumstances, the carrier is not liable for any damage as a result of the unseaworthiness. The onus of proof rests with the carrier. Article IV (1) HVR explicitly stipulates that the carrier bears the burden to prove that he had exercised due diligence for the seaworthiness of the ship at the beginning of the voyage.

The care for the cargo

Although the carrier's obligation to care for the cargo encompasses the entire voyage (and not just the beginning of the voyage), the difference in strength between the (overriding) obligation to provide a seaworthy ship and the (regular) obligation to care for the cargo immediately follows from the first words of article III (2) HVR:

> Subject to the provisions of Article IV, the carrier shall properly and carefully load, handle, stow, carry, keep, care for, and discharge the goods carried.

Article III (2) HVR gives way to the exceptions listed in article IV (2) HVR. The duty of care for the cargo is 'subject to the provisions of article IV HVR'. The carrier can therefore still rely on the exemptions of liability of article IV (2) HVR, even though he may have breached his duty of care for the cargo.

Exemptions of liability

Article IV (2) HVR lists the exemptions of liability available to the carrier. The classic exemptions such as the acts of God and the King's enemies are still in the

109 F. Berlingieri (ed.), *The Travaux Préparatoires of the Hague Rules and the Hague-Visby Rules* (CMI: Antwerp, 1997) 369.

catalogue, but their number has grown over the years. The carrier is not liable for damage as a result of any:

(a) Act, neglect, or default of the master, mariner, pilot, or the servants of the carrier in the navigation or in the management of the ship;

The navigation of the ship relates to the nautical movements of the ship, i.e. the sailing between two designated ports, the positioning of the ship and the actual manoeuvring both at sea and in the ports.[110] The management of the ship is then obviously something different, covering the non-nautical actions in the exploitation of the ship, for instance the ventilation of the ship during the voyage.

It is not always easy to distinguish between the management of the ship and the care for the cargo,[111] but it can be relevant as the qualification may either lead to liability for the damage (article III (2) HVR) or may produce an exemption from liability (article IV (2) (a) HVR). The House of Lords held in the *Canadian Highlander* that 'if the principle is clearly borne in mind of distinguishing between want of care of cargo and want of care of vessel indirectly affecting the cargo . . . there ought not to be very great difficulty in arriving at a proper conclusion.'[112] The objective of the carrier is thus decisive for the qualification of the act.

(b) Fire, unless caused by the actual fault or privity of the carrier;

The meaning of fire in the sense of article IV (2) (b) HVR is not different from the day-to-day meaning of the word. The fire exception requires actual, open fire. There must have been flames to invoke the exception; liability for damage as a result of scorching, heating or smoke development is not exempted.[113]

The fire exception does not just cover mistakes or innocent errors in judgment. The exception also covers serious errors in judgment, wilful misconduct and even intent, provided that the fire is not caused 'by the actual fault or privity of the carrier'.[114] As the carrier will (almost) always be a legal entity, only the actions of its legal representatives qualify as acts of the carrier.

(c) Perils, dangers and accidents of the sea or other navigable waters;

The exception of article IV (2) (c) HVR does not cover each and every peril at sea, but only the perils of the sea.[115] This exception therefore only applies to those

110 N.J. Margetson, *The system of liability of Articles III and IV of the Hague (Visby) Rules* (Paris: Zutphen, 2008) 93.

111 The example of the ventilation may indeed be for the benefit of the ship, and more in particular the crew on board the ship, but it may also be required to regulate the condition of a shipment of potatoes, onions or other perishable goods.

112 *The Canadian Highlander* (1929) A.C. 223.

113 R. Aikens, M. Bools & R. Lord, *Bills of lading* (LLP: London, 2006) 272.

114 The French text of article IV (2) (b) HVR may help to clarify the term; it reads 'le fait ou la faute' (the act or the fault) of the carrier. F. Berlingieri (ed.), *The Travaux Préparatoires of the Hague Rules and the Hague-Visby Rules* (CMI: Antwerp, 1997) 400.

115 The *Xantho* (1887) 12 App Cas 503; *The Giulia*, 218 Fed. 744 (2 Cir. 1914).

incidents that relate to the specific dangers of carriage of goods by sea, such as sudden ground swells, freak waves and extreme storms.[116]

Unfortunately, there is less consensus on the question whether these perils should have been unforeseeable. In the Australian case of the *Bunga Seroja* the master had received a weather bulletin just prior to the departure warning for gales and 'very rough to high seas and heavy swell'. The master sailed nevertheless, and several containers were lost in the 11 Beaufort storm. The High Court held that the weather conditions qualified as perils of the sea, but also held that 'the weather encountered had been forecast before the vessel left port does not deny that conclusion.'[117]

In spite of the thorough discussion of the history and objective of the exception in the High Court judgment, it is submitted that the foreseeability of the perils of the sea is indeed a deal breaker. Foreseeable perils are avoidable perils, and the carrier should then not be exempted from liability for the loss or damage.[118]

Apart from these three exemptions, article IV (2) HVR then lists 14 other exemptions from liability, namely:[119]

- (d) Act of God;
- (e) Act of war;
- (f) Act of public enemies;
- (g) Arrest or restraint of princes, rulers or people, or seizure under legal process;
- (h) Quarantine restrictions;
- (i) Act or omission of the shipper or owner of the goods, his agent or representative;
- (j) Strikes or lockouts or stoppage or restraint of labour from whatever cause, whether partial or general;
- (k) Riots and civil commotions;
- (l) Saving or attempting to safe life or property at sea;
- (m) Wastage in bulk or weight or any other loss or damage arising from inherent defect, quality or vice of the goods;
- (n) Insufficiency of packing;

116 Arguably, these circumstances might also qualify as an 'Act of God', see *Nugent v. Smith* (1876) 1 CPD 423.

117 The *Bunga Seroja* (1999) 1 Lloyd's Rep. 512. The approach in the *Bunga Seroja* was followed by the Rotterdam Court in its (interim) decision in the *Happy Rover* of 30 March 2016, ECLI:NL:RBROT:2016:6226.

118 R. Aikens, M. Bools & R. Lord, *Bills of lading* (LLP: London, 2006) 275; HOLG Bremen VersR 1967, 576, BGH Versr 69, 536 (Isarstein) and HR 11 June 1993, NJ 1995, 235 (ann. Japikse), S&S 1993/123 (Quo Vadis). The Supreme Court held in the *Quo Vadis* that 'the court of appeal's apparent decision that Kroezen cannot rely on the perils of the sea, because it cannot be said that Kroezen on 24 December (beginning of the voyage) and for the stage Northern Spain – Antwerp did not have to be prepared for a sudden lateral ground sea, so that he must be considered to have been capable of avoiding the circumstance that the water entered the engine room through the open ventilation grill, does not show an error in judgment.'

119 These exceptions are all individually discussed by S.D. Girvin, *Carriage of goods by sea* (OUP: Oxford, 2011) 479–88 and R. Aikens, M. Bools & R. Lord, *Bills of lading* (LLP: London. 2006) 275–84.

(o) Insufficiency or inadequacy of marks;
(p) Latent defects not discoverable by due diligence;
(q) Any other cause arising without the actual fault or privity of the carrier, or without the actual fault or neglect of the agents or servants of the carrier, but the burden of proof shall be on the person claiming the benefit of this exception to show that neither the actual fault or privity of the carrier nor the fault or neglect of the agents or servants of the carrier contributed to the loss or damage.

The division of the burden of proof

The combination of the provisions of articles III (1), (2), IV (1) and (2) HVR adds up to a balanced division of the burden of proof in cargo claims under the convention.[120]

First of all, the cargo-interested parties (shipper, consignee, owner of the goods, insurers) will need to state and prove that the goods were damaged in the mandatory period of liability. A clean on-board bill of lading shows the apparent good order and condition of the goods at the beginning of this period of responsibility,[121] and article III (4) HVR prescribes that it gives prima facie evidence between the carrier and the shipper,[122] and conclusive evidence between the carrier and a third-party bill of lading holder.[123]

If the cargo-interested parties succeed herein, then the carrier can state and prove that the damage was in fact caused by one of the exceptions listed under article IV (2) HVR. When the damage was also caused by a breach in the duty of care for the cargo, the carrier will also have to state and prove to which extent the exception contributed to the damage.

If the carrier in turn succeeds herein, then the cargo-interested parties can state and prove that the damage was in fact caused by the unseaworthiness of the ship at the beginning of the voyage. Article III (1) HVR gives an overriding obligation: the carrier is fully liable for the damage, even if it was also caused by one or more of the exceptions of article IV (2) HVR.[124]

120 H. Boonk, *Zeevervoer onder cognossement* (Kluwer: Deventer, 1993) 228.

121 The condition of the goods at discharge is usually assessed by local surveyors.

122 Prima facie evidence can still be disproved, e.g. by a remark on the mate's receipt or witness statements.

123 Most bills of lading will in practice provide for a so-called 'said to contain' clause, though, especially when the goods are carried in a container. When the carrier is unable to verify the goods, their number and condition, the evidentiary function of a clean bill of lading loses value. See in this respect the last sentence of article III (3) HVR: 'Provided that no carrier, master or agent of the carrier shall be bound to state or show in the bill of lading any marks, number, quantity or weight which he has reasonable ground for suspecting not accurately to represent the goods actually received, or which he has had no reasonable means of checking.' In that case, the shipper cannot simply rely on the clean bill of lading, but he may need to prove the sound condition of the goods in another way, for instance with pictures, health certificates and/or survey reports.

124 *Maxine Footwear v. Canadian Government Merchant Marine* (1959) 2 Lloyd's Rep. 105; HR 11 June 1993, NJ 1995, 235 (ann. Japikse), S&S 1993, 123 (*Quo Vadis*). Again, however, see also *The Vallescura* 293 U.S. 296, The *Irish Spruce* (1976) 1 Lloyd's Rep. 63 and article 17 (6) RR.

The carrier can still escape liability, though, even in the case of unseaworthiness of the ship. The carrier is in accordance with article IV (1) HVR not liable for damage as a result of the unseaworthiness of the ship if he states and proves that he had in fact exercised due diligence in making the ship seaworthy at the beginning of the voyage.

The limitation of liability

If the carrier is liable for loss or damage under the rules, the 'total amount recoverable shall be calculated by reference to the value of such goods at the place and time at which the goods are discharged from the ship'.[125] The destination value of the goods is in practice really the maximum amount recoverable as article IV (5) (a) HVR stipulates:[126]

> Unless the nature and value of such goods have been declared by the shipper before shipment and inserted in the bill of lading, neither the carrier nor the ship shall in any event be or become liable for any loss or damage to or in connection with the goods in an amount exceeding the equivalent of 666.67 units of account per package or unit or 2 units of account per kilo of gross weight of the goods lost or damaged, whichever is the higher.[127]

The explicit reference to 'loss or damage to or in connection with goods' suggests a wider scope than just the loss of the goods or damage to the goods themselves.[128] In fact, it would seem to include consequential losses in connection with the goods. Other consequential losses, such as economic losses caused by delay, are then arguably not regulated by the HVR.[129] The carrier's liability for these losses is subsequently often excluded in the bill of lading.[130]

125 Article IV (5) (b) HVR.

126 The declaration of the value hardly happens in practice, in part because it might give potential thieves an idea, but mostly because the carrier will then increase the freight.

127 A collo is a unit, a box or a coil, and not a container in which units are carried (article IV (5) (c) HVR), but see *El Greco* (2004) 2 Lloyd's Rep. 537.

128 Lord Morton identified four different categories in *Renton v. Palmyra* (1957) AC 149, i.e. '(a) loss of goods; (b) damage to goods; (c) loss in connection with goods; (d) damage in connection with goods'. Burton J. held in *The Limnos* that 'the goods by reference to which losses have been suffered consequential to the damage to the originally (physically) damaged goods fall into a different category from the goods originally damaged.' *The Limnos* (2008) 2 Lloyd's Rep. 166.

129 The Dutch courts have taken the view that the HVR 'do not regulate consequential and indirect losses'; see for instance Hof's-Gravenhage 22 March 2005, S&S 2005 113. Liability for such losses can therefore validly be excluded in the bill of lading. Conversely, M. Ganado & H.M. Kindred, *Marine cargo delays* (LLP: London, 1990) have argued at 23 that such a liability is (on balance) subject to the rules. See in this respect also S. Geense, *Vergoedbare schadevormen in het Engelse vervoerrecht en het leerstuk van 'remoteness of damage'* (TVR, 2010) 10. Geense's dissertation (Erasmus, Rotterdam) on the compensation of consequential loss in transport law is expected in the course of 2018.

130 Article 8 of the MSC bill of lading for instance stipulates: 'In no event shall the Carrier be liable for consequential damages or for any delay in scheduled departures or arrivals of any Vessel or

The carrier cannot rely on the limitation of liability if the damage resulted from an act or omission of the carrier, either with the intent to cause damage or recklessly with the knowledge that damage would probably result. The act or omission referred to is an act or omission of the carrier himself, and thus not of his agents, servants, subcontractors or even the master. The knowledge referred to is the subjective awareness of the carrier.[131] Since the carrier will often be a corporation, article IV (e) HVR requires its management's actual knowledge of the probability.[132]

5.3. The Montreal Convention

The Convention for the Unification of Certain Rules Relating to International Carriage by Air is actually not much younger than the Hague Rules. The Warsaw Convention was signed in 1929 and entered into force in 1933.[133] The convention was amended several times over the years;[134] so many times in fact that the patchwork Warsaw system was ultimately replaced in 1999 by an entirely new convention, the Montreal Convention (MC).

The material scope of application

Article 1 MC provides the material scope of application.[135] The convention governs the international carriage by air of goods (and passengers),[136] whether gratuitous or not:[137]

> This Convention applies to all international carriage of persons, baggage or cargo performed by aircraft for reward. It applies equally to gratuitous carriage by aircraft performed by an air transport undertaking.

other conveyances used to transport the Goods by sea or otherwise. If the Carrier should nevertheless be held legally liable for any such direct or indirect or consequential loss or damage caused by such alleged delay, such liability shall in no event exceed the Freight paid for the carriage.'

131 R. Aikens, M. Bools & R. Lord, *Bills of lading* (LLP: London, 2006) 299.

132 Article IV (5) (e) HVR – other than article 29 CMR – has not really provoked a lot of litigation. The goods carried by sea are not often worth more than the limitation of liability. Besides, the required 'intent to cause these damages or recklessness with the knowledge that the damage would probably result' makes it very difficult to break through the limitation.

133 The convention only required five ratifications for its entry into force; see article 37 (2) Warsaw Convention.

134 The Warsaw Convention was amended with the Hague Protocol of 1955, the Guadalajara Convention of 1961, the Guatemala City protocol of 1971 and four Montreal Protocols of 1975.

135 Other than article 1 CMR, article 1 MC does not explicitly require a 'contract for the carriage of goods by air'. See in that respect article 38 (1) MC: 'In the case of combined carriage performed partly by air and partly by any other mode of carriage, the provisions of this Convention shall, subject to paragraph 4 of Article 18, apply only to the carriage by air, provided that the carriage by air falls within the terms of Article 1.'

136 The MC is an anomaly in that respect; all the other conventions only regulate the carriage of goods.

137 The reference to 'whether gratuitous or not' appears to have little added value, but article 1 CMR for instance explicitly requires 'the carriage of goods … for reward'.

The convention does not define an aircraft. Instead, the definition is left to domestic law. Fortunately, there is a certain worldwide consensus as to its meaning.[138] An aircraft in the sense of the convention covers more than just airplanes. An aircraft obviously includes commercial freighters and passenger planes, but other devices capable of travelling through the air as well, such as helicopters, gliders and drones.[139]

The formal scope of application

Article 2 MC gives the formal scope of application of the convention. The convention deals with 'international carriage' only, and this means:

> any carriage in which, according to the agreement between the parties, the place of departure and the place of destination, whether or not there be a break in the carriage or a transhipment, are situated either within the territories of two States Parties, or within the territory of a single State Party if there is an agreed stopping place within the territory of another State, even if that State is not a State Party. Carriage between two points within the territory of a single State Party without an agreed stopping place within the territory of another State is not international carriage for the purposes of this Convention.

International carriage in the sense of the convention thus includes one-way carriage between two different contracting states, but it also covers international return flights departing from any one contracting state, irrespective of whether the return flight is made from a contracting state or from any other state.

The temporal scope of application

The temporal, and to some extent geographical, scope of application follows from article 18 MC. It is not an easy provision (at all). In fact, the MC needs three at first sight rather confusing paragraphs to describe the scope of the convention. Article 18 (1) MC initially provides for a limited scope of application, i.e. the convention applies during the carriage by air:

> The carrier is liable for damage sustained in the event of the destruction or loss of or damage to, cargo upon condition only that the event which caused the damage so sustained took place during the carriage by air.

Article 18 (3) MC then stretches 'carriage by air' beyond its normal meaning, and in the process aligns the temporal scope of application of the convention with the

138 See also Annex 6/7 of the Chicago Convention 1944.

139 Article 8:3a DCC defines aircraft as 'devices that can be maintained in the atmosphere as a result of the forces that the air exercises'. It is not a very strong definition, but it excludes hovercraft, for instance.

contract of carriage (running from the receipt of the goods for transportation to their delivery at the destination):

> The carriage by air within the meaning of paragraph 1 of this Article comprises the period during which the cargo is in the charge of the carrier.

Apparently, however, this extension again goes too far as the first sentence of article 18 (4) MC then confines the temporal/geographical scope of application to the airport-to-airport period:[140]

> The period of the carriage by air does not extend to any carriage by land, by sea or by inland waterway performed outside an airport.[141]

The upshot is that the convention always applies when the goods are in the air. In fact, the entire contract of carriage is governed by the MC if the goods are received for carriage at the departure airport and delivered to the consignee at the destination airport. The period before the receipt of the goods for carriage and after their delivery, however, is never governed by the MC as the goods are at that time simply not 'in the charge of the carrier'.

The system of liability

Once the convention governs the contract of carriage by air, article 18 (1) MC ensures that the carrier is liable for any loss of or damage to the goods unless he can rely on (one of) the exemptions of article 18 (2) MC. The carrier escapes liability if he can prove that the damage is the result of:

> (a) inherent defect, quality or vice of that cargo;
> (b) defective packing of that cargo performed by a person other than the carrier or its servants or agents;
> (c) an act of war or an armed conflict;
> (d) an act of public authority carried out in connection with the entry, exit or transit of the cargo.

140 The airport-to-airport period means 'the period of transport from the fence of the airport of departure to the fence of the airport of destination'. See in this respect G. Leloudas, *Door-to-door application of international air law conventions: commercially convenient, but doctrinally dubious* (LMCLQ, 2015) 368, but see also *Royce Plc v. Heavylift-Volga DNEPR* (2000) 1 Lloyd's Rep 653 and *Victoria Sales* (1990) 917 F.2d 705 (2nd Cir) for a wider interpretation.

141 The second and third sentence of article 18 (4) MC then again provide exceptions to the first sentence of article 18 (4) MC. The convention still governs loading, delivery and transhipment services in the course of the contract of carriage beyond the airport-to-airport period, namely in those cases whereby the cause of the damages has remained unknown. Furthermore, the convention also governs those cases whereby the carrier has one-sidedly chosen to use a different means of transportation (in violation of the contract of carriage). Given the obvious multimodal aspects of these exceptions, article 18 (4) MC is discussed in detail in Chapter 6.

The system of liability of the MC is pretty straightforward. There are only four exceptions to the main rule of article 18 (1) MC, and the onus of proof that one of more of these situations occurred and actually caused the loss or damage rests with the carrier.[142]

The (unbreakable) limitation of liability

The limits of liability follow from article 22 MC. Article 22 (3) MC ensures that only the destination value of the goods can be recovered.[143] Since the convention 'is intended to be uniform and to be exclusive' where the carrier's liability is at stake,[144] consequential and other losses under the MC should therefore remain for the account of the cargo-interested parties.[145]

The destination value is furthermore subject to a limitation of liability of 19 SDR per kilo.[146] The MC thus at first sight appears to give a very generous limitation of liability, but there is a catch. Whereas all the other conventional limitations of liability can (at least in theory) be broken, the MC limitation of liability for loss of or damage to the goods is unbreakable.

Article 22 (3) MC does not say in so many words that the limitation of liability for damages to the goods cannot be set aside, but it follows a contrario from the wording of article 22 (5) MC. Article 22 (5) MC at first sight resembles article IV (5) (e) HVR, but it specifically stipulates that the 'provisions of paragraphs 1 and 2 shall not apply if it is proved that the damage resulted from an act or omission of the carrier, its servants or agents, done with intent to cause damage or recklessly and with knowledge that the damage would probably result.'

Since article 22 (1) MC only relates to passenger delays, and article 22 (2) MC only relates to the baggage of passengers, the exception to the rule does not cover cargo damage. The carrier will therefore never be liable beyond 19 SDR per kilo, irrespective of the cause of the damage and the degree of his recklessness. Although this may arguably give the wrong (moral) signal, the straightforward unbreakable limitation of liability has in practice proved to be very attractive. As there is really not much left to disagree on anymore, litigation on the loss of or damage to the cargo has almost come to a halt under the MC.[147]

142 The MC does not regulate any 'special risks', but only lists regular exemptions from liability.

143 Article 22 (2) MC is not really very explicit with regard to the destination value. In fact, the provision only stipulates that the declared sum should not exceed the value of the goods at their destination, but it makes sense that the limitation of liability should not exceed the destination value either. Article 22 (6) MC does explicitly allow the court to render a cost order and award interest in accordance with the law fori.

144 *Sidhu v. British Airways* (1997) 2 Lloyd's Rep. 76, per Lord Hope of Craighead.

145 See, however, M. Clarke, *Contracts of carriage by air* (Lloyd's List: London, 2010), at 109: 'The measure of damage is also left to national law.'

146 Article 22 (3) MC mentions 17 SDR per kilo, but the limit has meanwhile been raised to 19 SDR per kilo.

147 The unbreakable limitation is particularly attractive from a macro-economic perspective. The cargo-interested parties will often have insured the goods in transit, and the air carrier's liability will often have been insured as well. The costs of litigation can be saved on both sides if the loss is simply borne where it falls.

5.4. The CMR

The Convention relative au contrat de transport international des Marchandises par Route (CMR) was signed in Geneva in 1956. Unlike the HVR and the MC, the CMR is not really a global convention, but its reach does extend far beyond the boundaries of Europe. A number of Eurasian, Middle Eastern and North African countries, including Kazakhstan, Iran and Tunisia, are also party to the convention. The CMR has never been revised since its entry into force. In fact, it is safe to say that the convention could use a thorough makeover by now.[148]

The material scope of the convention

The material scope of application of the convention is very straightforward. The convention applies 'to every contract for the carriage of goods by road in vehicles for reward', and article 1 (4) CMR lists only three exceptions, i.e. carriage governed by postal conventions, funeral consignments and furniture removal.

The specific reference to 'every contract' in article 1 CMR already implies that the convention does not require the issue of a consignment note,[149] and therefore also applies to verbal contracts, implied contracts and even umbrella contracts pursuant to which individual contracts of carriage (evidenced by a consignment note) are made.[150] Morritt LJ clearly supported a wide interpretation of a contract of carriage by road in *Gefco v. Mason*:[151]

> First, ... I do not accept that the contracts to which the Convention applies are necessarily limited to those relating to specific and ascertained goods. Second, art. 4 makes it plain that the absence of a note, for whatever reason, does not affect the validity of the contract or the application of the Convention. ... Third, ... the consignment note is, primarily, needed to enable a consignee to exercise the right to stop the goods in transit (art. 12) and to impose liability on a successive carrier (arts. 34 and 35). ... Fourthly I do not think that the implication contended for would be consistent with the overall intention of the authors of the Convention to provide for harmonization across national boundaries.

Gratuitous carriage is not covered by the convention. A contract of carriage by road in the sense of article 1 CMR needs to be 'for reward'. This reward will in

148 In particular articles 2 (piggyback transport), 23 (limitation of liability), 29 (wilful misconduct) in combination with 31 (competence) and 34 and further (successive carriage).

149 In fact, article 4 CMR explicitly stipulates that its absence 'shall not affect the existence or the validity of the contract of carriage which shall remain subject, to the provisions of this Convention'.

150 These umbrella contracts will in practice often stipulate a certain freedom for the carrier to choose the means of transportation. When the carrier then performs the (until that time still) optional contract of carriage by road, then the CMR applies; see *Datec v. UPS* (2007) 2 Lloyd's Rep. 114, and *DHL v. Landis*. This is different under Belgian law, see Hof van Cassatie 8 November 2004, *TNT v. Mitsui* (2006) ETL 228.

151 *Gefco v. Mason* (1998) 2 Lloyd's Rep. 585.

practice of course usually just be the freight, but the general reference to a reward suggests that any counter performance will do.

Article 2 CMR then extends the material scope of application to mode-on-mode transport, common practice when goods are for instance carried by truck from mainland Europe to the UK (or vice versa). The carrier can of course decide to offload the goods in France, Belgium or the Netherlands, and then bring them on board of a ship for the passage of the Channel. The carrier can also decide, however, to simply drive the truck with the goods onto a ro/ro vessel in Calais, Oostende or Hook of Holland, and drive off again in Dover. In the latter case, article 2 CMR ensures that the entire contract of carriage remains covered by the convention even though part of it has in fact been performed by another means of transportation.[152]

The formal scope of the convention

The formal scope of application of the convention is also defined in article 1 CMR. The application of the convention is triggered:

> when the place of taking over of the goods and the place designated for delivery, as specified in the contract, are situated in two different countries, of which at least one is a Contracting country, irrespective of the place of residence and the nationality of the parties.

As only one of the countries involved needs to be a contracting country, the CMR has a considerable reach.[153] Effectively, more or less every international contract for the carriage of goods by road in and around Europe will be governed by the convention.

The temporal scope of application

Article 17 (1) CMR gives the temporal scope of application. The convention applies during the entire period of time between the receipt of the goods by the carrier and their delivery to the consignee.[154] Article 17 (1) CMR stipulates:

> The carrier shall be liable for the total or partial loss of the goods and for damage thereto occurring between the time when he takes over the goods and the time of delivery, as well as for any delay in delivery.

152 Such a contract is a multimodal contract of carriage, and not a unimodal contract of carriage. The working of article 2 CMR is therefore discussed in more detail in Chapter 6.

153 See in comparison article 2 MC.

154 The difference in this respect with the HVR or MC can easily be explained as a truck does not necessarily have to depart from a certain designated area, such as a port or an airport. The rule is open to exceptions, though. When the parties to the contract agree that the sender will arrange for the loading and securing of the goods in the truck, the carrier will not be liable if the damages result from an inadequate loading or securing (see also article 17 (2) CMR).

The convention only regulates the liability of the carrier for the loss of or damage to the goods in his care, and it does not cover other loss or damage. When the carrier for instance delivers the wrong goods, albeit in a sound condition, his liability is governed by domestic law.[155] When the carrier delivers contaminated goods into a land tank with uncontaminated goods,[156] his liability for the damage to the goods in the land tank is again governed by domestic law.[157] In fact, the Dutch Supreme Court held very recently that the CMR does not apply to a claim against the carrier for fines, storage costs, demurrage and clearance costs:[158]

> The CMR does not provide for an exhaustive regulation of the carrier's liability. Article 17 only regulates the carrier's liability for the loss of or damage to goods that were carried by him, as well as for any delay in delivery. For other damages than these, the carrier may be liable under the applicable domestic law.

It is submitted that this is the wrong approach.[159] Article 17 (1) CMR actually contains two different rules, one to define the temporal scope of application and another to define the liability of the carrier. These two rules should not only be applied separately, but also in a certain (logical) sequence.[160] The court should first of all establish whether the convention applies, i.e. whether it is a contract of carriage by road between two different countries of which at least one is a contracting state, and if that is the case the convention applies between receipt and delivery. The second question, i.e. whether the carrier is liable under the provisions of the convention, only surfaces once the application of the convention has been established.[161]

155 BGH 27 October 1978, I ZR 30/77, VersR 1979, 276; *Shell Chemicals v. P&O Roadtanks* (1993) 1 Lloyd's Rep. 114.

156 See also J.H.J. Teunissen in *Verbindend Recht, Liber Amicorum K.F. Haak* (Kluwer: Deventer, 2012) 504.

157 HR 15 April 1994, NJ 1995, 114 (*Cargofoor*); Hof van Cassatie 16 January 2009, Rechtskundig Weekblad 2009–10, 738 (with annotation by F. Stevens). In this latter case, the Belgian Supreme Court held that the CMR did not regulate the carrier's liability for other damages, and 'more in particular not for the damage incurred to other goods than those carried, which is governed by the applicable domestic law'.

158 HR 18 December 2015, NJ 2016, 341 (ann. K.F. Haak), S&S 2016/37. Since the CMR did not apply, and Dutch domestic law did not provide for any limitation of liability, the claim was awarded in full.

German domestic law actually limits the carrier's liability in this situation. § 433 GCC stipulates: 'If the carrier is liable for the breach of a contractual duty connected with the performance of the carriage of the goods, his liability for damage which has not resulted from loss of or damage to the goods or from non-compliance with the delivery period and which is not damage to goods or persons, is limited also, namely to three times the amount payable in the event of loss of the goods.'

159 M. Spanjaart, *Transfennica v. Schenker, the system of articles 17 and 23 CMR* TranspR (2016) 383.

160 This sequence was followed in *Gefco v. Mason* (1998) 2 Lloyd's Rep. 585.

161 The observance of this sequence is likely to affect the outcome of the proceedings. Whereas the carrier may be liable for consequential loss, missed profits and other damage than damage to the goods under domestic law, he will escape liability under the convention as article 23 (4) CMR explicitly prescribes that 'no further damage shall be payable.'

The system of liability

The mandatory period of liability under the convention corresponds with the duration of the contract of carriage. The carrier is liable for any loss of or damage to the goods while they are in his care, unless he can rely on one of the listed exemptions of liability.

The convention provides for two different kinds of exemptions from liability: regular exemptions (listed in article 17 (2) CMR) and special exemptions relating to inherent risks (listed in article 18 (2) CMR). Article 17 (2) CMR resembles article 18 (2) sub (a) and (b) MC, but in addition mentions a (wrongful) fault of the cargo-interested parties and general force majeure:[162]

> The carrier shall however be relieved of liability if the loss, damage or delay was caused by the wrongful act or neglect of the claimant, by the instructions of the claimant given otherwise than as the result of a wrongful act or neglect on the part of the carrier, by inherent vice of the goods or through circumstances which the carrier could not avoid and the consequences of which he was unable to prevent.

The exemptions of article 17 (2) CMR are regular exemptions. Article 18 (1) CMR stipulates that the carrier will not only have to prove their existence, but he will also have to prove that they caused the loss or damage.[163]

Article 18 (2) CMR is less demanding with regard to the circumstances listed in article 17 (4) CMR. The carrier is relieved from liability if the damages could be attributed to certain special risks inherent to the:

(a) use of open unsheeted vehicles, when their use has been expressly agreed and specified in the consignment note;
(b) the lack of, or defective condition of packing in the case of goods which, by their nature, are liable to wastage or to be damaged when not packed or when not properly packed;
(c) handling, loading, stowage or unloading of the goods by the sender, the consignee or person acting on behalf of the sender or the consignee;
(d) the nature of certain kinds of goods which particularly exposes them to total or partial loss or to damage, especially through breakage, rust, decay, desiccation, leakage, normal wastage, or the action of moth or vermin;
(e) insufficiency or inadequacy of marks or numbers on the packages;
(f) the carriage of livestock.

162 This is in practice quite difficult; see HR 24 April 2009, S&S 2009/96 (*Amev v. Oegema*). The carrier had been forced to part with the goods by armed men, but he could still not rely on force majeure as these were not 'circumstances which the carrier could not avoid and the consequences of which he was unable to prevent'.

163 See article 18 (1) CMR: 'The burden of proving that loss, damage or delay was due to one of the causes specified in article 17 (2) shall rest upon the carrier.'

The key difference with article 17 (2) CMR is the division of the onus of proof. Since article 17 (4) CMR refers to special risks inherent to specific circumstances, the carrier will still need to prove the occurrence of such circumstances (as he would in case of article 17 (2) CMR), but he will only have to prove that these circumstances could have caused the damages. If he succeeds, the first sentence of article 18 (2) CMR then shifts the onus of proof to the cargo-interested parties:

> When the carrier establishes that in the circumstances of the case, the loss or damage could be attributed to one or more of the special risks referred to in art. 17, par. 4, it shall be presumed that it was so caused. The claimant shall however be entitled to prove that the loss or damage was not, in fact, attributable either wholly or partly to one of these risks.

The working of articles 17 (4) and 18 (2) CMR can perhaps best be explained with an example, one whereby the sender and the carrier agree (specified in the consignment note) on the carriage of a shipment of tyres in an open unsheeted vehicle. When the carrier delivers the shipment with a shortage, it is not unlikely that he simply lost a few of the tyres on the way. This is a risk inherent to the carriage of goods in an open unsheeted truck, and the carrier may rely on the protection of article 17 (4) (a) CMR in accordance with the first sentence of article 18 (2) CMR.[164]

Still, as follows from the second sentence of article 18 (2) CMR, the carrier is not off the hook yet. The cargo-interested parties may be able to disprove the inferred cause of the damages, for instance because the missing tyres were in fact stolen from the truck while the driver was having a coffee. Besides, article 18 (3) CMR dismantles the presumption of the first sentence of article 18 (2) CMR in the case of an 'abnormal shortage', i.e. when not just a few tyres but in fact half of the shipment of tyres was missing at the time of delivery.[165]

The limitation of liability

Article 23 CMR limits the carrier's exposure if he is indeed liable for the damage. Article 23 (1) CMR for instance provides that the 'compensation shall be calculated by reference to the value of the goods at the place and time at which they were accepted for carriage'.[166] This compensation is furthermore subject to a

164 Provided that the carrier has taken all the normal precautions and has complied with any special instructions; see article 18 (5) CMR.

165 Article 18 (3) CMR reads: 'This presumption shall not apply in the circumstances set out in article 17 (4) (*a*), if there has been an abnormal shortage, or a loss of any package.'

166 This value is the commodity exchange price or, if there is no such price, according to the current market price or, if there is no commodity exchange price or current market price. See article 23 (2) CMR.

limitation of liability of SDR 8.33 per kilo gross weight. On top of this amount, 'the carriage charges, customs duties and other charges incurred in respect of the carriage of the goods' will also be compensated,[167] but article 23 (4) CMR explicitly stipulates that 'no further damage shall be payable.'

These benefits are subject to article 29 CMR. The carrier cannot rely on the provisions of article 23 CMR when the damage was caused by his own wilful misconduct, the wilful misconduct of his servants, agents or subcontractors,[168] or by a default on his or their part that 'in accordance with the law of the court or tribunal seized of the case, is considered as equivalent to wilful misconduct'.

Unfortunately, article 29 CMR does not define such a default. Instead, the drafters have deliberately left the qualification hereof to the court seized. This has triggered an endless stream of litigation on the question of whether ignorance, sloppiness, stupidity, recklessness or recklessness with the knowledge that the damage would probably result thereof constitutes the equivalent of wilful misconduct.[169]

The number of different competent courts under article 31 CMR has increased the problem as the system encourages forum shopping. When the cargo-interested parties can choose between several different jurisdictions, surely they will select the most cargo-friendly jurisdiction. On the other hand, the carriers will obviously do the same. A prudent carrier will therefore not sit back

167 The convention does not define these charges and duties, and their qualification has produced different results in different countries, particularly with regard to excise duties. The courts in most contracting states will refuse to award excise duties on the basis of the last part of article 23 (4) CMR, i.e. that 'no further damage shall be payable.' All the same, the House of Lords held in *James Buchanan v. Babco* (1978) 1 Lloyd's Rep. 119 that excise duties qualify as 'carriage charges, customs duties and other charges incurred in respect of the carriage of the goods'.

168 Whereas the CIM 1999 and the HVR require an act or omission of the carrier (himself), article 29 (2) CMR ensures that the rule also applies to the acts or omissions of 'agents or servants of the carrier or by any other persons of whose services he makes use for the performance of the carriage, when such agents, servants or other persons are acting within the scope of their employment'.

169 The qualification of the equivalent of wilful misconduct varies in the various CMR countries. France, Spain, Italy and in practice also Germany adopt a more objective approach, i.e. really reckless behaviour (often cases whereby the driver parks his truck at an unguarded parking overnight) qualifies as the domestic equivalent, whereas the English and Dutch courts will require subjective knowledge of both the risks and the chances that the risks in fact materialize; see *Texas Instruments Ltd. v. Nason (Europe) Ltd.* (1991) 1 Lloyd's Rep. 146 and HR 5 January 2001, NJ 2001, 391/392; S&S 2001/ 61–2. Since it is so difficult to prove wilful misconduct in the UK and the Netherlands, judges will sometimes help the claimants out. In *Datec v. UPS* (2007) 2 Lloyd's Rep. 114 Lord Mance (with Richards LJ in appeal) accepted 'that theft involving a UPS employee was shown on a strong balance of probability to have been the cause of this loss'. The Dutch Supreme Court has accepted that the carrier cannot simply deny all responsibility (and let the claimants sort it out), but has to support his denial with the documents and information available on his side to be able to rely on the limitation; see HR 29 May 2009, NJ 2009, 245, S&S 2009, 97.

when he expects a claim for unlimited liability. Instead, he will anticipate. He will initiate proceedings in the most carrier-friendly jurisdiction to have the court declare before law that he is not or alternatively only limitedly liable.[170]

5.5. The CMNI

The Convention relative au contrat de transport des Marchandises en Navigation Interieure (CMNI) is the youngest of the (existing) conventions discussed in this book. The convention covers the carriage of goods by inland waterways. It was signed in Budapest in 2001.

The scope of application

Article 2 (2) CMNI provides the material scope of application. Whereas the name of the convention only refers to the carriage by 'Inland Waterway', the scope of the convention actually goes beyond inland waterways. The CMNI applies 'if the purpose of the contract of carriage is the carriage of goods,[171] without transhipment, both on inland waterways and in waters to which maritime regulations apply'.[172]

All the same, the application of the convention in maritime waters is restricted. Article 2 (2) CMNI ensures that the convention does not apply when (a) a 'maritime' bill of lading has been issued,[173] or (b) when the distance travelled in maritime waters exceeds the distance travelled on inland waterways.[174]

The explicit reference in article 2 (2) CMNI to 'without transhipment' requires the contract of carriage to be performed with one single vessel in one single voyage. In fact, it implies that the convention does not govern multimodal contracts of carriage (that include a leg by inland waterways).[175]

The formal scope of application follows from article 2 (1) CMNI. The convention applies to 'any contract of carriage according to which the port of loading

170 Mutatis mutandis the same applies for excise claims; see the wide interpretation of carriage charges, customs duties and other charges in the sense of article 23 (4) CMR in *James Buchanan v. Babco* (1978) 1 Lloyd's Rep. 119 and the strict interpretation in for instance HR 14 July 2006, NJ 2006, 599 (ann. K.F. Haak), S&S 2007/30 (*Philip Morris v. Van der Graaf*).

171 Article 1 (7) CMNI, however, excludes towed or pushed vessels from the scope of application.

172 This is particularly relevant if the goods need to be received from or delivered to a sea-going vessel. A contract of carriage by barge from Basel (Switzerland) to Rotterdam (the Netherlands) is then entirely governed by the CMNI, even though maritime regulations apply within the Rotterdam port area.

173 Obviously to avoid a possible collision with the HVR.

174 The flag of the vessel or its registration as either an inland or a sea-going vessel is irrelevant for the application of the convention; article 2 (3) CMNI.

175 K. Ramming, *Hamburger Handbuch zum Binnenschifffahrtsfrachtrecht* (C.H. Beck: München, 2009) 98; P.M. Bugden/S. Lamont-Black, *Goods in transit* (Sweet & Maxwell: London, 2013) 404; G.B. Czerwenka, *Das Budapester Übereinkommen über den Vertrag über die Güterbeförderung in der Binnenschiffahrt (CMNI)* TranspR (2001), 277.

or the place of taking over of the goods and the port of discharge or the place of delivery of the goods are located in two different States of which at least one is a State Party to this Convention'.[176] In principle, the convention therefore does not cover national carriage of goods by inland waterways.[177]

The temporal scope of application effectively corresponds with the tackle-to-tackle period.[178] The CMNI is not as explicit as the HVR in this respect, but it follows from article 16 (2) CMNI. This article prescribes that the carrier's liability 'during the time before the goods are loaded on the vessel or the time after they have been discharged from the vessel shall be governed by the law of the State applicable to the contract of carriage'.

Still, the convention will often govern the entire contract of carriage pursuant to the default rule of article 3 (2) CMNI. The shipper and the carrier are perfectly free to agree on the exact places of receipt and delivery (beyond the tackle-to-tackle period) in their contract, but when they have failed to do so, article 3 (2) CMNI prescribes that the 'taking over and delivery of the goods shall take place on board the vessel'. In that case, the CMNI governs the entire contract of carriage by inland waterways.

The system of liability

The main rule follows from article 3 (1) CMNI: 'The carrier shall carry the goods to the place of delivery within the specified time and deliver them to the consignee in the condition in which they were handed over to him.' It is submitted that this is not a scope rule, and that article 3 (1) CMNI therefore only applies when the convention applies.[179] This means that the mandatory period of liability under the convention is limited to the actual carriage on board,[180] and that the carrier's liability in the period between receipt and loading or discharge and delivery is therefore subject to the applicable domestic law.[181]

176 If the contract allows for several ports of discharge or places of delivery, the actual port of discharge or the place of delivery is decisive; article 2 (1) CMNI last sentence.

177 T.K. Hacksteiner, *Reikwijdte van het Verdrag van Boedapest inzake de overeenkomst van goederenvervoer over de binnenwateren* (CMNI) TVR (2007) 144. In principle, because the contracting states can declare that the convention governs national carriage by inland waterways as well, article 31 CMNI, and with regard to gratuitous carriage article 32 CMNI. Only Romania, Hungary, Switzerland and the Netherlands (subject to agreement) have done so, though. Article 8:889 DCC reads: 'Parties can agree that … the provisions of the Budapest convention on the contract for the carriage of goods by inland waterway (CMNI) apply to the transport.'

178 See also article I (e) and VII HVR. The key difference is that the carrier is free under the HVR to exclude his liability in the before and after period, whereas the carrier under the CMNI may then still find himself bound to mandatory domestic law.

179 See the discussion on the extent of article 17 (1) CMR in the previous section.

180 T.K. Hacksteiner, *Inwerkingtreding Verdrag van Boedapest inzake de overeenkomst van goederenvervoer over de binnenwateren* (CMNI) TVR (2006) 120.

181 Article 16 (2) CMNI.

The carrier is liable for loss, damage or delay in this mandatory period of liability, unless they were either caused by force majeure[182] or were the result of one of the circumstances listed in article 18 (1) CMNI:

(a) acts or omissions of the shipper, the consignee or the person entitled to dispose of the goods;
(b) handling, loading, stowage or discharge of the goods by the shipper, the consignee or third parties acting on behalf of the shipper or the consignee;
(c) carriage of the goods on deck or in open vessels, where such carriage has been agreed with the shipper or is in accordance with the practice of the particular trade, or if it is required by the regulations in force;
(d) nature of the goods which exposes them to total or partial loss or damage, especially through breakage, rust, decay, desiccation, leakage, normal wastage (in volume or weight), or the action of vermin or rodents;
(e) lack of or defective condition of packaging in the case of goods which, by their nature, are exposed to loss or damage when not packed or when the packaging is defective;
(f) insufficiency or inadequacy of marks identifying the goods;
(g) rescue or salvage operations or attempted rescue or salvage operations on inland waterways;
(h) carriage of live animals, unless the carrier has not taken the measures or observed the instructions agreed upon in the contract of carriage.

The system of liability with regard to these specific circumstances operates in line with articles 23 § 3 and 25 § 2 CIM 1999 and 17 (4) and 18 (2) CMR. The carrier needs to prove the occurrence of (one or more of) the listed circumstances. When he succeeds, these circumstances are presumed to have caused the loss or damage, and the carrier escapes liability.[183]

Error in navigation, fire, latent defects

The list of article 18 (1) CMNI does not really match the list of article IV (2) HVR. This is partially due to the obvious differences between the open sea and inland waterways, but mostly due to the different choices that were made in the drafting process.[184] The CMNI does not exempt the carrier from liability for loss

182 Article 16 (1) CMNI. The onus of proof rests with the carrier. The carrier is liable 'unless he can show that the loss was due to circumstances which a diligent carrier could not have prevented and the consequences of which he could not have averted'.

183 Article 18 (2) CMNI. The presumption is rebuttable, though; see the last sentence: 'This presumption does not apply if the injured party proves that the loss suffered does not result, or does not result exclusively, from one of the circumstances or risks listed in paragraph 1 of this article.'

184 T.K. Hacksteiner, *Inwerkingtreding Verdrag van Boedapest inzake de overeenkomst van goederenvervoer over de binnenwateren* (CMNI), TVR (2006), 121.

or damage as a result of an error in navigation, fire or latent defects, but instead allows contractual stipulations excluding liability resulting from:

(a) an act or omission by the master of the vessel, the pilot or any other person in the service of the vessel, pusher or tower during navigation or in the formation or dissolution of a pushed or towed convoy, provided that the carrier complied with the obligations set out for the crew in article 3, paragraph 3, unless the act or omission results from an intention to cause damage or from reckless conduct with the knowledge that such damage would probably result;
(b) fire or an explosion on board the vessel, where it is not possible to prove that the fire or explosion resulted from a fault of the carrier or the actual carrier or their servants or agents or a defect of the vessel;
(c) the defects existing prior to the voyage of his vessel or of a rented or chartered vessel if he can prove that such defects could not have been detected prior to the start of the voyage despite due diligence.

The contractual exemption of liability for errors in navigation is subject to the exercise of due diligence for the seaworthiness of the ship 'before and at the beginning of the voyage'.[185] Article 3 (3) CMNI at first sight resembles article III (1) HVR, but arguably lacks its strength as an overriding obligation.[186] The carrier's failure to comply with his obligation under article 3 (3) CMNI would therefore not necessarily deprive him in full of the exemptions of liability under the convention.

The limitation of liability

Article 19 (1) and (3) CMNI limits the carrier's exposure to the destination value of the goods.[187] Article 20 CMNI provides a 667 SDR/collo and 2 SDR/kilo limitation. This limitation is in line with article IV (5) (a) HVR, but the second sentence of the provision then reads:

> If the package or other shipping unit is a container and if there is no mention in the transport document of any package or shipping unit consolidated in

185 According to Ramming, the carrier is also bound to this obligation during the voyage ('während der Reise'); see K. Ramming, *Hamburger Handbuch zum Binnenschifffahrtsfrachtrecht* (C.H. Beck: München, 2009) 108. This may indeed be so in practice – see the main rule of article 3 (1) CMNI – but it does not seem to follow from the wording of the provision ('before and at the beginning of the voyage').

186 The German and English version of article 18 (1) CMNI are not the same. Whereas the English version exonerates the carrier 'when the loss, damage or delay are the result of one of the circumstances or risks listed below', the German version exonerates the carrier 'in as far as ('soweit') the loss, damage or delay are the result of one of the circumstances or risks listed below'. Authoritative case law on this point has yet to develop.

187 Article 19 (3) CMNI refers to the commodity exchange price, or alternatively the market price, or alternatively the 'normal value'.

> the container, the amount of 666.67 units of account shall be replaced by the amount of 1,500 units of account for the container without the goods it contains and, in addition, the amount of 25,000 units of account for the goods which are in the container.

The limitation of liability is semi-mandatory. The contract of carriage may stipulate a higher limitation of liability in accordance with article 20 (4) (b) CMNI.[188] A lower contractual limitation of liability remains subject to the main rule of article 25 (1) CMNI: it is null and void.

In line with the corresponding provisions in the CIM 1999 and HVR,[189] the carrier loses his right to limitation of liability 'if it is proved that he himself caused the damage by an act or omission, either with the intent to cause such damage, or recklessly and with the knowledge that such damage would probably result'.[190]

188 Article 20 (4) (a) stipulates that the limitation of liability does not apply either when the 'nature and higher value of the goods or articles of transport have been expressly specified in the transport document'.

189 Article 36 CIM 1999, article IV (e) HVR.

190 Article 21 (1) CMNI.

6 Multimodal situations governed by unimodal conventions

The HVR are silent on multimodal transportation.[1] The CMNI is strictly unimodal and does not apply to multimodal situations.[2] The CIM 1999, the MC and the CMR, however, do contain rules for multimodal situations. Article 1 §§ 3 and 4 CIM 1999 extends the scope of the convention to supplemental carriage. Article 18 (4) MC deals with unlocalized losses beyond the airport-to-airport period and 'vertragswidriges Transport'. Article 2 (1) CMR covers ro/ro and piggyback transportation in the course of international road carriage. The objective of these provisions is always the same, namely to extend the scope of application of a unimodal convention to (potentially) multimodal situations. However, the way in which these provisions try and reach this objective is very different.

6.1. Supplemental carriage, article 1 §§ 3 and 4 CIM 1999

The CIM 1999 regulates contracts for the international carriage of goods by rail. Such contracts will usually be unimodal, i.e. for the carriage by rail from one station to another, but the convention also governs certain multimodal contracts of

1 Still, the rules may apply to certain multimodal situations in the absence of specific provisions; see for instance the decision in *Mayhew Foods v. Overseas Containers* (1984) 1 Lloyd's Rep 317. The tackle-to-tackle period of article I (e) HVR runs from the tackle in the initial port of loading to the tackle in the ultimate port of discharge, and any transhipment, handling or movement of the goods by other means of transportation in between remains governed by the rules.

2 K. Ramming, *Hamburger Handbuch zum Binnenschifffahrtsfrachtrecht* (C.H. Beck: München, 2009) 98; P.M. Bugden/S. Lamont-Black, *Goods in transit* (Sweet & Maxwell: London, 2013) 404; G.B. Czerwenka, *Das Budapester Übereinkommen über den Vertrag über die Güterbeförderung in der Binnenschiffahrt* (CMNI) TranspR (2001) 277. The outcome in *Mayhew Foods v. Overseas Containers* would therefore have been different if the goods had travelled by inland waterways. Article 2 (2) CMNI specifically restricts the scope of application to contracts of carriage of goods 'without transhipment'. This implies that the contract of carriage can only be performed with one single vessel; so not two vessels, let alone one vessel and another means of transportation. Whereas transhipment in general requires two different ships or a ship and another means of transportation, the CMNI could theoretically still cover the handling or movement of the goods in the period between their discharge in an intermediate port and their (re)loading on board the same ship for the passage to their final destination.

carriage. In accordance with article 1 §§ 3 and 4 CIM 1999, the convention also applies to multimodal contracts of carriage whereby the carriage by land, sea or inland waterways is supplemental to the carriage by rail, irrespective of where the loss, damage or delay occurred.[3]

Supplemental domestic carriage

Whereas article 1 § 4 CIM 1999 covers supplemental cross-border carriage by sea and inland waterways, article 1 § 3 CIM 1999 only relates to supplemental domestic carriage by road and inland waterways. Article 1 § 3 CIM 1999 reads:

> When international carriage being the subject of a single contract includes carriage by road or inland waterway in internal traffic of a Member State as a supplement to transfrontier carriage by rail, these Uniform Rules shall apply.

The obvious question with regard to this provision is: when does the carriage by road or inland waterways qualify 'as a supplement' to the carriage by rail? Is supplemental carriage in the sense of article 1 § 3 CIM 1999 just an ancillary delivery service in the course of a contract of carriage by rail,[4] or does it also encompass domestic legs by road or inland waterways in the course of a multimodal contract of carriage that happens to include an international rail leg?

The question was brought before the German Supreme Court in 2013.[5] A manufacturer of consumer electronics had instructed its regular carrier under an existing umbrella contract to carry a container with merchandise from Istanbul (Turkey) to Nürnberg (Germany). The container was carried by rail between Istanbul and Nürnberg, but prior thereto it was carried by road from the factory to the Istanbul station, and again afterwards it was carried by road from the Nürnberg station to the consignee. The contract of carriage was therefore multimodal, yet predominantly performed by rail.

Upon arrival of the container at its final destination a part of the cargo proved to be missing. The manufacturer's insurers initiated proceedings against the carrier, and by the time the case had reached the Supreme Court the key issue was the applicable law. The contract of carriage was subject to German law in accordance with the choice of law in the umbrella contract, but it would be governed by the CIM 1999 if the two road legs were supplemental to the international carriage of the goods by rail. The German Supreme Court adopted an extensive interpretation of 'a supplement' in the sense of article 1 § 3 CIM 1999:

3 K. Ramming, *Hamburger Handbuch Multimodaler Transport* (C.H. Beck: München, 2011) Rn 150.

4 See the next section for a discussion of ancillary services in the sense of article 18 (4) MC.

5 BGH 9 October 2013 – I ZR 115/12. The case has also been discussed by R. Freise in TranspR 2013, 426.

> Hereby is meant that the principal subject matter of the uniform contract of carriage must be the carriage by rail. The road leg must therefore be short in relation to the rail leg. ... As such multimodal contracts of carriage could also be subject to the provisions of the CIM when the main part of the carriage is by rail and the carriage is governed by one single contract of carriage.

OTIF, the intergovernmental organization for international carriage by rail, welcomed this decision,[6] saying that 'the highest court in Germany interpreted the legal text exactly in accordance with the legislator's aim and hence rejected a restrictive interpretation.'[7]

Supplemental cross-border carriage by sea or inland waterways

Mutatis mutandis the same applies to supplemental, non-domestic carriage by sea or inland waterways, provided that these cross-border services are duly listed. Article 1 § 4 CIM 1999 stipulates:

> When international carriage being the subject of a single contract of carriage includes carriage by sea or transfrontier carriage by inland waterway as a supplement to carriage by rail, these Uniform Rules shall apply if the carriage by sea or inland waterway is performed on services included in the list of services provided for in Article 24 § 1 of the Convention.

Article 24 Cotif then ensures that these services are included in 'the CIM list of maritime and inland waterway services'.[8] This list contains a number of major ferry connections, for instance the services between Marseille (France) and Algiers (Algeria), Trelleborg (Sweden) and Rostock (Germany) and Liverpool (UK) and Dublin (Ireland).[9]

Obviously, the supplemental carriage by sea exposes the cargo to additional risks, and therewith exposes the carrier to additional liabilities. Article 38 CIM 1999 therefore allows Member States to make a reservation, i.e. that the carrier may rely on the following four (maritime) exemptions from liability in addition to the exemptions listed in article 23 CIM 1999:[10]

6 Bulletin of International Carriage by Rail No 4/2013, 20–1.

7 OTIF also quoted the Explanatory Re-port on Article 1 CIM saying: 'The term "as a supplement" is intended to express the idea that the principal subject matter of the contract of carriage is transfrontier carriage by rail.'

8 Article 24 Cotif reads: 'The maritime and inland waterway services referred to in Article 1 of the CIV Uniform Rules and of the CIM Uniform Rules, on which carriage is performed in addition to carriage by rail subject to a single contract of carriage, shall be included in two lists: (a) the CIV list of maritime and inland waterway services, (b) the CIM list of maritime and inland waterway services.'

9 See www.otif.org for an overview of the listed services.

10 These exemptions were borrowed from the HVR; see articles I (c) and IV (2) b, c and l.

a) fire, if the carrier proves that it was not caused by his act or default, or that of the master, a mariner, the pilot or the carrier's servants; b) saving or attempting to save life or property at sea; c) loading of goods on the deck of the ship, if they are so loaded with the consent of the consignor given on the consignment note and are not in wagons; d) perils, dangers and accidents of the sea or other navigable waters.

These extra exemptions only apply in the tackle-to-tackle period,[11] and article 38 § 3 CIM 1999 prescribes that the carrier cannot rely on these exemptions 'if the person entitled proves that the loss, damage or exceeding the transit period is due to the fault of the carrier, the master, a mariner, the pilot or the carrier's servants'.

6.2. Ancillary services, second sentence of article 18 (4) MC

The first sentence of article 18 (4) MC basically confines the geographical scope of the convention to an airport-to-airport range: 'The period of the carriage by air does not extend to any carriage by land, by sea or by inland waterway performed outside an airport.'[12] The second sentence of article 18 (4) MC, however, extends the scope of the convention to certain ancillary services performed outside the airport, provided that the cause of the loss remains unknown.

Loading, delivery or transhipment services

The obligations of the air carrier under the contract of carriage will in practice often run beyond the boundaries of the airport, 'the area of land devoted to carriage by air'.[13] The carrier has for instance agreed to collect the goods at the consignor's production plant, or to carry them by truck from the airport to their final destination, or from one airport to another in the course of the voyage.

Under such circumstances, and in spite of the provision in the first sentence of article 18 (4) MC, the convention may still play a role, namely when this carriage 'takes place in the performance of a contract for carriage by air, for the purpose of loading, delivery or transhipment' of the goods. These services need to be ancillary to the carriage of goods by air; they are not supposed to replace the carriage of goods by air.[14]

If these loading, delivery or transhipment services are performed in the course of a contract for the carriage of goods by air, and if the goods are damaged

11 Article 38 § 2 CIM 1999; see Chapter 5 and the discussion of article I (e) HVR.

12 Still, US courts have on occasion applied the convention throughout the entire period that the goods were in the care of the air carrier; see for instance *Magnus Electronics Inc v. Royal Bank of Canada* 71 (1985) 611 F. Supp. 436 (ND III); *Jaycees Patou Inc v. Pier Air International* (1989) 714 F. Supp. 81 (SDNY).

13 M. Clarke, *Contracts of carriage by air* (Informa: London, 2010) 117.

14 E. Giemulla/R. Schmidt (eds) *Montreal Convention* (Kluwer: Alphen aan de Rijn, 2006) under No. 88–9; OLG Hamburg 11 January 1996, TranspR 1997, 267.

somewhere during the voyage, but this damage cannot be localized afterwards, then the second sentence of article 18 (4) MC comes in:[15]

> If, however, such carriage takes place in the performance of a contract for carriage by air, for the purpose of loading, delivery or transhipment, any damage is presumed, subject to proof to the contrary, to have been the result of an event which took place during the carriage by air.

The second sentence of article 18 (4) MC provides for a presumption that is 'subject to proof to the contrary'.[16] This means that the convention does not apply to any loss or damage that actually occurred during these ancillary services. In the absence of mandatory conventional rules, the carrier's liability for these ancillary services is then governed by (mandatory) domestic legislation and/or the provisions of the contract of carriage.

In *Siemens v. Schenker* the parties had agreed on an umbrella contract for the carriage of goods from Frankfurt (Germany) to Melbourne (Australia).[17] The airport in Melbourne was not the final destination under the umbrella contract. Instead, the goods had to be delivered at a bonded warehouse just 4 kilometres from the airport. Schenker issued an air waybill for each individual voyage. This air waybill stipulated a 20 US/KG limitation of liability and furthermore mentioned the bonded warehouse as the place of delivery.

In the course of one of the voyages under the umbrella contract the goods were damaged during their carriage by road from the airport to the warehouse. Siemens sued Schenker for the damage, and argued that the carrier was fully liable in the absence of conventional protection. Schenker relied on the limitation of liability under the convention all the same,[18] but alternatively relied on the limitation of liability provided in the air waybill.

The majority of the court held that Schenker could not rely on the limitation of liability (or in fact any other provision) of the convention. The damage had occurred during the road leg from the airport to the warehouse and the convention therefore did not apply. Since this road leg was not governed by any mandatory domestic legislation either, Schenker could rely on the provisions of the contract of carriage, in particular the 20 US/KG limitation stipulated in the air waybill.

Ancillary services versus legs of a multimodal contract of carriage

The specific reference to 'the performance of a contract for carriage by air, for the purpose of loading, delivery or transhipment' in the second sentence of

15 The provision refers to 'loading' and 'delivery', a surprising choice as one would expect either 'loading' and 'discharging' or 'receipt' and 'delivery'.

16 This implies that the party alleging that the event took place in the course of the ancillary loading, delivery or transhipment services also bears the burden to prove that; see for instance BGH 10 May 2012, TranspR 2012, 466.

17 *Siemens v. Schenker* (2004) HCA 11.

18 The Warsaw Convention in his case.

article 18 (4) MC suggests a certain proximity to the airport. On the other hand, the wording of the provision does not require these ancillary services to take place in the immediate vicinity of the airport.[19] This raises a demarcation question: when are these services still ancillary to the unimodal contract of carriage by air, and when are they individual legs of a multimodal contract of carriage that happens to include an air leg?

The answer to the question affects the applicable law.[20] If the services qualify as 'loading, delivery or transhipment' in the sense of the second sentence of article 18 (4) MC, the convention applies to the entire contract of carriage by air.[21] If, however, the delivery or transhipment actually qualifies as an individual leg of a multimodal contract of carriage, article 38 (1) MC ensures that 'the provisions of this Convention shall . . . apply only to the carriage by air', and not to any of the other legs within the multimodal contract of carriage.[22]

The contract of carriage is obviously the primary source in search of an answer, but not all contracts of carriage specify the mode or modes of transportation,[23] and the intention of the parties may sometimes be difficult to (re)construct. In that case it is submitted that the relevant question is whether the delivery or transhipment can be detached from the air carriage.

If the delivery or transhipment service forms an integral part of the carriage of the goods by air, it is absorbed by the unimodal contract of carriage by air and the presumption of article 18 (4) MC applies to unlocalized losses in the course of that contract.[24]

If, however, the delivery or transhipment service can stand on its own feet, it qualifies as a separate leg within a multimodal contract of carriage. The convention then only governs the carriage by air in accordance with article 38 (1) MC as 'loading, delivery and transhipment as meant in Article 18 can certainly be no more than that; it can be no more than accessory carriage. The rationale behind the provision is to extend the scope of the Montreal regime to situations of unlocalized loss, but only in case the air carriage is supplemented by carriage by another mode that does not have an identity of its own'.[25]

The 'delivery or transhipment' services in the sense of the second sentence of article 18 (4) MC should therefore really be reserved for the transportation

19 The proximity is obvious enough where it concerns loading operations in the course of carriage by air, but the delivery of the goods at the final destination or the transhipment of the goods between two airports could theoretically cover a serious distance. The distance between Charles de Gaulle Airport and Orly Airport (the international airport to the north of Paris (France) and the domestic airport to the south of Paris) is for instance approximately 45 kilometres.

20 G. Leloudas, *Multimodal transport under the Warsaw and Montreal Convention Regimes: A velvet revolution?* (2014) 93; G. Miller, *Liability in international air transport* (Kluwer: Deventer, 1977) 152.

21 Provided of course that the losses remain unlocalized.

22 See Chapter 8 for the law applicable to the individual legs of a multimodal contract of carriage.

23 The contract may simply be silent on the matter, but parties may also have agreed on an optional contract of carriage.

24 M. Clarke, *Contracts of carriage by air* (Informa: London, 2010) 116.

25 M.A.I.H. Hoeks, *Multimodal transport law* (Diss.: Rotterdam, 2009) 200.

by land from and to the nearest airport.[26] The transportation by land can only assist, but not replace the transportation by air. Arguably, the distance covered and the presence of suitable airports along the way are then important clues to establish whether the 'delivery or transhipment' facilitates the performance of a unimodal contract of carriage by air or alternatively forms a separate leg within a multimodal contract of carriage that includes an air leg.[27]

The delivery of a shipment of telecommunication equipment to a bonded warehouse only 4 kilometres away from the airport then surely qualifies as an ancillary delivery service in the sense of article 18 (4) MC.[28] The delivery by truck of a shipment of mobile phones from Bochum (Germany) to Paris (France) for their carriage by air to Singapore qualifies as a separate leg within a multimodal contract of carriage.[29] Mutatis mutandis the same applies to the transhipment of photo cameras by truck from Amsterdam (the Netherlands) to Paris in the course of their carriage by air to Tripoli (Libya).[30]

These examples are rather straightforward; the distance covered is either just 4 kilometres or more than 300 kilometres with alternative air options. The difficulties obviously surface in the grey area where the delivery of the goods covers 10 kilometres, 20 kilometres or perhaps even 50 or 100 kilometres. The presumption of article 18 (4) MC then in principle still applies if such a delivery is instrumental to the performance of the contract of carriage by air, but as the mileage increases, the delivery is more likely to assume an identity of its own.

Still, the courts may in practice be tempted to adopt a rather loose approach,[31] and apply the convention to a road leg following or preceding the carriage of the goods by air. In *Commercial Union Insurance v. Alitalia Airlines* the delivery of the goods by road from the airport to the final destination covered approximately 150 miles. Nevertheless, the court applied the presumption of the second sentence of article 18 (4) MC as the contract was for 'primarily air transport, but where some ground transport is also performed'.[32]

It is submitted that this interpretation is too extensive. The 'delivery or transhipment' in the sense of the second sentence of article 18 (4) MC is clearly something different from 'supplemental carriage' in the sense of article 1 § 3 CIM.[33] Besides, a restrictive interpretation also follows from the wording of

26 K. Ramming, *Hamburger Handbuch Multimodaler Transport* (C.H. Beck: München, 2011) Rn 186.

27 The German Supreme Court held that when the goods were carried by land although 'the transportation by air was technically and systematically possible, the transportation by land is no longer ancillary'. BGH 13 June 2012, TranspR 2012, 456; BGH 10 December 2015 – I ZR 87/14.

28 *Siemens v. Schenker* (2004) HCA 11.

29 BGH 10 December 2015 – I ZR 87/14.

30 Hof Amsterdam 6 May 1993, S&S 1994, 110

31 In particular the US courts; see G. Leloudas, *Door-to-door application of international air law conventions: Commercially convenient, but doctrinally dubious*, LMCLQ (2015) 368.

32 *Commercial Union Insurance v. Alitalia Airlines* 347 F. 3d 448 (2nd Cir. 2003).

33 The criterion applied by the court in *Commercial Union Insurance v. Alitalia Airlines* looks very much like the criterion that the BGH applied to supplemental carriage under the CIM 1999 in BGH 9 October 2013 – I ZR 115/12. Bundesgerichtshof 9 October 2013 – I ZR 115/12.

the first sentence of article 18 (4) and (the presence of) article 38 (1) MC.[34] The application of the convention to other services than the carriage of goods by air is an exception to the main rule that the MC only applies to contracts of carriage by air.[35]

Cross-border ancillary services

The matter can be complicated even further with the introduction of an international component. The 'delivery or transhipment' of the goods in the sense of article 18 (4) MC will usually be a domestic affair, but it does not have to be. Some airports are situated on or very close to the border, such as the Geneva airport. The airport itself lies in Switzerland, but there are several warehouses within very close range on the other side of the border in France.

The ancillary delivery of the goods by truck from the Geneva airport to a French warehouse in the course of a contract of carriage by air may be governed by the second sentence of article 18 (4) MC,[36] but the delivery of the goods by truck between Switzerland and France may also qualify as a contract for the international carriage of goods by road in the sense of article 1 CMR.[37] This raises the question of whether the two conventions overlap, and if so, where the demarcation line should be drawn.

Again, the starting point is the qualification of the delivery by truck as either a separate road leg within a multimodal contract of carriage that includes an air leg or an ancillary service in the course of a unimodal contract of carriage by air. If the delivery by truck forms a separate leg within a multimodal contract of carriage, article 38 (1) MC prescribes that the provisions of the convention only apply to the 'carriage by air'.

Pursuant to article 18 (3) MC the carriage by air 'comprises the period during which the cargo is in the charge of the carrier', and in accordance with article 18 (4) MC it 'does not extend to any carriage by land, by sea or by inland waterway performed outside an airport'.

The temporal scope of application of the CMR starts when the carrier 'takes over the goods',[38] and this then implies that the CMR could operate from the moment that the road carrier receives the goods from the air carrier at the Geneva airport.[39] Even though the goods are indeed still at the airport at that time, the

34 The German Supreme Court held in this respect that 'it can only be considered as a delivery service in the sense of the second sentence of article 18 (4) MC if the transportation by land is strictly ancillary to the transportation by air.' See BGH 13 June 2012, TranspR 2012, 456; BGH 10 December 2015 – I ZR 87/14.

35 G. Leloudas, *Door-to-door application of international air law conventions: Commercially convenient, but doctrinally dubious*, LMCLQ (2015) 368.

36 The goods will usually leave the airport premises by truck (and occasionally by train), but not by ship so there will not be any overlap with the HVR.

37 *Quantum Corp. v. Plane Trucking* (2002) 2 Lloyd's Rep. 24; see the discussion in Chapter 8.

38 Article 17 CMR.

39 The operation of the CMR is not a given; see the discussion in Chapter 8.

two conventions would not overlap. The airport is only the outer boundary of the application of the MC, and article 18 (3) MC has by then already ensured that the contract of carriage by air ended at an earlier stage, namely when the air carrier delivered the goods to the road carrier.

If the delivery by truck is really just an ancillary service in the course of a unimodal contract of carriage by air, there is no risk of any overlap either, irrespective of whether the losses can be localized or not. An ancillary delivery service simply cannot stand alone; it does not qualify as a 'contract for the carriage of goods by road in vehicles', and it is effectively absorbed by the unimodal contract of carriage by air.[40] The air carrier's liability is then either governed by the MC in the case of unlocalized losses or governed by the law applicable to the contract and/or the provisions of the contract of carriage in the case of localized losses.

6.3. Another means of transportation than agreed, third sentence of article 18 (4) MC

Whereas the second sentence of article 18 (4) MC regulates the agreed (ancillary) transportation of goods other than by air, the third sentence of article 18 (4) MC deals with the carriage of the goods by any other means of transportation although the parties had agreed on carriage by air.

Vertragswidriges Transport

The working of the third sentence of article 18 (4) MC can perhaps best be explained with an example. Air France has agreed to carry a shipment of electronics by air from Singapore to Paris. The regular (and direct) Air France flight to Paris is already fully booked, but the Singapore Airlines flight to Munich that same day is not. Air France could then decide to (have Singapore Airlines) carry the shipment of electronics to Munich by air, tranship the goods into a truck and subsequently carry them by road to Paris. Article 18 (4) MC, third sentence, then ensures that this international road leg is governed by the convention:

> If a carrier, without the consent of the consignor, substitutes carriage by another mode of transport for the whole or part of a carriage intended by the agreement between the parties to be carriage by air, such carriage by another mode of transport is deemed to be within the period of carriage by air.

40 See for a different view on this point G. Leloudas in B. Soyer/A. Tettenborn (eds) *Carriage of goods by sea, land and air: Unimodal and multimodal transport in 21st century* (Informa: London, 2014) and *Multimodal transport under the Warsaw and Montreal Convention regimes: A velvet revolution?* He says at 97 that 'there is nothing in the international air law conventions to suggest that these operations cannot constitute an autonomous stage of combined carriage and thus be subject to an international convention, domestic laws or the road carrier's terms and conditions, as appropriate'.

The idea behind the rule is obvious enough: the cargo-interested parties should not suffer from the carrier's one-sided decision to use a different means of transportation than agreed. This objective will be reached in most of the cases as any loss or damage in the course of the carriage by another means of transportation is then reimbursed on the basis of the generous 19 SDR/KG limitation of liability of the MC. For two different reasons, however, the cargo-interested parties may nevertheless find themselves in an awkward position.

First of all, the carriage of goods by air is often reserved for the more valuable goods. The freight is higher, but this is well worth it as the passage is safer and faster. This advantage is lost when the goods are not (directly) carried by air to the agreed destination. It means that transhipment is necessary, an extra activity during which mistakes can be made. It also means that the safe and fast airplane is substituted for a slower means of transportation which significantly increases the transit time. The limitation of liability may then have remained the same, but the chance on incidents and accidents has increased along the way.

Second, the application of the MC limitation of liability will not always be beneficial to the cargo-interested parties. Indeed, the limitation of liability is higher, but it is also unbreakable. If the driver were to embezzle the shipment of electronics between Munich and Paris, article 18 (4) MC thus effectively limits Air France's liability to 19 SDR/KG whereas the carrier might otherwise have been exposed to an unlimited liability under the CMR.[41]

Given the obvious inequity of this result, it is tempting to try and find a way around this provision.[42] The problem is, however, that the MC provides for a uniform, exclusive and mandatory regime. In fact, its drafters have not only foreseen this situation, but they have even explicitly addressed it in the convention. The convention can under these circumstances not be circumvented if the outcome turns out to be unfair in individual cases.[43]

Besides, most (air) carriers will want to leave their options open. They will therefore negotiate the freedom to use any other means of transportation in their contracts of carriage. KLM for instance stipulates in its general conditions that the 'Carrier is authorized to carry the consignment without notice wholly or

41 *Quantum Corp. v. Plane Trucking* (2002) 2 Lloyd's Rep. 24.

42 See M.A.I.H. Hoeks, *Multimodal transport law* (Diss.: Rotterdam, 2009) 204–5 for some of the options. The choice for the carriage by road between Munich and Paris could perhaps be validated afterwards, so that it as a 'contract for the carriage of goods by road in vehicles' could still be brought under the CMR or the entire contract could perhaps be annulled. Another option might be to have the carrier's breach of contract qualified as a 'fundamental breach' of the contract or an 'unreasonable deviation' of the voyage so that the carrier would no longer have the benefit the protection under the convention. In *Z.I. Pompey v. Ecu-Line* (2000 AMC 142), the Canadian Federal Court denied the carrier the protection of the provisions in the bill of lading as the damage to a 'sophisticated photo-processor' had been the result of transhipment in breach of the contract.

43 *Sidhu v. British Airways* (1997) 2 Lloyd's Rep. 76.

partly by any other means of surface transportation or to arrange such Carriage'.[44] The result is then that the substitution for another means of transportation ultimately takes place with the consent of the consignor.[45]

6.4. Mode-on-mode transport, article 2 (1) CMR

The infamous article 2 (1) CMR covers mode-on-mode transport in the course of a contract for the carriage of goods by road.[46] The optimistic approach is that the article is difficult to read; the more realistic approach is that it is a lawyers' paradise and a nightmare for uniformity.[47]

The objective of uniformity

Article 2 (1) CMR consists of three sentences, and it can probably best be discussed sentence by sentence. The first sentence of article 2 (1) CMR breathes uniformity. This provision ensures that the convention applies to the entire voyage as long as the goods remain on the same set of wheels:

> Where the vehicle containing the goods is carried over part of the journey by sea, rail, inland waterways or air, and, except where the provisions of article 14 are applicable, the goods are not unloaded from the vehicle, this Convention shall nevertheless apply to the whole of the carriage.

The obvious example relates to roll on/roll off (ro/ro) ferry transportation, very common in the course of carriage between the UK and the Netherlands/France/Belgium or between the different Scandinavian countries. The truck (or just the trailer) carrying the goods boards the ship in Denmark, and drives off again in Sweden (still carrying the goods) to resume the carriage by road.

Another example is piggyback transportation over the Alps. This time the truck boards the train in Germany or Switzerland, crosses the Alps by rail road, and continues its voyage by road in Italy. The entire contract of carriage is then governed by the CMR, even though it was partially performed by another means of transportation.

44 The carrier could then at the same time protect his liability position for these surface legs. Article 38 (2) MC allows this as long as the air leg remains subject to the provisions of the MC: 'Nothing in this Convention shall prevent the parties in the case of combined carriage from inserting in the document of air carriage conditions relating to other modes of carriage, provided that the provisions of this Convention are observed as regards the carriage by air.'

45 Article 6.3.2 of General Conditions of Carriage KLM Cargo (July 2010), https://afklcargo.com/WW/common.

46 Article 2 (2) CMR ensures that the same rules apply when the road carrier and mode-on-mode carrier are one and the same entity.

47 R. Wijffels in Liber Amicorum Nicolas Mateesco Matte, Guido Rinaldi Bacelli (ed.) (Pedone Paris 1989) 336; J. Theunis, *International carriage of goods by road* (CMR) (Lloyd's of London 1987) 256; M. Bombeeck, P. Hamer, B. Verhoegen, *La responsabilité du transporteur routier dans le transport par car-ferries*, ETL 1990, saying at 158 that article 2 CMR is the 'paria of transport law'.

Three cumulative conditions

The first sentence of article 2 (1) CMR is straightforward enough; it is the second sentence that causes the problems. In spite of the (uniformity) rule in the first sentence, the second sentence then steers away from the provisions of the CMR,[48] and instead offers an alternative set of rules when certain conditions are met:

> Provided that to the extent it is proved that any loss, damage or delay in delivery of the goods which occurs during the carriage by the other means of transport was not caused by act or omission of the carrier by road, but by some event which could only have occurred in the course of and by reason of the carriage by that other means of transport, the liability of the carrier by road shall be determined not by this Convention but in the manner in which the liability of the carrier by the other means of transport would have been determined if a contract for the carriage of the goods alone had been made by the sender with the carrier by the other means of transport in accordance with the conditions prescribed by law for the carriage of goods by that means of transport.

The second sentence of article 2 (1) CMR lists three cumulative conditions. First, the damage must have occurred during the ro/ro or piggyback transportation. Second, the damage was not caused by the road carrier. And third, the damage could only have occurred during the ro/ro or piggyback transportation.

Whereas the first two conditions are pretty clear, the third condition has given rise to discussion. Does 'only' mean that the damage could not possibly have occurred during the carriage of the goods by road,[49] or does it simply mean that this specific damage could only have occurred during this specific carriage of the goods by sea or train?

The Dutch Supreme Court dealt with this question in the *St. Clair*.[50] The carrier had received a shipment of textiles in the Netherlands for transportation to Tunisia. The carrier drove the first part of the voyage to Marseille, and there the truck boarded the *St. Clair* for the passage to Tunisia. During the sea leg a fire broke out on board the ship and the textiles were damaged as a result.

The first two conditions were clearly fulfilled, but the cargo-interested parties argued that a fire could have happened anywhere, not just on the ship.[51]

48 The idea is that the road carrier thus avoids a potential recourse gap, for instance when he is liable for 8.33 SDR/KG under the CMR, yet he can only recover 2 SDR/KG from the sea carrier. R. Herber, *Die CMR und der Roll-on/Roll-off-Verkehr*, VersR (1988) 646; OLG Hamburg 15 September 1983, VersR 1984, 534.

49 The (also authentic) French text refers to 'et qu'il provient d'un fait qui n'a pu se produire qu'au cours et en raison du transport non routier'.

50 HR 14 June 1996, S&S 1996, 86 (*St. Clair*).

51 The discussion was obviously triggered by the fact that the road carrier would be able to rely on the fire exception (article IV (2) (b) HVR) if the HVR governed the sea leg, whereas the CMR does not provide for such an exemption, only a general (hence almost impossible to prove) force majeure escape.

The Supreme Court did not take the reference to 'only' too literally.[52] It held that the condition was met when the damage had actually occurred on board the ship as it should be read in connection with the second condition, i.e. that the damages had not been caused by the road carrier:[53]

> From the English text, requiring that the damage 'was not caused by an act or omission of the carrier by road, but by some event which could only have occurred in the course of and by reason of the carriage by that other means of transport,' it follows more clearly than from the earlier under (3.3) cited French text ... that it must concern a damage that occurred without any involvement of the road carrier.

A hypothetical regime

Once the three conditions have been met, the carrier's liability is governed by 'the conditions prescribed by law for the carriage of goods by that means of transport' when the sender would have concluded the contract directly with the sea/rail carrier. The second part of the second sentence thus provides for a hypothetical regime, prescribed by law for the carriage of goods by sea or train.

This hypothetical regime causes a problem as no one really knows what the sender of the goods and the ro/ro or piggyback carrier would have agreed upon. The court cannot look inside their heads, and a (one-sided) recollection afterwards might be biased because of a financial interest in the outcome of the case. The court could also take a more objective point of view, i.e. not to try and establish which contract *the* sender would have made, but to try and establish which contract *a* sender would have made in these circumstances.[54]

Having said that, it should not be too difficult to reconstruct the hypothetical regime in the case of international piggyback transport over the Alps. The contract of carriage will then be governed by the CIM 1999. Germany, Switzerland, Austria, France and Italy are all contracting states to the convention, and CIM

52 Other than the Court of Appeal, see Hof's Hertogenbosch 15 February 1995, S&S 1995, 67 (*St. Clair*).

53 The Dutch Supreme Court approach in the St. Clair is in line with the (older) judgment in *Thermo v. Ferrymasters* (1981) 1 Lloyd's Rep. 200. In this case Neill J held: 'One is concerned to consider not whether the loss or damage could only have occurred in the course of the other means of transport but whether the event could only have so occurred. It seems to me that any adequate description of the relevant events in this case would have to include a statement to the effect that a collision with the bulkhead of a ship had taken place in the course of loading the ship. Such an event could only have occurred in the course of, and by reason of, the carriage by sea. I therefore consider that the third condition is satisfied.'

54 The actual contract of carriage between the road carrier and the ro/ro carrier might then provide valuable information in that respect, especially if that contract is in line with the general practice in a certain trade; see the *European Enterprise* (1989) 2 Lloyd's Rep. 185.

1999 applies to 'every contract of carriage of goods by rail for reward when the place of taking over of the goods' between contracting states.[55]

The difficulty is to establish 'the conditions prescribed by law' for the carriage of goods by sea. The HVR would appear to be the regime of choice, but the problem is that it only has a limited scope of application. Article I (b) HVR requires the issuance of a bill of lading, and ro/ro carriers generally do not issue bills of lading.[56] In fact, the contract of carriage is often evidenced by a sea waybill, a consignment note or just a ticket,[57] and none of these documents qualifies as a bill of lading or similar document of title in the sense of article 1 (b) HVR.

The interpretation of the conditions prescribed by law

Courts over Europe have been struggling with this problem over the years, and their solutions are far from in line. Some courts have adopted a subjective approach, some have adopted an objective approach and some just follow the provision to the letter.

In *Thermo v. Ferrymasters* a heat exchanger had to be carried by road from Aylesbury (UK) to Copenhagen (Denmark), and the trailer was brought on board the Orion for the sea passage between the UK and Denmark.[58] When the heat exchanger was damaged in the course of the sea leg (during the loading operations in Felixstowe), the court had to establish which law applied in accordance with the second part of the second sentence of article 2 (1) CMR. Neill J stayed close to the wording of the provision and concluded:

> That the compensation payable to the plaintiffs is to be calculated in accordance with such conditions as they could, and would, have agreed with a carrier by sea in November, 1975, if a separate contract for the carriage of the heat exchanger alone from Felixstowe to Copenhagen had been made.

This reading of article 2 (1) CMR does justice to the wording of the article, but still leaves a considerable problem. How should the court establish the conditions that the parties 'could, and would, have agreed' upon?[59] The only possibility

55 The scope of application (in as far as relevant for the example) § 1 CIM reads in full: 'These Uniform Rules shall apply to every contract of carriage of goods by rail for reward when the place of taking over of the goods and the place designated for delivery are situated in two different Member States, irrespective of the place of business and the nationality of the parties to the contract of carriage.'

56 *European Enterprise* (1989) 2 Lloyd's Rep. 185 and W.E. Haak in his advice to the Supreme Court in HR 29 June 1990, NJ 1992, 106, S&S 1990/110 (*Gabriële Wehr*).

57 These consignment notes may then of course incorporate the HVR but only as a contractual set of rules and these do not qualify as 'the conditions prescribed by law'. See also the discussion below of the *Anna-Oden*, Cour de Cassation 5 July 1988, ETL 1990, 227.

58 *Thermo v. Ferrymasters* (1981) 1 Lloyd's Rep. 200.

59 Neill J did not have to answer this question, though; he merely needed to give the interpretation of the second sentence of article 2 CMR. See *Thermo v. Ferrymasters* (1981) 1 Lloyd's Rep. at 205:

would be to hear both the sender and the ro/ro carrier as witnesses afterwards to have them confirm that they would indeed have agreed on a certain set of conditions. This is not a very likely scenario.[60]

The French Supreme Court adopted a very strict approach in the *Anna-Oden*.[61] In the course of a contract of carriage by road between Sweden and France, the truck boarded the ro/ro vessel *Anna-Oden*, and was carried on deck during the sea passage. The vessel encountered heavy weather and the goods were damaged in the course of the sea leg.

The Court of Appeal had applied the HVR in accordance with the Paramount clause in the bill of lading,[62] but the Supreme Court reversed the decision as its rules were in that case not mandatorily prescribed.[63] The court stressed that article 2 CMR requires 'conditions prescribed by law for the carriage of goods by that means of transport', and held that:[64]

> in the absence of conditions prescribed by law for the carriage of goods by a means of transportation other than by road, the responsibility of the road carrier is determined by the CMR and the second text (i.e. article I (c) HVR, ms) excludes the carriage on deck from its scope of application; ... in deciding that the HVR were applicable in these circumstances, the court of appeal has referred to article X of that convention, which ... allows the parties to the contract of carriage by sea to stipulate in the bill of lading that the contract will be governed by this convention and that the clause headed 'Paramount'

'For the moment I am being asked to decide only the preliminary question: is the compensation to be determined in accordance with art. 4, r. 5, and art. 9 of The Hague Rules, or do the "conditions prescribed by law" in par. 1 of art. 2 of C.M.R. extend to such conditions as the sender and the sea carrier could legally, and would, have agreed in November, 1975?'

60 In fact, the judge appeared to have been impressed by the road carrier's argument that 'art. 5 of The Hague Rules allows a carrier to increase his responsibilities and liabilities under the rules provided such increase is embodied in the bill of lading'. Indeed, this may be possible in theory, but it is not very likely to happen in practice, and besides it is certainly not something that will eagerly be confirmed by the ro/ro carrier afterwards.

61 Cour de Cassation 5 July 1988, ETL 1990, 227 (*Anna-Oden*).

62 Cour d'Appel Paris 23 March 1988, ETL 1990, 221 (*Anna-Oden*).

63 See also the discussion in Chapter 7.

64 This is the author's translation, not an official one. The original French text reads: 'Vu l'article 2, paragraphe 1, de la CMR et l'article 1 c de la convention de Bruxelles pour l'unification de certaines règles en matière de connaissement; Attendu qu'aux termes du premier de ces textes, en l'absence de dispositions impératives de la loi concernant le transport de marchandises par un mode de transport autre que la route la responsabilité du transporteur par route est déterminée par la convention de transport international de marchandises par route et que le second texte exclut les transports sur le pont de son champ d'application; Attendu que pour décider que la convention de Bruxelles était applicable en l'espèce, la cour d'appel a retenu que l'article 10 de cette convention, tel qu'il a été modifié par le protocole du 23 février 1968, autorise les parties au contrat de transport maritime à stipuler dans le connaissement que le contrat sera régi par ladite convention et que la clause dite "Paramount" insérée en l'espèce dans le connaissement comporte une telle disposition; Attendu qu'en se déterminant ainsi alors que l'article 10 de la convention de Bruxelles n'a pas de caractère impératif, la cour d'appel a violé par fausse application les textes susvisés.'

> in the bill of lading shows the will thereto. ... in determining so even though article X lacks a mandatory character, the court of appeal has wrongfully applied the texts under consideration.

The French Supreme Court thus adopted a strict interpretation. The rules only apply mandatorily to the carriage of goods in the sense of article I (c) HVR. If the rules do not apply mandatorily, the requirement for the exception of the second sentence of article 2 CMR ('prescribed by law') has not been met, and the presence of a Paramount clause in the bill of lading does not change that. Consequently, the CMR governs the sea leg (as well).

In this reading of the second sentence of article 2 CMR, the actual circumstances were instrumental to establish the applicable rules. The wording of the article, however, clearly refers to the contract as it 'had been made by the sender with the carrier by the other means of transport', therefore not to the contract as it was made between the road carrier and the ro/ro carrier.

Finally, the Dutch Supreme Court has taken an (extremely) objective approach in the *Gabriële Wehr*.[65] This case related to the carriage of a shipment of auto components from Sweden to the Netherlands. The road carrier drove the first part of the voyage, and then boarded the *Gabriële Wehr* in Sweden for the passage to Amsterdam. The sea carrier had issued a sea waybill, and he had furthermore agreed with the road carrier that the trailer would be carried on deck. The goods were damaged during the sea passage, and again the question was which law applied.

The Dutch Supreme Court held that the reference to 'the conditions prescribed by law for the carriage of goods by that means of transport' could in light of the objective of the convention to ensure uniformity only be a reference to a uniform set of rules dealing with the carriage of goods by train, air or sea:[66]

> The contracting states apparently had in mind ... that these other conventions contained objective uniform law that was tailor made for the special nature and risks of the respective means of transportation, and under these circumstances held that it was best that this uniform law, where it concerns piggy back transport, would also govern the relation between the sender and the road carrier.

65 As has the German Supreme Court in the *UND Adrayatik*, BGH, 15 December 2011 – Az. I ZR 12/11.

66 The Supreme Court held: 'The contracting states apparently had in mind . . . that these other conventions contained objective uniform law that was tailor made for the special nature and risks of the respective means of transportation, and under these circumstances held that it was best that this uniform law, where it concerns piggy back transport, would also govern the relation between the sender and the road carrier.' See on this point also Roland Loewe Commentary on the Convention of 19 May 1956 on the Contract for the International Carriage of Goods by Road (CMR) *ETL* 1976, 503, F. Fremuth in Kommentar zur CMR (Verlag recht und Wirtschaft, Frankfurt, 2007) 142 and F. Ponet *De overeenkomst van internationaal wegvervoer* (Kluwer: Deventer, 2004) 84; 'The objective construction through a fictive contract aims to protect the shipper who was not present at the time of the conclusion of the contract between the road carrier and the sea carrier.'

Obviously, the HVR did not mandatorily apply to carriage under a sea waybill (or on deck for that matter), but the Supreme Court overcame this problem by saying that the agreement that was reached in reality cannot be taken into account to construct 'the manner in which the liability of the carrier by the other means of transport would have been determined if a contract for the carriage of the goods alone had been made by the sender with the carrier by the other means of transport'.[67] The HVR therefore applied even though no bill of lading had been issued, and even though the goods were carried on deck.

The Dutch Supreme Court ignored the actual contract between the road carrier and the ro/ro carrier, but also discarded the fact that it would have been very unlikely that any hypothetical contract would have produced a bill of lading (required to trigger the convention in accordance with article I (b) HVR). The mere fact that the HVR would have given the 'conditions prescribed by law' if they had applied to the contract of carriage is in this approach sufficient for their application to the sea leg.[68]

It is indeed safe to assume that the drafters of the CMR had uniformity in mind, but it is submitted that it is very unlikely that they also had in mind to bring each and every ro/ro sea leg under the working of the HVR.[69] If that had really been the objective, surely the second sentence would not so explicitly have referred to 'conditions prescribed by law'. The use of the word 'prescribed' implies a mandatory regime, and the HVR simply do not govern the carriage of goods under a sea waybill (or on deck) mandatorily.[70]

Ultimately these different interpretations of the second sentence of article 2 CMR all have their downsides, but that is perhaps more to blame on the wording of the provision than on the interpretation thereof by the different courts. It is submitted that a combination of the judgments in *Thermo v. Ferrymasters* and the *Anna-Oden* would produce the proper interpretation of article 2 (1) CMR. The ro/ro or piggyback leg is only governed by another international convention if that convention applies mandatorily to the contract that the sender and the ro/ro or piggyback carrier would have agreed upon.

As it is practically impossible to determine which kind of contract the sender and the ro/ro carrier would have agreed upon, it is submitted that the ro/ro carrier's actual behaviour in his relation to the road carrier in combination with generally accepted knowledge may play a role in the construction of this hypothetical contract. The court will then still not know for sure whether the ro/ro carrier would have issued a bill of lading in his relation to the sender, but if he has

67 Although acknowledging its shortcomings, the Supreme Court decision was supported by K.F. Haak Ro-ro transport under CMR, Art. 2: The Dutch solution (2005) *LMCLQ* 308.

68 J. Lojda, The impact of CMR on multimodal transport, in *International transportation* (Czech Yearbook of International Law, Vol. 6), New York: Huntington (2015) 162.

69 Or the Hague Rules, given the CMR's birth in 1956.

70 All the same, the objective approach has acquired a certain authority. The German Supreme Court followed the objective interpretation in the *UND Adrayatik*, *BGH*, 15 December 2011 – Az. I ZR 12/11.

not issued one in his relation to the road carrier, and if it is common practice not to issue one in certain trades,[71] the court may assume on a balance of probabilities that the ro/ro carrier would not have issued a bill of lading in his relation to this particular sender either.[72]

Admittedly, this implies that the road carrier's liability in the cross-Channel trade will in practice always be governed by the CMR,[73] but this is arguably a result that the drafters must have had in mind any way. In the absence of any prescribed conditions, the default rule in the third sentence of article 2 (1) CMR namely stipulates that 'the liability of the carrier by road shall be determined by this convention'. Besides, if nothing else, the application of the CMR to the entire voyage in any case benefits uniformity.

71 See the European Enterprise (1989) 2 Lloyd's Rep. 185 and W.E. Haak in his advice to the Supreme Court in HR 29 June 1990, NJ 1992, 106, S&S 1990/110 (Gabriële Wehr).

72 This assumption is open to counter-evidence, of course.

73 See in this respect Rechtbank Rotterdam, 21 June 1985, S&S 1986/56 (although reversed in appeal, Hof Den Haag 8 April 1988, S&S 1989/1), and LG Cologne 25 May 1985, VersR 1985, 985.

7 The law applicable in the absence of a mandatory convention

The unimodal conventions discussed in the last two chapters cover those contracts of carriage within their scope of application. All the same, not every international contract of carriage, and certainly not every multimodal contract of carriage, is governed by one of these conventions.[1]

This chapter deals with the conflict of laws, and more particularly the question of which law applies to (multimodal) contracts of carriage in the absence of conventional rules. As different countries have different rules of private international law, it is almost impossible to give an all-encompassing overview.[2] It is, however, certainly possible to provide a general idea through a discussion of the basic principles, the common law conflict rules, the provisions of Rome I and the general Paramount clause.[3]

7.1. The start and finish of private international law

The quest for the applicable law must have a beginning and an ending. This is a commonplace of course, but a rather important one, both from an academic and a practical point of view.

The application of the conflict rules of the lex fori

The question of which law applies to a (multimodal) contract of carriage is subject to a preliminary question: which law identifies the applicable conflict rules?

1 For instance, contracts for the carriage of commodities by sea under a charter party, the carriage of mobile phones by air between two non-contracting states or the carriage of furniture by road within Europe; see respectively article V HVR, article 2 MC and article 1 (4) (c) CMR. Besides, the law applicable to the contract also governs those issues that the conventions leave untouched.

2 Hence the focus on the common law conflict rules and Rome I in this chapter, but that then still leaves more than 150 countries unaccounted for. The courts in these other countries, including some major countries such as the US, China and Russia, but also most South American, African and Asian countries, will apply their domestic conflict rules to identify the law applicable to a (multimodal) contract of carriage.

3 The two systems take a different approach. The common law identifies the proper law of the contract on the basis of recognized precedents whereas Rome I provides for a code to that extent. As the principle of freedom of choice is closely followed under both the common law and Rome I, the outcome will in (the commercial) practice very often be the same.

The answer is fortunately generally accepted: the court seized applies its own conflict rules to establish the law applicable to the contract.[4]

The common law countries (with the exception of the UK, at least for the time being) will therefore apply their common law rules of private international law. The EU member states (thus still including the UK) will in turn apply the provisions of Rome I to determine the applicable law.[5]

The exclusion of renvoi

Another generally accepted principle is the exclusion of renvoi.[6] Once the applicable law has been established in accordance with the rules of private international law of the court seized, that law applies to the contract with the exception of its rules of private international law. This principle has been codified in article 20 Rome I:

> The application of the law of any country specified by this Regulation means the application of the rules of law in force in that country other than its rules of private international law, unless provided otherwise in this Regulation.

The exclusion of renvoi makes considerable sense. If the applicable law were to include conflict rules, the entire exercise could in theory go on indefinitely. The court would be going in circles as it would have to apply the rules of private international law of the just established applicable law, only to apply the rules of private international law of the then established applicable law and so on.

7.2. Common law conflict rules

At common law the law applicable in the absence of a mandatory convention is the proper law of the contract, i.e. 'the system of law by which the parties intended the contract to be governed, or, where their intention is neither expressed nor to be inferred from the circumstances, the system of law with which the transaction has its closest and most real connection'.[7]

To establish the proper law of the contract, the common law operates in three stages (in a logical order).[8] When the contracting parties have made an express

4 Lord Collins of Mapesbury et al (eds), *Dicey, Morris & Collins on the conflict of laws* (London: Sweet & Maxwell, 2012) 203.

5 Regulation 593/2008 of the European Parliament and the Council of 17 June 2008 on the law applicable to contractual obligations (Rome I). Rome I is the successor of the Rome Convention 1980, the Convention on the Law Applicable to Contractual Obligations.

6 Lord Collins of Mapesbury et al (eds), *Dicey, Morris & Collins on the conflict of laws* (London: Sweet & Maxwell, 2012) 1792.

7 *Rex v. International Trustee for the Protection of Bondholders Aktiengesellschaft* (1937) A.C. 500; (1937) 57 Ll.L.Rep. 145; *Vita Food v. Unus Shipping* (1939) AC 277; *Compagnie D'Armement Maritime v. Compagnie Tunisienne de Navigation* (1970) 2 Lloyd's Rep. 99; *The Komninos S* (1991) 1 Lloyd's Rep. 271.

8 *Pacific Recreation Pte Ltd v. S Y Technology Inc* (2008) 2 SLR(R) 491. The contract under consideration here had no specific connection with the carriage of goods but the rules apply to contracts

choice of law, the proper law is the chosen law. When the contracting parties have failed to make an express choice of law, the intended choice of law may sometimes be inferred from the circumstances. When the contracting parties have not made any (either express or implied) choice of law at all, the contract is governed by the law with the closest and most real connection.

The choice for the law of a country

A choice of law effectively means a choice for the law of a certain country.[9] The contracting parties are therefore free to choose English, Swedish or Brazilian law or in fact any other national law,[10] but they cannot choose an international convention,[11] a set of general mercantile principles[12] or a religious system of law.[13] In *Musawi v. RE International*, the contracting parties had agreed to have the 'Shia Sharia law' govern their contract. David Richards J held, however, that a valid choice of law can only be for the law of a country:[14]

> In my judgment, at common law the proper law of a contract had to be either English law or the law of another country, and the courts would not apply any other system to a contract. Although I am not aware of any decision to this effect, it was clearly stated as the applicable principle in successive editions of Dicey, Morris and Collins on the Conflict of Laws ... that the parties to a contract could choose the law of a country as its governing law, failing which the court would decide the proper law by applying its conflicts of laws rules which necessarily involve a choice between the laws of countries.

in general, including thus contracts of carriage: 'The first stage is to examine the contract itself to determine whether it states expressly what the governing law should be. In the absence of an express provision one moves to the second stage which is to see whether the intention of the parties as to the governing law can be inferred from the circumstances. If this cannot be done, the third stage is to determine with which system of law the contract has its most close and real connection.' See for other Singapore cases *Overseas Union Insurance Ltd v. Turegum Insurance Co* (2001) 2 SLR(R) 285 and the *Dolphina* (2012) 1 Lloyd's Rep. 304.

9 A contract cannot exist in a legal vacuum; see *Amin Rashid Shipping v. Kuwait Insurances* (1984) AC 50, per Lord Diplock. Still, there will arguably never really be a legal vacuum as the provisions of the convention (or in fact any other system) will always be supplemented or superseded by the proper domestic law of the contract.

10 In fact, they can also choose for the law of a certain part of a country when that country has adopted a federal system. Instead of choosing Canadian, US or Australian law, the parties would then for instance choose the law of Alberta, New York or Queensland. Lord Collins of Mapesbury et al (eds), *Dicey, Morris & Collins on the conflict of laws* (London: Sweet & Maxwell, 2012) 1793.

11 See paragraph 7.4 for discussion of the Paramount clause.

12 Such as the Unidroit Principles of International Commercial Contracts. See for their increasingly relevant role in the international trade R. Michaels, *The Unidroit Principles as global background law Unif. L. Rev.* (2014) 643.

13 Yong Pung How (ed.), *Halsbury's Laws of Singapore* (LexisNexis: Singapore, 2013) 299; M. Davies, A. Bell, P. Le Gay, *Brereton Nygh's Conflict of Laws in Australia* (LexisNexis Australia: Chatswood, 2013) 442.

14 *Musawi v. RE International* (2008) 1 Lloyd's Rep. 326.

Still, the requirement of a choice for the law of a country does not per definition preclude the involvement of another (international, mercantile or religious) system of law. First of all, the parties could for instance choose the law of Saudi Arabia, Iran, Yemen or another (Middle Eastern) Muslim country, and the Sharia would then apply after all as (part of) the domestic law in that country.

Besides, an international convention, a set of general mercantile principles or a religious system of law may have a contractual effect. A contract stipulating that 'subject to the principles of the Glorious Sharia'a, this Agreement shall be governed by and construed in accordance with the laws of England' is for instance governed by English law, but the Sharia could still be incorporated as a set of contractual provisions 'if the Sharia law proviso were sufficient to incorporate the principles of Sharia law into the parties' agreements'.[15]

Further restrictions

A choice of law may not validate a nullity. A contract for the sale of slaves is a worldwide nullity, but surely one very small country in the West Indies may have failed to repeal its eighteenth-century provisions on slave trade. If that were so, the contracting parties cannot choose the law of this country to validate their obviously invalid agreement.[16] Clearly, the example only serves to make the point, but the principle can also be applied to the sale of illegal arms, narcotics or endangered species.

The choice of law may furthermore not be contrary to public policy.[17] Again, this is unlikely to occur in commercial matters and the examples in case law and literature are often family law related.[18]

The last restriction is less academic: a choice of law cannot violate provisions of mandatory law. The unimodal conventions on carriage of goods all contain similar provisions to render contractual exclusions or limitations of the carrier's

15 *Shamil Bank v. Beximco* (2004) Lloyd's Rep. 1. This particular provision did not achieve that objective, though, 'since . . . the proviso is plainly inadequate for that purpose, the validity of the contract and the defendants' obligations thereunder fall to be decided according to English law'.

16 The Privy Council held in *Vita Food v. Unus Shipping* that the intention of the parties should be bona fide and legal, *Vita Food v. Unus Shipping* (1939) AC 277. See also Tan Yock Lin, *Good Faith Choice of a Law to Govern a Contract* (2014) SingJLS 307; M. Davies, A. Bell, P. Le Gay, *Brereton Nygh's conflict of laws in Australia* (LexisNexis Australia: Chatswood, 2013) 450 and the discussion therein of *Golden Acres v. Queensland* (1969) Qd R 378.

17 It is not always easy to make a clear distinction with a nullity. An illegal act is a nullity, and as such it will probably at the same time be an act contrary to a country's public policy. Still, a nullity suggests a certain absoluteness whereas public policy, for instance with regard to guns, drugs, working conditions and family life, is perhaps more of a gliding scale whereby the outcome in similar circumstances may be different from one country to the next.

18 See in this respect Lord Collins of Mapesbury et al (eds), *Dicey, Morris & Collins on the conflict of laws* (London: Sweet & Maxwell, 2012) 106–7. A more commercial example relates to sanction legislation. A contract for the sale of toxic chemicals by a seller in one state to a buyer in a blacklisted state surely violates the public policy in the country of the seller, and a choice for the law of the blacklisted state in question does not change that, even though the contract may be valid under that law.

liability 'null and void and of no effect'.[19] These provisions are primarily aimed at straightforward exoneration clauses in the contract of carriage, but they may also extend to law and jurisdiction clauses.

An asphalt road-finishing machine was carried on the *Morviken* from Leith (Scotland) to Bonaire (the Netherlands).[20] The requirements of article X (a) and (b) HVR were met, but the bill of lading provided for Dutch law and jurisdiction. As the Netherlands were still a party to the Hague Rules (and not the HVR) at that time, the clause effectively limited the carrier's liability to *f* 1,250.[21] As this was only a fraction of the limitation under the HVR,[22] the cargo-interested parties argued that the law and jurisdiction clause violated article III (8) HVR,[23] and with success:[24]

> The only sensible meaning to be given to the description of provisions in contracts of carriage which are rendered 'null and void and of no effect' by this rule is one which would embrace every provision in a contract of carriage which, if it were applied, would have the effect of lessening the carrier's liability otherwise than as provided in the rules. To ascribe to it the narrow meaning for which Counsel contended would leave it open to any shipowner to evade the provisions of art. III, r. 8 by the simple device of inserting in his bills of lading issued in, or for carriage from a port in, any contracting state a clause in standard form providing as the exclusive forum for resolution of disputes ... in a country ... whose law recognized an unfettered right in a shipowner by the terms of the bill of lading to relieve himself from all liability for loss or damage to the goods.

Obviously, the outcome of such cases depends on the port of loading and the place where the bill of lading was issued. If the *Morviken* had sailed from a port in a Hague Rules country (assuming that the bill of lading had also been issued there) instead of Leith, article X (a) or (b) HVR would not have triggered the mandatory application of the HVR in the first place.

At the same time, however, the outcome also depends on the court seized. If the cargo claim in the *Morviken* had been brought before the court of Amsterdam instead of the Admiralty court in London, the Amsterdam court would have

19 See article 5 CIM, article III (8) HVR, article 49 MC, article 41 CMR, article 49 MC and article 25 (1) CMNI.

20 The *Morviken* (1983) 1 Lloyd's Rep. 1.

21 The amount of 1,250 guilders was the Dutch currency conversion of 100*l* mentioned in article IV (5) of the Hague Rules. This corresponds with approximately EUR 600 per package, and there was only that single asphalt road-finishing machine.

22 The machine had a gross weight of 9,906 KG, so approximately EUR 22,000.

23 The machine was in fact carried on board of the *Morviken* after transhipment in Amsterdam but the (intended) arrest of the (carrier's ship) Hollandia (under which name this case is also known) in England triggered the jurisdiction of the Admiralty court.

24 Years later, the Dutch Court of Appeal in The Hague took the same approach in the *Vishva Apurva*, Hof's-Gravenhage 28 October 1997, S&S 2000/109 (*Vishva Apurva*). See also HR 12 December 1947, NJ 1948, 608 (*Celtic Star*).

limited the carrier's liability to *f* 1,250 in accordance with the Hague Rules. The bill of lading referred to Dutch law and jurisdiction, the Hague Rules were in force in the Netherlands at that time, and under these circumstances there would not have been any violation of mandatory law from a Dutch perspective.

The effect of mandatory conventions in non-party states

The discussion in the *Morviken* triggers a follow-up question, i.e. whether the courts of a country are actually held to apply a convention to which that country is not a party. This will often be a theoretical question,[25] but it is not too difficult to find an example. A contract for the carriage of computer chips by road from Madrid (Spain) to Moscow (Russia) may for instance be concluded through the branch offices of the contracting parties in New Zealand. The contract of carriage provides for jurisdiction Auckland (New Zealand),[26] and it also contains a choice for New Zealand law.

The contract of carriage by road between Spain and Russia falls within the scope of application of article 1 CMR, but New Zealand is not a contracting state. Should the court in Auckland then apply the mandatory provisions of the convention (as per article 1 and 41 CMR) or should it apply its domestic law (as per the choice of the parties thereto)?

It is submitted that the New Zealand courts should apply the mandatory provisions of CMR.[27] The convention has a direct effect between the contracting parties, and its provisions mandatorily govern their relation.[28] New Zealand may not be a contracting state to the convention, but in line with the rationale behind the *Morviken*,[29] the parties' choice for domestic New Zealand law in the contract should not be allowed to override the mandatory application of the CMR.[30]

25 There is hardly any case law on this question, and this suggests that the question is of little practical relevance.

26 This jurisdiction clause violates article 31 (1) CMR as it requires the court be situated in a contracting state. Since the agreement was reached through the New Zealand branch offices of the two contracting parties, however, the court of Auckland would still have jurisdiction in accordance with article 31 (1) (a) CMR.

27 Assuming that the case stays in New Zealand. Apart from the requirements of article 31 (1) CMR, the jurisdiction of the Auckland court may be challenged by the defendant on the basis of the common law principle of forum non conveniens. See for the test in this respect N. Meeson/J.A. Kimbell, *Admiralty jurisdiction and practice* (Informa: London, 2011) 244.

28 Article 1 jo 41 CMR. The CMR does not allow for 'contracting out'.

29 The *Morviken* (1983) 1 Lloyd's Rep. 1: a choice of law and jurisdiction should not achieve the circumvention of a mandatory regime.

30 Nevertheless, the courts of a country may feel a certain reluctance to apply a convention to which that country is not a contracting state. The Rotterdam court had for instance established in the Maipo that the Hamburg Rules applied to a contract of carriage between Valparaiso (Chili) and Bilbao (Spain) in accordance with article 1 (2) of the Hamburg Rules. All the same, the court still applied Dutch domestic law (chosen in the contract of carriage) as the Netherlands were not a party to the Hamburg Rules and Dutch law did not contain a provision that prescribed its application. Rechtbank Rotterdam 30 May 2002, S&S 2003/15 (*Maipo*).

Still, the Auckland court will not have to apply the CMR if its provisions would violate the public policy of New Zealand in any way.[31] In the *Komninos S.*, for instance, a shipment of steel coils was carried under a bill of lading from Thessaloniki (Greece) to Ravenna (Italy).[32] The HVR did not apply to this contract.[33] Leggatt J held on the circumstances of the case that Greek law was the proper law of the contract. Under Greek law, however, the claim would have been time-barred when the proceedings were instituted in London.[34] The judge held that this would constitute 'undue hardship' on the claimants, and that the application of Greek law on this point violated English public policy.[35]

On appeal Bingham LJ disagreed with the application of Greek law,[36] but clearly supported the decision to discard the time bar if Greek law had in fact applied: 'I agree with it and in any event regard it as a conclusion to which the Judge could properly come.'[37]

The express choice of law

Commercial contracts will often contain an express choice of law, e.g. 'This contract shall be subject to Queensland law' or 'The contract evidenced hereby or contained herein shall be governed by Singapore law.' The intention of the parties is obvious and the wording of the clause usually leaves little room for discussion.[38]

An express choice of law does not need to be carved in stone, though. The initial choice does not preclude later amendments, and the parties to a contract of carriage are free to change their mind along the way. In fact, an express choice of law can also relate to more than one single law, for instance when the parties to a multimodal contract of carriage agree to have the different legs governed by different laws.[39]

31 Y. Baatz (ed.), *Maritime law* (Routledge: London, 2014) 60.
32 The *Komninos S.* (1990) 1 Lloyd's Rep. 541; (1991) 1 Lloyd's Rep. 370.
33 Greece was at that time not a contracting state to the HVR. Articles X (a) and (b) HVR therefore failed to trigger the application of the rules. The bill of lading did not contain a (valid) paramount clause in the sense of article X (c) HVR either as the jurisdiction clause in the bill of lading for the 'British courts' did not satisfy article X (c) HVR.
34 Greek domestic law provided for a very short six months' time bar.
35 The 'undue hardship' test in the *Komnonis S.* suggests a rather flexible approach of the public policy. In fact, applying this criterion, the Auckland court would then arguably also by-pass the CMR if its provisions were to violate mandatory domestic law.
36 Bingham LJ held that the choice of forum in the bill of lading for the 'British courts' inferred that the parties had intended to have English law govern their contract. He referred to the authority of *Compagnie D'Armement Maritime v. Compagnie Tunisienne de Navigation* (1970) 2 Lloyd's Rep. 99; see also the discussion on the implied choice of law in this paragraph.
37 The *Komninos S.* (1991) 1 Lloyd's Rep. 370.
38 At common law the question of whether the parties have validly agreed on a choice of law is governed by the lex fori, i.e. the law of the court seized.
39 Lord Collins of Mapesbury et al (eds), *Dicey, Morris & Collins on the conflict of laws* (London: Sweet & Maxwell, 2012) 1806; The *Mariannina* (1983) 1 Lloyd's Rep. 12. Such a choice would qualify as a 'floating proper law' choice in the sense of *Bhatia Shipping v. Alcobex Metals* (2005)

Still, the choice of law cannot be too flexible. The choice cannot 'float in an indeterminate way'.[40] The choice of law clause in the Iran Vojdan for instance allowed the carrier to select either Iranian, German or English law.[41] Bingham J found that such a choice could not be upheld:[42]

> The proper law is something so fundamental to questions relating to the formation, validity, interpretation and performance of a contract that it must in my judgment, be built into the fabric of the contract from the start and cannot float in an indeterminate way until finally determined at the option of one party.

When the chosen law cannot be determined (objectively), the clause fails as an express choice of law. All the same, an ineffective express choice of law may still be relevant to establish whether the contracting parties have made an implied choice of law.[43]

The implied choice of law

Even though the contracting parties may have failed to make an express choice of law, their intention to select a certain law can sometimes be inferred from the

2 Lloyd's Rep. 336, but the terminology is unfortunately somewhat confusing as a 'floating choice' is sometimes also used to indicate a contractual provision whereby the applicable law can be determined afterwards. See for instance A. Beck, *Floating choice of law clauses LMCLQ* (1987) 523 and A. Briggs, *The validity of "floating" choices of law and jurisdiction clauses LMCLQ* (1986) 508.

40 See also A. Briggs, *On drafting agreements on choice of law LMCLQ* (2003) 389, saying that this clause 'partially failed the validity test on the ground that the common law was hostile to "floating" choices of law'.

41 The clause was not just indeterminable but also very difficult to read: 'The contract of carriage, the bill of lading and all disputes arising hereunder or in connection therewith, including the creation and the legal effects of maritime liens, shall, except as provided elsewhere herein, in the option of the carrier to be declared by him on the merchant's request, be governed (i) either by Iranian law, in particular by the Hague Rules contained in the International Convention for the unification of certain rules relating to bills of lading dated Brussels 25.8.1924, as enacted in the Iranian Maritime Code by statute of 24.1.1965 with exclusive jurisdiction of the courts in Teheran, Iran; (ii) or by German law, in particular by the Hague Rules as enacted in German Commercial Code (Handelgezetsbuch) by statute of 10.8.1937 with exclusive jurisdiction of the courts in Hamburg (German); (iii) or by English law, in particular by the Hague Rules as enacted in the Carriage of Goods by Sea Act, 1924, of the United Kingdom and the schedule thereto with exclusive jurisdiction of the courts in London (England). If in connection with the enactment of the Hague Rules and the law which will govern this bill of lading the amount of pounds sterling 100 mentioned in Article 4, paragraph 5, of the Hague Rules should be replaced by an amount in another currency, this latter amount shall also replace the amount of pounds sterling 100 wherever mentioned in this bill of lading in connection with the limitation of the carrier's liability. Notwithstanding their English wording, these conditions of carriage shall be exclusively construed and interpreted according to the law governing this bill of lading.'

42 The *Iran Vojdan* (1984) 2 Lloyd's Rep. 380; see also the *Armar* (1980) 2 Lloyd's Rep. 450.

43 *Compagnie D'Armement Maritime v. Compagnie Tunisienne de Navigation* (1971) AC 572.

circumstances at hand, and this implied choice of law then governs their contract. Lord Atkin said in *Rex v. International Trustee for the Protection of Bondholders Aktiengesellschaft*:[44]

> The legal principles which are to guide an English Court on the question of the proper law of a contract are now well settled. It is the law which the parties intended to apply. Their intention will be ascertained by the intention expressed in the contract if any, which will be conclusive. If no intention be expressed the intention will be presumed by the Court from the terms of the contract and the relevant surrounding circumstances. In coming to its conclusion the Court will be guided by rules which indicate that particular facts or conditions lead to a prima facie inference, in some cases an almost conclusive inference, as to the intention of the parties to apply a particular law.

These surrounding circumstances include the language of the contract, the underlying purpose of the agreement, any earlier contracts between these parties, their respective domiciles, the place designated for performance, the currency agreed upon and the inclusion of a jurisdiction or arbitration clause.[45] Most of these circumstances are far from decisive. The agreement to pay in EUR or US$ for instance hardly narrows things down and English is the *lingua franca* in international commercial contracts. The choice for the courts of a certain country or arbitration in a certain country gives a better indication, though certainly not a decisive one:[46]

> The circumstance that parties agree that any differences are to be settled by arbitration in a certain country may and very likely will lead to an inference that they intend the law of that country to apply. But it is not a necessary inference or an inevitable one though it will often be the reasonable and sensible one. Before drawing it, all the relevant circumstances are to be considered.

The closest and most real connection

When the contract contains neither an express nor an implied choice of law, it is governed by the law with the closest and most real connection. Perhaps not

44 *Rex v. International Trustee for the Protection of Bondholders Aktiengesellschaft* (1937) A.C. 500; (1937) 57 Ll.L.Rep. 145.

45 Another question is whether a choice for English law also works the other way around, i.e. whether it could identify the English courts as a convenient or appropriate forum; see in that respect *Novus Aviation v. Onur Air* (2009) 1 Lloyd's Rep. 576, The *Spiliada* (1987) Lloyd's Rep. 1 and *Bhatia Shipping v. Alcobex Metals* (2005) 2 Lloyd's Rep. 336 per Julian Flaux QC: 'Furthermore, since the contract(s) of carriage are governed by English law so far as the present dispute is concerned, that is a further reason why the English court is the appropriate forum.'

46 *Compagnie D'Armement Maritime v. Compagnie Tunisienne de Navigation* (1970) 2 Lloyd's Rep. 99 per Lord Morris at 108, more recently acknowledged in *Lupofresh v. Sapporo* (2013) 2 Lloyd's Rep. 445 per Tomlinson LJ and see also Y. Baatz, *Maritime law* (Routledge: London, 2014) 44.

surprisingly, the circumstances listed above are also relevant to determine the 'closest and most real connection'. Nevertheless, the test is different:[47]

> You must look at all the circumstances, and you must seek to find what just and reasonable persons ought to have intended if they had thought about the matter at the time they made the contract. If they had thought that they were likely to have a dispute, I hope it may be said that just and reasonable persons would like the dispute determined in the most convenient way and in a way in accordance with business efficacy.

The key difference between the implied choice of law and the establishment of the law with the 'closest and most real connection' is that the contracting parties in the latter case never intended to make any choice of law at all. At the end of the day it is then left to the court to balance the circumstances of the case at hand.[48]

7.3. Rome I

Rome I regulates the conflict of laws within the European Union (EU). Since the UK actively participated in the drafting of the regulation, its relevance arguably stretches beyond Europe. Rome I really codifies commune private international law, and its provisions are largely in line with the common law rules.[49]

The scope of application

Just as the unimodal conventions discussed in the previous chapters, Rome I defines its own material scope of application.[50] Article 1 (1) Rome I stipulates that the regulation applies 'to contractual obligations in civil and commercial matters'.[51]

47 The *Assunzione* (1953) 2 Lloyd's Rep. 716.

48 This is not always easy. In the *Assunzione* (1953) 2 Lloyd's Rep. 716 Singleton LJ listed the following relevant circumstances: 'The charterers, who were also shippers under the bills of lading, were French, . . . ; the contract was entered into by a charter-party which was made in France, . . . and the bills of lading were issued in France. . . . The ship was an Italian ship owned . . . , and a ship wearing the Italian flag; the owners were Italians; the master was an Italian; the contract was for carriage from a French port to an Italian port; the cargo was to be delivered at an Italian port . . . : the charter-party provided that freight and demurrage should be paid in Italian currency.' Balancing these circumstances, the Court of Appeal finally concluded that the contract was governed by Italian law.

49 Other than the common law, Rome I gives specific rules for contracts of carriage, and there is a difference in the law that applies to establish the validity of the choice of law.

50 The formal scope of application is not separately defined but follows from the fact that it is an EU regulation. An EU regulation is only binding for its EU members. Rome I has no temporal scope of application (other than it does not deal with contracts concluded before its entry into force on 17 December 2009; see article 28 Rome I).

51 And furthermore that the regulation does not apply 'to revenue, customs or administrative matters'.

Non-contractual obligations, and certain semi-contractual obligations,[52] are governed by another regulation, namely Rome II.[53]

Article 1 (2) Rome I identifies several contractual obligations that are not covered by the regulation. Most of these excluded obligations have nothing to do with (multimodal) contracts of carriage, but article 1 (2) (d) Rome I explicitly mentions 'obligations arising under bills of exchange, cheques and promissory notes and other negotiable instruments to the extent that the obligations under such other negotiable instruments arise out of their negotiable character'.[54]

This exclusion raises the question of whether a bill of lading contract is governed by Rome I. The bill of lading functions as a receipt and it evidences the contract of carriage, but it is also a document of title. In fact, whereas straight bills of lading are often referred to as non-negotiable bills of lading, order and bearer bills of lading might qualify as negotiable instruments in the sense of article 1 (2) (d) Rome I.

It is submitted that Rome I indeed covers bill of lading contracts. A negotiable instrument is first of all not the same as a document of title. Negotiable instruments are transferred free of equity; the transferee may therefore find himself in a better position that the transferor was prior to the transfer.[55] The transferee of a negotiable bill of lading acquires his rights subject to equities, but he may rely on the bill of lading to evidence his relation with the carrier, provided that he has acted in good faith.[56]

The exclusion of article 1 (2) (d) Rome I furthermore only relates to obligations that 'arise out of their negotiable character', i.e. obligations in relation to the endorsement and delivery of the document (of title). As long as the obligations arise from a contract of carriage evidenced by a bill of lading, however, the 'negotiable character' of the bill of lading (if any) does not play a role, and Rome I applies to the bill of lading contract.[57]

52 See e.g. article 18 Rome II on the direct action of third parties against insurers.

53 Regulation 864/2007 of the European Parliament and the Council of 11 July 2007 on the law applicable to non-contractual obligations (Rome II).

54 See also (9) of the Preamble of Rome I: 'Obligations under bills of exchange, cheques and promissory notes and other negotiable instruments should also cover bills of lading to the extent that the obligations under the bill of lading arise out of its negotiable character.'

55 J.S. Ewart *Negotiability and Estoppel* (1900) 16 LQR 141; R.E. Negus The negotiability of bills of lading (1921) 37 *LQR* 456: 'The most vital – indeed, the vital – characteristic of negotiability clearly is that the transferee for value takes a negotiable instrument in good faith and without notice of any defect in the title of his transferor, he acquires an indefeasible right to the property in the instrument and to the benefits represented thereby. . . . It is clear from the authorities above cited that bills of lading as heretofore understood do not satisfy the requisites of negotiability as thus defined.'

56 *Leduc v. Ward* (1888) 20 Q.B.D. 475.

57 This discussion is particularly relevant when Rome I collides with provisions of domestic law. Article 10:162 DCC for instance provides that certain rights and obligations under the bill of lading are governed by the law of the country where the goods were discharged, irrespective of any choice of law in the bill of lading. A valid choice of law in the bill of lading contract then overrides this domestic provision; see also F.G.M. Smeele in F.G.M. Smeele (ed.) *Conflictenrecht in ontwikkeling* (Paris: Zutphen, 2009) 43.

Choice of law

Article 3 (1) Rome I codifies the main principle: freedom of choice. When the parties have made a choice of law in their contract, the chosen law governs that contract:

> A contract shall be governed by the law chosen by the parties. The choice shall be made expressly or clearly demonstrated by the terms of the contract or the circumstances of the case. By their choice the parties can select the law applicable to the whole or to part only of the contract.

Although Rome I is less explicit than its predecessor in this respect,[58] a choice of law in the sense of article 3 (1) Rome I equals a choice for the law of a country,[59] and not an international convention, the Lex Mercatoria or a religious system.[60] The provisions of these alternative systems can still take effect as contractual provisions, though. Provision (13) of the preamble to Rome I stipulates that the regulation 'does not preclude parties from incorporating by reference into their contract a non-State body of law or an international convention'.

The incorporation of rules by reference is not the same as a choice of law. When a Swedish carrier and an Italian shipper select Japanese law to govern their contract of carriage by road between Singapore and Thailand,[61] Japanese domestic law applies pursuant to article 3 Rome I. When the contracting parties furthermore (validly) agree to incorporate the CMR by reference into their contract of carriage, the provisions of the CMR only take contractual effect.[62] The convention does not apply mandatorily and its provisions do not override Japanese law. The provisions of the CMR only function as contractual provisions.

Still, if the contracting parties wish to have the provisions of the CMR take a mandatory effect, then the choice for the law of a country may de facto achieve

58 Article 1 (1) Rome Convention spoke of 'contractual obligations involving a choice between the laws of different countries'.

59 Still, the Dutch Supreme Court accepted the (conflict) choice for the CMR in a contract for domestic carriage by road that formed part of an international agreement. The court held in *Zerstegen-Van der Harst v. Norfolk Line*, HR 26 May 1989, NJ 1992, 105 (ann. J.C. Schultsz), that 'in as far as that choice is made in connection with such an agreement, that can be qualified as international, this in principle leads to the application of the provisions of the CMR, also where they would deviate from the mandatory legal rules applicable to that agreement.' See in this respect also the discussion in paragraph 7.4.

60 J.J. Fawcett, J.M. Harris, M. Bridge, *International sale of goods in the conflicts of laws* (OUP: Oxford, 2005) 678; Y. Baatz (ed.) *Maritime law* (Routledge: London, 2014) 50.

61 The CMR does not apply directly to the contract as neither Singapore nor Thailand is a contracting state (article 1 CMR).

62 See for the same result under US law *Pannell v. United States Lines* 263 F. 2d 497 (2nd Cir. 1959): 'Where a statute is incorporated by reference its provisions are merely terms of the contract evidenced by the bill of lading.' See furthermore *The Westmoreland* 86 F. 2d 96 (2nd Cir. 1936) and *The Tregenna* 121 F. 2d 940 (2nd Cir. 1941).

that objective. If the contracting parties for instance agree on Belgian law, the provisions of the CMR will govern their relation after all as the convention has been incorporated into domestic Belgian law.[63]

Clearly demonstrated choices

The choice of law will often be express, but it is sufficient that it is 'clearly demonstrated by the terms of the contract or the circumstances of the case'. Provided that the choice is clearly demonstrated,[64] article 3 (1) Rome I therefore encompasses express, implied,[65] partial,[66] but also floating choices of law.[67]

The choice of law clause in Bhatia Shipping for instance stipulated that 'the liability . . . shall be determined by the applicable Indian law if the loss and damage occurs in India or by the provisions of the applicable law of the country where the loss or damage occurred.' Julian Flaux QC held that the effect of this clause was 'to provide for a floating proper law which is objectively ascertainable, here English law as the law of the country where the loss or damage occurred'.[68]

Article 3 (1) Rome I may furthermore cover 'principal place of business' clauses, again provided that the choice is clearly demonstrated. These principal place of business clauses are often included in standard contracts, suitable for the use by different parties. The Bimco Multimodal Transport Waybill for instance provides:

> Disputes arising under this MT Waybill shall be determined by the courts and in accordance with the law of the place where the MTO has his principal place of business.

A choice for the law of the country where the carrier has his principal place of business will not always provide instant clarity, but such a choice is valid when

63 There is an exception, though: the incorporation only relates to shipments over 500 kg.

64 A contractual provision allowing one of the parties to choose the applicable law is not a choice of law; see e.g. HR 14 June 1974, NJ 1976, 196 (*Taranger*).

65 *Egon Oldendorff v. Libera Corporation* (1995) 2 Lloyd's Rep. 64. This case on the question of whether a choice for arbitration in London demonstrates the intention of the parties to have their contract governed by English law was decided under the Rome Convention. The wording of article 3 (1) of the convention is slightly different, though: 'A contract shall be governed by the law chosen by the parties. The choice must be express or demonstrated with reasonable certainty by the terms of the contract or the circumstances of the case. By their choice the parties can select the law applicable to the whole or a part only of the contract.'

66 The last sentence of article 3 (1) Rome I explicitly allows a choice of law whereby different laws govern different parts of the contract, also known as 'depecage'. A choice for the US COGSA 1936 would for instance be such a partial choice of law, see H. Boonk in F.G.M. Smeele (ed.) *Conflictenrecht in ontwikkeling* (Paris: Zutphen, 2009) 115.

67 See also Chapter 8. A floating choice of law in a multimodal contract of carriage whereby the applicable law changes with each change in the means of transportation prevails over the applicable rules found on the basis of a domestic network system.

68 *Bhatia Shipping v. Alcobex Metals* (2005) 2 Lloyd's Rep. 336 (under the Rome Convention).

this principal place of business can objectively be ascertained.[69] Leggatt LJ had no problem in identifying Hamburg as the principal place of business in the *Rewia*,[70] i.e. the place where the company was managed and controlled:[71]

> That was the centre from which instructions were given when necessary, and ultimate control exercised. I do not consider that the reference to the 'principal place' of the third defendants' business requires the identification of a particular building. For purposes of cl. 3 of the bills of lading it is sufficient that the principal business of the third defendants should have been conducted from West Germany. Had it been necessary to determine the matter at this stage, I would therefore have held that the third defendants' principal place of business is in Hamburg where its central management and control is exercised.

The choice of law does not necessarily need to be stipulated in the contract itself; the choice of law may also be incorporated into the contract. This is in fact common practice, for instance when general terms and conditions are incorporated into a contract or when the provisions of a charter party are incorporated into the bill of lading contract. Males J accepted in the *Channel Ranger* that the choice of law from an underlying charter party had validly been incorporated in a bill of lading contract,[72] even when that underlying charter party had in fact incorporated the choice of law from an earlier charter party:[73]

> the express references to the governing law of the charterparty amount to an irrefutable case that the parties to the bill of lading intended their contract to be governed by the same law as was applicable to the charterparty, at any rate provided that the law so chosen was usual and proper for the trade.

The validity of the choice depends on the circumstances of the case at hand, more in particular whether the intention of the parties can easily be ascertained in the given circumstances. The validity of the choice of law is governed by the allegedly chosen law. Article 10 (1) Rome I prescribes:[74]

69 This in line with standard case law from the ECJ on forum choices for the court of the carrier's principal place of business, see e.g. ECJ 9 November 2000, NJ 2001, 599 (*Karl Liebknecht*).

70 The *Rewia* (1991) 2 Lloyd's Rep. 325 (under the Rome Convention).

71 *Palmer v. Caledonian Railway* (1892) 1 QB 823; *De Beers Consolidated Mines v. Howe* (1906) AC 455; *Daimler v. Continental Tyre* (1916) 2 AC 307.

72 Referring to *The Njegos* (1935) Ll L 53 Rep 286 and *The San Nicolas* (1976) 1 Lloyd's Rep. 8, Males J accepted that 'that general words of incorporation are sufficient to incorporate a proper law clause, or at any rate that there is at least a good arguable case that this is so'. On appeal Beatson LJ said that the dissenting opinion of Sellers LJ in *The Merak* (1964) 2 Lloyd's Rep. 527 would nowadays have prevailed. *The Channel Ranger* (2015) 1 Lloyd's Rep. 256.

73 *The Channel Ranger* (2014) 1 Lloyd's Rep. 337, affirmed in appeal (2015) 1 Lloyd's Rep. 256.

74 At common law the question of whether the parties have validly agreed on a choice of law is governed by the lex fori.

> The existence and validity of a contract, or of any term of a contract, shall be determined by the law which would govern it under this Regulation if the contract or term were valid.

The law applicable in the absence of a choice of law

In practice most contracts of carriage will contain a choice of law, and the contract of carriage will therefore usually be governed by the chosen law. Failing such a choice of law, however, article 5 (1) Rome I explicitly regulates the law applicable to contracts of carriage:[75]

> To the extent that the law applicable to a contract for the carriage of goods has not been chosen in accordance with Article 3, the law applicable shall be the law of the country of habitual residence of the carrier, provided that the place of receipt or the place of delivery or the habitual residence of the consignor is also situated in that country. If those requirements are not met, the law of the country where the place of delivery as agreed by the parties is situated shall apply.

In the absence of a choice of law, the law applicable to a contract of carriage must be determined in three steps. The first two steps follow from article 5 (1) Rome I. The law of the residence of the carrier governs the contract of carriage, but only if that law coincides with the law of the place of receipt, delivery or the residence of the consignor.[76] If not, the law applicable to the contract of carriage is the law of the contractual place of delivery.

The third step follows from article 5 (3) Rome I: 'Where it is clear from all the circumstances of the case that the contract, in the absence of a choice of law, is manifestly more closely connected with a country other than that indicated in paragraphs 1 or 2, the law of that other country shall apply.'[77]

The reference to 'all the circumstances' and 'manifestly' in this provision implies that the outcome on the basis of article 5 (1) Rome I will not easily be set aside. The Court of Appeal in 's-Hertogenbosch (the Netherlands) held very recently that 'mere geographical circumstances', such as the residence of the carrier and the place where the payment had to be made, were in any case not sufficient to depart from the main rule of article 5 (1) Rome I.[78]

The system of article 5 Rome I is limited to 'real' contracts of carriage. This follows from the decision in *ICF v. Balkenende*.[79] ICF had agreed to make train wagons available for the transportation of goods in a regular shuttle service

75 This is another significant difference between the common law and Rome I. Whereas the common law relies on the open norm of the closest and most real connection, article 5 Rome I instead gives very specific guidance.

76 Since Rome I deals with contractual relationships, the reference to the 'consignor' is likely to be a reference to the contractual counterpart of the carrier (the shipper, see Chapter 4).

77 Article 5 (2) Rome I relates to carriage of passengers.

78 Hof's-Hertogenbosch 21 June 2016, S&S 2016/114.

79 *ICF v. Balkenende* (2010) 2 Lloyd's Rep. 400; see also 23 October 2014, S&S 2015/50 (*El-Diablo*).

between Amsterdam (the Netherlands) and Frankfurt (Germany). ICF was not the actual carrier of the goods though; this was the Deutsche Bahn. The European Court of Justice adopted a narrow interpretation of a contract of carriage; article 5 Rome I only applies 'when the main purpose of the contract is not merely to make available a means of transport, but the actual carriage of goods'.

The law applicable to other contracts

When a contract is neither covered by article 3 nor by article 5 Rome I,[80] article 4 Rome I provides for a series of rules to establish the law that applies to these other contracts. Article 4 Rome I therefore governs several carriage related contracts such as bare boat charters, time charters (whereby the purpose of the contract is to make a means of transportation available),[81] and forwarding contracts.

Article 4 (1) Rome I provides a number of tailor-made rules for selected contracts, such as sale contracts, franchise contracts and distribution contracts.[82] Article 4 (1) (b) Rome I specifically relates to service providers, such as forwarders, and stipulates that 'a contract for the provision of services shall be governed by the law of the country where the service provider has his habitual residence.'

If a contract can either be brought under more than one or alternatively none of these selected contracts, the contract is in accordance with article 4 (2) Rome I governed by 'the law of the country where the party required to effect the characteristic performance of the contract has his habitual residence'.

The law found pursuant to article 4 (2) Rome I does not apply when 'the contract is manifestly more closely connected' with another country. In that case the law of that other country applies in accordance with article 4 (3) Rome I. Article 4 (4) Rome I then gives an open rule of last resort. If the applicable law cannot be identified in accordance with articles 4 (1) and (2), 'the contract shall be governed by the law of the country with which it is most closely connected.'

Universal application

Once the law applicable to the contract has been identified in accordance with Rome I, that law has universal application. Article 2 Rome I ensures that any 'law specified by this Regulation shall be applied whether or not it is the law of a Member State'.

Rome I does not require any connection with the law of the court seized, the nationality of the contracting parties or in fact the European Union. If a German court, dealing with a dispute between a Spanish shipper and an Irish carrier, identifies the law of Argentina as the law applicable to the contract, Argentinian law applies even though there is no connection with Germany, Spain or Ireland.

The rule is not absolute, though. Article 9 (1) Rome I stipulates that the applicable law found in accordance with Rome I cannot restrict the application of

80 Or one of the contracts governed by article 6 (consumer contracts) or 7 (insurance contracts) or article 8 (employment contracts), but these contracts will not be discussed in this book.

81 *ICF v. Balkenende* (2010) 2 Lloyd's Rep. 400.

82 Respectively article 4 (a), (e) and (g) Rome I, but other contracts are listed as well.

'overriding mandatory provisions' of the lex fori.[83] Article 21 Rome I furthermore prescribes that the applicable law may be refused (only) if its 'application is manifestly incompatible with the public policy' of the country of the court seized.[84]

7.4. Paramount clauses

The discussion of the Paramount clause merits a separate section within this chapter. Paramount clauses are commonly found in bills of lading, but they may also surface in charter parties and sea waybills. The clause contains a choice for the Hague (Visby) Rules.

The Paramount clause under the Hague Rules

The use of Paramount clauses was initially linked to the formal scope of application of the Hague Rules. Article X Hague Rules stipulated that the rules would 'apply to all bills of lading issued in any of the Contracting States',[85] but the Protocol of Signature provided:

> Contracting Parties may give effect to this Convention either by giving it the force of law or by including in their national legislation in a form appropriate to that legislation the rules adopted under this Convention.

The Hague Rules did therefore not apply directly.[86] The contracting states had to arrange for the application of the rules in their own national legislation. The UK

83 These 'overriding mandatory provisions' are according to article 9 (1) Rome I 'provisions the respect for which is regarded as crucial by a country for safeguarding its public interests, such as its political, social or economic organisation, to such an extent that they are applicable to any situation falling within their scope, irrespective of the law otherwise applicable to the contract under this Regulation'. Clearly, this is therefore something other than just mandatory domestic law. Boonk has for instance argued that these 'overriding mandatory provisions' cover the scope rules of those international conventions to which that country is a party. H. Boonk, *Zeerecht en IPR* (Kluwer: Deventer, 1998) 214. Article 9 (3) Rome I furthermore stipulates: 'Effect may be given to the overriding mandatory provisions of the law of the country where the obligations arising out of the contract have to be or have been performed, in so far as those overriding mandatory provisions render the performance of the contract unlawful. In considering whether to give effect to those provisions, regard shall be had to their nature and purpose and to the consequences of their application or non-application.'

84 Article 21 Rome I reads: 'The application of a provision of the law of any country specified by this Regulation may be refused only if such application is manifestly incompatible with the public policy (ordre public) of the forum.'

85 Article X HVR stipulates the same, but also reads: 'Each Contracting State shall apply the provisions of this Convention to the bills of lading.'

86 See HR 8 November 1968, NL 1969, 10 (*Portalon*) where the Dutch Supreme Court held 'that the protocol to the 25th August 1924 Brussels Convention establishing certain uniform rules on the Bill of Lading stipulates that contracting parties may give effect to the convention by either attributing force of law to it or incorporating the rules accepted in the convention in national law in a form fitting that law; that this stipulation shows that the rules laid down in the convention – The Hague Rules – do not directly apply'.

was one of the first countries to adopt the Hague Rules in 1924, and it gave force of law to these rules in its COGSA 1924.[87] Pursuant to S. 1 COGSA 1924, the rules had 'effect in relation to and in connexion with the carriage of goods by sea in ships carrying goods from any port in Great Britain or Northern Ireland to any other port whether in or outside Great Britain or Northern Ireland'.[88]

This provision ensured the application of the Hague Rules to outbound traffic under a bill of lading. To extend the reach of the rules to all bills of lading 'issued in Great Britain or Northern Ireland', S. 6 COGSA 1924 prescribed that the bill of lading 'shall contain an express statement that it is to have effect subject to the provisions of the Rules as applied by this Act'. Such an express statement became known as the Paramount clause.[89]

The consequences of non-compliance with this requirement were tested in *Vita Food v. Unus Shipping*.[90] A shipment of cured herring was carried on the Hurry On from Newfoundland to New York. Newfoundland was a British Dominion at that time, and its COGSA 1932 also required the inclusion of a Paramount clause in the bill of lading.[91] In violation of this requirement, though, the bill of lading did not contain a Paramount clause, but it did contain a choice for English law.[92]

The Hurry On stranded in Nova Scotia as a result of an error in navigation, an exempted event under the terms of the bill of lading. The carrier obviously relied on this exemption to escape liability for the damage to the shipment of herring, but Vita Food argued that the absence of a Paramount clause in the bill of lading affected its validity. As the bill of lading was illegal, the carrier would not be able to rely on the exemptions in that bill of lading. As the bill of lading was furthermore not subject to the Hague Rules, the carrier would in fact only be able to rely on the implied common law exceptions, i.e. an act of God or the King's enemies,[93] but not an error in navigation.

The Privy Council disagreed with Vita Food. The bill of lading contained a choice for English law, and the Privy Council held that English law was the proper law of the contract. As the parties were (under English law) free to agree on a contract of carriage by sea without the issuance of a bill of lading, they were (again under English law) equally free to agree on a contract of carriage by sea under a bill of lading without a Paramount clause:[94]

87 In fact, the COGSA 1924 (1 August 1024) even predated the Hague Rules (25 August 1924). The second sentence of the act actually refers to 'a meeting held at Brussels in October 1923'.

88 S. 4 (2) COGSA 1924 then provided that the act would not trigger the application of the rules to the carriage of goods by sea between two ports in the same state; see also article X HVR.

89 Paramount as it prevails over any regular choice of law. This 'regular' choice of law (if any) still remains effective, but only in as far as the Hague (Visby) Rules do not address the issue at stake.

90 *Vita Food v. Unus Shipping* (1939) AC 277.

91 S. 3 of the Newfoundland COGSA 1932.

92 Apparently, the bill of lading was taken from a rather old stack of bills of lading normally used in another trade.

93 *Forward v. Pittard* (1785) 99 ER 953; *Riley v. Horne* (1828) 130 ER 1044; see the discussion in Chapter 2.

94 *Vita Food v. Unus Shipping* (1939) AC 277. The reference to S. 3 in the quote is a reference to S. 3 of the Newfoundland COGSA 1932.

> All these reasons seem to justify the conclusion that the omission of what is called the clause paramount does not make the bills of lading illegal documents, in whole or in part, either within Newfoundland or outside it. Sect. 3 is, in their Lordships' judgment, directory. It is not obligatory nor does failure to comply with its terms nullify the contract contained in the bill of lading. This, in their Lordships' judgment, is the true construction of the statute, having regard to its scope and its purpose and to the inconvenience which would follow from any other conclusion. If that is so, the bills of lading are binding according to their terms and consequently the respondent is entitled to succeed in its defence.

Effectively, this meant that the application of the Hague Rules could be avoided,[95] a consequence also known as the Vita gap.[96] The gap was later closed with the Visby amendment.[97] Article X (a) and (b) HVR ensures the application of the rules to bills of lading either issued in or covering the carriage from a contracting state.[98] Article X (c) HVR allows the contracting parties to choose the HVR in the bill of lading contract, but this is an option, not an obligation:

> The provisions of this Convention shall apply to every bill of lading relating to the carriage of goods between ports in two different States if ... the Contract contained in or evidenced by the bill of lading provides that the rules of this Convention or legislation of any State giving effect to them are to govern the contract, whatever may be the nationality of the ship, the carrier, the shipper, the consignee, or any other interested person.

The reference to 'every' bill of lading in article X (c) HVR ensures its application to a multimodal bill of lading 'in so far as such document relates to the carriage of goods by sea'.[99] A choice for the HVR or any national legislation giving effect thereto will therefore trigger the mandatory application of the convention to the sea leg within a multimodal contract of carriage under a bill of lading.[100]

The effect of the clause in (multimodal) bills of lading

The Paramount clause is often rather difficult to read. The clause may refer to (some of) the Hague Rules, the HVR and sometimes even the US COGSA 1936 in one and the same provision. A typical Paramount clause could read:[101]

95 Provided that the bill of lading contained a choice for English law, and provided that the case was brought before an English court. See J.F. Wilson, *Carriage of goods by sea* (Pearson: Harlow, 2010) 184.

96 G.H. Treitel & F.M.B. Reynolds, *Carver on bills of lading* (Sweet & Maxwell: London, 2011) 628.

97 See the UK the COGSA 1971 (or similar legislation in other common law countries). The HVR have direct effect in several civil law countries, e.g. the Netherlands.

98 Irrespective of the presence of any 'express statement' to that extent in the bill of lading.

99 Article I (b) HVR.

100 The HVR may still apply to other legs performed by other means of transportation, but then only as a contractual set of rules incorporated by reference. See also Chapter 8 and the discussion of the *European Enterprise* (1989) 2 Lloyd's Rep. 185 later in this paragraph.

101 This is the wording of the clause in the *Happy Ranger* (2002) 2 Lloyd's Rep. 357.

> The Hague Rules contained in the International Convention for the Unification of certain rules relating to Bills of Lading, dated Brussels 25 August 1924, as enacted in the country of shipment shall apply to this contract. When no such enactment is in force in the country of shipment, Articles I to VIII of the Hague Rules shall apply. In such case the liability of the Carrier shall be limited to £100 sterling per package.
>
> Trades where Hague-Visby Rules apply
>
> In trades where the International Brussels Convention 1924 as amended by the Protocol signed at Brussels on 23 February 1968 – the Hague-Visby Rules – apply compulsorily, the provisions of the respective legislation shall be considered incorporated in this Bill of Lading.

The first paragraph of the clause refers to the Hague Rules 'as enacted in the country of shipment'. This implies that the rules only apply if the country of shipment is a Hague Rules country.[102] If the country of shipment is not a Hague Rules country, and provided that the requirements of article X (a) or (b) HVR have not been met, only some of the Hague Rules apply to the contract and the carrier's liability is limited to £100 sterling per package. This selection is possible in the absence of mandatory rules. Articles I to VIII of the Hague Rules only take effect as contractual provisions.[103]

The second paragraph of the clause relates to trades where the HVR apply.[104] This is in fact a provision with very little added value as it merely confirms that the HVR apply compulsorily if they apply pursuant to article X (a) or (b) HVR.[105] The first paragraph of the clause can then indeed be discarded, but that would also have been the case without the second paragraph.[106]

102 In the *Seijin* (1997 AMC 2705), however, the second circuit court of appeal agreed with the district court in holding 'that the language as enacted in the country of shipment incorporates the Hague Rules in the manner that England has enacted them: to wit, including the Visby Amendments and the 1979 Protocol.'

103 The *Tasman Discoverer* (2004) 2 Lloyd's Rep. 647.

104 Longmore LJ in the *MSC Amsterdam* (2007) 2 Lloyd's Rep. 622: 'A trade does, of course, start from a particular port but it also goes to a particular port.'

105 The last part of the second paragraph may have some added value in those cases whereby the port of loading is in a contracting state or the bill of lading was issued in a contracting state, yet the case is brought before the courts of a non-contracting state. The provisions of the HVR are then in any case incorporated in the bill of lading, and if they are not applied mandatorily, at least they still have contractual effect.

106 When the HVR indeed apply (because the port of loading is in a contracting state or the bill of lading was issued in a contracting state) the Hague Rules cannot contractually apply in addition to the HVR. Males J. recently held in the *Superior Pescadores* (2014) 1 Lloyd's Rep. 660: 'If they thought about the clause paramount at all, the parties must be taken to have understood that the original Hague Rules would not apply because Belgium was a Hague-Visby state. They would therefore have viewed the clause paramount purporting to incorporate the Hague Rules as surplusage which would have no application in this case and could for all practical purposes be ignored. It seems to me most unlikely that the parties intended a clause paramount which they knew would be

Although article X (c) HVR was designed to activate the HVR, the application of the rules is in practice generally avoided.[107] In *Pacific Electric v. NOL* 40 reels of power cable were carried by sea from Taiwan to Singapore.[108] The bill of lading was issued in Taiwan, and contained a Paramount clause, a limitation of liability and an express choice for Singapore law.

When Pacific initiated proceedings for damage to the goods in Singapore, NOL relied on the limitation of liability in the bill of lading.[109] This limitation of liability would be null and void in accordance with article III (8) HVR, but the application of the rules was not so obvious. Article X (a) and (b) did not activate the HVR, and that only left article X (c) HVR: a choice for either the HVR or a legislation giving effect to them in the bill of lading. The Paramount clause in *Pacific v. NOL* provided:

> This bill of lading shall have effect subject to any national law as enacted in the country of shipment, making the Hague Rules or the Hague Rules as amended by the Protocol signed at Brussels on 23 February 1968 (the Hague-Visby Rules) compulsorily applicable to this bill of lading. If any term of this bill of lading be repugnant to the said legislation to any extent, such terms shall be void to that extent, but no further. Neither the Hague Rules nor the Hague-Visby Rules shall apply to this contract where the goods carried hereunder consist of live animals or cargo which by this contract is stated as being carried on deck and is so carried. If no such national law shall be compulsorily applicable the carrier shall be entitled to the benefit of all privileges rights and immunities contained in the United Kingdom Carriage of Goods by Sea Act 1924, but without prejudice to his right to rely on the terms, conditions and exceptions set out herein notwithstanding that they may confer wider or more beneficial rights liberties or immunities upon the carrier than those set out in the said Convention.

The Singapore court held that this Paramount clause failed to trigger the application of the HVR. The clause only prescribed the application of the HVR

ineffective to result in some but not all cases to the application of the Hague Rules limit to the rather different Hague-Visby limitation regime. As Mr Goldstone QC put it, it seems improbable that the parties could have intended a single contract of carriage to be covered simultaneously by two differing limitation of liability regimes with differing provisions. The claimants' "pick and mix" approach, taking the benefit of whichever bits of the two package limitation regimes are in their favour, seems a surprising thing for rational business people to wish to agree.'

107 See in this respect for instance the *MSC Amsterdam* (2007) 2 Lloyd's Rep. 622. Longmore LJ held 'that the scheme of the bill of lading in the present case is that the owners, as a matter of contract, accept Hague Rules (1924) obligations but only accept HVR obligations if they are forced to do so. They can only be forced to do so if the proper law of the contract compels it (or if the place where the cargo owners choose to sue them compels it). Neither law compels it on the facts of the present case and they are not contractually obliged further than the law compels.'

108 *Pacific Electric v. Neptune Orient Lines* (1993) SGHC 122.

109 The maximum liability under this provision amounted to merely SG$ 22,000, far less than the actual damage to the goods.

(or Hague Rules) to the contract of carriage if those rules were 'compulsorily applicable'. In the absence of such a mandatory regulation, however, the contract of carriage was governed by Singapore law in accordance with the choice of law in the bill of lading. The last sentence of the Paramount clause secured an additional contractual protection for the carrier's benefit. The carrier may rely on all the 'privileges, rights and immunities' listed in the Hague Rules (in addition to his defences under Singapore law and the provisions of the bill of lading).

This result is probably not in line with the objective of the drafters of the Visby Amendment in 1968.[110] At the same time, however, it is probably very much in line with the objective of the drafters of this particular Paramount clause. The wording of the clause on the one hand avoids the mandatory application of the HVR, yet on the other hand gives the carrier the benefit of the Hague Rules as an extra set of contractual provisions.

The effect of the clause in other documents than a bill of lading

The effect of the clause obviously depends on its wording, but also on the nature of the document. Article I (b) HVR limits the material scope of the convention to 'contracts of carriage covered by a bill of lading or any similar document of title', and the inclusion of a Paramount clause in a charter party or sea waybill does not activate the mandatory regime. The provisions of the HVR then only apply as a contractual set of rules in addition (but without prejudice) to the bill of lading conditions.[111]

Browner had agreed to carry a shipment of meat by road from Cork (Ireland) to several destinations in France.[112] He obviously had to cross the Channel to reach France, and he booked the sea passage from Dover (UK) to Calais (France) on the *European Enterprise*. In line with the common practice of the cross-Channel operators, this contract of carriage by sea was evidenced by a consignment note, and not by a bill of lading.[113] The consignment note contained the following clause:

> The goods are received loaded stowed carried discharged and otherwise handled and kept by the Carrier under and subject to:- (a) the Rules (commonly known as the Hague-Visby Rules and hereinafter called 'the Rules') set out in the Schedule to the Carriers of Goods by Sea Act 1971, save as follows:-

110 See again Longmore LJ and his (rhetorical) question/remark on this point in the *MSC Amsterdam* (2007) 2 Lloyd's Rep. 622: 'Whether that is an attractive way for a shipowner to do business 40 years after the Hague-Visby Protocol was internationally agreed is a different matter.'

111 The *Tasman Discoverer* (2004) 2 Lloyd's Rep. 647.

112 The *European Enterprise* (1989) 2 Lloyd's Rep. 185.

113 A contract of carriage evidenced by a non-negotiable document may under English law still be governed by the HVR if the document expressly states so. See S. 1 (6) COGSA 1971: 'Without prejudice to Article X(C) of the Rules, the Rules shall have the force of law in relation to – (a) any bill of lading if the contract contained in or evidenced by it expressly provides that the Rules shall govern the contract and (b) any receipt which is a non-negotiable document marked as such if the contract contained in or evidenced by it is a contract for the carriage of goods by sea which expressly provides that the Rules are to govern the contract as if the receipt were a bill of lading.' This specific consignment note, however, did not meet this requirement.

> (i) each vehicle (whether consisting of a single unit, an articulated unit or a trailer or semi trailer) together with any container(s) flat(s) pallet(s) package(s) or other equipment and together with their respective contents (if any) shall be deemed to be one package or unit for the purposes of art. IV. par. 5(a) of the Rules; (ii) the Carrier shall be entitled to limit its liability to 10,000 frs. per package or unit, and par. 5(a) shall be read as though the words 'or 30 frs. per kilo of gross weight of the goods lost or damaged, whichever is the higher' were deleted; (iii) the value of a franc shall be as defined in the Sterling Equivalents Order made by the Secretary of State pursuant to Sec. 1(5) of the Carriage of Goods by Sea Act 1971 in force at the time the loss or damage occurs; (iv) art. IV, par. 5(c) of the Rules shall be deleted.

Accordingly, the contractual limitation was considerably less than the conventional limitation, and this raised the question of whether the Paramount clause caused the HVR to apply mandatorily. Browner argued that the HVR applied mandatorily,[114] but the sea carrier argued that the (selected) provisions of the HVR only had contractual force, and with success. Steyn J held:[115]

> that it would be curious if a voluntary paramount clause, which effected only a partial incorporation of the rules, had the result that a statutory binding character was given to all the rules, even when there was no primary contractual bond. It must be right that ... the legislation did not intend to override the agreement of the parties when the parties had freedom of choice whether or not to incorporate the rules into their contract.

The Paramount clause in the consignment note did not accomplish the mandatory application of the HVR to the contract of carriage.[116] Instead, the contracting parties retained their freedom of contract,[117] and only those selected provisions of the HVR were incorporated into the contract.[118]

114 Relying on an earlier decision to that extent in *The Vechscroon* (1982) 1 Lloyd's Rep. 301.

115 The *European Enterprise* (1989) 2 Lloyd's Rep. 185.

116 See in this respect also Schultsz in his annotation under the *Gabriëlle Wehr*, HR 29 June 1990, S&S 1990, 110, NJ 1992, 106: 'Where the parties do not intend to transfer the goods, they usually settle for a non-negotiable sea waybill. This then often stipulates the applicability of the Hague Rules or Hague-Visby Rules, yet such a stipulation may alter or exclude certain aspects of the Rules . . . since the Rules are not mandatorily applicable in absence of a bill of lading.'

117 Debattista remarks in his case comment on the *European Enterprise* that 'as the carrier was not bound to issue a bill of lading and only voluntarily incorporated the Rules into the contract, then the Act could not apply'. C. Debattista, Sea waybills and the Carriage of Goods by Sea Act 1971 *LMCLQ* (1989) 405.

118 Since the incorporated provisions only apply as contractual provisions, they can be set aside by provisions of mandatory (domestic) law; see e.g. *Colgate Palmolive v. S/S Dart Canada*, 724 F. 2d 313 (2nd Cir. 1983): 'Parties may contractually extend COGSA's application beyond its normal parameters. When they do so, however, COGSA does not apply of its own force, but merely as a contractual term. In this case, state law, the law of New Jersey, governs and invalidates the contractual limitation of liability upon which Global relies.'

The Paramount clause under Rome I

It is still an open question whether the application of Rome I affects the working of Paramount clauses in bills of lading. On the one hand, a choice of law in the sense of article 3 (1) Rome I means a choice for the law of a certain country, and not a choice for a convention. On the other hand, article 25 (1) Rome I gives precedence to the provisions on conflict rules in existing conventions:[119]

> This Regulation shall not prejudice the application of international conventions to which one or more Member States are parties at the time when this Regulation is adopted and which lay down conflict-of-law rules relating to contractual obligations.

The question therefore is whether article X (c) HVR is such a 'conflict-of-law rule' (in which case it prevails over Rome I), or whether article X (c) HVR merely defines the formal scope of application of the convention (in which case Rome I prevails over the HVR). The latter view is probably the more accurate of the two. The HVR do not identify the law applicable to the contract of carriage of goods by sea, but instead give material rules for the carriage of goods by sea within their scope of application.[120]

At the same time, however, this discussion probably has more academic than practical relevance. First of all, Paramount clauses in bills of lading are in practice often included to circumvent rather than activate the HVR. Second, the restrictions of Rome I only affect a choice for the HVR, and not a choice for the 'legislation of any State giving effect to' the HVR. If the parties really want to have the HVR govern their bill of lading contract, they can still choose a domestic law that gives effect to the HVR.[121]

119 This is a stricter rule than under the Rome Convention. Article 21 Rome Convention did not mention any conflict rules, but simply gave precedence to international conventions.

120 Still, the more accurate view is perhaps not the better view. It is submitted that there is really nothing wrong with contracting parties choosing a mandatory convention to govern their relation; see also H. Boonk in F.G.M. Smeele (ed.) *Conflictenrecht in ontwikkeling* (Paris: Zutphen, 2009) 117. Besides, the bill of lading contract will not exist in a 'legal vacuum' as the domestic law applicable to the contract will supplement the provisions of the HVR. The situation is then really just the same as when the convention had applied ex article X (a) or (b) HVR.

121 Apart from the rule of article X (c) HVR, the incorporation by reference also remains possible of course (see provision 13 of the preamble), but the HVR will then only take contractual effect, and they will not apply mandatorily.

8 The rules applicable to the individual legs of multimodal contracts of carriage

In the absence of an international convention on multimodal contracts of carriage, the rules of private international law identify the law applicable to a multimodal contract of carriage. That still leaves the question, though, of whether the law applicable to a multimodal contract of carriage law then also governs its individual legs.

As so often, there is not just one answer. An individual leg within a multimodal contract of carriage may be governed by a unimodal convention, for instance because that leg falls within its scope of application, or because that convention gives specific or implied rules to that extent.[1] In that case, the leg is mandatorily governed by the provisions of that convention.

If the individual legs within a multimodal contract of carriage are not governed by a unimodal convention, or when it cannot be established during which of the different legs the damage occurred, they are governed by these domestic law applicable to the multimodal contract of carriage.[2]

If this is mandatory law, the rights and obligations of the parties to a multimodal contract of carriage are obviously governed by its mandatory provisions. Otherwise, the contracting parties are free to define their rights and obligations. The individual legs are then regulated by the provisions of the contract of carriage, in practice often evidenced by a multimodal bill of lading or waybill, and supplemented by the applicable domestic law.

8.1. The application of the CMR to road legs within a multimodal contract of carriage

This section deals with the question of whether the CMR applies directly to road legs within multimodal contracts of carriage. This is one of the major bottlenecks in multimodal transport law as the question has produced two completely different answers.

1 Or because the multimodal contract of carriage is entirely governed by a unimodal convention; see the discussion in Chapter 6.

2 O. Hartenstein, *Die Bestimmung des Teilstreckenrechts im Multimodaltranportvertrag TranspR* (2005) 9; M.A.I.H. Hoeks, *Multimodal transport law* (Diss.: Rotterdam, 2009) 356; A. van Beelen, *Multimodaal vervoer* (Diss.: Leiden, 1996) 97–8.

The direct application of the CMR

In *Quantum Corp. v. Plane Trucking* a shipment of hard disc drives was carried by Air France from Singapore to Dublin (Ireland). The first leg was by air between Singapore and Paris (France); the second leg was by road between Paris and Dublin.[3] Air France had flown the shipment to Paris, but it had subcontracted the second leg to Plane Trucking, an English road haulier. The shipment was stolen in the course of this second leg, and the driver was in on the theft.

Air France had issued an air waybill for the entire transport. This air waybill referred to French law and jurisdiction. The air waybill furthermore provided for a limitation of liability of 17 SDR/Kg. Since the hard disc drives were quite valuable, but not very heavy, the maximum liability under the air waybill amounted to GBP 116,057.56, only a fraction of the actual damage of approximately US$ 1,500,000.

Quantum argued that the road leg between Paris and Dublin fell within the scope of application of the CMR. It initiated proceedings against Air France and Plane Trucking in England on the basis of article 31 (1) (a) CMR. Although Air France did not challenge the competence of the English court,[4] it did challenge the application of the CMR. In the absence of a mandatory regime, Air France argued that it could rely on the limitation of liability in its air waybill. Conversely, Quantum argued that article 41 CMR rendered the limitation of liability null and void. Since the driver had participated in the theft, Air France would instead be fully liable in accordance with articles 3 and 29 CMR.

Tomlinson J agreed with Air France and rejected the application of the CMR. He qualified the contract as 'a contract predominantly for carriage by air'. The CMR did not apply to the road leg as 'the nature of the contract . . . must be examined, not the nature of the carriage which happens at the time of the loss to be being undertaken'. He concluded that Air France's liability under the contract was limited to 17 SDR per kilo.[5]

The Court of Appeal agreed with Quantum.[6] Mance LJ accepted the direct application of the CMR to an international road leg within a multimodal contract of carriage as 'the concept of a contract for the carriage of goods by road embraces a contract providing for or permitting the carriage of goods by road on one leg, when such carriage actually takes place under such contract.' Paris was the place of receipt, Dublin was the place of delivery, and the Court of Appeal

3 The contract was evidenced by Air France's air waybill and allowed for the carriage by another means of transportation than an airplane. The discussion on the application of the CMR in light of article 18 (4) MC (vertragswidriges Transport, see Chapter 6) did not surface.

4 This is remarkable as article 31 CMR did not establish English jurisdiction between Quantum and Air France, irrespective of the question of whether the forum choice in the air waybill was exclusive or just one of the options under article 31 CMR. M.H. Claringbould, *Syllabus SVA Congress* (2012) 20.

5 *Quantum Corp. v. Plane Trucking* (2001) 2 Lloyd's Rep. 133.

6 *Quantum Corp. v. Plane Trucking* (2002) 2 Lloyd's Rep. 24.

held that the scope of application of the CMR extended to an international road leg within a multimodal contract of carriage.[7]

Although the wording of article 1 (1) CMR not immediately suggests the application of the convention to multimodal transportation, and it is not very likely that such a wide interpretation had been intended or foreseen by the drafters of the convention either,[8] the decision received a lot of support. The CMR was meant to unify the law, and this objective should not be restricted by a narrow interpretation of the wording of the scope of application. For this reason, the judgment in *Quantum Corp. v. Plane Trucking* was welcomed by Haak,[9] Clarke[10] and Hoeks:[11]

> All things considered the objective of the CMR to uniformly regulate the international carriage of goods by road is best served by applying its rules to such carriage even if the contract is multimodal.

The authority of *Quantum Corp. v. Plane Trucking* was later affirmed by the House of Lords in *Datec v. UPS*.[12] The carrier (UPS) had negotiated the freedom to decide on the routing and means of transportation. Exercising that freedom, the goods were carried by truck from Datec's warehouse to Luton Airport (UK), flown to Cologne (Germany), and then again carried by truck to Amsterdam (the Netherlands). Lord Mance held that it was 'common ground that CMR would

7 Referring to case law from (amongst others) courts in Germany and the Netherlands, namely BGH 24 June 1987, TranspR 1987, 447, BGH 17 May 1989, TranspR 1990, 19 and Rechtbank Rotterdam, 28 October 1999, S&S 2000, 35 (*Resolution Bay*). In the resolution Bay the goods were first carried by sea from Port Chalmers (New Zealand) to Rotterdam (the Netherlands), and then damaged in the course of the road leg between Rotterdam and Antwerp (Belgium). Although the combined transport bill of lading referred to English law and jurisdiction, the cargo-interested parties initiated proceedings in Rotterdam. They argued that the road leg between Rotterdam and Antwerp met the requirements of article 1 CMR, and that the court of Rotterdam therefore had jurisdiction in accordance with article 31 (1) (b) CMR. The court of Rotterdam agreed and accepted jurisdiction: 'Since under the combined transport of goods P & O has opted to arrange part of the transport, i.e. from Rotterdam to Antwerp, by truck/by road whereas the contract, as contained in the CT document allows it to do so, the place where P & O . . . took delivery for transport by road, i.e. Rotterdam, counts as the place of receipt stated in the contract for the purpose of article 1 (1) CMR.'

8 On the contrary, the CMR gives very specific rules on multimodal contracts of carriage in article 2 CMR. The application of the CMR beyond ro/ro and piggyback transportation would not seem to make sense in the absence of a specific provision to that extent, especially since article 2 CMR prescribes that the convention then 'nevertheless' applies. Moreover, the Protocol of Signature under the convention provides that the contracting states 'undertake to negotiate conventions governing contracts for furniture removals and combined transport'. This suggests that multimodal contracts of carriage were not (intended to be) covered under the convention at the time of its signing. All these arguments later surfaced in BGH 17 July 2008, TranspR 2008, 365 and HR 1 June 2012, NJ 2012, 516, S&S 2012/95 (*Godafoss*).

9 Haak was in fact one of the (three) judges in the Rotterdam court deciding on the *Resolution Bay*.

10 M.A. Clarke, *The line in law between land and sea*, JBL (2003) 522.

11 K.F. Haak & M.A.I.H. Hoeks, *Intermodal transport under unimodal arrangements*, TranspR (2005) 89; M.A.I.H. Hoeks, *Multimodal transport law* (Diss.: Rotterdam, 2009) 176.

12 *Datec v. UPS* (2007) 2 Lloyd's Rep. 114.

apply as between UPS and the respondents to the international road carriage which UPS was entitled, and chose, to undertake'.[13]

A different approach in Germany and the Netherlands

The Dutch Supreme Court chose a different approach in the *Godafoss*.[14] Eimskip agreed in November 2003 to carry a shipment of fish from Reykjavik (Iceland) to Naples (Italy). It issued a multimodal waybill for the entire voyage. This multimodal waybill explicitly referred to Icelandic law and jurisdiction. Eimskip carried the goods by sea on board of the *Godafoss* for the first leg between Reykjavik and Rotterdam. The shipment of fish was then discharged in Rotterdam to be carried by truck to Naples, but it was stolen in the course of this road leg.

The leading case in the Netherlands at that time was the Court of Rotterdam judgment in the *Resolution Bay*,[15] a decision that had furthermore just been embraced by the Court of Appeal in *Quantum Corp. v. Plane Trucking*.[16] Once the cargo insurers had reimbursed their assured for the loss of the fish, they therefore confidently ignored the jurisdiction clause in the waybill and initiated proceedings in Rotterdam. In line with the judgments in the *Resolution Bay* and *Quantum Corp. v. Plane Trucking*, the Rotterdam court indeed assumed jurisdiction on the basis of articles 31 and 41 CMR,[17] and awarded the claim.

Eimskip appealed, and its timing was impeccable. Shortly after the judgment in the first instance, but well before the judgment in appeal, the German Supreme Court rendered its landmark decision of 17 July 2008.[18] The shipper and the carrier had agreed on the carriage of a shipment of copiers from Tokyo (Japan) to Monchengladbach (Germany) under a multimodal waybill. This waybill referred to Japanese law and jurisdiction. The copiers were first carried by sea from Tokyo to Rotterdam, and then by road from Rotterdam to Monchengladbach. They arrived at their destination in a damaged condition, and the cargo-interested parties initiated proceedings in Germany.

The carrier relied on the jurisdiction clause in the waybill. In fact, he challenged the competence of the German courts up to the Supreme Court.[19] The German Supreme Court had several objections against the application of the CMR.[20] It held that the wording of article 1 (1) CMR did not cover multimodal

13 This outcome was hardly a surprise (although the decision was unanimous) as Lord Mance had also written the leading judgment in *Quantum Corp. v. Plane Trucking* (2002) 2 Lloyd's Rep. 24.

14 HR 1 June 2012, NJ 2012, 516, S&S 2012/95 (*Godafoss*).

15 Rechtbank Rotterdam, 28 October 1999, S&S 2000, 35 (*Resolution Bay*).

16 *Quantum Corp. v. Plane Trucking* (2002) 2 Lloyd's Rep. 24.

17 The first instance decision in the Godafoss is in fact a copy of the decision in the Resolution Bay, Rechtbank Rotterdam 11 April 2007, S&S 2009/55 (*Godafoss*).

18 BGH 17 July 2008, TranspR 2008, 365.

19 The court of appeal, OLG Düsseldorf 28 September 2005-I-18U 162/02, had held that the competence of the German courts followed from article 31 CMR.

20 The Supreme Court decision in fact mentions a total of six arguments. Only arguments one, two, three and five are discussed here; the remaining two relate to German (case) law.

transportation, that the exception of article 2 CMR only applied to ro/ro and piggyback transportation, that the Protocol of Signature suggested that the convention failed to apply to multimodal transportation, and that the objective of the CMR was just to provide uniform rules for unimodal contracts of carriage by road.[21]

Whereas the Rotterdam court only had the benefit of the judgments in the *Resolution Bay* and *Quantum Corp. v. Plane Trucking*, the Court of Appeal in The Hague could now also draw arguments from the 2008 German Supreme Court decision,[22] and indeed it did. The court followed the German approach, and in the process also introduced a new argument. The court stressed the potential difficulties for the identification of the competent court in the case of ongoing or unlocalized losses:[23]

> These rules link the jurisdiction to the place where the goods are taken over respectively the place designated for delivery, but in the case of multimodal transport these places do not always correspond with the beginning or final destination of the road leg. Especially when damage occurs during several legs, or when it cannot be localized, undesirable issues regarding the jurisdiction may surface, which would not benefit legal certainty. This is an argument to allow an exclusive choice of forum for multimodal contracts.

This is indeed a convincing argument.[24] The damage in the *Godafoss* had occurred solely in the course of the road leg between Rotterdam and Naples, but it would have been difficult to isolate the road leg and label Rotterdam as the 'place where the goods were taken over by the carrier' if the damage had in fact occurred continuously throughout the entire voyage from Reykjavik to Naples.[25]

The problem becomes even bigger if an extra leg is added to the multimodal contract of carriage for argument's sake. Italy is obviously a contracting state

21 The Supreme Court also discussed the decision in *Quantum*, and specifically the reference of the Court of Appeal in that case to the BGH judgment of 24 June 1987, 'a case that was subject to German law', and therefore not subject to the direct application of the CMR. BGH 17 July 2008, TranspR 2008, 365.

22 Although De Meij and Spiegel/De Vos had also already defended this position before 2008. See P. de Meij, *Samenloop van CMR-Verdrag en EEX-Verordening* (Kluwer: Deventer, 2003); J. Spiegel/G.J.H. de Vos in M.L Hendrikse/Ph.H.J.G. van Huizen (eds) *CMR: Internationaal vervoer van goederen over de weg* (Paris: Zutphen, 2005).

23 Hof's-Gravenhage 22 June 2010, S&S 2010/104 (*Godafoss*).

24 Mutatis mutandis the same problem may surface for the beginning of the time bar or for the question who has the right of disposal; see J. Lojda, 'The impact of CMR on multimodal transport' in *International transportation* (Czech Yearbook of International Law, Vol. 6) (New York: Huntington, 2015) 150; J. Spiegel/G.J.H. de Vos in M.L Hendrikse/Ph.H.J.G. van Huizen (eds) *CMR: Internationaal vervoer van goederen over de weg* (Paris: Zutphen, 2005) 68.

25 From a practical point of view, the jurisdiction issue in the case of an unlocalized loss could arguably be solved by the division of the burden of proof. If the claimant relies on article 31 (1) (b) CMR alone for the competence of the court seized, he will have to prove that the damage occurred during the road leg. If he succeeds, the jurisdiction problem does not surface. If he does not succeed, however, the jurisdiction problem does not surface either as the court then simply lacks jurisdiction.

to the CMR, but what would happen if the shipment of fish were subsequently carried from Naples to Singapore? Since neither Iceland nor Singapore is a contracting party to the CMR, the convention might then not even apply at all.

The Court of Appeal decision was affirmed by the Dutch Supreme Court two years later.[26] Weighing all the available arguments, the court followed its German counterpart, and affirmed the decision by the Court of Appeal. The Supreme Court found 'that it must be accepted that the CMR in general does not apply to multimodal transport other than mode-on-mode transport'.[27] It is submitted that this is the correct approach.[28]

8.2. The direct application of the other unimodal conventions to individual legs

The arguments for and against the direct application of the CMR are not always helpful, let alone decisive, to determine whether the CIM 1999, HVR, MC and CMNI apply directly to rail, sea, air and inland navigation legs within multimodal contracts of carriage.

Rail legs within multimodal contracts of carriage

It is safe to say that the discussion on the direct application of the CIM 1999 to rail legs within multimodal contracts of carriage has been prejudiced by the developments under the CMR. There is hardly any light between the scope of

26 HR 1 June 2012, NJ 2012, 516, S&S 2012/95 (*Godafoss*).

27 The decision has been extensively discussed afterwards; see e.g. M.A.I.H. Hoeks, *Vallend water en verdwenen vis* NTHR (2012) 237; M.H. Claringbould, *Multimodaal vervoer en de CMR: De Hoge Raad heeft gesproken*, W&W (26) (2012) 10 and M. Spanjaart, *Godafoss, the applicability of the CMR within multimodal contracts of carriage* TranspR (2012) 278.

28 One of the few reported US judgments on the application of the CMR is in the *OOCL Bravery*, but the decision is (unfortunately in both instances) not very helpful in the discussion at hand. A shipment of bicycle parts was carried from Wisconsin to the Netherlands, the first leg by road, the second leg by rail, the third leg by sea to Belgium and the fourth leg from Belgium to the Netherlands by road. The goods went (partially) missing during this last road leg. The bill of lading contained two 'choice of law' provisions; article 23 said: 'All carriage under this Bill of Lading to or from the United States of America shall have effect subject to the provisions of COGSA.' Article 4 said: 'Each stage of the transport shall be governed according to any law and tariffs applicable to such stage.' In the first instance, the court held that the US COGSA 1936 applied mandatorily to the entire contract; see *OOCL Bravery* (2000) 1 Lloyd's Rep. 394. This was wrong as these provisions only apply mandatorily from tackle-to-tackle. They can be extended to apply to the entire voyage, but then only as contractual rules that do not override other provisions in the bill of lading. On appeal (2001 AMC 25 2nd Cir. 2000), the court thus had a chance to choose for either the Quantum or Godafoss option, but instead it chose neither option. The court held that the CMR applied, but it reached this outcome by arguing that the goods were stolen in Belgium, a CMR country, and that the CMR applied by force of law between Belgium and the Netherlands, and since it applied to that stage, the CMR was the applicable law in accordance with article 4. The Court of Appeal thus still needed article 4 to come to the application of the CMR, but that would have meant that the floating choice of law in article 4 was effectively the choice for a convention and not for the law of a country.

application of the two conventions. Whereas the CMR applies to 'every contract for the carriage of goods by road in vehicles for reward', the CIM 1999 applies to 'every contract of carriage of goods by rail for reward'. Besides, both conventions link the jurisdiction to 'the place where the goods were taken over by the carrier or the place designated for delivery is situated'.

The exact same arguments for and against the direct application of the CMR will therefore steer the discussion on the reach of the CIM 1999. The UK courts will apply the convention to rail legs within multimodal contracts of carriage.[29] The German and Dutch will apply the law applicable to the multimodal contract of carriage.[30]

For obvious reasons, there are not that many US decisions on the (direct) application of the CIM 1999 within multimodal contracts of carriage, but the US Supreme Court decision in *Norfolk v. Kirby*,[31] and more in particular its decision in *KKK v. Regal-Beloit*,[32] suggest that the US courts would have followed the German/Dutch approach.

The Japanese carrier KKK accepted a shipment of fireworks for transportation from China to several destinations in the US. KKK carried the goods by sea from China to Long Beach (US), and then instructed Union Pacific for the second leg by train to the various destinations in the Midwest. KKK issued a multimodal bill of lading to evidence the contract of carriage.[33] This multimodal bill of lading stipulated that the US COGSA governed the entire voyage, and furthermore provided for Japanese law and jurisdiction.

This time the tension was not between the provisions of the contract and the scope of application of the CMR or CIM 1999, but instead between the provisions of the contract and the scope of application of the Carmack Amendment.[34] This amendment gives mandatory rules for the interstate carriage of goods by rail. Amongst others it provides that claims 'may be brought in a district court of the United States or in a State court'. The application of the Carmack Amendment, however, is subject to certain conditions. The Carmack Amendment for instance prescribes that the 'rail carrier . . . shall issue a receipt or a bill of lading for property it receives for transportation under this part', and this was something that Union Pacific had not done.

29 *Quantum Corp. v. Plane Trucking* (2001) Lloyd's Rep. 133; *Datec v. UPS* (2007) 2 Lloyd's Rep. 114.

30 BGH 17 July 2008, TranspR 2008, 365; HR 1 June 2012, NJ 2012, 516, S&S 2012/95 (*Godafoss*). If the applicable law is either German or Dutch law, the rail leg may then very well be governed by the CIM 1999 after all, but then via the application of the domestic network system (see section 8.3).

31 *Norfolk v. Kirby* (2004) AMC 2705.

32 *KKK v. Regal-Beloit* (2010) AMC 1521.

33 The judgment consequently refers to a through bill of lading instead of a multimodal bill of lading but the two are not the same; see the discussion in Chapter 3. The reference to a through bill of lading should best be reserved for a(n in principle) port-to-port bill of lading that allows for transhipment in combination with sub-contracting; see D. Rhidian Thomas, *Multimodalism and through transport: Language, concepts, and categories* Tul. Mar. L.J. (2012) 761.

34 The Carmack Amendment of 1906 to the Interstate Commerce Act, 49 U.S.C. § 11706.

The train derailed in Colorado and the goods were damaged. Regal-Beloit (and its insurers) initiated proceedings against KKK in Los Angeles (US), and thus not in Japan as prescribed by the contract of carriage. Regal-Beloit argued that the Carmack Amendment applied to the contract, and that the jurisdiction clause Tokyo was overruled by its mandatory application.

KKK on the other hand relied on the jurisdiction clause in the multimodal bill of lading and challenged the competence of the US courts. Hence the dispute in a nutshell: did the Carmack Amendment govern this domestic rail leg within a multimodal contract of carriage? In the absence of a separately issued receipt or bill of lading, the Supreme Court held that Union Pacific was only a delivering carrier under KKK's multimodal bill of lading contract, and therefore not a receiving carrier regulated by the Carmack Amendment:

> 'K' Line received the goods in China, under through bills for shipment into the United States. 'K' Line was thus not a receiving rail carrier under Carmack and was not required to issue bills of lading under that Amendment. Union Pacific is also not a receiving carrier for this carriage and was thus not required to issue Carmack-compliant bills. Because the journey included no receiving rail carrier that had to issue bills of lading under Carmack, Carmack does not apply. The parties' agreement to litigate these cases in Tokyo is binding. The cargo owners must abide by the contracts they made.

The situation is obviously different, but still to some extent comparable. The US Supreme Court refused to stretch the reach of the Carmack Amendment to domestic carriage by rail under a multimodal bill of lading. The jurisdiction clause in the contract therefore remained perfectly valid in the absence of mandatory rules on jurisdiction.

Sea legs within multimodal contracts of carriage

Obviously, the discussion on the application of the HVR to sea legs within multimodal contracts of carriage only surfaces when the contract of carriage is covered by 'a bill of lading or any similar document of title'. Once a (multimodal) bill of lading has been issued, however, it is submitted that the HVR indeed govern the sea leg within a multimodal contract of carriage.

There are several good arguments for this submission.[35] The first of these arguments relates to the wording of article I (b) HVR. Whereas article 1 (1) CMR refers to 'every contract for the carriage of goods by road', article I (b) HVR in fact refers to 'contracts of carriage covered by a bill of lading or any similar document of title, in so far as such document relates to the carriage of

35 Although hardly an argument in this discussion, it is in any case noteworthy that the COGSA 1992 also applies to multimodal bills of lading; see *The Law Commission and The Scottish Law Commission Rights of suit in respect of carriage of goods by sea* (HMSO: London, 1991) 20.

goods by sea'. The decisive difference comes from the words 'in so far as'. These words imply that the HVR also govern sea legs in the performance of a wider contract, provided of course that this contract is covered by a (multimodal) bill of lading or similar document of title.

This textual argument is closely related to the second argument, i.e. that the drafters of the Hague Rules explicitly contemplated the effect of the rules on sea legs under through bills of lading.[36] When the delegates first met in The Hague, the proposed wording of article I (b) still referred to 'a bill of lading or any similar document of title relating to the carriage of goods by sea'. Delegate Paine, representing the Banker's Association, made the following remarks on the scope of the rules and suggested a wider definition:[37]

> We have to remember that there are such things as through bills of lading, and we want these Rules to govern that part of through bills of lading which relates to contracts of carriage by sea. I suggest, therefore, the insertion after the word 'relating' of the words 'wholly or in part', so as to cover the question of through bills of lading. ... I think we are all in agreement (I think it is only a question of drafting) that where a banker, or anybody else, is dealing with a through bill of lading, he does get the benefit of these rules in so far as that bill of lading relates to carriage of goods by sea.

The last argument relates to the Court of Appeal (and Supreme Court) decision in the *Godafoss*.[38] Apart from the interpretation of the scope of the convention, the application of the CMR on road legs within multimodal contracts of carriage could be problematic in the case of an ongoing or unlocalized loss. This is indeed an argument against the application of the CMR, but it does not play any role in the application of the HVR as the rules do not give any provisions on jurisdiction.

All in all, the arguments against the application of the CMR on road legs within multimodal contracts of carriage do not affect the application of the HVR to sea legs within multimodal contracts of carriage.[39] The wording of article I (b) HVR is wider than the wording of article 1 (1) CMR; its application to sea legs was furthermore explicitly discussed in the drafting process and complicating jurisdictional issues do not arise.

36 Through bills of lading are not the same as multimodal bills of lading. The difference between the two documents was discussed in Chapter 3, but does not affect the relevance of Delegate Paine's remark. In fact, see D.A. Glass, *Freight forwarding and multimodal transport contracts* (Informa: London, 2012) saying at 248 that 'the development of combined transport documentation took the form of adaptation of through transport documents.'

37 F. Berlingieri (ed.) *The Travaux Préparatoires of the Hague and Hague-Visby Rules* (CMI: Antwerp, 1997) 90–1.

38 Hof's-Gravenhage 22 June 2010, S&S 2010/104; HR 1 June 2012, NJ 2012, 516, S&S 2012/95 (*Godafoss*).

39 M.A.I.H. Hoeks, *Multimodal transport law* (Diss.: Rotterdam, 2009) 319.

Air legs within multimodal contracts of carriage

There can be little doubt that the MC applies to air legs within multimodal contracts of carriage. First of all, the wording of article 1 (1) MC is again wider than the wording of article 1 (1) CMR. Whereas article 1 (1) CMR refers to 'every contract for the carriage of goods by road', article 1 (1) MC refers to 'all international carriage . . . performed by aircraft'. A specific contract for the carriage of goods by air is therefore not required by article 1 (1) MC.

More importantly, however, the drafters have explicitly addressed multimodal contracts of carriage including an air leg in the convention. Once the contract has been identified as a multimodal contract of carriage, as opposed to a unimodal contract of carriage with ancillary services,[40] article 38 (1) MC provides that the convention only governs the air leg within this multimodal contract of carriage:

> In the case of combined carriage performed partly by air and partly by any other mode of carriage, the provisions of this Convention shall, subject to paragraph 4 of Article 18, apply only to the carriage by air, provided that the carriage by air falls within the terms of Article 1.

Admittedly, article 38 (1) MC has been worded somewhat restrictively ('only'), but with regard to the question at hand, it is quite clear that the provisions of the convention apply to an air leg within a multimodal contract of carriage.[41] If the damage occurred during the carriage by air, and provided that the requirements of article 1 MC have been met, the liability of the multimodal carrier is governed by the convention.[42] The direct application of the convention then implies that the plaintiff may initiate proceedings against the carrier before any court identified by article 33 (1) MC.[43]

Obviously, this leaves a jurisdiction problem as article 33 (1) MC (amongst others) links the jurisdiction to the place of destination.[44] It is submitted, however, that this jurisdiction problem does not affect the rule of article 38 (1) MC.

First of all, the drafters of the convention clearly contemplated the convention's role in multimodal contracts of carriage, and they explicitly addressed the

40 Consequently, the presumption of the second sentence of article 18 (4) MC is limited to unimodal contracts of carriage by air; it cannot apply to multimodal contracts of carriage that include an air leg.

41 I. Koning, *Aansprakelijkheid in het luchtvervoer* (Paris: Zutphen, 2007) 125; W. Verheyen, *Afbakening toepassingsgebied vervoerverdragen door nationale wetgever: aanleiding tot parallelle procedures onder Brussel I (bis)?* NTHR (2016) 51; J. Spiegel/G.J.H. de Vos in M.L Hendrikse/Ph.H.J.G. van Huizen (eds) *CMR: Internationaal vervoer van goederen over de weg* (Paris: Zutphen, 2005) 71.

42 E. Giemulla/R. Schmid, *Montreal Convention* (Kluwer: New York, 2007) under 38 (1) MC.

43 Article 33 (1) MC reads: 'An action for damages must be brought, at the option of the plaintiff, in the territory of one of the States Parties, either before the court of the domicile of the carrier or of its principal place of business, or where it has a place of business through which the contract has been made or before the court at the place of destination.'

44 Hof's-Gravenhage 22 June 2010, S&S 2010, 104; HR 1 June 2012, NJ 2012, 516, S&S 2012/95 (*Godafoss*).

issue in article 38 (1) MC. Such a provision in a uniform, mandatory convention cannot be set aside because of jurisdictional inconveniences.[45]

Second, but that is really more of a practical than a legal argument, the jurisdiction problem under the MC is only half the size of the jurisdiction issues under the CMR and CIM 1999. Article 33 (1) MC only refers to the place of destination, and does not mention the place of receipt.

Third, the jurisdiction problem is arguably just academic. Article 38 (1) MC prescribes that the convention shall 'apply only to the carriage by air, provided that the carriage by air falls within the terms of Article 1'. Article 1 MC in turn requires 'international carriage . . . performed by aircraft'. The wording of these two provisions combined suggests that the convention, including thus article 33 (1) MC, does not apply to multimodal contracts of carriage when it cannot be established that damage occurred in the course of the air leg.[46]

Inland navigation legs within multimodal contracts of carriage

The CMNI is still a very young convention. There have not been very many cases on carriage of goods by inland waterways yet, and certainly not on inland navigation legs within multimodal contracts of carriage. Since the convention fails to give specific guidance in this respect,[47] the question of whether the CMNI applies to these individual legs is theoretically still open.

Again, however, the answer may have been prejudiced by the discussion on the scope of application of the CMR. Whereas the CMR applies to 'every contract for the carriage of goods by road in vehicles for reward', the CMNI applies 'if the purpose of the contract of carriage is the carriage of goods . . . on inland waterways'. Although the UK is not a contracting state to the convention, it seems likely that the English courts would be tempted to apply *Quantum v. Plane Trucking* to an inland navigation leg within a multimodal contract of carriage.[48]

In fact, an extra argument in favour of its direct application is that the convention does not give any jurisdiction rules. Consequently, the jurisdiction problem does not surface under the CMNI. Another argument in favour may be derived from article 16 (2) CMNI.[49] This provision prescribes that the carrier's liability beyond the tackle-to-tackle period, including thus any prior or subsequent carriage

45 *Sidhu v. British Airways* (1997) 2 Lloyd's Rep. 76.

46 The application of the convention cannot be assumed just to have article 33 (1) MC take effect, and the air leg would in that case be governed by the law applicable to the multimodal contract of carriage and the provisions of the contract. The provisions of the contract, for instance evidenced by a multimodal waybill, will probably include a jurisdiction clause.

47 See M.A.I.H. Hoeks, *Multimodal transport law* (Diss.: Rotterdam, 2009), observing at 238 that 'its designers must have known of the ambiguity concerning the interpretation of the scope of application rules of the CMR, yet they failed to take appropriate measures to prevent the CMNI from following the same path.'

48 M.A. Clarke, *Carriers' liability in cross border air cargo substitute transportation* TranspR (2005), 182; M.A.I.H. Hoeks, *Multimodal transport law* (Diss.: Rotterdam, 2009) 237.

49 M.A.I.H. Hoeks, *Multimodal transport law* (Diss.: Rotterdam, 2009) 238.

by other means of transportation 'shall be governed by the law of the State applicable to the contract of carriage'.[50]

In spite of all these arguments, however, it is submitted that the material scope of the convention provides a decisive argument against its direct application to inland navigation legs within multimodal contracts of carriage. Article 2 (2) CMNI stipulates that the convention applies 'if the purpose of the contract of carriage is the carriage of goods, without transhipment, both on inland waterways and in waters to which maritime regulations apply'.

The key lies in the words 'without transhipment'. Since the transfer from one means of transportation to the next more or less necessarily requires the transhipment of the goods,[51] this restriction implies that the convention only governs unimodal contracts of carriage by inland waterways, on occasion extended to waterways on which maritime regulations apply.[52]

8.3. The application of a domestic network system

When the individual legs of a multimodal contract of carriage are not directly governed by one of the unimodal conventions, they are governed by the law applicable to the multimodal contract of carriage.[53] Obviously, there are as many domestic systems as there are countries. Some countries will not have any specific provisions on contracts of carriage in place at all,[54] others will just have one set of provisions to govern contracts of carriage in general and again others will have separate provisions for the different unimodal contracts of carriage.[55] Several countries, however, including Argentina, Brazil, China, Germany, India, Mexico and the Netherlands, have incorporated mandatory provisions on multimodal contracts of carriage in their legislation.[56]

The network/chameleon system

It obviously goes beyond the scope of this book to discuss all these legislations one by one, but that is really not necessary. All these different legislations have

50 Other than article 38 (1) MC, though, article 16 (2) CMNI does not explicitly target multimodal transport, it just restricts the application of the convention to the tackle-to-tackle period.

51 Transhipment is not always required, though; see for instance ro/ro or piggyback transport. In theory, the CMNI could therefore apply to the carriage of a shipment of gravel in a push barge, first pushed by an inland navigation vessel, and later relieved by a sea-going vessel.

52 K. Ramming, *Hamburger Handbuch zum Binnenschifffahrtsfrachtrecht* (C.H. Beck: München, 2009) 98.

53 O. Hartenstein, *Die Bestimmung des Teilstreckenrechts im Multimodaltranportvertrag TranspR* (2005) 9; M.A.I.H. Hoeks, *Multimodal transport law* (Diss.: Rotterdam, 2009) 356; A. van Beelen *Multimodaal vervoer* (Diss.: Leiden, 1996) 97.

54 The contract of carriage is then governed by the provisions on contractual obligations in general.

55 France, for instance, has regulated several unimodal contracts of carriage in its Code des Transports, but multimodal contracts of carriage have not specifically been regulated. P. Seck 'De vernieuwde', *Franse Code des Transports TVR* (2016) 118.

56 See the Unctad report UNCTAD/SDTE/TLB/2/Add. 1 of 9 October 2001.

adopted a more or less similar network system, also known as the chameleon system.[57] The regime changes colour with each change in the means of transportation; see for instance article 8:41 DCC prescribing that 'each leg of the carriage shall be governed by the legal rules applicable to that leg.'[58] The provision does not distinguish between mandatory and supplementary legal rules, and therefore encompasses both.[59]

The network system does not settle the conflict of laws.[60] In fact, the domestic network system that governs the multimodal contract of carriage was found as a result of the prior application of conflict rules,[61] and further renvoi is not allowed.[62] The reference to the 'legal rules applicable to that leg' is therefore not a reference to the law of a certain country, but instead a reference to the rules that govern contracts of carriage by a certain means of transportation.[63]

The network system can perhaps best be explained with an example of a multimodal contract of carriage, for instance for the carriage of a shipment of tea from Sri Lanka to Poland. The tea is first carried by truck from the interior to the port of Colombo (Sri Lanka), then by sea to Hamburg (Germany) and then by road again to Warsaw (Poland). The multimodal contract of carriage in this example contains a choice for Dutch law and jurisdiction of the court of Rotterdam.

Once the application of Dutch law has been established on the basis of the rules of private international law, the network system of article 8:41 DCC then ensures that the road leg within Sri Lanka is governed by Dutch domestic law on carriage of goods by road. It is perhaps tempting to apply local domestic law to the carriage by road within Sri Lanka, but incorrect. The network system does not identify the applicable law; the law that applies to the multimodal contract

57 R. de Wit, *Multimodal transport* (LLP: London, 1995) 138.

58 Mutatis mutandis the same applies when the domestic legislation of a country prescribes different rules for different means of transportation, and the network system is applied to multimodal contracts of carriage by its courts. See for the UK for instance *Datec v. UPS* (2007) 2 Lloyd's Rep. 114 and *Quantum Corp. v. Plane Trucking* (2002) 2 Lloyd's Rep. 24, discussed in Chapter 8. See for the US S.G. Wood in A. Kiantou-Pampouki (ed.) *Multimodal transport* (Bruylant: Brussels, 2000) 249. See for Belgium for instance Rechtbank van Koophandel Antwerpen 25 June 1976, ETL 1976, 691; Rechtbank van Koophandel Antwerpen 18 January 2005, ETL 2006, 543 and Hof van Beroep Antwerpen 25 October 2004, ETL 2006, 79 where the Court of Appeal held 'that, when, as in this case, not all legs are maritime, for those legs that have been performed by another means of transportation, the regime will apply that applies to that specific means of transportation'.

59 M.H. Claringbould (ed.) *Parliamentary history book 8 DCC* (Kluwer: Deventer, 1992) 93.

60 A. van Beelen, *Multimodaal vervoer* (Diss.: Leiden, 1996) 90; O. Hartenstein, *Die Bestimmung des Teilstreckenrechts im Multimodaltranportvertrag TranspR* (2005) 9; J. Spiegel/G.J.H. de Vos in M.L Hendrikse/Ph.H.J.G. van Huizen (eds) *CMR: Internationaal vervoer van goederen over de weg* (Paris: Zutphen, 2005) 74.

61 This necessarily implies that domestic network systems will not take effect if the multimodal contract of carriage contains a valid floating choice of law whereby the applicable law changes with each new leg. The chosen law then governs that leg and the domestic network system does not come into play.

62 J. Spiegel/G.J.H. de Vos in M.L Hendrikse/Ph.H.J.G. van Huizen (eds) *CMR: Internationaal vervoer van goederen over de weg* (Paris: Zutphen, 2005) 74; see also the discussion of the basic principles in Chapter 7.

63 A. van Beelen, *Multimodaal vervoer* (Diss.: Leiden, 1996) 91.

of carriage has already been identified. The network system only identifies the applicable legal rules.[64]

The regime that applies to the sea leg depends on the transport documentation. The domestic network system cannot override the direct application of mandatory conventions. If the sea leg is therefore covered by a bill of lading or any similar document of title, or if the entire multimodal contract of carriage is evidenced by a multimodal bill of lading,[65] it is mandatorily governed by the HVR.[66] If the sea leg is not covered by any transport document,[67] the HVR do not apply directly.[68] Since Dutch law applies to the multimodal contract of carriage, the sea leg is in that case governed by Dutch domestic law on carriage of goods by sea pursuant to article 8:41 DCC.[69]

Finally, the road leg from Germany to Poland is governed by the CMR. The convention does not apply directly, though;[70] the convention only applies to the road leg because article 8:41 DCC prescribes its application.[71] The CMR forms part of Dutch law, it gives the 'legal rules applicable' to an international contract of carriage of goods by road and its provisions mandatorily regulate the multimodal carrier's liability during the road leg.

The application of conventional rules via a domestic network system

The different unimodal conventions discussed in this book are meant to be uniform and exclusive.[72] The application of a convention via a domestic network system, however, affects its uniform and exclusive character.

64 Obviously, the contract of sub-carriage between the multimodal carrier and his Sri Lankan sub-carrier for the road leg may be subject to Sri Lankan law. This then also implies that any recourse proceedings between the multimodal carrier and the sub-carrier may be subject to a different law than the law that applies between the multimodal carrier and the shipper/consignee. See the discussion of the recourse gap in Chapter 4.

65 See the previous section for a discussion on the application of the HVR to sea legs within multimodal contracts of carriage covered by 'a bill of lading or any similar document of title'.

66 Articles I (b), III (8) and X HVR.

67 Dutch law has a peculiar tendency to apply uniform rules whenever the opportunity arises. See in this respect the Supreme Court decision in HR 29 June 1990, NJ 1992, 106, S&S 1990/110 (Gabriëla Wehr), but also article 8:46 DCC: 'For the part of the transport, that will take place as carriage by sea or inland waterways in accordance with the contract between the parties, the multimodal transport document is deemed to be a bill of lading.'

68 Or if the sea leg is subject to a charter party, see articles I (b) and V HVR.

69 The contract would then be subject to more or less the same rules (as the HVR have been incorporated with a few alterations in the DCC), but Dutch domestic law on carriage of goods by sea is supplementary in the absence of a bill of lading or any similar document of title (article 8:382 DCC).

70 Hof's-Gravenhage 22 June 2010, S&S 2010, 104; HR 1 June 2012, NJ 2012, 516, S&S 2012/95 (*Godafoss*).

71 The CMR could have applied directly if the circumstances were only slightly different. If the port of Hamburg in the example were substituted for the port of Southampton (UK), the English courts would have assumed jurisdiction on the basis of article 31 (1) (b) CMR; see *Datec v. UPS* (2007) 2 Lloyd's Rep. 114 and *Quantum Corp. v. Plane Trucking* (2002) 2 Lloyd's Rep. 24.

72 *Sidhu v. British Airways* (1997) 2 Lloyd's Rep. 76, and see Chapter 5.

If the CMR, for example, applies to a contract for the carriage of goods by road because the requirements of articles 1 and 17 CMR have been met, the convention applies in full force. Article 13 CMR deals with the right of suit, article 31 CMR regulates the jurisdiction and article 32 CMR sets the limitation period, and all these rules apply mandatorily pursuant to article 41 CMR. If, however, the CMR applies to the road leg within a multimodal contract of carriage because a domestic network system prescribes its application, this is no longer possible as the application of the convention cannot change the course of events with retroactive effect.

The example of the multimodal contract of carriage from Sri Lanka to Poland may again be helpful to explain this. The contract refers to jurisdiction of the court of Rotterdam. Once the Rotterdam court has assumed jurisdiction on the basis of the forum choice in a multimodal contract of carriage, it applies its own conflict rules to determine the law applicable to the contract. Dutch law then governs the contract in accordance with article 3 Rome I, and the application of the network system of article 41 and further leads to CMR. Clearly, the provisions of articles 31 and 33 CMR are then no longer relevant as the jurisdiction of the Rotterdam court has already been established.

In fact, it is submitted that the provisions in the CMR on the right of suit, successive carriage and even the limitation period are also ineffective.[73] The application of the convention cannot affect the law applicable to the multimodal contract of carriage, the law in fact that led to its application to the road leg in the first place. The application of the CMR via a domestic network system therefore really just means the mandatory application of those provisions of the CMR relating to the carrier's liability.

The liability of the carrier for localized losses

The multimodal carrier's liability under the network system is governed by the legal rules that apply to the leg where the damage occurred.[74] Arguably, this is

73 This also follows from articles 8:42, 43 and 1722 DDC. This last provision regulates the limitation period (of in principle one year) in multimodal contracts of carriage under Dutch law. This limitation cannot be suspended in accordance with article 32 CMR, not even when the CMR were to govern the road leg. In fact, article 8:1722 DDC explicitly stipulates that the period starts running on 'the day of delivery under the multimodal contract of carriage'. § 452b GCC gives a similar provision for the notice period: '§ 438 applies irrespective of whether the place of damage is unknown, is known or becomes known later. The form and time limit prescribed for the notice of damage shall be deemed to have been observed as well if the corresponding provisions which would have been applicable to a contract of carriage covering the last leg of the carriage have been complied with.' The result is arguably the same in the absence of such explicit provisions, though.

74 The German network system of § 452 GCC is only activated when 'at least two of these contracts would have been subject to different legal rules'. Given the uniform approach of 'Landschaden' under German law, a multimodal contract of carriage by road and rail would therefore not be subject to the network system of § 452 GCC, but would instead be subject to the general provisions of § 407 and further GCC.

already an implicit consequence of the network system,[75] but the first sentence of § 452a GCC stipulates for good measure:[76]

> If it has been established that the loss, damage or event which caused delay in delivery occurred on a specific leg of the carriage, the liability of the carrier shall, contrary to the provisions of the first sub-chapter, be determined in accordance with the legal provisions which would apply to a contract of carriage covering this leg of carriage.

The reference to 'the legal provisions which would apply', instead of 'the legal rules applicable' as in article 8:41 DCC, has caused several German authors to read this provision as a conflict rule. The leg in question would then be governed by the hypothetically applicable law.[77]

It is submitted that this is a wrong approach.[78] § 452a GCC does not deal with the conflict of laws.[79] The conflict of laws has already been settled by the applicable conflict rules at an earlier stage. When German law applies as a result thereof, § 452a GCC cannot reopen this discussion once again as it could lead to renvoi.[80] The reference to 'legal provisions which would apply' is therefore the exact same criterion as 'the legal rules applicable to that leg' or 'the regime . . . that applies to that specific means of transportation'.[81] German law applies to the individual legs, and § 452a GCC settles the question which rules of German law govern the carrier's liability for a specific leg.

Given the different rules (on limitation of liability) for the different means of transportation, the carrier and the cargo-interested parties will often disagree on the question during which leg the damage occurred. When the localization of the damage is indeed in dispute, the second sentence of § 452a

75 The Indian Multimodal Transportation of Goods Act (IMTGA) only contains a reference to the limits, and not to the rules. Article 15 of the IMTGA stipulates that the carrier's 'limit of liability . . . shall be determined in accordance with the provisions of the relevant law applicable in relation to the mode of transport during the course of which the loss or damage occurred and any stipulation in the multimodal transport contract to the contrary shall be void and unenforceable'.

76 Article 105 of the Chinese Maritime Code (CMC) gives a similar rule: 'If loss of or damage to the goods has occurred in a certain section of the transport, the provisions of the relevant laws and regulations governing that specific section of the multimodal transport shall be applicable to matters concerning the liability of the multimodal transport operator and the limitation thereof.'

77 See for instance I. Koller, *Die Haftung des Multimodalbeförders bei bekannten Schadensort VersR* (2000), 1188; D. Rabe, *Die Probleme bei einer multimodalen beförderung unter Einslchluss einer Seestrecke – Sind Lösungen in Sicht?* TranspR (2000) 194, and very recently D. Merkt, *Becksche Kurzkommentare HGB* (2016) 1651: '§ 452a contains a special provision for the applicable law.'

78 The original German text does not support this approach either. § 452a GCC specifically refers to 'Rechtsvorschriften' that would apply, and not the 'Recht' (law) that would apply.

79 O. Hartenstein, *Die Bestimmung des Teilstreckenrechts im Multimodaltranportvertrag TranspR* (2005) 9.

80 See article 20 Rome I: 'The application of the law of any country specified by this Regulation means the application of the rules of law in force in that country other than its rules of private international law, unless provided otherwise in this Regulation.'

81 See respectively article 8:41 DCC and Hof van Beroep Antwerpen 25 October 2004, ETL 2006, 79.

GCC ensures that 'the burden of proving that the loss, damage or event which caused delay in delivery occurred on a particular leg of carriage is borne by the person alleging this'.[82]

The liability of the carrier for unlocalized losses

The network system has an obvious blind spot. Which legal rules govern the carrier's liability if it cannot be determined during which leg the damage occurred? There is no general answer to this question. In fact, the different domestic network systems have actually produced three possible answers to the question.

If the leg where the damage occurred cannot be identified, one obvious possibility is to apply the provisions on contracts of carriage in general. This is for instance the fall-back solution of § 452a GCC. The network system applies to localized losses only, and if the leg where the losses occurred cannot be established (or if the losses occurred in the course of several legs), the carrier's liability is governed by the general provisions of § 407 and further GCC.[83] Article 106 CMC in fact provides for the same solution:

> If the section of transport in which the loss of or damage to the goods occurred could not be ascertained, the multimodal transport operator shall be liable for compensation in accordance with the stipulations regarding the carrier's liability and the limitation thereof as set out in this Chapter.

A second possibility is to regulate the liability of the carrier for unlocalized losses in the specific provisions on multimodal contracts of carriage. Article 13 of the IMTGA prescribes that the carrier is liable for the loss of and damage to the goods in his charge, but article 14 (1) and (2) of the IMTGA stipulates that:

> the liability of the multimodal transport operator to pay compensation shall not exceed two Special Drawing Rights per kilogram of the gross weight of the consignment lost or damaged or 666.67 Special Drawing Rights per package or unit lost or Damaged, whichever is higher.
>
> ... if the multimodal transportation does not, according to the multimodal transport contract, include carriage of goods by sea or by inland waterways, the liability of the multimodal transport operator shall be limited to an amount not exceeding 8.33 Special Drawing Rights per kilogram of the gross weight of the goods lost or damaged.

82 Again, this division of the onus of proof more or less already follows from the network system itself, but the rule is also in line with generally accepted principles of civil procedure.

83 § 407 (1) GCC codifies the receptum nautarum: 'By virtue of the contract of carriage the carrier is obliged to carry the goods to their destination and there to deliver them to the consignee.' § 431 GCC limits the liability of the carrier to 8.33 SDR for each kilogram of gross weight. The paradox is that the legal certainty actually increases in the case of unlocalized losses, W. Verheyen, *Contractuele aansprakelijkheid van vervoersintegratoren* (Diss.: Leuven, 2013) 373.

Article 8:43 (1) DCC provides a third possibility, and this is surely the most adventurous of the options. The fact that damage cannot be localized fully remains for the account of the carrier, and the cargo-interested parties may invoke the highest limitation available:[84]

> If the multimodal carrier is liable for the damage ... and it has not been established where the event leading to the damage occurred then his liability is determined in accordance with the legal rules applicable to the leg or legs of the transport where this event could have occurred and which results in the highest award for the damage.[85]

8.4. The application of contractual (network) provisions

If a multimodal contract of carriage is not governed by conventional or domestic mandatory law, and if the individual legs of that multimodal contract of carriage are not subject to conventional or domestic mandatory law either,[86] the contracting parties are free to regulate their relation in the multimodal contract of carriage. This freedom of contract is rather relative, though. Multimodal contracts of carriage are seldom negotiated line for line; instead they are often evidenced by standard documents issued by the carrier.

The last section of this chapter discusses the relevant (network) provisions of two of these standard multimodal contracts of carriage, the Multidoc 1995 and the multipurpose MSC Bill of Lading.[87] There are of course numerous other transport documents in circulation, but their provisions will often resemble the contractual network system of one of these two documents.[88]

The Multidoc 1995

The Multimodal Transport Bill of Lading (Multidoc 1995) was drafted by the Baltic and the International Maritime Council (Bimco), and its network system is subject

84 This is mandatory law, article 8:43 (2) DCC.

85 The same rule applies under Belgian law, see for instance Rechtbank van Koophandel Antwerpen 13 May 2010, ETL 2011, 223: 'When the carrier in a case of multimodal transportation is liable for damage, and, as in this case, it has not been established where the event leading thereto occurred . . . the liability of carrier must be determined in accordance with the regime that leads to the highest amount of compensation.'

86 This mandatory law can be a convention (sections 8.1 and 8.2) or a domestic network system (section 8.3).

87 The Multimodal Transport Waybill (Multiwaybill 1995, also drafted and issued by Bimco) is the non-negotiable sister of the Multidoc 1995. Its article 12 is almost identical to article 12 of the Multidoc 1995.

88 These two documents are (primarily) maritime documents, and this is for a reason. It is not really customary for (road or rail) consignment notes to evidence multimodal contracts of carriage. Air waybills will occasionally evidence multimodal contract of carriage (just think of *Quantum Corp. v. Plane Trucking* discussed earlier in this chapter). The air leg within such a contract of carriage will on the basis of article 38 MC often be subject to the MC (or one of its predecessors) anyhow, but if one of the legs or an ancillary service is not governed by a mandatory convention, the carrier's liability may be subject to contractual exclusions and limitations listed in the air waybill.

to the UNCTAD/ICC Rules for Multimodal Transport Documents.[89] Article 10 makes the carrier responsible for the goods from the time of receipt to the time of their delivery. Article 12 then regulates the limitation of liability under the (different legs of the) multimodal contract of carriage.[90] Article 12 (a) reads:

> Unless the nature and value of the Goods have been declared by the Consignor before the Goods have been taken in charge by the MTO and inserted in the MT Bill of Lading, the MTO shall in no event be or become liable for any loss of or damage to the Goods in an amount exceeding: (i) when the Carriage of Goods by Sea Act of the United States of America, 1936 (US COGSA) applies USD 500 per package or customary freight unit; or (ii) when any other law applies, the equivalent of 666.67 SDR per package or unit or two SDR per kilogramme of gross weight of the Goods lost or damaged, whichever is the higher.

Article 12 (a) is not a Paramount clause. The provision does not select the US COGSA 1936, but only confirms that the carrier's liability is subject to its USD 500 per package limitation if the US COGSA 1936 applies. When any other law applies, the carrier's liability is limited to the HVR/CMNI limitation of 666.67 SDR per collo or 2 SDR per kilo.[91]

These 'wet' limits of liability do not apply, however, if the multimodal contract of carriage lacks a sea or inland waterways leg. In that case article 12 (c) prescribes that 'the liability of the MTO shall be limited to an amount not exceeding 8.33 SDR per kilogramme of gross weight of the Goods lost or damaged.' This corresponds with the CMR limitation of liability, but the limit is significantly lower than the CIM 1999/MC limitation of liability. The potential conflict is addressed in article 12 (d):[92]

> In any case, when the loss of or damage to the Goods occurred during one particular stage of the Multimodal Transport, in respect of which an applicable international convention or mandatory national law would have provided

89 ICC Publication No 481; J. Richardson, *Combined Transport Documents* (LLP: Hong Kong, 2000) 202–3. The ICC 1992 are a compromise between the earlier ICC 1975 and the MTC 1980, see H.M. Kindred/M.R. Brooks, *Multimodal transport rules* (Kluwer: The Hague, 1997) 35 and onwards.

90 See P.M. Bugden/S. Lamont-Black, *Goods in transit* (Sweet & Maxwell: London, 2013) at 455 in this respect: 'BIMCO Multidoc 95 is not a traditional document and like the Multimodal Convention, the basis of liability in uniform but the limits of liability vary.'

91 Article 12 (b) stipulates: 'Where a container, pallet or similar article of transport is loaded with more than one package or unit, the packages or other shipping units enumerated in the MT Bill of Lading as packed in such article of transport are deemed packages or shipping units. Except as aforesaid, such article of transport shall be considered the package or unit.'

92 This will not always be a problem, though. The contractual solution of article 12 (d) is redundant when the individual legs of the multimodal contract of carriage are directly governed by a convention; see sections 8.1 and 8.2.

> another limit of liability if a separate contract of carriage had been made for that particular stage of transport, then the limit of the MTO's liability for such loss or damage shall be determined by reference to the provisions of such convention or mandatory national law.

Article 12 (d) is really the only true network provision in the Multidoc 1995. It works on the basis of chain of fictive unimodal contracts of carriage and regulates the limits of liability. The limitation of liability that would have applied to each fictive unimodal contract of carriage applies to each individual leg within the multimodal contract of carriage. Article 12 (d) does not incorporate the different unimodal conventions; it only incorporates their respective limits.

The carrier's liability under a multimodal contract of carriage from Busan (South Korea) to Ljubljana (Slovenia) would then be subject to different limitations for the different legs. The sea leg from Busan to Piraeus (Greece) would be subject to the 666.67 SDR/collo or 2 SDR/Kg limitation.[93] The road leg from Piraeus to Ljubljana would then be subject to an 8.33 SDR/Kg limit.

The reference to 'In any case' ensures that article 12 (d) prevails over the other provisions of article 12.[94] If the sea leg from Busan to Piraeus were substituted for an air leg from Seoul (South Korea) to Athens (Greece), the multimodal contract of carriage would lack a sea or inland waterways leg. The air leg would then not be subject to the 8.33 SDR/Kg limit, though, but would instead be subject to the 19 SDR/Kg limit of the MC as article 12 (d) supersedes article 12 (c).[95]

Article 12 (e) limits the carrier's liability for consequential and immaterial losses to the amount of the freight,[96] article 12 (f) ensures that the limited liability cannot exceed the total loss,[97] and article 12 (g) stipulates:

> The MTO is not entitled to the benefit of the limitation of liability if it is proved that the loss, damage or delay in Delivery resulted from a personal act or omission of the MTO done with the intent to cause such loss, damage or delay, or recklessly and with knowledge that such loss, damage or delay would probably result.

93 The Multidoc 1995 is a bill of lading in the sense of article I (b) HVR and the sea leg is therefore subject to the HVR limitation. Article 12 (a) (ii) ensures that the sea leg under a charter party or waybill is subject to the exact same limitation. In fact, since article 12 (a) (i) only refers to the COGSA 1936, the provision also ensures that a bill of lading contract under the Hague Rules is subject to the (higher) HVR limitation.

94 See the Explanatory Notes to the Multidoc 1995.

95 The 19 SDR limit arguably applies anyhow on the basis of article 38 MC, but the right of way of article 12 (d) also ensures that international rail legs are subject to a 17 SDR/Kg limit.

96 Article 12 (e) reads: 'If the MTO is liable in respect of loss following from delay in Delivery, or consequential loss or damage other than loss of or damage to the Goods, the liability of the MTO shall be limited to an amount not exceeding the equivalent of the freight under the Multimodal Transport Contract for the Multimodal Transport.'

97 The aggregate liability of the MTO shall not exceed the limits of liability for total loss of the Goods.

This criterion is in line with articles 36 CIM 1999, IV (e) HVR and 21 (1) CMNI, but it is stricter than article 29 CMR (since it requires a personal act), and more lenient again than article 22 (3) MC (since it can be broken). Still, there is no conflict between these different provisions. If an international air leg is directly governed by the MC, article 22 (3) MC applies mandatorily and the provision of article 12 (g) is null and void.[98] Mutatis mutandis the same applies if the CMR applies directly to an international road leg.[99] If the CMR does not apply directly, though,[100] its 8.33 SDR/Kg limitation of liability is only incorporated as a contractual rule on the basis of article 12 (d), and the contracting parties are free to agree on stricter requirements than those of the CMR in the absence of mandatory law.

The Multidoc 1995 does not explicitly regulate unlocalized losses. The limitation of liability for unlocalized losses is therefore governed by the provisions of article 12 (a) and (c). If the multimodal contract of carriage includes a sea leg, the limitation of liability for unlocalized losses is basically subject to a 666.67 SDR/collo or 2 SDR/Kg limitation.[101] If the multimodal contract of carriage does not include a sea leg, the carrier's liability for unlocalized losses is limited to 8.33 SDR/Kg.

The multipurpose MSC bill of lading

For obvious reasons the network system of article 5 of the MSC bill of lading is more carrier-friendly. The provisions of this document were first of all drafted by MSC's own lawyers, and its network system is furthermore not subject to the UNCTAD/ICC Rules.[102]

The bill of lading differentiates between port-to-port and multimodal carriage. Article 5.1 deals with port-to-port carriage (only). Article 5.1 (a) contains a before and after clause, article 5.1 (b) makes the bill of lading subject to the Hague Rules unless the HVR are compulsorily applicable, and article 5.1 (c) ensures that the carrier can still rely on the provisions of the Hague Rules if he were for any reason liable for damage beyond the tackle-to-tackle period.

Article 5.2 governs the carrier's liability in the case of multimodal transportation. The presence of other legs does not affect the carrier's liability for the sea leg. Article 5.2.1 ensures that where 'the loss or damage occurred during the Port-to-Port section of the carriage, the liability of the Carrier is in accordance with clause 5.1 above', including therefore the before and after clause of article 5.1 (a). It is submitted that this is a rather awkward combination as the clause shoots

98 Article 38 jo 49 MC.

99 *Datec v. UPS* (2007) 2 Lloyd's Rep. 114; *Quantum Corp. v. Plane Trucking* (2002) 2 Lloyd's Rep. 24, and then in combination with article 41 CMR.

100 BGH 17 July 2008, TranspR 2008, 365; HR 1 June 2012, NJ 2012, 516, S&S 2012/95 (*Godafoss*).

101 Unless the US COGSA 1936 applies, then the carrier's liability is limited to USD 500 per package.

102 www.msc.com/nga/contract-of-carriage/bl-standard-terms-conditions.

(two) liability holes in the carrier's period of responsibility under the multimodal contract of carriage.[103] All the same, the before and after clause also applies to sea legs within multimodal contracts of carriage.[104]

In the *Iris* a container with deep-frozen butter had to be carried from Tuitjenhorn (the Netherlands) to Leek (UK) under a multimodal contract of carriage.[105] The container was first carried by truck from Tuitjenhorn to the port of Rotterdam to be brought on board of the *Iris* for the subsequent sea leg to Hull (UK). The container arrived in Rotterdam, was placed in the carrier's outgoing stack, but was never brought on board of the *Iris*. Instead, the container was brought on board of the Cardigan Bay, bound for Hong Kong. Upon arrival of the ship in Hong Kong, the butter was no longer fit for consumption.

The cargo-interested parties initiated proceedings against the carrier, and the carrier relied on the before and after clause in the bill of lading. The Dutch Supreme Court established that the road leg had ended with the delivery of the container to the sea carrier in the port of Rotterdam, and that the sea leg had begun upon receipt of the container by the sea carrier. From then on, including therefore all the events between the outgoing stack and the passing of the ship's rail of the Cardigan Bay, the carrier's liability was governed by the applicable maritime rules.[106] Since these rules allowed for a contractual exclusion of liability for damage to the goods 'before they have crossed ships' rail in loading or after they have crossed the ship's rail in discharging operation', the carrier could successfully rely on the before and after clause in the bill of lading.[107]

The carrier's liability for damage in the course of any of the other legs is then regulated through a contractual network system in article 5.2.2. (a). The carrier's liability is determined 'by the provisions contained in any international convention, national law or regulation applicable to the means of transport utilized, if such convention, national law or regulation would have been compulsorily applicable in the case where a separate contract had been made in respect to the particular stage of transport concerned'.

103 See in this way also J.H.J. Teunissen in his comment on the Supreme Court decision in the *Iris*, JutD (1995) 7.

104 In the *Arawa* a shipment of frozen lamb carcasses was carried by sea from Auckland (NZ) to London (UK). Initially, the plan was to discharge the carcasses at King George V Dock, but the parties later agreed to discharge the goods into lighters to bring them to Chambers Wharf instead. Unfortunately, however, the carcasses could not be discharged from the lighters into the wharf because of a strike, and deteriorated as a result of the delay. The carrier relied on the before and after clause in the bill of lading, and the Court of Appeal denied the claim of the cargo-interested parties. Obviously, the varied discharge procedure did not convert the unimodal contract into a multimodal contract, but the decision does underline the extent of the before and after clause. The *Arawa* (1980) 2 Lloyd's Rep. 137.

105 HR 24 March 1995, S&S 1995/72 (*Iris*).

106 Article 8:41 and further DCC; see the discussion in section 8.3.

107 Still, the working of the before and after can of course be restricted by mandatory domestic law. See for instance *Eutectic Corp. v. M/V Gudmundra* (1973) 367 F. Supp. 681 (SDNY) where the court held that 'the liability of the carrier prior to loading and after discharge is made subject to the Harter Act.'

Whereas the Multidoc 1995 only incorporates the limitation of liability of the mandatory law that would applied, the MSC bill of lading incorporates the provisions of the entire convention, national law or regulation that would have applied mandatorily. The full system of liability is therewith incorporated in the multimodal contract of carriage, albeit solely as a set of contractual rules.[108]

Article 5.2.2 (b) and (c) then regulates the situation whereby the leg (or legs) in the course of which the damage occurred would not have been governed by mandatory law.[109] In that case, the carrier's liability is in principle subject to the provisions as they apply between the carrier and his subcontractor for the leg in question.[110] If for some reason the carrier cannot rely on the provisions of the contract of sub-carriage, his liability is determined in accordance with article 5.1. The carrier's liability, either under the provisions of the contract of sub-carriage or under article 5.1, is subject to a maximum of GBP 100 per package.

Finally, article 5.2.2 (d) tackles any unlocalized losses in the course of the multimodal contract of carriage. The burden to proof that the damage occurred during a specific leg rests with the cargo-interested parties, and 'if the place of loss or damage cannot be established by the Merchant, then the loss or damage shall be presumed to have occurred during the Port-to-Port section of carriage and the Carrier's liability shall be determined as provided at 5.1 above.'[111]

108 See the discussion in Chapter 7 and the *European Enterprise* (1989) 2 Lloyd's Rep. 185.

109 Article 5.2.2 (b) (c) stipulates that 'where no international convention, national law or regulation would have been compulsorily applicable, by the contract of carriage issued by the Subcontractor carrier for that stage of transport, including any limitations and exceptions contained therein, which contract the Merchant and the Carrier adopt and incorporate by reference, it being agreed that the Carrier's rights and liabilities shall be the same as those of the Subcontractor carrier, but in no event whatsoever shall the Carrier's liability exceed GBP 100 sterling legal tender per package, or if any court shall determine that no international convention, national law or regulation would have been compulsorily applicable and that the Carrier may not determine its liability, if any, by reference to the applicable Subcontractor's contract of carriage or where said Subcontractor carrier does not have a contract of carriage, then it is contractually agreed as between the Merchant and the Carrier that the Carrier's liability shall be determined as if the loss and/or damage complained of occurred during the Port-to-Port section of carriage as provided at 5.1 above, but in no event whatsoever shall the Carrier's liability exceed GBP 100 sterling legal tender per package.'

110 The objective of article 5.2.2 (b) is to create a back-to-back situation whereby a possible recourse gap is avoided. The carrier is then perhaps liable for the damage, but he knows that his recourse on the subcontractor is subject to the exact same terms and conditions.

111 The different terms and conditions for different situations on the reverse of the multipurpose bill of lading will not always be equally compatible; see for instance *Finagra v. O.T. Africa Line* (1998) 2 Lloyd's Rep. 622.

9 The Rotterdam Rules

The last chapter of this book deals with the United Nations Convention on Contracts for the International Carriage of Goods wholly or partly by Sea, better known as the Rotterdam Rules (RR). The RR were signed in 2009, but they have not entered into force yet. Whereas 20 ratifications are required,[1] only three countries have ratified the convention so far. In due course, however, the rules may prescribe a mandatory network system for multimodal contracts of carriage that include a sea leg.

The new system was deemed necessary because the HVR (or any of the other existing unimodal conventions) were never really designed to cover multimodal contracts of carriage. Besides, the limitation of liability has meanwhile not been amended for half a century,[2] and the traditional (physical) transport documents (of title) are in practice more and more often replaced by (electronic) equivalents.[3] All these factors were recognized by the drafters of the rules,[4] and have consequently been addressed in the convention.[5]

Still, there are a few problems with the RR.[6] A general problem is that the rules are not very accessible. The convention struggles with its identity,[7] overregulates

1 Article 94 (1) RR.

2 The SDR protocol of 1980 has changed the 'currency', but not the corresponding amount.

3 The bill of lading has for instance almost disappeared in short sea carriage.

4 See the Preamble: 'Concerned that the current legal regime governing the international carriage of goods by sea lacks uniformity and fails to adequately take into account modern transport practices, including containerization, door-to-door transport contracts and the use of electronic transport documents.'

5 See respectively articles 59, 1 (17/20) and 5 (1) RR.

6 A. Diamond, *The Rotterdam Rules* LMCLQ (2009) 536. His overall conclusion was: no substantial degree of uniformity, little balance and too much uncertainty. A. Tettenborn in D. Rhidian Thomas (ed.) *The carriage of goods by sea under Rotterdam Rules* (Informa: London, 2010) 89 concluded that 'the changes it introduces are of doubtful utility, and the uncertainties it leaves us with are a disgrace.' T. Nikaki/B. Soyer, 'A new international regime for carriage of goods by sea: Contemporary, certain, inclusive and efficient, or just another one for the shelves?', 30 *Berkeley J. Int'l Law.* 303 (2012) 348 also stressed the rather practical problem 'that the implementation of the Rules might lead to an increase in the liability of a maritime performing parties such as terminal handlers, multimodal transport operators and freight forwarders, and any such increase might lead to irrational purchase of liability insurance, thereby increasing the cost of international carriage of goods by sea'.

7 M.A.I.H. Hoeks, *Multimodal transport law* (Diss.: Rotterdam, 2009) 284.

with too many (96) provisions[8] and the wording of these provisions is often very difficult.[9] With regard to multimodal contracts of carriage in particular, an obvious problem is that the RR only govern those multimodal contracts of carriage that include a sea leg.

9.1. The scope of application

Just as with each of the unimodal conventions on carriage of goods discussed in Chapter 5, the RR have a material, a formal and a temporal scope of application. Article 79 (1) RR ensures that the convention in the basis applies mandatorily to those contracts within its scope of application:

> Unless otherwise provided in this Convention, any term in a contract of carriage is void to the extent that it … excludes or limits the obligations … or … the liability of the carrier or a maritime performing party for breach of an obligation under this Convention.

Article 79 (2) RR mirrors this provision with regard to the obligations and liability of the cargo-interested parties, but with one subtle difference. Whereas the liability of the carrier/maritime performing party cannot be excluded or limited, the liability of the cargo-interested parties cannot be excluded, limited or increased.

The material scope of application

Other than the HVR, the RR do not require 'a bill of lading or any similar document of title'. In fact, the RR merely require freight and a sea leg. Article 1 (1) RR defines the contract of carriage in the first sentence, and gives the convention's material scope of application in the second:

> 'Contract of carriage' means a contract in which a carrier, against the payment of freight, undertakes to carry goods from one place to another. The contract shall provide for carriage by sea and may provide for carriage by other modes of transport in addition to the sea carriage.

Still, not every contract of carriage within the definition of article 1 (1) RR is governed by the rules. Article 6 (1) RR excludes charter parties and (other) contracts for the use of a ship from the scope of application.[10] Article 6 (2) RR in

8 D. Rhidian Thomas in D. Rhidian Thomas (ed.) *The carriage of goods by sea under Rotterdam Rules* (Informa: London, 2010) 25: 'a dangerous cocktail of too many ingredients of the wrong kind'.

9 See for instance the provisions on the transport documents, the right of control and the jurisdiction and arbitration.

10 Charter parties are not defined by the rules (and they are not defined by the HVR either), but it seems safe to assume that the exclusion covers bare boat, time, voyage and slot charter parties. F. Lorenzon in Y. Baatz, C. Debattista, F. Lorenzon, A. Serdy, H. Staniland, M. Tsimplis, *The*

principle excludes tramp shipping (non-liner transportation) from the scope of application,[11] but a contract of non-liner transportation is in fact covered by the rules when a transport document or electronic transport record is issued.[12]

Article 7 RR has the same objective as the final part of article I (b) HVR, but its scope is wider.[13] The rules do not apply between the initial parties to the contracts listed under article 6 RR, but they do apply 'between the carrier and the consignee, controlling party or holder that is not an original party to the charter party or other contract of carriage excluded from the application of this Convention'.

In addition to the different contracts excluded in article 6 RR, the convention furthermore does not apply to certain carriage-related matters, such as global limitation of liability, general average, passenger claims and damage caused by nuclear incidents.[14]

Volume contracts, live animals and deck cargo

The drafters of the rules have created a carve-out position for so-called volume contracts, for the carriage of live animals and for the carriage of goods on deck. These different situations are still governed by the convention, but subject to a more relaxed regime.

Volume contracts cover 'the carriage of a specified quantity of goods in a series of shipments during an agreed period of time'.[15] A volume contract is in principle regulated by the convention, but not mandatorily. Article 80 RR allows the parties to the contract to depart from the provisions of the convention,[16] albeit under specific conditions.[17]

Rotterdam Rules: A practical annotation (Informa: London, 2009) 20. S.D. Girvin, *Carriage of goods by sea* (OUP: Oxford, 2011) 286–7 suggests an analogy with article 1 (4) LLMC. F. Berlingieri, *Revisiting the Rotterdam Rules* LMCLQ (2010) 591 refers to corresponding provision in article 1 (f) of the Arrest Convention 1999. See in this respect also *MSC Napoli* (2009) 1 Lloyd's Rep. 246; The *Tychy* (1999) 2 Lloyd's Rep 11.

11 See, however, M.F. Sturley, T. Fujita, G. van der Ziel, *The Rotterdam Rules* (Sweet & Maxwell: London, 2010), saying at 41 that tramp shipping is a narrower concept. Liner transportation and non-liner transportation are in any case defined in article 1 (3) and (4) RR.

12 The use of the word 'issued', instead of 'covered' as in article I (b) HVR, suggests that the intention to issue a document or record is not enough to trigger the application of the rules. This is different under the HVR. Tuckey LJ said in *The Happy Ranger* (2002) 2 Lloyd's Rep. 357: 'It does not seem to me that the rules are concerned with whether the bill of lading contains terms which have been previously agreed or not. It is the fact that it is issued or that it is contemplated which matters. If a bill of lading is or is to be issued the contract is "covered" by it or "provides for its issue" within the definition of art. 1(b) and s. 1(4) of the 1971 Act.'

13 M.F. Sturley, T. Fujita, G. van der Ziel, *The Rotterdam Rules* (Sweet & Maxwell: London, 2010) 43.

14 Articles 83, 84, 85 and 86 RR.

15 Article 1 (2) RR defines the volume contract.

16 Article 80 RR only refers to the carrier and the shipper in this respect, but will equally apply to a maritime performing party. R. Williams in B. Soyer/A. Tettenborn (eds) *Carriage of goods by sea, land and air: Unimodal and multimodal transport in 21st century* (Informa: London, 2014) 231.

17 See article 80 (2) RR.

Article 81 RR gives a similar rule for the carriage of live animals and other goods of which the 'character or condition of the goods or the circumstances and terms and conditions under which the carriage is to be performed are such as reasonably to justify a special agreement'.[18] This time the rule only works one way. The contracting parties are free to exclude or limit the liability of the carrier and maritime performing party.[19]

Article 25 RR regulates the carriage of goods by sea on deck.[20] Article 25 (1) RR prescribes that goods may only be carried on deck if this is required by law, if they are carried in containers or vehicles that are fit for deck carriage and for which the decks are specially fitted, or if the carriage on deck is either agreed upon or customary.

If the goods are carried on deck in the case of either of these three circumstances, the carrier is not liable if the damage, loss or delay results from the special risks of the carriage of goods on deck. The carriage of goods on deck in containers or vehicles that are fit for deck carriage and for which the decks are specially fitted does not create such a special risk, though, and such carriage therefore remains subject to the main liability regime of the rules.[21]

If, however, the goods are carried on deck in other circumstances than those permitted by article 25 (1) RR, the carrier is liable for any loss, damage or delay as a result of the carriage on deck. In fact, article 25 (3) RR stipulates that he can then no longer rely on the exemptions from liability of article 17 RR.

The formal scope of application

Article 5 RR gives the formal scope of application of the convention. The rules apply to all contracts of carriage (within the material scope of application) whereby either the place of receipt and the place of delivery or the port of loading and the port of discharge are situated in different countries,[22] and if, according to the contract of carriage, any one of the following places is located in a Contracting State:

18 Provided, however, that 'such contract of carriage is not related to ordinary commercial shipments made in the ordinary course of trade and that no negotiable transport document or negotiable electronic transport record is issued for the carriage of the goods'.

19 Article 81 (a) RR Article 81 (a) RR stipulates that 'any such exclusion or limitation will not be effective if the claimant proves that the loss of or damage to the goods, or delay in delivery, resulted from an act or omission of the carrier or of a person referred to in article 18, done with the intent to cause such loss of or damage to the goods or such loss due to delay or done recklessly and with knowledge that such loss or damage or such loss due to delay would probably result.'

20 The rule on deck cargo in article 25 RR deviates from the HVR at this point. Under the HVR 'cargo which by the contract of carriage is stated as being carried on deck and is so carried' does not qualify as 'goods' in the sense of article I (c) HVR, and is therefore not governed by the HVR. The solution of the RR is really more in line with article 17 (4) (a) CMR.

21 F. Berlingieri, *Revisiting the Rotterdam Rules* LMCLQ (2010) 605.

22 These different countries are not necessarily contracting states, H. Staniland in Y. Baatz, C. Debattista, F. Lorenzon, A. Serdy, H. Staniland, M. Tsimplis, *The Rotterdam Rules: A practical annotation* (Informa: London, 2009) 17.

(a) The place of receipt;
(b) The port of loading;
(c) The place of delivery; or
(d) The port of discharge.

The option of article X (c) HVR has not returned in the RR. The parties to the contract can therefore not establish the mandatory application of the convention contractually, but they can still incorporate its provisions by reference. The rules then apply as contractual provisions.[23]

The temporal scope of application

Since the convention (also) governs multimodal contracts of carriage that include a sea leg, the temporal scope of application obviously stretches beyond the tackle-to-tackle period.[24] Article 12 (1) RR defines the period of responsibility:[25]

> The period of responsibility of the carrier for the goods under this Convention begins when the carrier or a performing party receives the goods for carriage and ends when the goods are delivered.

The parties to the contract are obviously free to determine the place of receipt and delivery as they see fit,[26] but article 12 (3) RR also allows them to determine the time of receipt and delivery in their contract, provided that the agreed time of receipt lies before loading and the agreed time of delivery lies beyond discharge. This ensures that the rules at least apply tackle-to-tackle.[27]

The definition of the period of responsibility in article 12 RR already suggests that the loading and discharge operations are the responsibility of the carrier, and article 13 (1) RR indeed requires the carrier to 'properly and carefully receive, load, handle, stow, carry, keep, care for, unload and deliver the goods'.[28] At the same time, however, article 13 (2) RR stipulates:

> Notwithstanding paragraph 1 of this article, and without prejudice to the other provisions in chapter 4 and to chapters 5 to 7, the carrier and the shipper may agree that the loading, handling, stowing or unloading of the goods is to be performed by the shipper, the documentary shipper or the consignee. Such an agreement shall be referred to in the contract particulars.

23 The *Tasman Discoverer* (2004) 2 Lloyd's Rep. 647; The *European Enterprise* (1989) 2 Lloyd's Rep. 185.
24 Article 1 (e) HVR.
25 This provision closes the 'before and after loop hole' discussed in Chapter 8.
26 Article 12 (3) RR specifically says so, but this also touches on the essence of a contract of carriage.
27 M.F. Sturley, T. Fujita, G. van der Ziel, *The Rotterdam Rules* (Sweet & Maxwell: London, 2010) 62.
28 This provision obviously resembles article III (2) HVR, but the reference to 'properly and carefully' is probably inconsequential from a liability perspective; see section 9.2.

The generally accepted practice of FIOS clauses has this been codified in article 13 (2) RR.[29] The carrier may delegate the loading, handling, stowing or unloading of the goods to the cargo-interested parties. In that case, these activities are not a part of the contract of carriage, and as such they are not governed by the rules either.[30]

The relation between the RR and existing conventions

Even when all these material, formal and temporal requirements have been met, the rules may still not apply to the contract of carriage. Article 82 RR namely ensures that the rules give way to the already existing international conventions on carriage of goods (other than by sea):[31]

> Nothing in this Convention affects the application of any of the following international conventions in force at the time this Convention enters into force, including any future amendment to such conventions, that regulate the liability of the carrier for loss of or damage to the goods:
>
> (a) Any convention governing the carriage of goods by air to the extent that such convention according to its provisions applies to any part of the contract of carriage; (b) Any convention governing the carriage of goods by road to the extent that such convention according to its provisions applies to the carriage of goods that remain loaded on a road cargo vehicle carried on board a ship; (c) Any convention governing the carriage of goods by rail to the extent that such convention according to its provisions applies to carriage of goods by sea as a supplement to the carriage by rail; or (d) Any convention governing the carriage of goods by inland waterways to the extent that such convention according to its provisions applies to a carriage of goods without trans-shipment both by inland waterways and sea.

Article 82 RR only relates to the non-maritime conventions,[32] i.e. CIM (1999), MC (and WC), CMR and CMNI. These are at basis all unimodal conventions, but they may also apply to the carriage of goods by sea,[33] for instance a supplemental

29 The *Jordan II* (2005) 1 Lloyd's Rep. 57; *Pyrene v. Scindia* (1954) 2 QB 402; *Renton v. Palmyra* (1957) AC 149.

30 The provision does not distinguish between loading, handling, stowing and unloading operations at the beginning, at the end or in the course of the voyage. Surely, however, given the period of responsibility defined by article 12 (3) RR, the delegation of these activities only relates to the loading, handling, stowing and unloading operations at the beginning or at the end of the voyage. See in this respect also *Mayhew Foods v. Overseas Containers* (1984) 1 Lloyd's Rep. 317.

31 The provision only relates to conventions that are already in force or any amendments thereto. The RR will therefore not give way to future conventions. F. Berlingieri, *International maritime conventions: The carriage of goods and passengers by sea, Vol. 1* (Routledge: London, 2014) 132.

32 This makes sense as article 89 RR requires contracting states to denounce the Hague Rules, HVR and Hamburg Rules.

33 These are the multimodal situations discussed in Chapter 6.

sea leg in the sense of article 1 § 4 CIM 1999, the carriage by sea in violation of the agreement to carry the goods by air in the sense of article 18 (4) MC,[34] a ro/ro sea leg in the course of a road transport in the sense of article 2 (1) CMR or inland navigation yet partly by sea in the sense of article 2 (2) CMNI. These (multimodal) contracts of carriage remain governed by the existing conventions, and they are not governed by the RR.

Some of these non-maritime conventions also apply directly to unimodal legs within multimodal contracts of carriage. Article 38 MC for instance ensures that international air legs within multimodal contracts of carriage are governed by the convention, and the House of Lords has held that international road legs within multimodal contracts of carriage are governed by the CMR.[35] Arguably, these unimodal legs within a multimodal contract of carriage (that includes a sea leg) also remain governed by the MC and the CMR, and not governed by the RR.[36]

Article 82 RR, in spite of its position near the end of the convention, is thus essentially a scope rule as it restricts the operation of the rules.[37] The convention basically applies to a contract of carriage (partially) by sea, but it does not apply if such a contract falls within the scope of application of one of the existing conventions on the carriage of goods.[38]

9.2. The system of liability

Apart from the (network) provisions in article 26 RR, the system of liability of the RR is really not very different from the systems discussed in Chapter 5. The carrier must deliver the goods to the consignee, on time, and in the same condition as in which he received them for transport.[39] If the carrier fails to achieve this result, he is liable for the loss, damage or delay unless the convention prescribes otherwise.

The liability of the carrier

Article 17 RR deals with the (basis of) liability under the convention. These provisions apply to the contract of carriage irrespective of whether the goods were carried by a sea-going ship or by any other means of transportation. Article 17 (1) RR gives the main rule:[40]

34 Ancillary carriage by sea in the sense of article 18 (4) MC is not very likely.

35 *Datec v. UPS* (2007) 2 Lloyd's Rep. 114; *Quantum Corp. v. Plane Trucking* (2002) 2 Lloyd's Rep. 24. Arguably, given the similar scope of application of the CMR and CIM 1999, this case law mutatis mutandis also applies to international rail legs within multimodal contracts of carriage.

36 M.F. Sturley, T. Fujita, G. van der Ziel *The Rotterdam Rules* (Sweet & Maxwell London 2010) 72.

37 Chapter 17 RR is in fact titled: 'Matters not governed by this convention'.

38 M.A.I.H. Hoeks, *Multimodal transport law* (Diss.: Rotterdam, 2009) 302.

39 The obligation to deliver the goods without delay is not regulated in the HVR, and as such is not subject to its mandatory regime either. Article 21 RR speaks of delay in delivery 'when the goods are not delivered at the place of destination provided for in the contract of carriage within the time agreed'.

40 The HVR do not contain such an explicit provision, but the same rule follows from its system of liability (articles III (1), III (2), IV (1) and IV (2) HVR).

> The carrier is liable for loss of or damage to the goods, as well as for delay in delivery, if the claimant proves that the loss, damage, or delay, or the event or circumstance that caused or contributed to it took place during the period of the carrier's responsibility as defined in chapter 4.[41]

Article 17 (2) RR provides the first escape. The carrier avoids liability if he 'proves that the cause or one of the causes of the loss, damage, or delay is not attributable to its fault or to the fault of any person referred to in article 18'. This provision closely resembles the catch-all exception of article IV (2) (q) HVR. In spite of its prominent and separate position in the rules, article 17 (2) RR is therefore not very likely to produce a successful defence against cargo claims.[42]

Article 17 (3) RR then lists the carrier's exemptions from liability. Some of these exemptions were borrowed from the catalogue of article IV (2) HVR without further amendments, but there are actually quite a few differences. The most important changes (to the detriment of the carrier) are that the error in navigation has been deleted and the fire exception has been trimmed.[43] On the other hand, the rules have introduced three new exceptions (for the benefit of the carrier) in article 17 (3) (i), (n) and (o) RR. The carrier is exempted from liability if the loss, damage or delay was caused by:

> (a) Act of God;
> (b) Perils, dangers, and accidents of the sea or other navigable waters;
> (c) War, hostilities, armed conflict, piracy, terrorism, riots, and civil commotions;
> (d) Quarantine restrictions; interference by or impediments created by governments, public authorities, rulers, or people including detention, arrest, or seizure not attributable to the carrier or any person referred to in article 18;
> (e) Strikes, lockouts, stoppages, or restraints of labour;
> (f) Fire on the ship;
> (g) Latent defects not discoverable by due diligence;
> (h) Act or omission of the shipper, the documentary shipper, the controlling party, or any other person for whose acts the shipper or the documentary shipper is liable pursuant to article 33 or 34;
> (i) Loading, handling, stowing, or unloading of the goods performed pursuant to an agreement in accordance with article 13, paragraph 2, unless the carrier or a performing party performs such activity on behalf of the shipper, the documentary shipper or the consignee;

41 The last part of this provision is arguably a redundant and perhaps even undesirable addition. The claimant would have to state this in the proceedings anyhow, but he would probably only need to prove this if it were contested by the carrier.

42 S.D. Girvin, *Carriage of goods by sea* (OUP: Oxford, 2011) 490.

43 The words 'unless caused by the actual fault or privity of the carrier' have been left out, and this means that the carrier is more exposed. M. Tsimplis in Y. Baatz, C. Debattista, F. Lorenzon, A. Serdy, H. Staniland, M. Tsimplis, *The Rotterdam Rules: A practical annotation* (Informa: London, 2009) 55.

(j) Wastage in bulk or weight or any other loss or damage arising from inherent defect, quality, or vice of the goods;
(k) Insufficiency or defective condition of packing or marking not performed by or on behalf of the carrier;
(l) Saving or attempting to save life at sea;
(m) Reasonable measures to save or attempt to save property at sea;
(n) Reasonable measures to avoid or attempt to avoid damage to the environment; or
(o) Acts of the carrier in pursuance of the powers conferred by articles 15 and 16.

The carrier cannot rely on these exemptions from liability if either his own fault or a fault of his agents, servants and subcontractors caused or contributed to the events listed in article 17 (3) RR.[44] When the loss, damage or delay was only partially caused by (one of) the exemptions of article 17 (3) RR, article 17 (6) RR reduces the liability of the carrier accordingly.[45]

The seaworthiness of the ship

Article 14 RR requires the carrier to exercise due diligence for the seaworthiness of the ship.[46]

In fact, the carrier is bound before, at the beginning of and during the voyage by sea to exercise due diligence to:

(a) Make and keep the ship seaworthy;
(b) Properly crew, equip and supply the ship and keep the ship so crewed, equipped and supplied throughout the voyage; and
(c) Make and keep the holds and all other parts of the ship in which the goods are carried, and any containers supplied by the carrier in or upon which the goods are carried, fit and safe for their reception, carriage and preservation.

Article 14 RR is almost an exact copy of article III (1) HVR, but there are two significant changes in the wording. The obligation to exercise due diligence for the seaworthiness of the ship has been extended to the entire voyage by sea,[47] and furthermore covers containers supplied by the carrier.[48]

44 Article 17 (4) (a) RR. In light of the framework of article 17 (1), (2) and (3), article 17 (4) (b) RR would seem to have little added value.

45 The rule of article 17 (6) RR refers to the situation whereby the carrier is relieved 'pursuant to this article', and the rule therefore also applies to the exception of article 17 (2) RR.

46 This obligation obviously relates to the carriage of the goods during the sea leg, but a carrier-supplied container in the sense of article 14 (c) RR may also be used to carry the goods from door to door. Arguably, the obligation of article 14 (c) RR should then really apply before, at the beginning of and during the voyage (by sea).

47 Article III (1) HVR only requires such due diligence 'before and at the beginning of the voyage'.

48 The Dutch Supreme Court already anticipated on article 14 (c) RR in the *NDS Provider*, HR 1 February 2008, NJ 2008, 505 (ann. K.F. Haak).

The most important change, however, lies in the strength of the obligation.[49] The exercise of due diligence for the seaworthiness of the ship is not an overriding obligation under the rules.[50] Article 17 (5) RR deals with the relation between (one of) the exempted events and the carrier's shortcomings in exercising due diligence for the seaworthiness of the ship. The carrier remains liable for (part of) the loss, damage or delay if:

> (a) The claimant proves that the loss, damage, or delay was or was probably caused by or contributed to by (i) the unseaworthiness of the ship; (ii) the improper crewing, equipping, and supplying of the ship; or (iii) the fact that the holds or other parts of the ship in which the goods are carried, or any containers supplied by the carrier in or upon which the goods are carried, were not fit and safe for reception, carriage, and preservation of the goods; and
> (b) The carrier is unable to prove either that: (i) none of the events or circumstances referred to in subparagraph 5 (a) of this article caused the loss, damage, or delay; or (ii) it complied with its obligation to exercise due diligence pursuant to article 14.

Multimodal contracts of carriage with a sea leg

The provisions of the convention regulate the carrier's liability during the sea leg, but they do not take precedence over provisions of other 'international instruments' beyond the tackle-to-tackle period.[51] On the contrary, in fact: article 26 RR prescribes a network system for localized losses only.[52] The liability of the carrier is then governed by the provisions of the instrument that would have applied if the parties had made a separate contract for that individual leg:

> When loss of or damage to goods, or an event or circumstance causing a delay in their delivery, occurs during the carrier's period of responsibility but solely before their loading onto the ship or solely after their discharge

49 See for the strength under the Hague (Visby) Rules paragraph 5.2, and the discussion of *Maxine Footwear v. Canadian Government Merchant Marine* (1959) 2 Lloyd's Rep. 105 and HR 11 June 1993, NJ 1995, 235 (ann. Japikse), S&S 1993/123 (*Quo Vadis*).

50 See also article 17 (6) RR: 'When the carrier is relieved of part of its liability pursuant to this article, the carrier is liable only for that part of the loss, damage or delay that is attributable to the event or circumstance for which it is liable pursuant to this article.'

51 Article 26 RR relates to international instruments, and not to international conventions (as in article 82 RR). An instrument seems wider than a convention; it could for instance include an EU or other international regulation. Besides, article 82 RR only relates to existing conventions whereas article 26 RR may in due course also relate to future conventions. M.F. Sturley, T. Fujita, G. van der Ziel, *The Rotterdam Rules* (Sweet & Maxwell: London, 2010) 69.

52 Given the reference in article 2 (2) CMNI to 'without transhipment', article 26 RR is unlikely to incorporate the provisions of the CMNI. The CMNI either applies if the voyage is partly by sea, and then the RR do not apply (article 82 RR), or the CMNI does not apply, and its provisions are then not incorporated via article 26 RR.

from the ship, the provisions of this Convention do not prevail over those provisions of another international instrument that, at the time of such loss, damage or event or circumstance causing delay:

(a) Pursuant to the provisions of such international instrument (that, ms) would have applied to all or any of the carrier's activities if the shipper had made a separate and direct contract with the carrier in respect of the particular stage of carriage where the loss of, or damage to goods, or an event or circumstance causing delay in their delivery occurred;
(b) Specifically provide for the carrier's liability, limitation of liability, or time for suit; and
(c) Cannot be departed from by contract either at all or to the detriment of the shipper under that instrument.

Article 26 RR is not a conflict rule. In fact, there is no need to settle any conflict as the application of the rules to the contract of carriage has already been established.[53] Instead, article 26 RR incorporates the mandatory provisions on the carrier's liability and the limitation period of an international instrument that would have applied to all or any of the carrier's activities if the shipper had made a separate and direct contract with the carrier.[54]

The network system of article 26 RR works in a different way from the (Dutch) domestic network system(s) discussed in Chapter 8. The application of articles 8:40 and further DCC only settles the question of which rules of Dutch law apply to a specific leg within a multimodal contract of carriage. The application of Dutch law itself has already been established at that point, and cannot be set aside anymore, not even when that specific leg would have been governed by a different mandatory domestic law if the shipper and the carrier had made a separate contract for that leg.

Article 26 RR, on the other hand, explicitly prescribes that the carrier's liability is governed by the mandatory provisions of an international convention that 'would have applied to all or any of the carrier's activities if the shipper had made a separate and direct contract with the carrier' for that specific leg.

53 The first sentence of article 26 RR to some extent resembles the rule of article 82 RR, but article 26 RR is not a scope rule. Referring to the report of the 18th session of the working group, Berlingieri has suggested that 'it appears that art. 26 should come first, because art. 82 has been adopted as a compliment to art. 26'. F. Berlingieri, *International maritime conventions: The carriage of goods and passengers by sea, Vol. 1* (Routledge: London, 2014) 121. The same approach seems to be adopted by M.F. Sturley, T. Fujita, G. van der Ziel, *The Rotterdam Rules* (Sweet & Maxwell: London, 2010) 73. It is submitted, however, that it must be the other way around. The application of the convention must have been established, amongst others, on the (restrictive) basis of article 82 RR, for article 26 RR to be applied in the first place. See for the same view on this point P. Neels, *The Rotterdam Rules and maritime transport practices: A successful marriage?* TVR (2011) 7.

54 Article 26 (b) RR suggests that the provisions that relate to the carrier's liability include the limitation period. The provisions of the international instrument on jurisdiction, right of suit, successive carriage and so on are all ineffective as these issues are already regulated by the RR.

The wording of the provision to some extent resembles the wording of § 452a GCC, but this time the renvoi discussion does not surface.[55] When the convention applies, it applies exclusively with regard to the carrier's liability (as regulated amongst others in article 26 RR).[56] The domestic law applicable to the contract then governs the unregulated issues, for instance the carrier's right of retention, and this domestic law remains unaffected by the operation of article 26 RR. In other words: if German law is applicable to certain unregulated issues, German law remains applicable to these issues, irrespective of whether article 26 RR incorporates the provisions of an international instrument. The operation of article 26 RR cannot result in renvoi.

The liability regime for the individual legs within a multimodal contract of carriage under the rules thus ultimately depends on the circumstances of the case. A contract for the carriage of goods by sea from Yokohama (Japan) to Bremen (Germany), and then by road from Bremen to Prague (Czech Republic), is then subject to two different liability regimes. The sea leg is obviously governed by the provisions of the RR. The road leg is governed by articles 17, 18, 23 and 32 CMR as that instrument would have applied if the shipper and carrier had made a separate contract for the carriage of goods by road between Bremen and Prague.[57]

Conversely, a contract for the carriage of goods by sea from Yokohama (Japan) to Los Angeles (US), and then by road from Los Angeles to Belize, is only subject to one liability regime. The sea leg is obviously governed by the provisions of the RR, but so is the road leg as the CMR (or any other international instrument) would not have applied if the shipper and carrier had made a separate contract for the carriage of goods by road between Los Angeles and Belize.

Article 26 RR only refers to the provisions of an international instrument, and not to the provisions of mandatory domestic law. A domestic road leg within China from Shanghai all the way to Urumqi (close to the Kazakhstan border), subsequent to a relatively short sea leg from Yokohama (Japan) to Shanghai, would therefore not be governed by domestic Chinese law, but instead by the provisions of the RR.[58]

The network system of article 26 RR furthermore only regulates localized losses. If the loss, damage or delay cannot 'solely' be traced back to an individual

55 See the discussion in Chapter 8.

56 *Sidhu v. British Airways* (1997) 2 Lloyd's Rep. 76.

57 If such a case were brought before a Dutch (or German) court, the CMR would not apply directly to the international road leg. BGH 17 July 2008, TranspR 2008, 365; HR 1 June 2012, NJ 2012, 516, S&S 2012/95 (*Godafoss*). This means that article 82 RR does not restrict the convention's scope of application, that the entire contract of carriage is then governed by the RR and that the liability and limitation rules of the CMR would regulate the claims for loss, damage or delay that occurred during the road leg in accordance with article 26 RR. If, however, such a claim were brought before a UK court, the CMR would apply directly to the road leg. *Datec v. UPS* (2007) 2 Lloyd's Rep. 114. This means that not just the liability and limitation rules of the CMR, but instead the entire CMR, including the rules on jurisdiction, would regulate the claims for loss, damage or delay that occurred during the road leg.

58 This consequence could prove to be a serious ratification hurdle for bigger countries.

leg beyond the tackle-to-tackle period,[59] the carrier's liability for the unlocalized losses remains governed by the general provisions of article 17 RR.[60]

The division of the burden of proof

Just as under the HVR, the burden of proof in cargo claims shifts from the cargo-interested parties to the carrier and back again, but it shifts in a different way. The starting point is article 26 RR as the division of the burden of proof may very well follow from the mandatory provisions of an international instrument.[61]

In the absence of an international instrument that would have applied or in the case of unlocalized loss, the division of the burden of proof follows from article 17 (1) RR: the cargo-interested parties have to prove that the goods were lost, damaged or delayed between their receipt and delivery.

If they succeed, the carrier can prove that the loss, damage or delay was not attributable to his fault or the fault of someone for whom he is vicariously liable.[62] If the carrier succeeds herein, the discussion ends right there. The carrier is relieved of all liability, or part of his liability if the loss, damage or delay remains to some extent attributable to the fault.

Alternatively, the carrier can prove that the loss, damage or delay was (in part) caused by one of the exceptions listed in article 17 (3) RR. If he succeeds, the cargo-interested parties can prove that the occurrence of the exempted event was (in part) attributable to the carrier's fault or the fault of someone for whom he is vicariously liable.[63]

If the goods were carried by sea, the cargo-interested parties can also prove that the loss, damage or delay was probably caused by the unseaworthiness of the ship. The drafters have burdened the cargo-interested parties with the onus of

59 The reference to 'solely' implies that a damage that occurred during both the sea leg and another leg is also governed by the general provisions of article 17 RR. Contra this point, however, M.A.I.H. Hoeks, *Multimodal transport law* (Diss.: Rotterdam, 2009) 301. This still leaves the question, though, of whether the RR would apply to damage to the goods that occurred during both an international rail leg and an international road leg, yet after their discharge from the ship. The reference to 'such international instrument' and 'the particular stage of carriage' (both singular) in article 26 (a) RR suggests that the rules would govern the carrier's liability in such a (probably rather theoretical) case.

60 This is in line with the German network system (see Chapter 8): if the leg where the loss occurred cannot be established, the carrier's liability is governed by the general provisions of § 407 GCC.

61 If the loss occurred during the international road leg between Bremen and Prague in the example above, the division of the burden of proof would be governed by articles 17 and 18 CMR.

62 See article 17 (2) RR.

63 Article 17 (4) (b) RR stipulates that the carrier would still be liable 'if the claimant proves that an event or circumstance not listed in paragraph 3 of this article contributed to the loss, damage, or delay, and the carrier cannot prove that this event or circumstance is not attributable to its fault or to the fault of any person referred to in article 18'. It is submitted that this is a redundant provision. If it is not an exempted cause, surely the carrier's liability already follows from article 17 (1) RR. If the carrier could prove, however, that the non-exempted cause was not attributable to his fault or the fault of someone for whom he is vicariously liable, he would already escape liability on the basis of article 17 (2) RR.

proof, but the reference to 'probably' certainly eases the threshold. If they succeed, the carrier is liable for the loss, damage or delay, unless he proves either that the unseaworthiness did not cause the loss, damage or delay or that he had in fact exercised due diligence to provide a seaworthy ship.

The limitation of liability

If the carrier is liable for loss, damage or delay under the convention, the extent of his liability is regulated by articles 22, 59, 60 and 61 RR. Whereas article IV (5) (b) HVR refers to the discharge value, article 22 RR prescribes that the compensation for loss or damage is calculated on the basis of the delivery value of the goods. The delivery value is in turn subject to the provisions of article 59 RR, and the carrier's exposure to cargo claims is then limited to 875 SDR per package or 3 SDR per kilo, whichever is higher.[64]

The carrier's liability for delay follows from article 60 RR. The limit equals two and one-half times the freight on the delayed goods. The limited liability for delay may not exceed the limited amount that would have applied ex article 59 RR if the goods had been a total loss.

The carrier cannot rely on the limitation of liability if the loss, damage or delay in delivery 'resulted from a personal act or omission of the person claiming a right to limit done with the intent to cause the loss due to delay or recklessly and with knowledge that such loss would probably result'. This criterion of article 61 RR falls in line with the criteria of articles 36 CIM 1999, IV (e) HVR and 21 (1) CMNI.

The limitation period

The drafters of the RR have decided on a generous two-year period from the day of delivery to initiate proceedings.[65] Article 62 (1) RR prescribes that 'no judicial or arbitral proceedings in respect of claims or disputes arising from a breach of an obligation under this Convention may be instituted after the expiration of a period of two years.'[66]

Article 62 RR does not distinguish between claims against the carrier or the cargo-interested parties. All claims under the RR are therefore subject to the two-year limitation period. The two-year period cannot be interrupted or suspended, but it can be extended in mutual agreement.[67]

The RR allow for an extra 90 days to initiate an action for indemnity, unless such a recourse claim would be subject to a more lenient limitation period under the law of the court seized.[68]

64 Packages in a container are still individual packages, unless they have not been enumerated. In that case, the container is the package; see article 59 (2) RR.

65 Alternatively, if no goods were delivered, this period starts on the day that the goods should have been delivered. Article 62 (2) RR.

66 Still, article 62 (3) RR allows the defendant to set his expired claim off.

67 Article 63 RR.

68 Articles 64 (a) and 65 (a) RR.

9.3. Dispute resolution

Whereas the HVR are completely silent on this point, the RR spend no fewer than 13 articles discussing dispute resolution.[69] Chapter 14 deals with jurisdiction and chapter 15 deals with arbitration.[70]

Jurisdiction for claims against the carrier

The provisions on jurisdiction concentrate on claims against the carrier.[71] In accordance with article 66 (a) RR, claims against the carrier can be brought before the courts of:

(i) The domicile of the carrier;
(ii) The place of receipt agreed in the contract of carriage;
(iii) The place of delivery agreed in the contract of carriage; or
(iv) The port where the goods are initially loaded on a ship or the port where the goods are finally discharged from a ship.

Article 66 (b) RR furthermore recognizes the jurisdiction of the court selected by an agreement of the contracting parties to decide on claims against the carrier. In view of the last word of article 66 (a) (iv) RR ('or'), the jurisdiction of the court chosen by agreement gives the cargo-interested parties an extra option,[72] unless the choice of jurisdiction qualifies as an exclusive choice pursuant to article 67 RR.

An exclusive choice of jurisdiction

Article 67 RR deals with exclusive choices of jurisdiction for claims against the carrier.[73] These exclusive choices of jurisdiction are reserved for volume contracts,

69 This is also the main reason to depart from the format used in chapter 5. Another reason is that these provisions are unfortunately not always easy to read. Just to give one example: article 67 (2) RR refers to 'an exclusive choice of court agreement concluded in accordance with paragraph 1 of this article'. Article 67 (1) RR in turn, however, refers to the 'jurisdiction of a court chosen in accordance with article 66, subparagraph (b)', and article 66 gives general rules for actions against the carrier that apply 'unless the contract of carriage contains an exclusive choice of court agreement that complies with article 67'.

70 In accordance with articles 74 and 78 RR, these provisions of these two chapters only bind those contracting states that have declared to be bound by them.

71 Except for the situation covered by article 72 RR, this implies that the jurisdiction for claims by the carrier against cargo-interested parties (for unpaid freight, for instance) follows from the provisions of their contract, and/or the provisions of Brussels I or the lex fori.

72 There is tension between this provision and article 25 Brussels I that prescribes that forum choices are in principle exclusive, but article 71 (1) Brussels I stipulates that 'this Regulation shall not affect any conventions to which the Member States are parties and which, in relation to particular matters, govern jurisdiction or the recognition or enforcement of judgments.'

73 This follows from the first part of article 67 RR: 'The jurisdiction of a court chosen in accordance with article 66, subparagraph (b) is exclusive.' Article 66 (b) RR only relates to claims against the carrier.

and they are subject to several formalities. A choice of jurisdiction is only exclusive if the parties agree thereto and if this agreement:

(a) Is contained in a volume contract that clearly states the names and addresses of the parties and either (i) is individually negotiated or (ii) contains a prominent statement that there is an exclusive choice of court agreement and specifies the sections of the volume contract containing that agreement; and
(b) Clearly designates the courts of one Contracting State or one or more specific courts of one Contracting State.

The exclusive choice of jurisdiction can bind other parties than the initial parties to the contract, particularly the consignee, controlling party or bill of lading holder, provided that the conditions of article 67 (2) RR have been met. The exclusive choice of jurisdiction is only binding for these other parties if (a) the seat of the chosen court corresponds with one of the courts listed under article 66 (a) RR, (b) the agreement is contained in the transport document or electronic transport record, (c) timely and adequate notice is given of the court where the action shall be brought and the jurisdiction of that court is exclusive, and (d) the law of the court seized recognizes that that person may be bound by such an agreement.

Claims against the maritime performing party

Article 68 RR covers claims against the maritime performing party.[74] The plaintiff may sue the maritime performing party before the courts of either:[75]

(a) The domicile of the maritime performing party; or
(b) The port where the goods are received by the maritime performing party, the port where the goods are delivered by the maritime performing party or the port in which the maritime performing party performs its activities with respect to the goods.

Claims against a performing party (other than a maritime performing party) are not governed by article 68 RR. The jurisdiction for claims against performing parties therefore follows from the forum choice in the contract and/or the provisions of Brussels I or the lex fori.[76]

74 Claims against the maritime performing party will in practice often be combined with claims against the (contractual) carrier. These claims can be consolidated in accordance with article 71 RR.

75 Article 68 RR does not regulate its relation to a choice of jurisdiction, and this may have consequences as the 'plaintiff' is not defined by the rules. A (recourse) claim by a carrier based on his volume contract with a subcarrier (and maritime performing party) may therefore perhaps be brought before the courts identified by article 68 RR, even though their volume contract contains a perfectly valid choice for the exclusive competence of another court. Mutatis mutandis the same could then apply to claims by a maritime performing party (for freight, for instance) against a carrier under a volume contract.

76 Claims by a performing party (other than a maritime performing party) against a carrier are also governed by the provisions of their contract, the provisions of Brussels I (on tort) and the lex fori as that contract does not qualify as a 'contract of carriage' under the rules.

A choice of jurisdiction afterwards

The parties may also agree on jurisdiction once their dispute has already arisen. Article 72 RR does not require any form formalities in this case. Any agreement, including a tacit agreement whereby the defendant appears in court yet fails to contest the competence of the court, will do:

1 After a dispute has arisen, the parties to the dispute may agree to resolve it in any competent court.
2 A competent court before which a defendant appears, without contesting jurisdiction in accordance with the rules of that court, has jurisdiction.

Article 72 RR applies to disputes governed by the convention in general. The provision does not distinguish between claims by or against the carrier or maritime performing party, and therefore applies to every claim under a contract of carriage governed by the rules.

Arbitration

Although article 75 RR starts by saying that parties may refer 'any dispute' to arbitration, chapter 15 mainly relates to arbitration claims against the carrier. In accordance with article 75 (2) RR, these claims against the carrier can at the option of the claimant be brought in arbitration at:[77]

(a) Any place designated for that purpose in the arbitration agreement; or
(b) Any other place situated in a State where any of the following places is located:

(i) The domicile of the carrier;
(ii) The place of receipt agreed in the contract of carriage;
(iii) The place of delivery agreed in the contract of carriage; or
(iv) The port where the goods are initially loaded on a ship or the port where the goods are finally discharged from a ship.

The designation of the place of arbitration in a volume contract is exclusive, though, if the agreement clearly mentions the names and addresses of the parties and is either individually negotiated or specifically identified in the contract.[78] The choice for a place of arbitration in a volume contract is in accordance with article 75 (4) RR furthermore binding on third parties if:

(a) The place of arbitration designated in the agreement is situated in one of the places referred to in subparagraph 2 (b) of this article;

77 This implies that the claimant may have as many as six different options for the place of arbitration. See in this respect Y. Baatz in Y. Baatz, C. Debattista, F. Lorenzon, A. Serdy, H. Staniland, M. Tsimplis, *The Rotterdam Rules: A practical annotation* (Informa: London, 2009) 237, calling it 'a major stumbling block'.
78 Article 75 (3) RR.

(b) The agreement is contained in the transport document or electronic transport record;
(c) The person to be bound is given timely and adequate notice of the place of arbitration; and
(d) Applicable law permits that person to be bound by the arbitration agreement.[79]

The enforceability of an arbitration agreement in a non-liner contract, although such a contract is in principle excluded from the scope of application of the rules in article 6 RR, is not affected by the rules if they either apply pursuant to article 7 RR,[80] or if the convention has been incorporated into the contract of carriage.[81]

The parties to the contract of carriage are free to agree on arbitration at any place once their dispute has already arisen. Article 77 RR does not distinguish between claims against the carrier or other claims, and therefore encompasses any claim under a contract of carriage governed by the rules.

79 The mere reference to 'applicable, and law' leaves the question of whether this is the (procedural) lex fori or the (substantive) lex causae that does not benefit the (indispensable) legal certainty. Y. Baatz in Y. Baatz, C. Debattista, F. Lorenzon, A. Serdy, H. Staniland, M. Tsimplis, *The Rotterdam Rules: A practical annotation* (Informa: London, 2009) 239. The explicit reference to the 'law of the court seized' in article 67 (2) (d) RR, and the absence thereof here, suggests that it is the (substantive) lex causae.

80 Article 76 (1) (a) RR. Article 7 RR ensures the application of the convention between the carrier and the consignee, controlling party or bill of lading holder that were not initial contracting parties. Article 76 (2) RR, however, prescribes that the arbitration provisions of the rules do not apply if the 'transport document or electronic transport record: (a) Identifies the parties to and the date of the charter party or other contract excluded from the application of this Convention by reason of the application of article 6; and (b) Incorporates by specific reference the clause in the charter party or other contract that contains the terms of the arbitration agreement'.

81 The incorporation of a convention only achieves the contractual operation of its provisions, and not the mandatory operation. This would imply that the enforceability could then still be affected by mandatory domestic law.

Annexes

Uniform Rules Concerning the Contract of International Carriage of Goods by Rail (CIM – Appendix B to the Convention) (CIM 1999)

Article 1 Scope

§ 1 These Uniform Rules shall apply to every contract of carriage of goods by rail for reward when the place of taking over of the goods and the place designated for delivery are situated in two different Member States, irrespective of the place of business and the nationality of the parties to the contract of carriage.

§ 2 These Uniform Rules shall apply also to contracts of carriage of goods by rail for reward, when the place of taking over of the goods and the place designated for delivery are situated in two different States, of which at least one is a Member State and the parties to the contract agree that the contract is subject to these Uniform Rules.

§ 3 When international carriage being the subject of a single contract includes carriage by road or inland waterway in internal traffic of a Member State as a supplement to transfrontier carriage by rail, these Uniform Rules shall apply.

§ 4 When international carriage being the subject of a single contract of carriage includes carriage by sea or transfrontier carriage by inland waterway as a supplement to carriage by rail, these Uniform Rules shall apply if the carriage by sea or inland waterway is performed on services included in the list of services provided for in Article 24 § 1 of the Convention.

§ 5 These Uniform Rules shall not apply to carriage performed between stations situated on the territory of neighbouring States, when the infrastructure of these stations is managed by one or more infrastructure managers subject to only one of those States.

§ 6 Any State which is a party to a convention concerning international through carriage of goods by rail comparable with these Uniform Rules may, when it makes an application for accession to the Convention, declare that it will apply these Uniform Rules only to carriage performed on part of the railway infrastructure situated on its territory. This part of the railway infrastructure must be precisely defined and connected to the railway infrastructure of a Member State. When a State has made the above-mentioned declaration, these Uniform Rules shall apply only on the condition

a) that the place of taking over of the goods or the place designated for delivery, as well as the route designated in the contract of carriage, is situated on the specified infrastructure or
b) that the specified infrastructure connects the infrastructure of two Member States and that it has been designated in the contract of carriage as a route for transit carriage.

§ 7 A State which has made a reservation in accordance with § 6 may withdraw it at any time by notification to the Depositary. This withdrawal shall take effect one month after the day on which the Depositary notifies it to the Member States. The declaration shall cease to have effect when the convention referred to in § 6, first sentence, ceases to be in force for that State.

Article 2 Prescriptions of public law

Carriage to which these Uniform Rules apply shall remain subject to the prescriptions of public law, in particular the prescriptions relating to the carriage of dangerous goods as well as the prescriptions of customs law and those relating to the protection of animals.

Article 3 Definitions

For purposes of these Uniform Rules the term

a) "carrier" means the contractual carrier with whom the consignor has concluded the contract of carriage pursuant to these Uniform Rules, or a subsequent carrier who is liable on the basis of this contract;
b) "substitute carrier" means a carrier, who has not concluded the contract of carriage with the consignor, but to whom the carrier referred to in letter a) has entrusted, in whole or in part, the performance of the carriage by rail;
c) "General Conditions of Carriage" means the conditions of the carrier in the form of general conditions or tariffs legally in force in each Member State and which have become, by the conclusion of the contract of carriage, an integral part of it;
d) "intermodal transport unit" means a container, swap body, semi-trailer or other comparable loading unit used in intermodal transport.

Article 4 Derogations

§ 1 Member States may conclude agreements which provide for derogations from these Uniform Rules for carriage performed exclusively between two stations on either side of the frontier, when there is no other station between them.

§ 2 For carriage performed between two Member States, passing through a State which is not a Member State, the States concerned may conclude agreements which derogate from these Uniform Rules.

§ 3 Agreements referred to in §§ 1 and 2 as well as their coming into force shall be notified to the Intergovernmental Organisation for International Carriage by Rail. The Secretary General of the Organisation shall inform the Member States and interested undertakings of these notifications.

Article 5 Mandatory law

Unless provided otherwise in these Uniform Rules, any stipulation which, directly or indirectly, would derogate from these Uniform Rules shall be null and void. The nullity of such a stipulation shall not involve the nullity of the other provisions of the contract of carriage. Nevertheless, a carrier may assume a liability greater and obligations more burdensome than those provided for in these Uniform Rules.

Article 6 Contract of carriage

§ 1 By the contract of carriage, the carrier shall undertake to carry the goods for reward to the place of destination and to deliver them there to the consignee.

§ 2 The contract of carriage must be confirmed by a consignment note which accords with a uniform model. However, the absence, irregularity or loss of the consignment note shall not affect the existence or validity of the contract which shall remain subject to these Uniform Rules.

§ 3 The consignment note shall be signed by the consignor and the carrier. The signature can be replaced by a stamp, by an accounting machine entry or in any other appropriate manner.

§ 4 The carrier must certify the taking over of the goods on the duplicate of the consignment note in an appropriate manner and return the duplicate to the consignor.

§ 5 The consignment note shall not have effect as a bill of lading.

§ 6 A consignment note must be made out for each consignment. In the absence of a contrary agreement between the consignor and the carrier, a consignment note may not relate to more than one wagon load.

§ 7 In the case of carriage which enters the customs territory of the European Community or the territory on which the common transit procedure is applied, each consignment must be accompanied by a consignment note satisfying the requirements of Article 7.

§ 8 The international associations of carriers shall establish uniform model consignment notes in agreement with the customers' international associations and the bodies having competence for customs matters in the Member States as well as any intergovernmental regional economic integration organisation having competence to adopt its own customs legislation.

§ 9 The consignment note and its duplicate may be established in the form of electronic data registration which can be transformed into legible written symbols. The procedure used for the registration and treatment of data must be equivalent from the functional point of view, particularly so far as concerns the evidential value of the consignment note represented by those data.

Article 7 Wording of the consignment note

§ 1 The consignment note must contain the following particulars:

a) the place at which and the day on which it is made out;
b) the name and address of the consignor;
c) the name and address of the carrier who has concluded the contract of carriage;
d) the name and address of the person to whom the goods have effectively been handed over if he is not the carrier referred to in letter c);
e) the place and the day of taking over of the goods;
f) the place of delivery;
g) the name and address of the consignee;
h) the description of the nature of the goods and the method of packing, and, in case of dangerous goods, the description provided for in the Regulation concerning the International Carriage of Dangerous Goods by Rail (RID);
i) the number of packages and the special marks and numbers necessary for the identification of consignments in less than full wagon loads;
j) the number of the wagon in the case of carriage of full wagon loads;
k) the number of the railway vehicle running on its own wheels, if it is handed over for carriage as goods;
l) in addition, in the case of intermodal transport units, the category, the number or other characteristics necessary for their identification;
m) the gross mass or the quantity of the goods expressed in other ways;
n) a detailed list of the documents which are required by customs or other administrative authorities and are attached to the consignment note or held at the disposal of the carrier at the offices of a duly designated authority or a body designated in the contract;
o) the costs relating to carriage (the carriage charge, incidental costs, customs duties and other costs incurred from the conclusion of the contract until delivery) in so far as they must be paid by the consignee or any other statement that the costs are payable by the consignee;
p) a statement that the carriage is subject, notwithstanding any clause to the contrary, to these Uniform Rules.

§ 2 Where applicable the consignment note must also contain the following particulars:

a) in the case of carriage by successive carriers, the carrier who must deliver the goods when he has consented to this entry in the consignment note;
b) the costs which the consignor undertakes to pay;
c) the amount of the cash on delivery charge;
d) the declaration of the value of the goods and the amount representing the special interest in delivery;
e) the agreed transit period;
f) the agreed route;

g) a list of the documents not mentioned in § 1, letter n) handed over to the carrier;
h) the entries made by the consignor concerning the number and description of seals he has affixed to the wagon.

§ 3 The parties to the contract may enter on the consignment note any other particulars they consider useful.

Article 8 Responsibility for particulars entered on the consignment note

§ 1 The consignor shall be responsible for all costs, loss or damage sustained by the carrier by reason of

a) the entries made by the consignor in the consignment note being irregular, incorrect, incomplete or made elsewhere than in the allotted space, or
b) the consignor omitting to make the entries prescribed by RID.

§ 2 If, at the request of the consignor, the carrier makes entries on the consignment note, he shall be deemed, unless the contrary is proved, to have done so on behalf of the consignor.

§ 3 If the consignment note does not contain the statement provided for in Article 7 § 1, letter p), the carrier shall be liable for all costs, loss or damage sustained through such omission by the person entitled.

Article 9 Dangerous goods

If the consignor has failed to make the entries prescribed by RID, the carrier may at any time unload or destroy the goods or render them innocuous, as the circumstances may require, without payment of compensation, save when he was aware of their dangerous nature on taking them over.

Article 10 Payment of costs

§ 1 Unless otherwise agreed between the consignor and the carrier, the costs (the carriage charge, incidental costs, customs duties and other costs incurred from the time of the conclusion of the contract to the time of delivery) shall be paid by the consignor.

§ 2 When by virtue of an agreement between the consignor and the carrier, the costs are payable by the consignee and the consignee has not taken possession of the consignment note nor asserted his rights in accordance with Article 17 § 3, nor modified the contract of carriage in accordance with Article 18, the consignor shall remain liable to pay the costs.

Article 11 Examination

§ 1 The carrier shall have the right to examine at any time whether the conditions of carriage have been complied with and whether the consignment corresponds with the entries in the consignment note made by the consignor. If the examination concerns the contents of the consignment, this shall be carried out as far as possible in the presence of the person entitled; where this is not possible, the carrier shall require the presence of two independent witnesses, unless the laws and prescriptions of the State where the examination takes place provide otherwise.

§ 2 If the consignment does not correspond with the entries in the consignment note or if the provisions relating to the carriage of goods accepted subject to conditions have not been complied with, the result of the examination must be entered in the copy of the consignment note which accompanies the goods, and also in the duplicate of the consignment note, if it is still held by the carrier. In this case the costs of the examination shall be charged against the goods, if they have not been paid immediately.

§ 3 When the consignor loads the goods, he shall be entitled to require the carrier to examine the condition of the goods and their packaging as well as the accuracy of statements on the consignment note as to the number of packages, their marks and numbers as well as the gross mass of the goods or their quantity otherwise expressed. The carrier shall be obliged to proceed with the examination only if he has appropriate means of carrying it out. The carrier may demand the payment of the costs of the examination. The result of the examination shall be entered on the consignment note.

Article 12 Evidential value of the consignment note

§ 1 The consignment note shall be prima facie evidence of the conclusion and the conditions of the contract of carriage and the taking over of the goods by the carrier.

§ 2 If the carrier has loaded the goods, the consignment note shall be prima facie evidence of the condition of the goods and their packaging indicated on the consignment note or, in the absence of such indications, of their apparently good condition at the moment they were taken over by the carrier and of the accuracy of the statements in the consignment note concerning the number of packages, their marks and numbers as well as the gross mass of the goods or their quantity otherwise expressed.

§ 3 If the consignor has loaded the goods, the consignment note shall be prima facie evidence of the condition of the goods and of their packaging indicated in the consignment note or, in the absence of such indication, of their apparently good condition and of the accuracy of the statements referred to in § 2 solely in the case where the carrier has examined them and recorded on the consignment note a result of his examination which tallies.

§ 4 However, the consignment note will not be prima facie evidence in a case where it bears a reasoned reservation. A reason for a reservation could be that the carrier does not have the appropriate means to examine whether the consignment corresponds to the entries in the consignment note.

Article 13 Loading and unloading of the goods

§ 1 The consignor and the carrier shall agree who is responsible for the loading and unloading of the goods. In the absence of such an agreement, for packages the loading and unloading shall be the responsibility of the carrier whereas for full wagon loads loading shall be the responsibility of the consignor and unloading, after delivery, the responsibility of the consignee.

§ 2 The consignor shall be liable for all the consequences of defective loading carried out by him and must in particular compensate the carrier for the loss or damage sustained in consequence by him. The burden of proof of defective loading shall lie on the carrier.

Article 14 Packing

The consignor shall be liable to the carrier for any loss or damage and costs due to the absence of, or defects in, the packing of goods, unless the defectiveness was apparent or known to the carrier at the time when he took over the goods and he made no reservations concerning it.

Article 15 Completion of administrative formalities

§ 1 With a view to the completion of the formalities required by customs and other administrative authorities, to be completed before delivery of the goods, the consignor must attach the necessary documents to the consignment note or make them available to the carrier and furnish him with all the requisite information.

§ 2 The carrier shall not be obliged to check whether these documents and this information are correct and sufficient. The consignor shall be liable to the carrier for any loss or damage resulting from the absence or insufficiency of, or any irregularity in, such documents and information, save in the case of fault of the carrier.

§ 3 The carrier shall be liable for any consequences arising from the loss or misuse of the documents referred to in the consignment note and accompanying it or deposited with the carrier, unless the loss of the documents or the loss or damage caused by the misuse of the documents has been caused by circumstances which the carrier could not avoid and the consequences of which he was unable to prevent. Nevertheless any compensation payable shall not exceed that provided for in the event of loss of the goods.

§ 4 The consignor, by so indicating in the consignment note, or the consignee by giving orders as provided for in Article 18 § 3 may ask

a) to be present himself or to be represented by an agent when the customs or other administrative formalities are carried out, for the purpose of furnishing any information or explanation required;
b) to complete the customs or other administrative formalities himself or to have them completed by an agent, in so far as the laws and prescriptions of the State in which they are to be carried out so permit;

c) to pay customs duties and other charges, when he or his agent is present at or completes the customs or other administrative formalities, in so far as the laws and prescriptions of the State in which they are carried out permit such payment.

In such circumstances neither the consignor, nor the consignee who has the right of disposal, nor the agent of either may take possession of the goods.

§ 5 If, for the completion of the customs or other administrative formalities, the consignor has designated a place where the prescriptions in force do not permit their completion, or if he has stipulated for the purpose any other procedure which cannot be followed, the carrier shall act in the manner which appears to him to be the most favourable to the interests of the person entitled and shall inform the consignor of the measures taken.

§ 6 If the consignor has undertaken to pay customs duties, the carrier shall have the choice of completing customs formalities either in transit or at the destination place.

§ 7 However, the carrier may proceed in accordance with § 5 if the consignee has not taken possession of the consignment note within the period fixed by the prescriptions in force at the destination place.

§ 8 The consignor must comply with the prescriptions of customs or other administrative authorities with respect to the packing and sheeting of the goods. If the consignor has not packed or sheeted the goods in accordance with those prescriptions the carrier shall be entitled to do so; the resulting cost shall be charged against the goods.

Article 16 Transit periods

§ 1 The consignor and the carrier shall agree the transit period. In the absence of an agreement, the transit period must not exceed that which would result from the application of §§ 2 to 4.

§ 2 Subject to §§ 3 and 4, the maximum transit periods shall be as follows:

a) for wagon-load consignments

- period for consignment 12 hours,
- period for carriage, for each 400 km or fraction thereof 24 hours;

b) for less than wagon-load consignment

- period for consignments 24 hours,
- period for carriage, for each 200 km or fraction thereof 24 hours.

The distances shall relate to the agreed route or, in the absence thereof, to the shortest possible route.

§ 3 The carrier may fix additional transit periods of specified duration in the following cases:

a) consignments to be carried
   - by lines of a different gauge, by sea or inland waterway, by road if there is no rail link;

b) exceptional circumstances causing an exceptional increase in traffic or exceptional operating difficulties.

The duration of the additional transit periods must appear in the General Conditions of Carriage.

§ 4 The transit period shall start to run after the taking over of the goods; it shall be extended by the duration of a stay caused without any fault of the carrier. The transit period shall be suspended on Sundays and statutory holidays.

Article 17 Delivery

§ 1 The carrier must hand over the consignment note and deliver the goods to the consignee at the place designated for delivery against receipt and payment of the amounts due according to the contract of carriage.

§ 2 It shall be equivalent to delivery to the consignee if, in accordance with the prescriptions in force at the place of destination,

a) the goods have been handed over to customs or octroi authorities at their premises or warehouses, when these are not subject to the carrier's supervision;

b) the goods have been deposited for storage with the carrier, with a forwarding agent or in a public warehouse.

§ 3 After the arrival of the goods at the place of destination, the consignee may ask the carrier to hand over the consignment note and deliver the goods to him. If the loss of the goods is established or if the goods have not arrived on the expiry of the period provided for in Article 29 § 1, the consignee may assert, in his own name, his rights against the carrier under the contract of carriage.

§ 4 The person entitled may refuse to accept the goods, even when he has received the consignment note and paid the charges resulting from the contract of carriage, so long as an examination which he has demanded in order to establish alleged loss or damage has not been carried out.

§ 5 In other respects, delivery of the goods shall be carried out in accordance with the prescriptions in force at the place of destination.

§ 6 If the goods have been delivered without prior collection of a cash on delivery charge, the carrier shall be obliged to compensate the consignor up to the amount of the cash on delivery charge without prejudice to his right of recourse against the consignee.

Article 18 Right to dispose of the goods

§ 1 The consignor shall be entitled to dispose of the goods and to modify the contract of carriage by giving subsequent orders. He may in particular ask the carrier

a) to discontinue the carriage of the goods;
b) to delay the delivery of the goods;
c) to deliver the goods to a consignee different from the one entered on the consignment note;
d) to deliver the goods at a place other than the place of destination entered on the consignment note.

§ 2 The consignor's right to modify the contract of carriage shall, notwithstanding that he is in possession of the duplicate of the consignment note, be extinguished in cases where the consignee

a) has taken possession of the consignment note;
b) has accepted the goods;
c) has asserted his rights in accordance with Article 17 § 3;
d) is entitled, in accordance with § 3, to give orders; from that time onwards, the carrier shall comply with the orders and instructions of the consignee.

§ 3 The consignee shall have the right to modify the contract of carriage from the time when the consignment note is drawn up, unless the consignor indicates to the contrary on the consignment note.

§ 4 The consignee's right to modify the contract of carriage shall be extinguished in cases where he has

a) taken possession of the consignment note;
b) accepted the goods;
c) asserted his rights in accordance with Article 17 § 3;
d) given instructions for delivery of the goods to another person in accordance with § 5 and when that person has asserted his rights in accordance with Article 17 § 3.

§ 5 If the consignee has given instructions for delivery of the goods to another person, that person shall not be entitled to modify the contract of carriage.

Article 19 Exercise of the right to dispose of the goods

§ 1 If the consignor or, in the case referred to in Article 18 § 3, the consignee wishes to modify the contract of carriage by giving subsequent orders, he must produce to the carrier the duplicate of the consignment note on which the modifications have to be entered.

§2 The consignor or, in the case referred to in Article 18 § 3, the consignee must compensate the carrier for the costs and the prejudice arising from the carrying out of subsequent modifications.

§ 3 The carrying out of the subsequent modifications must be possible, lawful and reasonable to require at the time when the orders reach the person who is to carry them out, and must in particular neither interfere with the normal working of the carrier's undertaking nor prejudice the consignors or consignees of other consignments.

§ 4 The subsequent modifications must not have the effect of splitting the consignment.

§ 5 When, by reason of the conditions provided for in § 3, the carrier cannot carry out the orders which he receives he shall immediately notify the person from whom the orders emanate.

§ 6 In the case of fault of the carrier he shall be liable for the consequences of failure to carry out an order or failure to carry it out properly. Nevertheless, any compensation payable shall not exceed that provided for in case of loss of the goods.

§ 7 If the carrier implements the consignor's subsequent modifications without requiring the production of the duplicate of the consignment note, the carrier shall be liable to the consignee for any loss or damage sustained by him if the duplicate has been passed on to the consignee. Nevertheless, any compensation payable shall not exceed that provided for in case of loss of the goods.

Article 20 Circumstances preventing carriage

§ 1 When circumstances prevent the carriage of goods, the carrier shall decide whether it is preferable to carry the goods as a matter of course by modifying the route or whether it is advisable, in the interest of the person entitled, to ask him for instructions while giving him any relevant information available to the carrier.

§ 2 If it is impossible to continue carrying the goods, the carrier shall ask for instructions from the person who has the right to dispose of the goods. If the carrier is unable to obtain instructions within a reasonable time he must take such steps as seem to him to be in the best interests of the person entitled to dispose of the goods.

Article 21 Circumstances preventing delivery

§ 1 When circumstances prevent delivery, the carrier must without delay inform the consignor and ask him for instructions, save where the consignor has requested, by an entry in the consignment note, that the goods be returned to him as a matter of course in the event of circumstances preventing delivery.

§ 2 When the circumstances preventing delivery cease to exist before arrival of instructions from the consignor to the carrier the goods shall be delivered to the consignee. The consignor must be notified without delay.

§ 3 If the consignee refuses the goods, the consignor shall be entitled to give instructions even if he is unable to produce the duplicate of the consignment note.

§ 4 When the circumstances preventing delivery arise after the consignee has modified the contract of carriage in accordance with Article 18 §§ 3 to 5 the carrier must notify the consignee.

Article 22 Consequences of circumstances preventing carriage and delivery

§ 1 The carrier shall be entitled to recover the costs occasioned by

a) his request for instructions,
b) the carrying out of instructions received,
c) the fact that instructions requested do not reach him or do not reach him in time,
d) the fact that he has taken a decision in accordance with Article 20 § 1, without having asked for instructions, unless such costs were caused by his fault. The carrier may in particular recover the carriage charge applicable to the route followed and shall be allowed the transit periods applicable to such route.

§ 2 In the cases referred to in Article 20 § 2 and Article 21 § 1 the carrier may immediately unload the goods at the cost of the person entitled. Thereupon the carriage shall be deemed to be at an end. The carrier shall then be in charge of the goods on behalf of the person entitled. He may, however, entrust them to a third party, and shall then be responsible only for the exercise of reasonable care in the choice of such third party. The charges due under the contract of carriage and all other costs shall remain chargeable against the goods.

§ 3 The carrier may proceed to the sale of the goods, without awaiting instructions from the person entitled, if this is justified by the perishable nature or the condition of the goods or if the costs of storage would be out of proportion to the value of the goods. In other cases he may also proceed to the sale of the goods if within a reasonable time he has not received from the person entitled instructions to the contrary which he may reasonably be required to carry out.

§ 4 If the goods have been sold, the proceeds of sale, after deduction of the costs chargeable against the goods, must be placed at the disposal of the person entitled. If the proceeds of sale are less than those costs, the consignor must pay the difference.

§ 5 The procedure in the case of sale shall be determined by the laws and prescriptions in force at, or by the custom of, the place where the goods are situated.

§ 6 If the consignor, in the case of circumstances preventing carnage or delivery, fails to give instructions within a reasonable time and if the circumstances preventing carriage or delivery cannot be eliminated in accordance with §§ 2 and 3, the carrier may return the goods to the consignor or, if it is justified, destroy them, at the cost of the consignor.

Article 23 Basis of liability

§ 1 The carrier shall be liable for loss or damage resulting from the total or partial loss of, or damage to, the goods between the time of taking over of the goods and the time of delivery and for the loss or damage resulting from the transit period being exceeded, whatever the railway infrastructure used.

§ 2 The carrier shall be relieved of this liability to the extent that the loss or damage or the exceeding of the transit period was caused by the fault of the person entitled, by an order given by the person entitled other than as a result of the fault of the carrier, by an inherent defect in the goods (decay, wastage etc.) or by circumstances which the carrier could not avoid and the consequences of which he was unable to prevent.

§ 3 The carrier shall be relieved of this liability to the extent that the loss or damage arises from the special risks inherent in one or more of the following circumstances:

a) carriage in open wagons pursuant to the General Conditions of Carriage or when it has been expressly agreed and entered in the consignment note; subject to damage sustained by the goods because of atmospheric influences, goods carried in intermodal transport units and in closed road vehicles carried on wagons shall not be considered as being carried in open wagons; if for the carriage of goods in open wagons, the consignor uses sheets, the carrier shall assume the same liability as falls to him for carriage in open wagons without sheeting, even in respect of goods which, according to the General Conditions of Carriage, are not carried in open wagons;
b) absence or inadequacy of packaging in the case of goods which by their nature are liable to loss or damage when not packed or when not packed properly;
c) loading of the goods by the consignor or unloading by the consignee;
d) the nature of certain goods which particularly exposes them to total or partial loss or damage, especially through breakage, rust, interior and spontaneous decay, desiccation or wastage;
e) irregular, incorrect or incomplete description or numbering of packages;
f) carriage of live animals;
g) carriage which, pursuant to applicable provisions or agreements made between the consignor and the carrier and entered on the consignment note, must be accompanied by an attendant, if the loss or damage results from a risk which the attendant was intended to avert.

Article 24 Liability in case of carriage of railway vehicles as goods

§ 1 In case of carriage of railway vehicles running on their own wheels and consigned as goods, the carrier shall be liable for the loss or damage resulting from the loss of, or damage to, the vehicle or to its removable parts arising between the time of taking over for carriage and the time of delivery and for loss or damage resulting from exceeding the transit period, unless he proves that the loss or damage was not caused by his fault.

§ 2 The carrier shall not be liable for loss or damage resulting from the loss of accessories which are not mentioned on both sides of the vehicle or in the inventory which accompanies it.

Article 25 Burden of proof

§ 1 The burden of proving that the loss, damage or exceeding of the transit period was due to one of the causes specified in Article 23 § 2 shall lie on the carrier.

§ 2 When the carrier establishes that, having regard to the circumstances of a particular case, the loss or damage could have arisen from one or more of the special risks referred to in Article 23 § 3, it shall be presumed that it did so arise. The person entitled shall, however, have the right to prove that the loss or damage was not attributable either wholly or in part to one of those risks.

§ 3 The presumption according to § 2 shall not apply in the case provided for in Article 23 § 3, letter a) if an abnormally large quantity has been lost or if a package has been lost.

Article 26 Successive carriers

If carriage governed by a single contract is performed by several successive carriers, each earner, by the very act of taking over the goods with the consignment note, shall become a party to the contract of carriage in accordance with the terms of that document and shall assume the obligations arising therefrom. In such a case each carrier shall be responsible in respect of carriage over the entire route up to delivery.

Article 27 Substitute carrier

§ 1 Where the carrier has entrusted the performance of the carriage, in whole or in part, to a substitute carrier, whether or not in pursuance of a right under the contract of carriage to do so, the carrier shall nevertheless remain liable in respect of the entire carriage.

§ 2 All the provisions of these Uniform Rules governing the liability of the carrier shall also apply to the liability of the substitute carrier for the carriage performed by him. Articles 36 and 41 shall apply if an action is brought against the servants and any other persons whose services the substitute carrier makes use of for the performance of the carriage.

§ 3 Any special agreement under which the carrier assumes obligations not imposed by these Uniform Rules or waives rights conferred by these Uniform Rules shall be of no effect in respect of the substitute carrier who has not accepted it expressly and in writing. Whether or not the substitute carrier has accepted it, the carrier shall nevertheless remain bound by the obligations or waivers resulting from such special agreement.

§ 4 Where and to the extent that both the carrier and the substitute carrier are liable, their liability shall be joint and several.

§ 5 The aggregate amount of compensation payable by the carrier, the substitute carrier and their servants and other persons whose services they make use of for the performance of the carriage shall not exceed the limits provided for in these Uniform Rules.

§ 6 This article shall not prejudice rights of recourse which may exist between the carrier and the substitute carrier.

Article 28 Presumption of loss or damage in case of reconsignment

§ 1 When a consignment consigned in accordance with these Uniform Rules has been reconsigned subject to these same Rules and partial loss or damage has been ascertained after that reconsignment, it shall be presumed that it occurred under the latest contract of carriage if the consignment remained in the charge of the carrier and was reconsigned in the same condition as when it arrived at the place from which it was reconsigned.

§ 2 This presumption shall also apply when the contract of carriage prior to the reconsignment was not subject to these Uniform Rules, if these Rules would have applied in the case of a through consignment from the first place of consignment to the final place of destination.

§ 3 This presumption shall also apply when the contract of carriage prior to the reconsignment was subject to a convention concerning international through carriage of goods by rail comparable with these Uniform Rules, and when this convention contains the same presumption of law in favour of consignments consigned in accordance with these Uniform Rules.

Article 29 Presumption of loss of the goods

§ 1 The person entitled may, without being required to furnish further proof, consider the goods as lost when they have not been delivered to the consignee or placed at his disposal within thirty days after the expiry of the transit periods.

§ 2 The person entitled may, on receipt of the payment of compensation for the goods lost, make a written request to be notified without delay should the goods be recovered within one year after the payment of compensation. The carrier shall acknowledge such request in writing.

§ 3 Within thirty days after receipt of a notification referred to in § 2, the person entitled may require the goods to be delivered to him against payment of the costs resulting from the contract of carriage and against refund of the compensation received, less, where appropriate, costs which may have been included therein. Nevertheless he shall retain his rights to claim compensation for exceeding the transit period provided for in Articles 33 and 35.

§ 4 In the absence of the request referred to in § 2 or of instructions given within the period specified in § 3, or if the goods are recovered more than one year after the payment of compensation, the carrier shall dispose of them in accordance with the laws and prescriptions in force at the place where the goods are situated.

Article 30 Compensation for loss

§ 1 In case of total or partial loss of the goods, the carrier must pay, to the exclusion of all other damages, compensation calculated according to the commodity exchange quotation or, if there is no such quotation, according to the current market price, or if there is neither such quotation nor such price, according to the usual value of goods of the same kind and quality on the day and at the place where the goods were taken over.

§ 2 Compensation shall not exceed 17 units of account per kilogramme of gross mass short.

§ 3 In case of loss of a railway vehicle running on its own wheels and consigned as goods, or of an intermodal transport unit, or of their removable parts, the compensation shall be limited, to the exclusion of all other damages, to the usual value of the vehicle or the intermodal transport unit, or their removable parts, on the day and at the place of loss. If it is impossible to ascertain the day or the place of the loss, the compensation shall be limited to the usual value on the day and at the place where the vehicle has been taken over by the carrier.

§ 4 The carrier must, in addition, refund the carriage charge, customs duties already paid and other sums paid in relation to the carriage of the goods lost except excise duties for goods carried under a procedure suspending those duties.

Article 31 Liability for wastage in transit

§ 1 In respect of goods which, by reason of their nature, are generally subject to wastage in transit by the sole fact of carriage, the carrier shall only be liable to the extent that the wastage exceeds the following allowances, whatever the length of the route:

a) two per cent of the mass for liquid goods or goods consigned in a moist condition;
b) one per cent of the mass for dry goods.

§ 2 The limitation of liability provided for in § 1 may not be invoked if, having regard to the circumstances of a particular case, it is proved that the loss was not due to causes which would justify the allowance.

§ 3 Where several packages are carried under a single consignment note, the wastage in transit shall be calculated separately for each package if its mass on consignment is shown separately on the consignment note or can be ascertained otherwise.

§ 4 In case of total loss of goods or in case of loss of a package, no deduction for wastage in transit shall be made in calculating the compensation.

§ 5 This Article shall not derogate from Articles 23 and 25.

Article 32 Compensation for damage

§ 1 In case of damage to goods, the carrier must pay compensation equivalent to the loss in value of the goods, to the exclusion of all other damages. The amount shall be calculated by applying to the value of the goods defined in accordance with Article 30 the percentage of loss in value noted at the place of destination.

§ 2 The compensation shall not exceed:

a) if the whole consignment has lost value through damage, the amount which would have been payable in case of total loss;
b) if only part of the consignment has lost value through damage, the amount which would have been payable had that part been lost.

§ 3 In case of damage to a railway vehicle running on its own wheels and consigned as goods, or of an intermodal transport unit, or of their removable parts, the compensation shall be limited, to the exclusion of all other damages, to the cost of repair. The compensation shall not exceed the amount payable in case of loss.

§ 4 The carrier must also refund the costs provided for in Article 30 § 4, in the proportion set out in § 1.

Article 33 Compensation for exceeding the transit period

§ 1 If loss or damage results from the transit period being exceeded, the carrier must pay compensation not exceeding four times the carriage charge.

§ 2 In case of total loss of the goods, the compensation provided for in § 1 shall not be payable in addition to that provided for in Article 30.

§ 3 In case of partial loss of the goods, the compensation provided for in § 1 shall not exceed four times the carriage charge in respect of that part of the consignment which has not been lost.

§ 4 In case of damage to the goods, not resulting from the transit period being exceeded, the compensation provided for in § 1 shall, where appropriate, be payable in addition to that provided for in Article 32.

§ 5 In no case shall the total of compensation provided for in § 1 together with that provided for in Articles 30 and 32 exceed the compensation which would be payable in case of total loss of the goods.

§ 6 If, in accordance with Article 16 § 1, the transit period has been established by agreement, other forms of compensation than those provided for in § 1 may be so agreed. If, in this case, the transit periods provided for in Article 16 §§ 2 to 4 are exceeded, the person entitled may claim either the compensation provided for in the agreement mentioned above or that provided for in §§ 1 to 5.

Article 34 Compensation in case of declaration of value

The consignor and the carrier may agree that the consignor shall declare in the consignment note a value for the goods exceeding the limit provided for in Article 30 § 2. In such a case the amount declared shall be substituted for that limit.

Article 35 Compensation in case of interest in delivery

The consignor and the carrier may agree that the consignor may declare, by entering an amount in figures in the consignment note, a special interest in delivery, in case of loss, damage or exceeding of the transit period. In case of a declaration of interest in delivery further compensation for loss or damage proved may be claimed, in addition to the compensation provided for in Articles 30, 32 and 33, up to the amount declared.

Article 36 Loss of right to invoke the limits of liability

The limits of liability provided for in Article 15 § 3, Article 19 §§ 6 and 7, Article 30 and Articles 32 to 35 shall not apply if it is proved that the loss or damage results from an act or omission, which the carrier has committed either with intent to cause such loss or damage, or recklessly and with knowledge that such loss or damage would probably result.

Article 37 Conversion and interest

§ 1 Where the calculation of the compensation requires the conversion of sums expressed in foreign currency, conversion shall be at the exchange rate applicable on the day and at the place of payment of compensation.

§ 2 The person entitled may claim interest on compensation, calculated at five per cent per annum, from the day of the claim provided for in Article 43 or, if no such claim has been made, from the day on which legal proceedings were instituted.

§ 3 If the person entitled does not submit to the carrier, within a reasonable time allotted to him, the supporting documents required for the amount of the claim to be finally settled, no interest shall accrue between the expiry of the time allotted and the actual submission of such documents.

Article 38 Liability in respect of rail-sea traffic

§ 1 In rail-sea carriage by the services referred to in Article 24 § 1 of the Convention any Member State may, by requesting that a suitable note be included in the list of services to which these Uniform Rules apply, add the following grounds for exemption from liability in their entirety to those provided for in Article 23 :

a) fire, if the carrier proves that it was not caused by his act or default, or that of the master, a mariner, the pilot or the carrier's servants;

b) saving or attempting to save life or property at sea;
c) loading of goods on the deck of the ship, if they are so loaded with the consent of the consignor given on the consignment note and are not in wagons;
d) perils, dangers and accidents of the sea or other navigable waters.

§ 2 The carrier may only avail himself of the grounds for exemption referred to in § 1 if he proves that the loss, damage or exceeding the transit period occurred in the course of the journey by sea between the time when the goods were loaded on board the ship and the time when they were unloaded from the ship.

§ 3 When the carrier relies on the grounds for exemption referred to in § 1, he shall nevertheless remain liable if the person entitled proves that the loss, damage or exceeding the transit period is due to the fault of the carrier, the master, a mariner, the pilot or the carrier's servants.

§ 4 Where a sea route is served by several undertakings included in the list of services in accordance with Article 24 § 1 of the Convention, the liability regime applicable to that route must be the same for all those undertakings. In addition, where those undertakings have been included in the list at the request of several Member States, the adoption of this regime must be the subject of prior agreement between those States.

§ 5 The measures taken in accordance with §§ 1 and 4 shall be notified to the Secretary General. They shall come into force at the earliest at the expiry of a period of thirty days from the day on which the Secretary General notifies them to the other Member States. Consignments already in transit shall not be affected by such measures.

Article 39 Liability in case of nuclear incidents

The carrier shall be relieved of liability pursuant to these Uniform Rules for loss or damage caused by a nuclear incident when the operator of a nuclear installation or another person who is substituted for him is liable for the loss or damage pursuant to the laws and prescriptions of a State governing liability in the field of nuclear energy.

Article 40 Persons for whom the carrier is liable

The carrier shall be liable for his servants and other persons whose services he makes use of for the performance of the carriage, when these servants and other persons are acting within the scope of their functions. The managers of the railway infrastructure on which the carriage is performed shall be considered as persons whose services the carrier makes use of for the performance of the carriage.

Article 41 Other actions

§ 1 In all cases where these Uniform Rules shall apply, any action in respect of liability, on whatever grounds, may be brought against the carrier only subject to the conditions and limitations laid down in these Uniform Rules.

§ 2 The same shall apply to any action brought against the servants or other persons for whom the carrier is liable pursuant to Article 40.

Article 42 Ascertainment of partial loss or damage

§ 1 When partial loss or damage is discovered or presumed by the carrier or alleged by the person entitled, the carrier must without delay, and if possible in the presence of the person entitled, draw up a report stating, according to the nature of the loss or damage, the condition of the goods, their mass and, as far as possible, the extent of the loss or damage, its cause and the time of its occurrence.

§ 2 A copy of the report must be supplied free of charge to the person entitled.

§ 3 Should the person entitled not accept the findings in the report, he may request that the condition and mass of the goods and the cause and amount of the loss or damage be ascertained by an expert appointed either by the parties to the contract of carriage or by a court or tribunal. The procedure to be followed shall be governed by the laws and prescriptions of the State in which such ascertainment takes place.

Article 43 Claims

§ 1 Claims relating to the contract of carriage must be addressed in writing to the carrier against whom an action may be brought.

§ 2 A claim may be made by persons who have the right to bring an action against the carrier.

§ 3 To make the claim the consignor must produce the duplicate of the consignment note. Failing this he must produce an authorisation from the consignee or furnish proof that the consignee has refused to accept the goods.

§ 4 To make the claim the consignee must produce the consignment note if it has been handed over to him.

§ 5 The consignment note, the duplicate and any other documents which the person entitled thinks fit to submit with the claim must be produced either in the original or as copies, the copies, where appropriate, duly certified if the carrier so requests.

§ 6 On settlement of the claim the carrier may require the production, in the original form, of the consignment note, the duplicate or the cash on delivery voucher so that they may be endorsed to the effect that settlement has been made.

Article 44 Persons who may bring an action against the carrier

§ 1 Subject to §§ 3 and 4 actions based on the contract of carriage may be brought:

a) by the consignor, until such time as the consignee has

  1 taken possession of the consignment note,

2 accepted the goods, or
3 asserted his rights pursuant to Article 17 § 3 or Article 18 § 3;

b) by the consignee, from the time when he has

1 taken possession of the consignment note,
2 accepted the goods, or
3 asserted his rights pursuant to Article 17 § 3 or Article 18 § 3.

§ 2 The right of the consignee to bring an action shall be extinguished from the time when the person designated by the consignee in accordance with Article 18 § 5 has taken possession of the consignment note, accepted the goods or asserted his rights pursuant to Article 17 § 3.

§ 3 An action for the recovery of a sum paid pursuant to the contract of carriage may only be brought by the person who made the payment.

§ 4 An action in respect of cash on delivery payments may only be brought by the consignor.

§ 5 In order to bring an action the consignor must produce the duplicate of the consignment note. Failing this he must produce an authorisation from the consignee or furnish proof that the consignee has refused to accept the goods. If necessary, the consignor must prove the absence or the loss of the consignment note.

§ 6 In order to bring an action the consignee must produce the consignment note if it has been handed over to him.

Article 45 Carriers against whom an action may be brought

§ 1 Subject to §§ 3 and 4 actions based on the contract of carriage may be brought only against the first carrier, the last carrier or the carrier having performed the part of the carriage on which the event giving rise to the proceedings occurred.

§ 2 When, in the case of carriage performed by successive carriers, the carrier who must deliver the goods is entered with his consent on the consignment note, an action may be brought against him in accordance with § 1 even if he has received neither the goods nor the consignment note.

§ 3 An action for the recovery of a sum paid pursuant to the contract of carriage may be brought against the carrier who has collected that sum or against the carrier on whose behalf it was collected.

§ 4 An action in respect of cash on delivery payments may be brought only against the carrier who has taken over the goods at the place of consignment.

§ 5 An action may be brought against a carrier other than those specified in §§ 1 to 4 when instituted by way of counter-claim or by way of exception in proceedings relating to a principal claim based on the same contract of carriage.

§ 6 To the extent that these Uniform Rules apply to the substitute carrier, an action may also be brought against him.

§ 7 If the plaintiff has a choice between several carriers, his right to choose shall be extinguished as soon as he brings an action against any one of them; this shall also apply if the plaintiff has a choice between one or more carriers and a substitute carrier.

Article 46 Forum

§ 1 Actions based on these Uniform Rules may be brought before the courts or tribunals of Member States designated by agreement between the parties or before the courts or tribunals of a State on whose territory

a) the defendant has his domicile or habitual residence, his principal place of business or the branch or agency which concluded the contract of carriage, or
b) the place where the goods were taken over by the carrier or the place designated for delivery is situated.

Other courts or tribunals may not be seized.

§ 2 Where an action based on these Uniform Rules is pending before a court or tribunal competent pursuant to § 1, or where in such litigation a judgment has been delivered by such a court or tribunal, no new action may be brought between the same parties on the same grounds unless the judgment of the court or tribunal before which the first action was brought is not enforceable in the State in which the new action is brought.

Article 47 Extinction of right of action

§ 1 Acceptance of the goods by the person entitled shall extinguish all rights of action against the carrier arising from the contract of carriage in case of partial loss, damage or exceeding of the transit period.
§ 2 Nevertheless, the right of action shall not be extinguished:

a) in case of partial loss or damage, if
   1 the loss or damage was ascertained in accordance with Article 42 before the acceptance of the goods by the person entitled;
   2 the ascertainment which should have been carried out in accordance with Article 42 was omitted solely through the fault of the carrier;
b) in case of loss or damage which is not apparent whose existence is ascertained after acceptance of the goods by the person entitled, if he
   1 asks for ascertainment in accordance with Article 42 immediately after discovery of the loss or damage and not later than seven days after the acceptance of the goods, and
   2 in addition, proves that the loss or damage occurred between the time of taking over and the time of delivery;
c) in cases where the transit period has been exceeded, if the person entitled has, within sixty days, asserted his rights against one of the carriers referred to in Article 45 § 1;
d) if the person entitled proves that the loss or damage results from an act or omission, done with intent to cause such loss or damage, or recklessly and with knowledge that such loss or damage would probably result.

§ 3 If the goods have been reconsigned in accordance with Article 28 rights of action in case of partial loss or in case of damage, arising from one of the previous contracts of carriage, shall be extinguished as if there had been only a single contract of carriage.

Article 48 Limitation of actions

§ 1 The period of limitation for an action arising from the contract of carriage shall be one year. Nevertheless, the period of limitation shall be two years in the case of an action

a) to recover a cash on delivery payment collected by the carrier from the consignee;
b) to recover the proceeds of a sale effected by the carrier;
c) for loss or damage resulting from an act or omission done with intent to cause such loss or damage, or recklessly and with knowledge that such loss or damage would probably result;
d) based on one of the contracts of carriage prior to the reconsignment in the case provided for in Article 28.

§ 2 The period of limitation shall run for actions

a) for compensation for total loss, from the thirtieth day after expiry of the transit period;
b) for compensation for partial loss, damage or exceeding of the transit period, from the day when delivery took place;
c) in all other cases, from the day when the right of action may be exercised.

The day indicated for the commencement of the period of limitation shall not be included in the period.

§ 3 The period of limitation shall be suspended by a claim in writing in accordance with Article 43 until the day that the carrier rejects the claim by notification in writing and returns the documents submitted with it. If part of the claim is admitted, the period of limitation shall start to run again in respect of the part of the claim still in dispute. The burden of proof of receipt of the claim or of the reply and of the return of the documents shall lie on the party who relies on those facts. The period of limitation shall not be suspended by further claims having the same object.

§ 4 A right of action which has become time-barred may not be exercised further, even by way of counter-claim or relied upon by way of exception.

§ 5 Otherwise, the suspension and interruption of periods of limitation shall be governed by national law.

Article 49 Settlement of accounts

§ 1 Any carrier who has collected or ought to have collected, either at departure or on arrival, charges or other costs arising out of the contract of carriage must pay to the carriers concerned their respective shares. The methods of payment shall be fixed by agreement between the carriers.

§ 2 Article 12 shall also apply to the relations between successive carriers.

Article 50 Right of recourse

§ 1 A carrier who has paid compensation pursuant to these Uniform Rules shall have a right of recourse against the carriers who have taken part in the carriage in accordance with the following provisions:

a) the carrier who has caused the loss or damage shall be solely liable for it;
b) when the loss or damage has been caused by several carriers, each shall be liable for the loss or damage he has caused; if such distinction is impossible, the compensation shall be apportioned between them in accordance with letter c);
c) if it cannot be proved which of the carriers has caused the loss or damage, the compensation shall be apportioned between all the carriers who have taken part in the carriage, except those who prove that the loss or damage was not caused by them; such apportionment shall be in proportion to their respective shares of the carriage charge.

§ 2 In the case of insolvency of any one of these carriers, the unpaid share due from him shall be apportioned among all the other carriers who have taken part in the carriage, in proportion to their respective shares of the carriage charge.

Article 51 Procedure for recourse

§ 1 The validity of the payment made by the carrier exercising a right of recourse pursuant to Article 50 may not be disputed by the carrier against whom the right of recourse is exercised, when compensation has been determined by a court or tribunal and when the latter carrier, duly served with notice of the proceedings, has been afforded an opportunity to intervene in the proceedings. The court or tribunal seized of the principal action shall determine what time shall be allowed for such notification of the proceedings and for intervention in the proceedings.

§ 2 A carrier exercising his right of recourse must make his claim in one and the same proceedings against all the carriers with whom he has not reached a settlement, failing which he shall lose his right of recourse in the case of those against whom he has not taken proceedings.

§ 3 The court or tribunal must give its decision in one and the same judgment on all recourse claims brought before it.

§ 4 The carrier wishing to enforce his right of recourse may bring his action in the courts or tribunals of the State on the territory of which one of the carriers participating in the carriage has his principal place of business, or the branch or agency which concluded the contract of carriage.

§ 5 When the action must be brought against several carriers, the plaintiff carrier shall be entitled to choose the court or tribunal in which he will bring the proceedings from among those having competence pursuant to § 4.

§ 6 Recourse proceedings may not be joined with proceedings for compensation taken by the person entitled under the contract of carriage.

Article 52 Agreements concerning recourse

The carriers may conclude agreements which derogate from Articles 49 and 50.

The Hague Rules as Amended by the Brussels Protocol 1968 (HVR)

Article I

In these Rules the following words are employed, with the meanings set out below:

(a) 'Carrier' includes the owner or the charterer who enters into a contract of carriage with a shipper.
(b) 'Contract of carriage' applies only to contracts of carriage covered by a bill of lading or any similar document of title, in so far as such document relates to the carriage of goods by sea, including any bill of lading or any similar document as aforesaid issued under or pursuant to a charter party from the moment at which such bill of lading or similar document of title regulates the relations between a carrier and a holder of the same.
(c) 'Goods' includes goods, wares, merchandise, and articles of every kind whatsoever except live animals and cargo which by the contract of carriage is stated as being carried on deck and is so carried.
(d) 'Ship' means any vessel used for the carriage of goods by sea.
(e) 'Carriage of goods' covers the period from the time when the goods are loaded on to the time they are discharged from the ship.

Article II

Subject to the provisions of Article VI, under every contract of carriage of goods by sea the carrier, in relation to the loading, handling, stowage, carriage, custody, care and discharge of such goods, shall be subject to the responsibilities and liabilities and entitled to the rights and immunities hereinafter set forth.

Article III

1 The carrier shall be bound before and at the beginning of the voyage to exercise due diligence to:

(a) Make the ship seaworthy;
(b) Properly man, equip and supply the ship;

(c) Make the holds, refrigerating and cool chambers, and all other parts of the ship in which goods are carried, fit and safe for their reception, carriage and preservation.

2 Subject to the provisions of Article IV, the carrier shall properly and carefully load, handle, stow, carry, keep, care for, and discharge the goods carried.

3 After receiving the goods into his charge the carrier or the master or agent of the carrier shall, on demand of the shipper, issue to the shipper a bill of lading showing among other things:

(a) The leading marks necessary for identification of the goods as the same are furnished in writing by the shipper before the loading of such goods starts, provided such marks are stamped or otherwise shown clearly upon the goods if uncovered, or on the cases or coverings in which such goods are contained, in such a manner as should ordinarily remain legible until the end of the voyage.

(b) Either the number of packages or pieces, or the quantity, or weight, as the case may be, as furnished in writing by the shipper.

(c) The apparent order and condition of the goods.

Provided that no carrier, master or agent of the carrier shall be bound to state or show in the bill of lading any marks, number, quantity or weight which he has reasonable ground for suspecting not accurately to represent the goods actually received, or which he has had no reasonable means of checking.

4 Such a bill of lading shall be prima facie evidence of the receipt by the carrier of the goods as therein described in accordance with paragraph 3 (a), (b) and (c). However, proof to the contrary shall not be admissible when the bill of lading has been transferred to a third party acting in good faith.

5 The shipper shall be deemed to have guaranteed to the carrier the accuracy at the time of shipment of the marks, number, quantity and weight, as furnished by him, and the shipper shall indemnify the carrier against all loss, damages and expenses arising or resulting from inaccuracies in such particulars. The right of the carrier to such indemnity shall in no way limit his responsibility and liability under the contract of carriage to any person other than the shipper.

6 Unless notice of loss or damage and the general nature of such loss or damage be given in writing to the carrier or his agent at the port of discharge before or at the time of the removal of the goods into the custody of the person entitled to delivery thereof under the contract of carriage, or, if the loss or damage be not apparent, within three days, such removal shall be prima facie evidence of the delivery by the carrier of the goods as described in the bill of lading.

The notice in writing need not be given if the state of the goods has, at the time of their receipt, been the subject of joint survey or inspection.

Subject to paragraph 6bis the carrier and the ship shall in any event be discharged from all liability whatsoever in respect of the goods, unless suit is brought within one year of their delivery or of the date when they should have been delivered. This period, may however, be extended if the parties so agree after the cause of action has arisen.

In the case of any actual or apprehended loss or damage the carrier and the receiver shall give all reasonable facilities to each other for inspecting and tallying the goods.

6 An action for indemnity against a third person may be brought even after the expiration of the year provided for in the preceding paragraph if brought within the time allowed by the law of the Court seized of the case. However, the time allowed shall be not less than three months, commencing from the day when the person bringing such action for indemnity has settled the claim or has been served with process in the action against himself.

7 After the goods are loaded the bill of lading to be issued by the carrier, master, or agent of the carrier, to the shipper shall, if the shipper so demands be a 'shipped' bill of lading, provided that if the shipper shall have previously taken up any document of title to such goods, he shall surrender the same as against the issue of the 'shipped' bill of lading, but at the option of the carrier such document of title may be noted at the port of shipment by the carrier, master, or agent with the name or names of the ship or ships upon which the goods have been shipped and the date or dates of shipment, and when so noted, if it shows the particulars mentioned in paragraph 3 of Article III, shall for the purpose of this article be deemed to constitute a 'shipped' bill of lading.

8 Any clause, covenant, or agreement in a contract of carriage relieving the carrier or the ship from liability for loss or damage to, or in connection with, goods arising from negligence, fault, or failure in the duties and obligations provided in this article or lessening such liability otherwise than as provided in these Rules, shall be null and void and of no effect. A benefit of insurance in favour of the carrier or similar clause shall be deemed to be a clause relieving the carrier from liability.

Article IV

1 Neither the carrier nor the ship shall be liable for loss or damage arising or resulting from unseaworthiness unless caused by want of due diligence on the part of the carrier to make the ship seaworthy, and to secure that the ship is properly manned, equipped and supplied, and to make the holds, refrigerating and cool chambers and all other parts of the ship in which goods are carried fit and safe for their reception, carriage and preservation in accordance with the provisions of paragraph 1 of Article III. Whenever loss or damage has resulted from unseaworthiness the burden of proving the exercise of due diligence shall be on the carrier or other person claiming exemption under this article.

2 Neither the carrier nor the ship shall be responsible for loss or damage arising or resulting from:

(a) Act, neglect, or default of the master, mariner, pilot, or the servants of the carrier in the navigation or in the management of the ship.
(b) Fire, unless caused by the actual fault or privity of the carrier.
(c) Perils, dangers and accidents of the sea or other navigable waters.
(d) Act of God.
(e) Act of war.
(f) Act of public enemies.
(g) Arrest or restraint of princes, rulers or people, or seizure under legal process.
(h) Quarantine restrictions.
(i) Act or omission of the shipper or owner of the goods, his agent or representative.
(j) Strikes or lockouts or stoppage or restraint of labour from whatever cause, whether partial or general.
(k) Riots and civil commotions.
(l) Saving or attempting to save life or property at sea.
(m) Wastage in bulk of weight or any other loss or damage arising from inherent defect, quality or vice of the goods.
(n) Insufficiency of packing.
(o) Insufficiency or inadequacy of marks.
(p) Latent defects not discoverable by due diligence.
(q) Any other cause arising without the actual fault or privity of the carrier, or without the fault or neglect of the agents or servants of the carrier, but the burden of proof shall be on the person claiming the benefit of this exception to show that neither the actual fault or privity of the carrier nor the fault or neglect of the agents or servants of the carrier contributed to the loss or damage.

3 The shipper shall not be responsible for loss or damage sustained by the carrier or the ship arising or resulting from any cause without the act, fault or neglect of the shipper, his agents or his servants.

4 Any deviation in saving or attempting to save life or property at sea or any reasonable deviation shall not be deemed to be an infringement or breach of these Rules or of the contract of carriage, and the carrier shall not be liable for any loss or damage resulting therefrom.

5 (a) Unless the nature and value of such goods have been declared by the shipper before shipment and inserted in the bill of lading, neither the carrier nor the ship shall in any event be or become liable for any loss or damage to or in connection with the goods in an amount exceeding the equivalent of 666.67 units of account per package or unit or units of account per kilo of gross weight of the goods lost or damaged, whichever is the higher.

(b) The total amount recoverable shall be calculated by reference to the value of such goods at the place and time at which the goods are discharged from the ship in accordance with the contract or should have been so discharged.

The value of the goods shall be fixed according to the commodity exchange price, or, if there be no such price, according to the current market price, or, if there be no commodity exchange price or current market price, by reference to the normal value of goods of the same kind and quality.

(c) Where a container, pallet or similar article of transport is used to consolidate goods, the number of packages or units enumerated in the bill of lading as packed in such article of transport shall be deemed the number of packages or units for the purpose of this paragraph as far as these packages or units are concerned. Except as aforesaid such article of transport shall be considered the package or unit.
(d) The unit of account mentioned in this Article is the special drawing right as defined by the International Monetary Fund. The amounts mentioned in sub-paragraph (a) of this paragraph shall be converted into national currency on the basis of the value of that currency on a date to be determined by the law of the Court seized of the case.
(e) Neither the carrier nor the ship shall be entitled to the benefit of the limitation of liability provided for in this paragraph if it is proved that the damage resulted from an act or omission of the carrier done with intent to cause damage, or recklessly and with knowledge that damage would probably result.
(f) The declaration mentioned in sub-paragraph (a) of this paragraph, if embodied in the bill of lading, shall be prima facie evidence, but shall not be binding or conclusive on the carrier.
(g) By agreement between the carrier, master or agent of the carrier and the shipper other maximum amounts than those mentioned in sub-paragraph (a) of this paragraph may be fixed, provided that no maximum amount so fixed shall be less than the appropriate maximum mentioned in that sub-paragraph.
(h) Neither the carrier nor the ship shall be responsible in any event for loss or damage to, or in connection with, goods if the nature or value thereof has been knowingly mis-stated by the shipper in the bill of lading.

6 Goods of an inflammable, explosive or dangerous nature to the shipment whereof the carrier, master or agent of the carrier has not consented with knowledge of their nature and character, may at any time before discharge be landed at any place, or destroyed or rendered innocuous by the carrier without compensation and the shipper of such goods shall be liable for all damages and expenses directly or indirectly arising out of or resulting from such shipment. If any such goods shipped with such knowledge and consent

shall become a danger to the ship or cargo, they may in like manner be landed at any place, or destroyed or rendered innocuous by the carrier without liability on the part of the carrier except to general average, if any.

Article IV bis

1 The defences and limits of liability provided for in these Rules shall apply in any action against the carrier in respect of loss or damage to goods covered by a contract of carriage whether the action be founded in contract or in tort.
2 If such an action is brought against a servant or agent of the carrier (such servant or agent not being an independent contractor), such servant or agent shall be entitled to avail himself of the defences and limits of liability which the carrier is entitled to invoke under these Rules.
3 The aggregate of the amounts recoverable from the carrier, and such servants and agents, shall in no case exceed the limit provided for in these Rules.
4 Nevertheless, a servant or agent of the carrier shall not be entitled to avail himself of the provisions of this article, if it is proved that the damage resulted from an act or omission of the servant or agent done with intent to cause damage or recklessly and with knowledge that damage would probably result.

Article V

A carrier shall be at liberty to surrender in whole or in part all or any of his rights and immunities or to increase any of his responsibilities and obligations under these Rules, provided such surrender or increase shall be embodied in the bill of lading issued to the shipper. The provisions of these Rules shall not be applicable to charter parties, but if bills of lading are issued in the case of a ship under a charter party they shall comply with the terms of these Rules. Nothing in these Rules shall be held to prevent the insertion in a bill of lading of any lawful provision regarding general average.

Article VI

Notwithstanding the provisions of the preceding articles, a carrier, master or agent of the carrier and a shipper shall in regard to any particular goods be at liberty to enter into any agreement in any terms as to the responsibility and liability of the carrier for such goods, and as to the rights and immunities of the carrier in respect of such goods, or his obligation as to seaworthiness, so far as this stipulation is not contrary to public policy, or the care or diligence of his servants or agents in regard to the loading, handling, stowage, carriage, custody, care and discharge of the goods carried by sea, provided that in this case no bill of lading has been or shall be issued and that the terms agreed shall be embodied in a receipt which shall be a non-negotiable document and shall be marked as such.

Any agreement so entered into shall have full legal effect.

Provided that this article shall not apply to ordinary commercial shipments made in the ordinary course of trade, but only to other shipments where the character or condition of the property to be carried or the circumstances, terms and conditions under which the carriage is to be performed are such as reasonably to justify a special agreement.

Article VII

Nothing herein contained shall prevent a carrier or a shipper from entering into any agreement, stipulation, condition, reservation or exemption as to the responsibility and liability of the carrier or the ship for the loss or damage to, or in connection with, the custody and care and handling of goods prior to the loading on, and subsequent to the discharge from, the ship on which the goods are carried by sea.

Article VIII

The provisions of these Rules shall not affect the rights and obligations of the carrier under any statute for the time being in force relating to the limitation of the liability of owners of sea-going vessels.

Article IX

These Rules shall not affect the provisions of any international Convention or national law governing liability for nuclear damage.

Article X

The provisions of these Rules shall apply to every bill of lading relating to the carriage of goods between ports in two different States if

(a) the bill of lading is issued in a contracting State, or
(b) the carriage is from a port in a contracting State, or
(c) the contract contained in or evidenced by the bill of lading provides that these Rules or legislation of any State giving effect to them are to govern the contract;

whatever may be the nationality of the ship, the carrier, the shipper, the consignee, or any other interested person.

Each contracting state shall apply the provisions of the convention to the bills of lading mentioned above.

This article shall not prevent a contracting state from applying the rules of this convention to bills of lading not included in the preceding paragraphs.

Convention for the Unification of Certain Rules for International Carriage by Air (MC)

Article 1 Scope of application

1 This Convention applies to all international carriage of persons, baggage or cargo performed by aircraft for reward. It applies equally to gratuitous carriage by aircraft performed by an air transport undertaking.

2 For the purposes of this Convention, the expression international carriage means any carriage in which, according to the agreement between the parties, the place of departure and the place of destination, whether or not there be a break in the carriage or a transhipment, are situated either within the territories of two States Parties, or within the territory of a single State Party if there is an agreed stopping place within the territory of another State, even if that State is not a State Party. Carriage between two points within the territory of a single State Party without an agreed stopping place within the territory of another State is not international carriage for the purposes of this Convention.

3 Carriage to be performed by several successive carriers is deemed, for the purposes of this Convention, to be one undivided carriage if it has been regarded by the parties as a single operation, whether it has been agreed upon under the form of a single contract or of a series of contracts, and it does not lose its international character merely because one contract or a series of contracts is to be performed entirely within the territory of the same State.

4 This Convention applies also to carriage as set out in Chapter V, subject to the terms contained therein.

Article 2 Carriage performed by State and carriage of postal items

1 This Convention applies to carriage performed by the State or by legally constituted public bodies provided it falls within the conditions laid down in Article 1.

2 In the carriage of postal items, the carrier shall be liable only to the relevant postal administration in accordance with the rules applicable to the relationship between the carriers and the postal administrations.

3 Except as provided in paragraph 2 of this Article, the provisions of this Convention shall not apply to the carriage of postal items.

Article 3 Passengers and baggage

1 In respect of carriage of passengers, an individual or collective document of carriage shall be delivered containing:

(a) an indication of the places of departure and destination;
(b) if the places of departure and destination are within the territory of a single State Party, one or more agreed stopping places being within the territory of another State, an indication of at least one such stopping place.

2 Any other means which preserves the information indicated in paragraph 1 may be substituted for the delivery of the document referred to in that paragraph. If any such other means is used, the carrier shall offer to deliver to the passenger a written statement of the information so preserved.
3 The carrier shall deliver to the passenger a baggage identification tag for each piece of checked baggage.
4 The passenger shall be given written notice to the effect that where this Convention is applicable it governs and may limit the liability of carriers in respect of death or injury and for destruction or loss of, or damage to, baggage, and for delay.
5 Non-compliance with the provisions of the foregoing paragraphs shall not affect the existence or the validity of the contract of carriage, which shall, nonetheless, be subject to the rules of this Convention including those relating to limitation of liability.

Article 4 Cargo

1 In respect of the carriage of cargo, an air waybill shall be delivered.
2 Any other means which preserves a record of the carriage to be performed may be substituted for the delivery of an air waybill. If such other means are used, the carrier shall, if so requested by the consignor, deliver to the consignor a cargo receipt permitting identification of the consignment and access to the information contained in the record preserved by such other means.

Article 5 Contents of air waybill or cargo receipt

The air waybill or the cargo receipt shall include:

(a) an indication of the places of departure and destination;
(b) if the places of departure and destination are within the territory of a single State Party, one or more agreed stopping places being within the territory of another State, an indication of at least one such stopping place; and
(c) an indication of the weight of the consignment.

Article 6 Document relating to the nature of the cargo

The consignor may be required, if necessary, to meet the formalities of customs, police and similar public authorities to deliver a document indicating the nature of the cargo. This provision creates for the carrier no duty, obligation or liability resulting therefrom.

Article 7 Description of air waybill

1 The air waybill shall be made out by the consignor in three original parts.
2 The first part shall be marked "for the carrier"; it shall be signed by the consignor. The second part shall be marked "for the consignee"; it shall be signed by the consignor and by the carrier. The third part shall be signed by the carrier who shall hand it to the consignor after the cargo has been accepted.
3 The signature of the carrier and that of the consignor may be printed or stamped.
4 If, at the request of the consignor, the carrier makes out the air waybill, the carrier shall be deemed, subject to proof to the contrary, to have done so on behalf of the consignor.

Article 8 Documentation for multiple packages

When there is more than one package:

(a) the carrier of cargo has the right to require the consignor to make out separate air waybills;
(b) the consignor has the right to require the carrier to deliver separate cargo receipts when the other means referred to in paragraph 2 of Article 4 are used.

Article 9 Non-compliance with documentary requirements

Non-compliance with the provisions of Articles 4 to 8 shall not affect the existence or the validity of the contract of carriage, which shall, nonetheless, be subject to the rules of this Convention including those relating to limitation of liability.

Article 10 Responsibility for particulars of documentation

1 The consignor is responsible for the correctness of the particulars and statements relating to the cargo inserted by it or on its behalf in the air waybill or furnished by it or on its behalf to the carrier for insertion in the cargo receipt or for insertion in the record preserved by the other means referred to in paragraph 2 of Article 4. The foregoing shall also apply where the person acting on behalf of the consignor is also the agent of the carrier.

2 The consignor shall indemnify the carrier against all damage suffered by it, or by any other person to whom the carrier is liable, by reason of the irregularity, incorrectness or incompleteness of the particulars and statements furnished by the consignor or on its behalf.

3 Subject to the provisions of paragraphs 1 and 2 of this Article, the carrier shall indemnify the consignor against all damage suffered by it, or by any other person to whom the consignor is liable, by reason of the irregularity, incorrectness or incompleteness of the particulars and statements inserted by the carrier or on its behalf in the cargo receipt or in the record preserved by the other means referred to in paragraph 2 of Article 4.

Article 11 Evidentiary value of documentation

1 The air waybill or the cargo receipt is prima facie evidence of the conclusion of the contract, of the acceptance of the cargo and of the conditions of carriage mentioned therein.

2 Any statements in the air waybill or the cargo receipt relating to the weight, dimensions and packing of the cargo, as well as those relating to the number of packages, are prima facie evidence of the facts stated; those relating to the quantity, volume and condition of the cargo do not constitute evidence against the carrier except so far as they both have been, and are stated in the air waybill or the cargo receipt to have been, checked by it in the presence of the consignor, or relate to the apparent condition of the cargo.

Article 12 Right of disposition of cargo

1 Subject to its liability to carry out all its obligations under the contract of carriage, the consignor has the right to dispose of the cargo by withdrawing it at the airport of departure or destination, or by stopping it in the course of the journey on any landing, or by calling for it to be delivered at the place of destination or in the course of the journey to a person other than the consignee originally designated, or by requiring it to be returned to the airport of departure. The consignor must not exercise this right of disposition in such a way as to prejudice the carrier or other consignors and must reimburse any expenses occasioned by the exercise of this right.

2 If it is impossible to carry out the instructions of the consignor, the carrier must so inform the consignor forthwith.

3 If the carrier carries out the instructions of the consignor for the disposition of the cargo without requiring the production of the part of the air waybill or the cargo receipt delivered to the latter, the carrier will be liable, without prejudice to its right of recovery from the consignor, for any damage which may be caused thereby to any person who is lawfully in possession of that part of the air waybill or the cargo receipt.

4 The right conferred on the consignor ceases at the moment when that of the consignee begins in accordance with Article 13. Nevertheless, if the consignee declines to accept the cargo, or cannot be communicated with, the consignor resumes its right of disposition.

Article 13 Delivery of the cargo

1 Except when the consignor has exercised its right under Article 12, the consignee is entitled, on arrival of the cargo at the place of destination, to require the carrier to deliver the cargo to it, on payment of the charges due and on complying with the conditions of carriage.
2 Unless it is otherwise agreed, it is the duty of the carrier to give notice to the consignee as soon as the cargo arrives.
3 If the carrier admits the loss of the cargo, or if the cargo has not arrived at the expiration of seven days after the date on which it ought to have arrived, the consignee is entitled to enforce against the carrier the rights which flow from the contract of carriage.

Article 14 Enforcement of the rights of consignor and consignee

The consignor and the consignee can respectively enforce all the rights given to them by Articles 12 and 13, each in its own name, whether it is acting in its own interest or in the interests of another, provided that it carries out the obligations imposed by the contract of carriage.

Article 15 Relations of consignor and consignee or mutual relations of third parties

1 Articles 12, 13 and 14 do not affect either the relations of the consignor and the consignee with each other or the mutual relations of third parties, whose rights are derived either from the consignor or from the consignee.
2 The provisions of Articles 12, 13 and 14 can only be varied by express provision in the air waybill or the cargo receipt.

Article 16 Formalities of customs, police or other public authorities

1 The consignor must furnish such information and such documents as are necessary to meet the formalities of customs, police and any other public authorities before the cargo can be delivered to the consignee. The consignor is liable to the carrier for any damage occasioned by the absence, insufficiency or irregularity of any such information or documents, unless the damage is due to the fault of the carrier, its servants or agents.
2 The carrier is under no obligation to enquire into the correctness or sufficiency of such information or documents.

Article 17 Death and injury of passengers - damage to baggage

1 The carrier is liable for damage sustained in case of death or bodily injury of a passenger upon condition only that the accident which caused the death or

injury took place on board the aircraft or in the course of any of the operations of embarking or disembarking.

2 The carrier is liable for damage sustained in case of destruction or loss of, or of damage to, checked baggage upon condition only that the event which caused the destruction, loss or damage took place on board the aircraft or during any period within which the checked baggage was in the charge of the carrier. However, the carrier is not liable if and to the extent that the damage resulted from the inherent defect, quality or vice of the baggage. In the case of unchecked baggage, including personal items, the carrier is liable if the damage resulted from its fault or that of its servants or agents.

3 If the carrier admits the loss of the checked baggage, or if the checked baggage has not arrived at the expiration of 21 days after the date on which it ought to have arrived, the passenger is entitled to enforce against the carrier the rights which flow from the contract of carriage.

4 Unless otherwise specified, in this Convention the term "baggage" means both checked baggage and unchecked baggage.

Article 18 Damage to cargo

1 The carrier is liable for damage sustained in the event of the destruction or loss of, or damage to, cargo upon condition only that the event which caused the damage so sustained took place during the carriage by air.

2 However, the carrier is not liable if and to the extent it proves that the destruction, or loss of, or damage to, the cargo resulted from one or more of the following:

(a) inherent defect, quality or vice of that cargo;
(b) defective packing of that cargo performed by a person other than the carrier or its servants or agents;
(c) an act of war or an armed conflict;
(d) an act of public authority carried out in connection with the entry, exit or transit of the cargo.

3 The carriage by air within the meaning of paragraph 1 of this Article comprises the period during which the cargo is in the charge of the carrier.

4 The period of the carriage by air does not extend to any carriage by land, by sea or by inland waterway performed outside an airport. If, however, such carriage takes place in the performance of a contract for carriage by air, for the purpose of loading, delivery or transhipment, any damage is presumed, subject to proof to the contrary, to have been the result of an event which took place during the carriage by air. If a carrier, without the consent of the consignor, substitutes carriage by another mode of transport for the whole or part of a carriage intended by the agreement between the parties to be carriage by air, such carriage by another mode of transport is deemed to be within the period of carriage by air.

Article 19 Delay

The carrier is liable for damage occasioned by delay in the carriage by air of passengers, baggage or cargo. Nevertheless, the carrier shall not be liable for damage occasioned by delay if it proves that it and its servants and agents took all measures that could reasonably be required to avoid the damage or that it was impossible for it or them to take such measures.

Article 20 Exoneration

If the carrier proves that the damage was caused or contributed to by the negligence or other wrongful act or omission of the person claiming compensation, or the person from whom he or she derives his or her rights, the carrier shall be wholly or partly exonerated from its liability to the claimant to the extent that such negligence or wrongful act or omission caused or contributed to the damage. When by reason of death or injury of a passenger compensation is claimed by a person other than the passenger, the carrier shall likewise be wholly or partly exonerated from its liability to the extent that it proves that the damage was caused or contributed to by the negligence or other wrongful act or omission of that passenger. This Article applies to all the liability provisions in this Convention, including paragraph 1 of Article 21.

Article 21 Compensation in case of death or injury of passengers

1 For damages arising under paragraph 1 of Article 17 not exceeding 100000 Special Drawing Rights for each passenger, the carrier shall not be able to exclude or limit its liability.

2 The carrier shall not be liable for damages arising under paragraph 1 of Article 17 to the extent that they exceed for each passenger 100000 Special Drawing Rights if the carrier proves that:

   (a) such damage was not due to the negligence or other wrongful act or omission of the carrier or its servants or agents; or
   (b) such damage was solely due to the negligence or other wrongful act or omission of a third party.

Article 22 Limits of liability in relation to delay, baggage and cargo

1 In the case of damage caused by delay as specified in Article 19 in the carriage of persons, the liability of the carrier for each passenger is limited to 4150 Special Drawing Rights.

2 In the carriage of baggage, the liability of the carrier in the case of destruction, loss, damage or delay is limited to 1000 Special Drawing Rights for each passenger unless the passenger has made, at the time when the checked

baggage was handed over to the carrier, a special declaration of interest in delivery at destination and has paid a supplementary sum if the case so requires. In that case the carrier will be liable to pay a sum not exceeding the declared sum, unless it proves that the sum is greater than the passenger's actual interest in delivery at destination.

3 In the carriage of cargo, the liability of the carrier in the case of destruction, loss, damage or delay is limited to a sum of 17 Special Drawing Rights per kilogram, unless the consignor has made, at the time when the package was handed over to the carrier, a special declaration of interest in delivery at destination and has paid a supplementary sum if the case so requires. In that case the carrier will be liable to pay a sum not exceeding the declared sum, unless it proves that the sum is greater than the consignor's actual interest in delivery at destination.

4 In the case of destruction, loss, damage or delay of part of the cargo, or of any object contained therein, the weight to be taken into consideration in determining the amount to which the carrier's liability is limited shall be only the total weight of the package or packages concerned. Nevertheless, when the destruction, loss, damage or delay of a part of the cargo, or of an object contained therein, affects the value of other packages covered by the same air waybill, or the same receipt or, if they were not issued, by the same record preserved by the other means referred to in paragraph 2 of Article 4, the total weight of such package or packages shall also be taken into consideration in determining the limit of liability.

5 The foregoing provisions of paragraphs 1 and 2 of this Article shall not apply if it is proved that the damage resulted from an act or omission of the carrier, its servants or agents, done with intent to cause damage or recklessly and with knowledge that damage would probably result; provided that, in the case of such act or omission of a servant or agent, it is also proved that such servant or agent was acting within the scope of its employment.

6 The limits prescribed in Article 21 and in this Article shall not prevent the court from awarding, in accordance with its own law, in addition, the whole or part of the court costs and of the other expenses of the litigation incurred by the plaintiff, including interest. The foregoing provision shall not apply if the amount of the damages awarded, excluding court costs and other expenses of the litigation, does not exceed the sum which the carrier has offered in writing to the plaintiff within a period of six months from the date of the occurrence causing the damage, or before the commencement of the action, if that is later.

Article 23 Conversion of monetary units

1 The sums mentioned in terms of Special Drawing Right in this Convention shall be deemed to refer to the Special Drawing Right as defined by the International Monetary Fund. Conversion of the sums into national currencies shall, in case of judicial proceedings, be made according to the value of such currencies in

terms of the Special Drawing Right at the date of the judgment. The value of a national currency, in terms of the Special Drawing Right, of a State Party which is a Member of the International Monetary Fund, shall be calculated in accordance with the method of valuation applied by the International Monetary Fund, in effect at the date of the judgment, for its operations and transactions. The value of a national currency, in terms of the Special Drawing Right, of a State Party which is not a Member of the International Monetary Fund, shall be calculated in a manner determined by that State.

2 Nevertheless, those States which are not Members of the International Monetary Fund and whose law does not permit the application of the provisions of paragraph 1 of this Article may, at the time of ratification or accession or at any time thereafter, declare that the limit of liability of the carrier prescribed in Article 21 is fixed at a sum of 1500000 monetary units per passenger in judicial proceedings in their territories; 62500 monetary units per passenger with respect to paragraph 1 of Article 22; 15000 monetary units per passenger with respect to paragraph 2 of Article 22; and 250 monetary units per kilogram with respect to paragraph 3 of Article 22. This monetary unit corresponds to 65,5 milligrams of gold of millesimal fineness nine hundred. These sums may be converted into the national currency concerned in round figures. The conversion of these sums into national currency shall be made according to the law of the State concerned.

3 The calculation mentioned in the last sentence of paragraph 1 of this Article and the conversion method mentioned in paragraph 2 of this Article shall be made in such manner as to express in the national currency of the State Party as far as possible the same real value for the amounts in Articles 21 and 22 as would result from the application of the first three sentences of paragraph 1 of this Article. State Parties shall communicate to the depositary the manner of calculation pursuant to paragraph 1 of this Article, or the result of the conversion in paragraph 2 of this Article as the case may be, when depositing an instrument of ratification, acceptance, approval of or accession to this Convention and whenever there is a change in either.

Article 24 Review of limits

1 Without prejudice to the provisions of Article 25 of this Convention and subject to paragraph 2 below, the limits of liability prescribed in Articles 21, 22 and 23 shall be reviewed by the Depositary at five-year intervals, the first such review to take place at the end of the fifth year following the date of entry into force of this Convention, or if the Convention does not enter into force within five years of the date it is first open for signature, within the first year of its entry into force, by reference to an inflation factor which corresponds to the accumulated rate of inflation since the previous revision or in the first instance since the date of entry into force of the Convention. The measure of the rate of inflation to be used in determining the inflation factor shall be the weighted average of the annual rates of increase or decrease

in the Consumer Price Indices of the States whose currencies comprise the Special Drawing Right mentioned in paragraph 1 of Article 23.

2 If the review referred to in the preceding paragraph concludes that the inflation factor has exceeded 10 per cent, the Depositary shall notify States Parties of a revision of the limits of liability. Any such revision shall become effective six months after its notification to the States Parties. If within three months after its notification to the States Parties a majority of the States Parties register their disapproval, the revision shall not become effective and the Depositary shall refer the matter to a meeting of the States Parties. The Depositary shall immediately notify all States Parties of the coming into force of any revision.

3 Notwithstanding paragraph 1 of this Article, the procedure referred to in paragraph 2 of this Article shall be applied at any time provided that one-third of the States Parties express a desire to that effect and upon condition that the inflation factor referred to in paragraph 1 has exceeded 30 per cent since the previous revision or since the date of entry into force of this Convention if there has been no previous revision. Subsequent reviews using the procedure described in paragraph 1 of this Article will take place at five-year intervals starting at the end of the fifth year following the date of the reviews under the present paragraph.

Article 25 Stipulation on limits

A carrier may stipulate that the contract of carriage shall be subject to higher limits of liability than those provided for in this Convention or to no limits of liability whatsoever.

Article 26 Invalidity of contractual provisions

Any provision tending to relieve the carrier of liability or to fix a lower limit than that which is laid down in this Convention shall be null and void, but the nullity of any such provision does not involve the nullity of the whole contract, which shall remain subject to the provisions of this Convention.

Article 27 Freedom to contract

Nothing contained in this Convention shall prevent the carrier from refusing to enter into any contract of carriage, from waiving any defences available under the Convention, or from laying down conditions which do not conflict with the provisions of this Convention.

Article 28 Advance payments

In the case of aircraft accidents resulting in death or injury of passengers, the carrier shall, if required by its national law, make advance payments without delay to a natural person or persons who are entitled to claim compensation in order to meet the immediate economic needs of such persons. Such advance payments shall not constitute a recognition of liability and may be offset against any amounts subsequently paid as damages by the carrier.

Article 29 Basis of claims

In the carriage of passengers, baggage and cargo, any action for damages, however founded, whether under this Convention or in contract or in tort or otherwise, can only be brought subject to the conditions and such limits of liability as are set out in this Convention without prejudice to the question as to who are the persons who have the right to bring suit and what are their respective rights. In any such action, punitive, exemplary or any other non-compensatory damages shall not be recoverable.

Article 30 Servants, agents – aggregation of claims

1 If an action is brought against a servant or agent of the carrier arising out of damage to which the Convention relates, such servant or agent, if they prove that they acted within the scope of their employment, shall be entitled to avail themselves of the conditions and limits of liability which the carrier itself is entitled to invoke under this Convention.

2 The aggregate of the amounts recoverable from the carrier, its servants and agents, in that case, shall not exceed the said limits.

3 Save in respect of the carriage of cargo, the provisions of paragraphs 1 and 2 of this Article shall not apply if it is proved that the damage resulted from an act or omission of the servant or agent done with intent to cause damage or recklessly and with knowledge that damage would probably result.

Article 31 Timely notice of complaints

1 Receipt by the person entitled to delivery of checked baggage or cargo without complaint is prima facie evidence that the same has been delivered in good condition and in accordance with the document of carriage or with the record preserved by the other means referred to in paragraph 2 of Article 3 and paragraph 2 of Article 4.

2 In the case of damage, the person entitled to delivery must complain to the carrier forthwith after the discovery of the damage, and, at the latest, within seven days from the date of receipt in the case of checked baggage and 14 days from the date of receipt in the case of cargo. In the case of delay, the complaint must be made at the latest within 21 days from the date on which the baggage or cargo have been placed at his or her disposal.

3 Every complaint must be made in writing and given or dispatched within the times aforesaid.

4 If no complaint is made within the times aforesaid, no action shall lie against the carrier, save in the case of fraud on its part.

Article 32 Death of person liable

In the case of the death of the person liable, an action for damages lies in accordance with the terms of this Convention against those legally representing his or her estate.

Article 33 Jurisdiction

1 An action for damages must be brought, at the option of the plaintiff, in the territory of one of the States Parties, either before the court of the domicile of the carrier or of its principal place of business, or where it has a place of business through which the contract has been made or before the court at the place of destination.

2 In respect of damage resulting from the death or injury of a passenger, an action may be brought before one of the courts mentioned in paragraph 1 of this Article, or in the territory of a State Party in which at the time of the accident the passenger has his or her principal and permanent residence and to or from which the carrier operates services for the carriage of passengers by air, either on its own aircraft, or on another carrier's aircraft pursuant to a commercial agreement, and in which that carrier conducts its business of carriage of passengers by air from premises leased or owned by the carrier itself or by another carrier with which it has a commercial agreement.

3 For the purposes of paragraph 2,

(a) "commercial agreement" means an agreement, other than an agency agreement, made between carriers and relating to the provision of their joint services for carriage of passengers by air;

(b) "principal and permanent residence" means the one fixed and permanent abode of the passenger at the time of the accident. The nationality of the passenger shall not be the determining factor in this regard.

4 Questions of procedure shall be governed by the law of the court seised of the case.

Article 34 Arbitration

1 Subject to the provisions of this Article, the parties to the contract of carriage for cargo may stipulate that any dispute relating to the liability of the carrier under this Convention shall be settled by arbitration. Such agreement shall be in writing.

2 The arbitration proceedings shall, at the option of the claimant, take place within one of the jurisdictions referred to in Article 33.

3 The arbitrator or arbitration tribunal shall apply the provisions of this Convention.

4 The provisions of paragraphs 2 and 3 of this Article shall be deemed to be part of every arbitration clause or agreement, and any term of such clause or agreement which is inconsistent therewith shall be null and void.

Article 35 Limitation of actions

1 The right to damages shall be extinguished if an action is not brought within a period of two years, reckoned from the date of arrival at the destination, or from the date on which the aircraft ought to have arrived, or from the date on which the carriage stopped.

2 The method of calculating that period shall be determined by the law of the court seised of the case.

Article 36 Successive carriage

1 In the case of carriage to be performed by various successive carriers and falling within the definition set out in paragraph 3 of Article 1, each carrier which accepts passengers, baggage or cargo is subject to the rules set out in this Convention and is deemed to be one of the parties to the contract of carriage in so far as the contract deals with that part of the carriage which is performed under its supervision.

2 In the case of carriage of this nature, the passenger or any person entitled to compensation in respect of him or her can take action only against the carrier which performed the carriage during which the accident or the delay occurred, save in the case where, by express agreement, the first carrier has assumed liability for the whole journey.

3 As regards baggage or cargo, the passenger or consignor will have a right of action against the first carrier, and the passenger or consignee who is entitled to delivery will have a right of action against the last carrier, and further, each may take action against the carrier which performed the carriage during which the destruction, loss, damage or delay took place. These carriers will be jointly and severally liable to the passenger or to the consignor or consignee.

Article 37 Right of recourse against third parties

Nothing in this Convention shall prejudice the question whether a person liable for damage in accordance with its provisions has a right of recourse against any other person.

Article 38 Combined carriage

1 In the case of combined carriage performed partly by air and partly by any other mode of carriage, the provisions of this Convention shall, subject to paragraph 4 of Article 18, apply only to the carriage by air, provided that the carriage by air falls within the terms of Article 1.

2 Nothing in this Convention shall prevent the parties in the case of combined carriage from inserting in the document of air carriage conditions relating to other modes of carriage, provided that the provisions of this Convention are observed as regards the carriage by air.

Article 39 Contracting carrier actual carrier

The provisions of this Chapter apply when a person (hereinafter referred to as "the contracting carrier") as a principal makes a contract of carriage governed by this Convention with a passenger or consignor or with a person acting on behalf of the passenger or consignor, and another person (hereinafter referred to as "the actual carrier") performs, by virtue of authority from the contracting carrier, the whole or part of the carriage, but is not with respect to such part a successive carrier within the meaning of this Convention. Such authority shall be presumed in the absence of proof to the contrary.

Article 40 Respective liability of contracting and actual carriers

If an actual carrier performs the whole or part of carriage which, according to the contract referred to in Article 39, is governed by this Convention, both the contracting carrier and the actual carrier shall, except as otherwise provided in this Chapter, be subject to the rules of this Convention, the former for the whole of the carriage contemplated in the contract, the latter solely for the carriage which it performs.

Article 41 Mutual liability

1 The acts and omissions of the actual carrier and of its servants and agents acting within the scope of their employment shall, in relation to the carriage performed by the actual carrier, be deemed to be also those of the contracting carrier.

2 The acts and omissions of the contracting carrier and of its servants and agents acting within the scope of their employment shall, in relation to the carriage performed by the actual carrier, be deemed to be also those of the actual carrier. Nevertheless, no such act or omission shall subject the actual carrier to liability exceeding the amounts referred to in Articles 21, 22, 23 and 24. Any special agreement under which the contracting carrier assumes obligations not imposed by this Convention or any waiver of rights or defences conferred by this Convention or any special declaration of interest in delivery at destination contemplated in Article 22 shall not affect the actual carrier unless agreed to by it.

Article 42 Addressee of complaints and instructions

Any complaint to be made or instruction to be given under this Convention to the carrier shall have the same effect whether addressed to the contracting carrier or to the actual carrier. Nevertheless, instructions referred to in Article 12 shall only be effective if addressed to the contracting carrier.

Article 43 Servants and agents

In relation to the carriage performed by the actual carrier, any servant or agent of that carrier or of the contracting carrier shall, if they prove that they acted within the scope of their employment, be entitled to avail themselves of the conditions and limits of liability which are applicable under this Convention to the carrier whose servant or agent they are, unless it is proved that they acted in a manner that prevents the limits of liability from being invoked in accordance with this Convention.

Article 44 Aggregation of damages

In relation to the carriage performed by the actual carrier, the aggregate of the amounts recoverable from that carrier and the contracting carrier, and from their servants and agents acting within the scope of their employment, shall not exceed the highest amount which could be awarded against either the contracting carrier or the actual carrier under this Convention, but none of the persons mentioned shall be liable for a sum in excess of the limit applicable to that person.

Article 45 Addressee of claims

In relation to the carriage performed by the actual carrier, an action for damages may be brought, at the option of the plaintiff, against that carrier or the contracting carrier, or against both together or separately. If the action is brought against only one of those carriers, that carrier shall have the right to require the other carrier to be joined in the proceedings, the procedure and effects being governed by the law of the court seised of the case.

Article 46 Additional jurisdiction

Any action for damages contemplated in Article 45 must be brought, at the option of the plaintiff, in the territory of one of the States Parties, either before a court in which an action may be brought against the contracting carrier, as provided in Article 33, or before the court having jurisdiction at the place where the actual carrier has its domicile or its principal place of business.

Article 47 Invalidity of contractual provisions

Any contractual provision tending to relieve the contracting carrier or the actual carrier of liability under this Chapter or to fix a lower limit than that which is applicable according to this Chapter shall be null and void, but the nullity of any such provision does not involve the nullity of the whole contract, which shall remain subject to the provisions of this Chapter.

Article 48 Mutual relations of contracting and actual carriers

Except as provided in Article 45, nothing in this Chapter shall affect the rights and obligations of the carriers between themselves, including any right of recourse or indemnification.

Article 49 Mandatory application

Any clause contained in the contract of carriage and all special agreements entered into before the damage occurred by which the parties purport to infringe the rules laid down by this Convention, whether by deciding the law to be applied, or by altering the rules as to jurisdiction, shall be null and void.

Article 50 Insurance

States Parties shall require their carriers to maintain adequate insurance covering their liability under this Convention. A carrier may be required by the State Party into which it operates to furnish evidence that it maintains adequate insurance covering its liability under this Convention.

Article 51 Carriage Performed in Extraordinary Circumstances

The provisions of Articles 3 to 5, 7 and 8 relating to the documentation of carriage shall not apply in the case of carriage performed in extraordinary circumstances outside the normal scope of a carrier's business.

Article 52 Definition of days

The expression "days" when used in this Convention means calendar days, not working days.

Article 53 Signature, ratification and entry into force

1 This Convention shall be open for signature in Montreal on 28 May 1999 by States participating in the International Conference on Air Law held at Montreal from 10 to 28 May 1999. After 28 May 1999, the Convention shall be open to all States for signature at the Headquarters of the International Civil Aviation Organization in Montreal until it enters into force in accordance with paragraph 6 of this Article.

2 This Convention shall similarly be open for signature by Regional Economic Integration Organisations. For the purpose of this Convention, a "Regional Economic Integration Organisation" means any organisation which is constituted by sovereign States of a given region which has competence in respect

of certain matters governed by this Convention and has been duly authorized to sign and to ratify, accept, approve or accede to this Convention. A reference to a "State Party" or "States Parties" in this Convention, otherwise than in paragraph 2 of Article 1, paragraph 1(b) of Article 3, paragraph (b) of Article 5, Articles 23, 33, 46 and paragraph (b) of Article 57, applies equally to a Regional Economic Integration Organisation. For the purpose of Article 24, the references to "a majority of the States Parties" and "one-third of the States Parties" shall not apply to a Regional Economic Integration Organisation.

3 This Convention shall be subject to ratification by States and by Regional Economic Integration Organisations which have signed it.

4 Any State or Regional Economic Integration Organisation which does not sign this Convention may accept, approve or accede to it at any time.

5 Instruments of ratification, acceptance, approval or accession shall be deposited with the International Civil Aviation Organization, which is hereby designated the Depositary.

6 This Convention shall enter into force on the sixtieth day following the date of deposit of the thirtieth instrument of ratification, acceptance, approval or accession with the Depositary between the States which have deposited such instrument. An instrument deposited by a Regional Economic Integration Organisation shall not be counted for the purpose of this paragraph.

7 For other States and for other Regional Economic Integration Organisations, this Convention shall take effect 60 days following the date of deposit of the instrument of ratification, acceptance, approval or accession.

8 The Depositary shall promptly notify all signatories and States Parties of:
   (a) each signature of this Convention and date thereof;
   (b) each deposit of an instrument of ratification, acceptance, approval or accession and date thereof;
   (c) the date of entry into force of this Convention;
   (d) the date of the coming into force of any revision of the limits of liability established under this Convention;
   (e) any denunciation under Article 54.

Article 54 Denunciation

1 Any State Party may denounce this Convention by written notification to the Depositary.

2 Denunciation shall take effect 180 days following the date on which notification is received by the Depositary.

Article 55 Relationship with other Warsaw Convention Instruments

This Convention shall prevail over any rules which apply to international carriage by air:

1 between States Parties to this Convention by virtue of those States commonly being Party to

(a) the Convention for the Unification of Certain Rules Relating to International Carriage by Air signed at Warsaw on 12 October 1929 (hereinafter called the "Warsaw Convention");
(b) the Protocol to Amend the Convention for the Unification of Certain Rules Relating to International Carriage by Air Signed at Warsaw on 12 October 1929, done at The Hague on 28 September 1955 (hereinafter called The Hague Protocol);
(c) the Convention, Supplementary to the Warsaw Convention, for the Unification of Certain Rules Relating to International Carriage by Air Performed by a Person Other than the Contracting Carrier, signed at Guadalajara on 18 September 1961 (hereinafter called the Guadalajara Convention);
(d) the Protocol to Amend the Convention for the Unification of Certain Rules Relating to International Carriage by Air Signed at Warsaw on 12 October 1929 as Amended by the Protocol Done at The Hague on 28 September 1955 signed at Guatemala City on 8 March 1971 (hereinafter called the Guatemala City Protocol);
(e) Additional Protocol Nos 1 to 3 and Montreal Protocol No 4 to amend the Warsaw Convention as amended by The Hague Protocol or the Warsaw Convention as amended by both The Hague Protocol and the Guatemala City Protocol signed at Montreal on 25 September 1975 (hereinafter called the Montreal Protocols); or

2 within the territory of any single State Party to this Convention by virtue of that State being Party to one or more of the instruments referred to in subparagraphs (a) to (e) above.

Article 56 States with more than one system of law

1 If a State has two or more territorial units in which different systems of law are applicable in relation to matters dealt with in this Convention, it may at the time of signature, ratification, acceptance, approval or accession declare that this Convention shall extend to all its territorial units or only to one or more of them and may modify this declaration by submitting another declaration at any time.
2 Any such declaration shall be notified to the Depositary and shall state expressly the territorial units to which the Convention applies.
3 In relation to a State Party which has made such a declaration:

(a) references in Article 23 to "national currency" shall be construed as referring to the currency of the relevant territorial unit of that State; and
(b) the reference in Article 28 to "national law" shall be construed as referring to the law of the relevant territorial unit of that State.

Article 57 Reservations

No reservation may be made to this Convention except that a State Party may at any time declare by a notification addressed to the Depositary that this Convention shall not apply to:

(a) international carriage by air performed and operated directly by that State Party for non-commercial purposes in respect to its functions and duties as a sovereign State; and/or
(b) the carriage of persons, cargo and baggage for its military authorities on aircraft registered in or leased by that State Party, the whole capacity of which has been reserved by or on behalf of such authorities.

The Convention relative au contrat de transport international des Marchandises par Route (CMR)

Article 1

1 This Convention shall apply to every contract for the carriage of goods by road in vehicles for reward, when the place of taking over of the goods and the place designated for delivery, as specified in the contract, are situated in two different countries, of which at least one is a contracting country, irrespective of the place residence and the nationality of the parties.
2 For the purposes of this Convention, "vehicles" means motor vehicles, articulated vehicles, trailers and semi-trailers as defined in article 4 of the Convention on Road Traffic dated 19 September 1949.
3 This Convention shall apply also where carriage coming within its scope is carried out by States or by governmental institutions or organizations.
4 This Convention shall not apply:

(a) To carriage performed under the terms of any international postal convention;
(b) To funeral consignments;
(c) To furniture removal.

5 The Contracting Parties agree not to vary any of the provisions of this Convention by special agreements between two or more of them, except to make it inapplicable to their frontier traffic or to authorize the use in transport operations entirely confined to their territory of consignment notes representing a title to the goods.

Article 2

1 Where the vehicle containing the goods is carried over part of the journey by sea, rail, inland waterways or air, and except where the provisions of article 14 are applicable, the goods are not unloaded from the vehicle, this Convention shall nevertheless apply to the whole of the carriage. Provided that to the extent that it is proved that any loss, damage or delay in delivery of the goods which occurs during the carriage by the other means of transport was not caused by an act or omission of the carrier by road, but by some event which could only have occurred in the course of and by reason of the carriage by that other means of transport, the liability of the carrier by road

shall be determined not by this Convention but in the manner in which the liability of the carrier by the other means of transport would have been determined if a contract for the carriage of the goods alone had been made by the sender with the carrier by the other means of transport in accordance with the conditions prescribed by law for the carriage of goods by that means of transport. If, however, there are no such prescribed conditions, the liability of the carrier by road shall be determined by this Convention.

2 If the carrier by road is also himself the carrier by the other means of transport, his liability shall also be determined in accordance with the provisions of paragraph 1 of this article, but as if, in his capacities as carrier by road and as carrier by the other means of transport, he were two separate persons.

Article 3

For the purposes of this Convention the carrier shall be responsible for the acts and omissions of his agents and servants and of any other persons of whose services he makes use for the performance of the carriage, when such agents, servants or other persons are acting within the scope of their employment, as if such acts or omissions were his own.

Article 4

The contract of carriage shall be confirmed by the making out of a consignment note. The absence, irregularity or loss of the consignment note shall not affect the existence or the validity of the contract of carriage which shall remain subject to the provisions of this Convention.

Article 5

1 The consignment note shall be made out in three original copies signed by the sender and by the carrier. These signatures may be printed or replaced by the stamps of the sender and the carrier if the law of the country in which the consignment note has been made out so permits. The first copy shall be handed to the sender, second shall accompany the goods and the third shall be retained by the carrier.

2 When the goods which are to be carried have to be loaded in different vehicles, or are of different kinds or are divided into different lots, the sender or the carrier have the right to require a separate consignment note to be made out for each vehicle used, or for each kind or lot of goods.

Article 6

1 The consignment note shall contain the following particulars:

(a) The date of the consignment note and the place at which it is made out;
(b) The name and address of the sender;

(c) The name and address of the carrier;
(d) The place and the date of taking over of the goods and the place designated for delivery;
(e) The name and address of the consignee;
(f) The description in common use of the nature of the goods and the method of packing, and, in the case of dangerous goods, their generally recognized description:
(g) The number of packages and their special marks and numbers;
(h) The gross weight of the goods or their quantity otherwise expressed;
(i) Charges relating to the carriage (carriage charges, supplementary charges, customs duties and other charges incurred from the making of the contract to the time of delivery);
(j) The requisite instructions for Customs and other formalities;
(k) A statement that the carriage is subject, notwithstanding any clause to the contrary, to the provisions of this Convention.

2 Where applicable, the consignment note shall also contain the following particulars:

(a) A statement that transhipment is not allowed;
(b) The charges which the sender undertakes to pay;
(c) The amount of "cash on delivery" charges;
(d) A declaration of the value of the goods and the amount representing special interest in delivery;
(e) The sender's instructions to the carrier regarding insurance of the goods;
(f) The agreed time-limit within which the carriage is to be carried out;
(g) A list of the documents handed to the carrier.

3 The parties may enter in the consignment note any other particulars which they may deem useful.

Article 7

1 The sender shall be responsible for all expenses, loss and damage sustained by the carrier by reason of the inaccuracy or inadequacy of:

(a) The particulars specified in article 6, paragraph 1, (b), (d), (e), (f), (g), (h) and (j);
(b) The particulars specified in article 6, paragraph 2;
(c) Any other particulars or instructions given by him to enable the consignment note to be made out or for the purpose of their being entered therein.

2 If, at the request of the sender, the carrier enters in the consignment note the particulars referred to in paragraph 1 of this article, he shall be deemed, unless the contrary is proved, to have done so on behalf of the sender.

3 If the consignment note does not contain the statement specified in article 6, paragraph 1 (k), the carrier shall be liable for all expenses, loss and damage sustain through such omission by the person entitled to dispose of the goods.

Article 8

1 On taking over the goods, the carrier shall check:

(a) The accuracy of the statements in the consignment note as to the number of packages and their marks and numbers, and
(b) The apparent condition of the goods and their packaging.

2 Where the carrier has no reasonable means of checking the accuracy of the statements referred to in paragraph 1 (a) of this article, he shall enter his reservation: the consignment note together with the grounds on which they are based. He shall likewise specify the grounds for any reservations which he makes with regard i the apparent condition of the goods and their packaging. Such reservations shall not bind the sender unless he has expressly agreed to be bound by them in the consignment note.

3 The sender shall be entitled to require the carrier to check the gross weight of the goods or their quantity otherwise expressed. He may also require the contents < the packages to be checked. The carrier shall be entitled to claim the cost of such checking. The result of the checks shall be entered in the consignment note.

Article 9

1 The consignment note shall be prima facie evidence of the making of the contract of carriage, the conditions of the contract and the receipt of the goods by the carrier.

2 If the consignment note contains no specific reservations by the carrier, it shall be presumed, unless the contrary is proved, that the goods and their packaging appeared to be in good condition when the carrier took them over and that the number of packages, their marks and numbers corresponded with the statements the consignment note.

Article 10

The sender shall be liable to the carrier for damage to persons, equipment or other goods, and for any expenses due to defective packing of the goods, unless the defect apparent or known to the carrier at the time when he took over the goods and he made no reservations concerning it.

Article 11

1 For the purposes of the Customs or other formalities which have to be completed before delivery of the goods, the sender shall attach the necessary documents to the consignment note or place them at the disposal of the carrier and shall furnish him with all the information which he requires.

2 The carrier shall not be under any duty to enquire into either the accuracy or the adequacy of such documents and information. The sender shall be liable

to the carrier for any damage caused by the absence, inadequacy or irregularity of such documents and information, except in the case of some wrongful act or neglect on the part of the carrier.

3 The liability of the carrier for the consequences arising from the loss or incorrect use of the documents specified in and accompanying the consignment note or deposited with the carrier shall be that of an agent, provided that the compensation payable by the carrier shall not exceed that payable in the event of loss of the goods.

Article 12

1 The sender has the right to dispose of the goods, in particular by asking the carrier to stop the goods in transit, to change the place at which delivery is to take place or to deliver the goods to a consignee other than the consignee indicated in the consignment note.

2 This right shall cease to exist when the second copy of the consignment note is handed to the consignee or when the consignee exercises his right under article 1! paragraph 1; from that time onwards the carrier shall obey the orders of the consignee.

3 The consignee shall, however, have the right of disposal from the time when the consignment note is drawn up, if the sender makes an entry to that effect in the consignment note.

4 If in exercising his right of disposal the consignee has ordered the delivery of the goods to another person, that other person shall not be entitled to name other consignees.

5 The exercise of the right of disposal shall be subject to the following conditions:

(a) That the sender or, in the case referred to in paragraph 3 of this article, the consignee who wishes to exercise the right produces the first copy of the consignment note on which the new instructions to the carrier have been entered and indemnifies the carrier against all expenses, loss and damage involve carrying out such instructions;

(b) That the carrying out of such instructions is possible at the time when the instructions reach the person who is to carry them out and does not either intend with the normal working of the carrier's undertaking or prejudice the senders or consignees of other consignments;

(c) That the instructions do not result in a division of the consignment.

6 When, by reason of the provisions of paragraph 5 (b) of this article, the carrier cannot carry out the instructions which he receives, he shall immediately notify the person who gave him such instructions.

7 A carrier who has not carried out the instructions given under the conditions provided for in this article, or who has carried them out without requiring the first copy of the consignment note to be produced, shall be liable to the person entitled to make a claim for any loss or damage caused thereby.

Article 13

1 After arrival of the goods at the place designated for delivery, the consignee shall be entitled to require the carrier to deliver to him, against a receipt, the second of the consignment note and the goods. If the loss of the goods is established or if the goods have not arrived after the expiry of the period provided for in article the consignee shall be entitled to enforce in his own name against the carrier any rights arising from the contract of carriage.

2 The consignee who avails himself of the rights granted to him under paragraph 1 of this article shall pay the charges shown to be due on the consignment note, but in the event of dispute on this matter the carrier shall not be required to deliver the goods unless security has been furnished by the consignee.

Article 14

1 If for any reason it is or becomes impossible to carry out the contract in accordance with the terms laid down in the consignment note before the goods reach the place designated for delivery, the carrier shall ask for instructions from the person entitled to dispose of the goods in accordance with the provisions of article 12.

2 Nevertheless, if circumstances are such as to allow the carriage to be carried out under conditions differing from those laid down in the consignment note and if the carrier has been unable to obtain instructions in reasonable time from the person entitled to dispose of the goods in accordance with the provisions of article 12, he shall take such steps as seem to him to be in the best interests of the person entitled to dispose of the goods.

Article 15

1 Where circumstances prevent delivery of the goods after their arrival at the place designated for delivery, the carrier shall ask the sender for his instructions. If the consignee refuses the goods the sender shall be entitled to dispose of them without being obliged to produce the first copy of the consignment note.

2 Even if he has refused the goods, the consignee may nevertheless require delivery so long as the carrier has not received instructions to the contrary from the sender.

3 When circumstances preventing delivery of the goods arise after the consignee, in exercise of his rights under article 12, paragraph 3, has given an order for the goods to be delivered to another person, paragraphs 1 and 2 of this article shall apply as if the consignee were the sender and that other person were the consignee.

Article 16

1 The carrier shall be entitled to recover the cost of his request for instructions and any expenses entailed in carrying out such instructions, unless such expenses were caused by the wrongful act or neglect of the carrier.

2 In the cases referred to in article 14, paragraph 1, and in article 15, the carrier may immediately unload the goods for account of the person entitled to dispose of them and thereupon the carriage shall be deemed to be at an end. The carrier shall then hold the goods on behalf of the person so entitled. He may however entrust them to a third party, and in that case he shall not be under any liability except for the exercise of reasonable care in the choice of such third party. The charges due under the consignment note and all other expenses shall remain chargeable against the goods.

3 The carrier may sell the goods, without awaiting instructions from the person entitled to dispose of them, if the goods are perishable or their condition warrants such a course, or when the storage expenses would be out of proportion to the value of the goods. He may also proceed to the sale of the goods in other cases if after the expiry of a reasonable period he has not received from the person entitled to dispose of the goods instructions to the contrary which he may reasonably be required to carry out.

4 If the goods have been sold pursuant to this article, the proceeds of sale, after deduction of the expenses chargeable against the goods, shall be placed at the disposal of the person entitled to dispose of the goods. If these charges exceed the proceeds of sale, the carrier shall be entitled to the difference.

5 The procedure in the case of sale shall be determined by the law or custom of the place where the goods are situated.

Article 17

1 The carrier shall be liable for the total or partial loss of the goods and for damage thereto occurring between the time when he takes over the goods and the time delivery, as well as for any delay in delivery.

2 The carrier shall however be relieved of liability if the loss, damage or delay was caused by the wrongful act or neglect of the claimant, by the instructions of the claimant given otherwise than as the result of a wrongful act or neglect on the part of the carrier, by inherent vice of the goods or through circumstances which the carrier could not avoid and the consequences of which he was unable to prevent.

3 The carrier shall not be relieved of liability by reason of the defective condition of the vehicle used by him in order to perform the carriage, or by reason of the wrongful act or neglect of the person from whom he may have hired the vehicle or of the agents or servants of the latter.

4 Subject to article 18, paragraphs 2 to 5, the carrier shall be relieved of liability when the loss or damage arises from the special risks inherent in one or more of the following circumstances:

(a) Use of open unsheeted vehicles, when their use has been expressly agreed and specified in the consignment note;
(b) The lack of, or defective condition of packing in the case of goods which, by their nature, are liable to wastage or to be damaged when not packed or when properly packed;
(c) Handling, loading, stowage of unloading of the goods by the sender, the consignee or persons acting on behalf of the sender or the consignee;
(d) The nature of certain kinds of goods which particularly exposes them to total or partial loss or to damage, especially through breakage, rust, decay, desiccation, leakage, normal wastage, or the action of moth or vermin;
(e) Insufficiency or inadequacy of marks or numbers on the packages;
(f) The carriage of livestock.

5 Where under this article the carrier is not under any liability in respect of some of the factors causing the loss, damage or delay, he shall only be liable to the extent that those factors for which he is liable under this article have contributed to the loss, damage or delay.

Article 18

1 The burden of proving that loss, damage or delay was due to one of the causes specified in article 17, paragraph 2, shall rest upon the carrier.
2 When the carrier establishes that in the circumstances of the case, the loss or damage could be attributed to one or more of the special risks referred to in article paragraph 4, it shall be presumed that is was so caused. The claimant shall however be entitled to prove that the loss or damage was not, in fact, attributable either wholly or partly to one of these risks.
3 This presumption shall not apply in the circumstances set out in article 17, paragraph 4 (a), if there has been an abnormal shortage, or a loss of any package.
4 If the carriage is performed in vehicles specially equipped to protect the goods from the effects of heat, cold, variations in temperature or the humidity of the air, carrier shall not be entitled to claim the benefit of article 17, paragraph 4 (d), unless he proves that all steps incumbent on him in the circumstances with respect the choice, maintenance and use of such equipment were taken and that he complied with any special instructions issued to him.
5 The carrier shall not be entitled to claim the benefit of article 17, paragraph 4 (f), unless he proves that all steps normally incumbent on him in the circumstances were taken and that he complied with any special instructions issued to him.

Article 19

Delay in delivery shall be said to occur when the goods have not been delivered within the agreed time-limit or when, failing an agreed time-limit, the actual duration of carriage having regard to the circumstances of the case, and in particular, in the case of partial loads, the time required for making up a complete load in the normal way exceeds the time it would be reasonable to allow a diligent carrier.

Article 20

1 The fact that goods have not been delivered within thirty days following the expiry of the agreed time-limit, or, if there is no agreed time-limit, within sixty days fi the time when the carrier took over the goods, shall be conclusive evidence of the loss of the goods, and the person entitled to make a claim may thereupon treat them as lost.

2 The person so entitled may, on receipt of compensation for the missing goods, request in writing that he shall be notified immediately should the goods be recovered in the course of the year following the payment of compensation. He shall be given a written acknowledgement of such request.

3 Within the thirty days following receipt of such notification, the person entitled as aforesaid may require the goods to be delivered to him against payment of the charges shown to be due on the consignment note and also against refund of the compensation he received less any charges included therein but without prejudice any claims to compensation for delay in delivery under article 23 and, where applicable, article 26.

4 In the absence of the request mentioned in paragraph 2 or of any instructions given within the period of thirty days specified in paragraph 3, or if the goods are not recovered until more than one year after the payment of compensation, the carrier shall be entitled to deal with them in accordance with the law of the place where the goods are situated.

Article 21

Should the goods have been delivered to the consignee without collection of the "cash on delivery" charge which should have been collected by the carrier under the ten the contract of carriage, the carrier shall be liable to the sender for compensation not exceeding the amount of such charge without prejudice to his right of action against the consignee.

Article 22

1 When the sender hands goods of a dangerous nature to the carrier, he shall inform the carrier of the exact nature of the danger and indicate, if necessary, the precautions to be taken. If this information has not been entered in the consignment note, the burden of proving, by some other means, that the carrier knew the exact nature of the danger constituted by the carriage of the said goods shall rest upon the sender or the consignee.

2 Goods of a dangerous nature which, in the circumstances referred to in paragraph 1 of this article, the carrier did not know were dangerous, may, at any

time or place, be unloaded, destroyed or rendered harmless by the carrier without compensation; further, the sender shall be liable for all expenses, loss or damage arising out of their handing over for carriage or of their carriage.

Article 23

1 When, under the provisions of this Convention, a carrier is liable for compensation in respect of total or partial loss of goods, such compensation shall be calculate reference to the value of the goods at the place and time at which they were accepted for carriage.

2 The value of the goods shall be fixed according to the commodity exchange price or, if there is no such price, according to the current market price or, if there is no commodity exchange price or current market price, by reference to the normal value of goods of the same kind and quality.

3 Compensation shall not, however, exceed 8.33 units of account per kilogram of gross weight short.

4 In addition, the carriage charges, Customs duties and other charges incurred in respect of the carriage of the goods shall be refunded in full in case of total loss and in proportion to the loss sustained in case of partial loss, but no further damages shall be payable.

5 In the case of delay, if the claimant proves that damage has resulted therefrom the carrier shall pay compensation for such damage not exceeding the carriage charges.

6 Higher compensation may only be claimed where the value of the goods or a special interest in delivery has been declared in accordance with articles 24 and 26.

7 The unit of account mentioned in this Convention is the Special Drawing Right as defined by the International Monetary Fund. The amount mentioned in paragraph 3 of this article shall be converted into the national currency of the State of the Court seized of the case on the basis of the value of that currency on the date of the judgment or the date agreed upon by the Parties. The value of the national currency, in terms of the Special Drawing Right, of a State which is a member of the International Monetary Fund, shall be calculated in accordance with the method of valuation applied by the International Monetary Fund in effect at the date in question for its operations and transactions. The value of the national currency, in terms of the Special Drawing Right, of a State which is not a member of the International Monetary Fund, shall be calculated in a manner determined by that State.

8 Nevertheless, a State which is not a member of the International Monetary Fund and whose law does not permit the application of the provisions of paragraph 7 c this article may, at the time of ratification of or accession to the Protocol to the CMR or at any time thereafter, declare that the limit of liability provided for in paragraph 3 of this article to be applied in its territory

shall be 25 monetary units. The monetary unit referred to in this paragraph corresponds to 10/31 gram of gold of millesimal fineness nine hundred. The conversion of the amount specified in this paragraph into the national currency shall be made according to the law of the State concerned.

9 The calculation mentioned in the last sentence of paragraph 7 of this article and the conversion mentioned in paragraph 8 of this article shall be made in such a manner as to express in the national currency of the State as far as possible the same real value for the amount in paragraph 3 of this article as is expressed therein units of account. States shall communicate to the Secretary-General of the United Nations the manner of calculation pursuant to paragraph 7 of this article or the result of the conversion in paragraph 8 of this article as the case may be, when depositing an instrument referred to in article 3 of the Protocol to the CMR and whenever there is a change in either.

Article 24

The sender may, against payment of a surcharge to be agreed upon, declare in the consignment note a value for the goods exceeding the limit laid down in article 23, paragraph 3, and in that case the amount of the declared value shall be substituted for that limit.

Article 25

1 In case of damage, the carrier shall be liable for the amount by which the goods have diminished in value, calculated by reference to the value of the goods fixed accordance with article 23, paragraphs 1, 2 and 4.

2 The compensation may not, however, exceed:

(a) If the whole consignment has been damaged, the amount payable in the case of total loss;

(b) If part only of the consignment has been damaged, the amount payable in the case of loss of the part affected.

Article 26

1 The sender may, against payment of a surcharge to be agreed upon, fix the amount of a special interest in delivery in the case of loss or damage or of the agreed time-limit being exceeded, by entering such amount in the consignment note.

2 If a declaration of a special interest in delivery has been made, compensation for the additional loss or damage proved may be claimed, up to the total amount of interest declared, independently of the compensation provided for in articles 23, 24 and 25.

Article 27

1 The claimant shall be entitled to claim interest on compensation payable. Such interest, calculated at five per centum per annum, shall accrue from the date on which the claim was sent in writing to the carrier or, if no such claim has been made, from the date on which legal proceedings were instituted.

2 When the amounts on which the calculation of the compensation is based are not expressed in the currency of the country in which payment is claimed, conversion shall be at the rate of exchange applicable on the day and at the place of payment of compensation.

Article 28

1 In cases where, under the law applicable, loss, damage or delay arising out of carriage under this Convention gives rise to an extra-contractual claim, the carrier may avail himself of the provisions of this Convention which exclude his liability or which fix or limit the compensation due.

2 In cases where the extra-contractual liability for loss, damage or delay of one of the persons for whom the carrier is responsible under the terms of article 3 is in issue, such person may also avail himself of the provisions of this Convention which exclude the liability of the carrier or which fix or limit the compensation due.

Article 29

1 The carrier shall not be entitled to avail himself of the provisions of this chapter which exclude or limit his liability or which shift the burden of proof if the damage caused by his wilful misconduct or by such default on his part as, in accordance with the law of the court or tribunal seized of the case, is considered as equivalent to wilful misconduct.

2 The same provision shall apply if the wilful misconduct or default is committed by the agents of servants of the carrier or by any other persons of whose services he makes use for the performance of the carriage, when such agents, servants or other persons are acting within the scope of their employment. Furthermore, in sue case such agents, servants or other persons shall not be entitled to avail themselves, with regard to their personal liability, of the provisions of this chapter referred to in paragraph 1.

Article 30

1 If the consignee takes delivery of the goods without duly checking their condition with the carrier or without sending him reservations giving a general indication of the loss or damage, not later than the time of delivery in the case of apparent loss or damage and within seven days of delivery, Sundays

and public holidays excepted, in the case of loss or damage which is not apparent, the fact of his taking delivery shall be prima facie evidence that he has received the goods in the condition described in the consignment note. In the case of loss or damage which is not apparent the reservation referred to shall be made in writing.

2 When the condition of the goods has been duly checked by the consignee and the carrier, evidence contradicting the result of this checking shall only be admissible in the case of loss or damage which is not apparent and provided that the consignee has duly sent reservations in writing to the carrier within seven days, Sundays and public holidays excepted, from the date of checking.

3 No compensation shall be payable for delay in delivery unless a reservation has been sent in writing to the carrier, within twenty-one days from the time that the goods were placed at the disposal of the consignee.

4 In calculating the time-limits provided for in this article the date of delivery, or the date of checking, or the date when the goods were placed at the disposal of the consignee, as the case may be, shall not be included.

5 The carrier and the consignee shall give each other every reasonable facility for making the requisite investigations and checks.

Article 31

1 In legal proceedings arising out of carriage under this Convention, the plaintiff may bring an action in any court or tribunal of a contracting country designated by agreement between the parties and, in addition, in the courts or tribunals of a country within whose territory:

(a) The defendant is ordinarily resident, or has his principal place of business, or the branch or agency through which the contract of carriage was made, or

(b) The place where the goods were taken over by the carrier or the place designated for delivery is situated, and in no other courts or tribunals.

2 Where in respect of a claim referred to in paragraph 1 of this article an action is pending before a court or tribunal competent under that paragraph, or where in respect of such a claim a judgment has been entered by such a court or tribunal no new action shall be started between the same parties on the same grounds unless the judgment of the court or tribunal before which the first action was brought is not enforceable in the country in which the fresh proceedings are brought.

3 When a judgment entered by a court or tribunal of a contracting country in any such action as is referred to in paragraph 1 of this article has become enforceable in that country, it shall also become enforceable in each of the other contracting States, as soon as the formalities required in the country concerned have been com with. These formalities shall not permit the merits of the case to be re-opened.

4 The provisions of paragraph 3 of this article shall apply to judgments after trial, judgments by default and settlements confirmed by an order of the court, but shall not apply to interim judgments or to awards of damages, in addition to costs against a plaintiff who wholly or partly fails in his action.
5 Security for costs shall not be required in proceedings arising out of carriage under this Convention from nationals of contracting countries resident or having their place of business in one other of those countries.

Article 32

1 The period of limitation for an action arising out of carriage under this Convention shall be one year. Nevertheless, in the case of wilful misconduct, or such default in accordance with the law of the court or tribunal seised of the case, is considered as equivalent to wilful misconduct, the period of limitation shall be three years. The period of limitation shall begin to run:

(a) In the case of partial loss, damage or delay in delivery, from the date of delivery;
(b) In the case of total loss, from the thirtieth day after the expiry of the agreed time-limit or where there is no agreed time-limit from the sixtieth day from the date on which the goods were taken over by the carrier;
(c) In all other cases, on the expiry of a period of three months after the making of the contract of carriage.

The day on which the period of limitation begins to run shall not be included in the period.

2 A written claim shall suspend the period of limitation until such date as the carrier rejects the claim by notification in writing and returns the documents attached thereto. If a part of the claim is admitted the period of limitation shall start to run again only in respect of that part of the claim still in dispute. The burden of proof of the receipt of the claim, or of the reply and of the return of the documents, shall rest with the party relying upon these facts. The running of the period of limitation shall not be suspended by further claims having the same object.
3 Subject to the provisions of paragraph 2 above, the extension of the period of limitation shall be governed by the law of the court or tribunal seised of the case. That law shall also govern the fresh accrual of rights of action.
4 A right of action which has become barred by lapse of time may not be exercised by way of counter-claim or set-off.

Article 33

The contract of carriage may contain a clause conferring competence on an arbitration tribunal if the clause conferring competence on the tribunal provides that the tribunal shall apply this Convention.

Article 34

If carriage governed by a single contract is performed by successive road carriers, each of them shall be responsible for the performance of the whole operation, the second carrier and each succeeding carrier becoming a party to the contract of carriage, under the terms of the consignment note, by reason of his acceptance of the goods and consignment note.

Article 35

1 A carrier accepting the goods from a previous carrier shall give the latter a dated and signed receipt. He shall enter his name and address on the second copy of the consignment note. Where applicable, he shall enter on the second copy of the consignment note and on the receipt reservations of the kind provided for in article paragraph 2.
2 The provisions of article 9 shall apply to the relations between successive carriers.

Article 36

Except in the case of a counter-claim or a set-off raised in an action concerning a claim based on the same contract of carriage, legal proceedings in respect of liability for loss, damage or delay may only be brought against the first carrier, the last carrier or the carrier who was performing that portion of the carriage during which the event causing the loss, damage or delay occurred; an action may be brought at the same time against several of these carriers.

Article 37

A carrier who has paid compensation in compliance with the provisions of this Convention, shall be entitled to recover such compensation, together with interest thereon all costs and expenses incurred by reason of the claim, from the other carriers who have taken part in the carriage, subject to the following provisions:

(a) The carrier responsible for the loss or damage shall be solely liable for the compensation whether paid by himself or by another carrier;
(b) When the loss or damage has been caused by the action of two or more carriers, each of them shall pay an amount proportionate to his share of liability should it be impossible to apportion the liability, each carrier shall be liable in proportion to the share of the payment for the carriage which is due to him;
(c) If it cannot be ascertained to which carriers liability is attributable for the loss or damage, the amount of the compensation shall be apportioned between all the carriers as laid down in (b) above.

Article 38

If one of the carriers is insolvent, the share of the compensation due from him and unpaid by him shall be divided among the other carriers in proportion to the share of payment for the carriage due to them.

Article 39

1 No carrier against whom a claim is made under articles 37 and 38 shall be entitled to dispute the validity of the payment made by the carrier making the claim if t amount of the compensation was determined by judicial authority after the first mentioned carrier had been given due notice of the proceedings and afforded an opportunity of entering an appearance.
2 A carrier wishing to take proceedings to enforce his right of recovery may make his claim before the competent court or tribunal of the country in which one of the carriers concerned is ordinarily resident, or has his principal place of business or the branch or agency through which the contract of carriage was made. All the carriers concerned may be made defendants in the same action.
3 The provisions of article 31, paragraphs 3 and 4, shall apply to judgments entered in the proceedings referred to in articles 37 and 38.
4 The provisions of article 32 shall apply to claims between carriers. The period of limitation shall, however, begin to run either on the date of the final judicial decision fixing the amount of compensation payable under the provisions of this Convention, or, if there is no such judicial decision, from the actual date of payment.

Article 40

Carriers shall be free to agree among themselves on provisions other than those laid down in articles 37 and 38.

Article 41

1 Subject to the provisions of article 40, any stipulation which would directly or indirectly derogate from the provisions of this Convention shall be null and void. The nullity of such a stipulation shall not involve the nullity of the other provisions of the contract.
2 In particular, a benefit of insurance in favour of the carrier or any other similar clause, or any clause shifting the burden of proof shall be null and void.

Article 42

1 This Convention is open for signature or accession by countries members of the Economic Commission for Europe and countries admitted to the

Commission in a consultative capacity under paragraph 8 of the Commission's terms of reference.

2 Such countries as may participate in certain activities of the Economic Commission for Europe in accordance with paragraph 11 of the Commission's terms of refer may become Contracting Parties to this Convention by acceding thereto after its entry into force.

3 The Convention shall be open for signature until 31 August 1956 inclusive. Thereafter, it shall be open for accession.

4 This Convention shall be ratified.

5 Ratification or accession shall be effected by the deposit of an instrument with the Secretary-General of the United Nations.

Article 43

1 This Convention shall come into force on the ninetieth day after five of the countries referred to in article 42, paragraph 1, have deposit their instruments of ratification or accession.

2 For any country ratifying or acceding to it after five countries have deposited their instruments of ratification or accession, this Convention shall enter into force or ninetieth day after the said country has deposited its instrument of ratification or accession.

Article 44

1 Any Contracting Party may denounce this Convention by so notifying the Secretary-General of the United Nations.

2 Denunciation shall take effect twelve months after the date of receipt by the Secretary-General of the notification of denunciation.

Article 45

If, after the entry into force of this Convention, the number of Contracting Parties is reduced, as a result of denunciations, to less than five, the Convention shall cease to be in force from the date on which the last of such denunciations takes effect.

Article 46

1 Any country may, at the time of depositing its instrument of ratification or accession or at any time thereafter, declare by notification addressed to the Secretary-General of the United Nations that this Convention shall extend to all or any of the territories for the international relations of which it is responsible. The Convent shall extend to the territory or territories named in the notification as from the ninetieth day after its receipt by the Secretary-General or, if on that day the Convention has not yet entered into force, at the time of its entry into force.

2 Any country which has made a declaration under the preceding paragraph extending this Convention to any territory for whose international relations it is responsible may denounce the Convention separately in respect of that territory in accordance with the provisions of article 44.

Article 47

Any dispute between two or more Contracting Parties relating to the interpretation or application of this Convention, which the parties are unable to settle by negotiations other means may, at the request of any one of the Contracting Parties concerned, be referred for settlement to the International Court of Justice.

Article 48

1 Each Contracting Party may, at the time of signing, ratifying, or acceding to, this Convention, declare that it does not consider itself as bound by article 47 of the Convention. Other Contracting Parties shall not be bound by article 47 in respect of any Contracting Party which has entered such a reservation.
2 Any Contracting Party having entered a reservation as provided for in paragraph 1 may at any time withdraw such reservation by notifying the Secretary-General the United Nations.
3 No other reservation to this Convention shall be permitted.

Article 49

1 After this Convention has been in force for three years, any Contracting Party may, by notification to the Secretary-General of the United Nations, request that a conference be convened for the purpose of reviewing the Convention. The Secretary-General shall notify all Contracting Parties of the request and a review confer shall be convened by the Secretary-General if, within a period of four months following the date of notification by the Secretary-General, not less than one-fourth the Contracting Parties notify him of their concurrence with the request.
2 If a conference is convened in accordance with the preceding paragraph, the Secretary-General shall notify all the Contracting Parties and invite them to submit w a period of three months such proposals as they may wish the Conference to consider. The Secretary-General shall circulate to all Contracting Parties the provisional agenda for the conference together with the texts of such proposals at least three months before the date on which the conference is to meet.
3 The Secretary-General shall invite to any conference convened in accordance with this article all countries referred to in article 42, paragraph 1, and countries which have become Contracting Parties under article 42, paragraph 2.

Article 50

In addition to the notifications provided for in article 49, the Secretary-General of the United Nations shall notify the countries referred to in article 42, paragraph 1, and countries which have become Contracting Parties under article 42, paragraph 2, of:

(a) Ratifications and accessions under article 42;
(b) The dates of entry into force of this Convention in accordance with article 43;
(c) Denunciations under article 44;
(d) The termination of this Convention in accordance with article 45;
(e) Notifications received in accordance with article 46;
(f) Declarations and notifications received in accordance with article 48, paragraphs 1 and 2.

Article 51

After 31 August 1956, the original of this Convention shall be deposited with the Secretary-General of the United Nations, who shall transmit certified true copies to each of the countries mentioned in article 42, paragraphs 1 and 2.

Protocol of Signature

On proceeding to sign the Convention on the Contract for the International Carriage of Goods by Road, the undersigned, being duly authorized, have agreed on the following statement and explanation:

1 This Convention shall not apply to traffic between the United Kingdom of Great Britain and Northern Ireland and the Republic of Ireland.
2 Ad article 1, paragraph 4

The undersigned undertake to negotiate conventions governing contracts for furniture removals and combined transport.

Budapest Convention on the Contract for the Carriage of Goods by Inland Waterway (CMNI)

Article 1 Definitions

In this Convention,

1 "Contract of carriage" means any contract, of any kind, whereby a carrier undertakes against payment of freight to carry goods by inland waterway;
2 "Carrier" means any person by whom or in whose name a contract of carriage has been concluded with a shipper;
3 "Actual carrier" means any person, other than a servant or an agent of the carrier, to whom the performance of the carriage or of part of such carriage has been entrusted by the carrier;
4 "Shipper" means any person by whom or in whose name or on whose behalf a contract of carriage has been concluded with a carrier;
5 "Consignee" means the person entitled to take delivery of the goods;
6 "Transport document" means a document which evidences a contract of carriage and the taking over or loading of goods by a carrier, made out in the form of a bill of lading or consignment note or of any other document used in trade;
7 "Goods" does not include either towed or pushed vessels or the luggage or vehicles of passengers; where the goods are consolidated in a container, on a pallet or in or on a similar article of transport or where they are packed, "goods" includes such article of transport or packaging if supplied by the shipper;
8 "In writing" includes, unless otherwise agreed between the parties concerned, the transmission of information by electronic, optical or similar means of communication, including, but not limited to, telegram, facsimile, telex, electronic mail or electronic data interchange (EDI), provided the information is accessible so as to be usable for subsequent reference.
9 The law of a State applicable in accordance with this Convention means the rules of law in force in that State other than its rules of private international law.

Article 2 Scope of application

1 This Convention is applicable to any contract of carriage according to which the port of loading or the place of taking over of the goods and the port of

discharge or the place of delivery of the goods are located in two different States of which at least one is a State Party to this Convention. If the contract stipulates a choice of several ports of discharge or places of delivery, the port of discharge or the place of delivery to which the goods have actually been delivered shall determine the choice.

2 This Convention is applicable if the purpose of the contract of carriage is the carriage of goods, without transshipment, both on inland waterways and in waters to which maritime regulations apply, under the conditions set out in paragraph 1, unless:

(a) a maritime bill of lading has been issued in accordance with the maritime law applicable, or
(b) the distance to be travelled in waters to which maritime regulations apply is the greater.

3 This Convention is applicable regardless of the nationality, place of registration or home port of the vessel or whether the vessel is a maritime or inland navigation vessel and regardless of the nationality, domicile, registered office or place of residence of the carrier, the shipper or the consignee.

Article 3 Taking over, carriage and delivery of the goods

1 The carrier shall carry the goods to the place of delivery within the specified time and deliver them to the consignee in the condition in which they were handed over to him.

2 Unless otherwise agreed, the taking over and delivery of the goods shall take place on board the vessel.

3 The carrier shall decide which vessel is to be used. He shall be bound, before and at the beginning of the voyage, to exercise due diligence to ensure that, taking into account the goods to be carried, the vessel is in a state to receive the cargo, is seaworthy and is manned and equipped as prescribed by the regulations in force and is furnished with the necessary national and international authorizations for the carriage of the goods in question.

4 Where it has been agreed that the carriage shall be performed by a specific vessel or type of vessel, the carrier shall be entitled to load or tranship the goods in whole or in part on to another vessel or on to another type of vessel without the consent of the shipper, only:

(a) in circumstances, such as low water or collision or any other obstacle to navigation, which were unforeseeable at the time when the contract of carriage was concluded and in which the loading or transshipment of the goods is necessary in order to perform the contract of carriage, and when the carrier is unable to obtain within an appropriate period of time instructions from the shipper, or
(b) when it is in accordance with the practice prevailing in the port where the vessel is located.

5 Except as provided by the obligations incumbent on the shipper, the carrier shall ensure that the loading, stowage and securing of the goods do not affect the safety of the vessel.
6 The carrier is entitled to carry the goods on deck or in open vessels only if it has been agreed with the shipper or if it is in accordance with the usage of the particular trade or is required by the statutory regulations.

Article 4 Actual carrier

1 A contract complying with the definition set out in article 1, paragraph 1, concluded between a carrier and an actual carrier constitutes a contract of carriage within the meaning of this Convention. For the purpose of such contract, all the provisions of this Convention concerning the shipper shall apply to the carrier and those concerning the carrier to the actual carrier.
2 Where the earner has entrusted the performance of the carriage or part thereof to an actual carrier, whether or not in pursuance of a liberty under the contract of carriage to do so, the carrier nevertheless remains responsible for the entire carriage according to the provisions of this Convention. All the provisions of this Convention governing the responsibility of the carrier also apply to the responsibility of the actual carrier for the carriage performed by him.
3 The carrier shall in all cases inform the shipper when he entrusts the performance of the carriage or part thereof to an actual carrier.
4 Any agreement with the shipper or the consignee extending the carrier's responsibility according to the provisions of this Convention affects the actual carrier only to the extent that he has agreed to it expressly and in writing. The actual carrier may avail himself of all the objections invocable by the carrier under the contract of carriage.
5 If and to the extent that both the carrier and the actual carrier are liable, their liability is joint and several. Nothing in this article shall prejudice any right of recourse as between them.

Article 5 Delivery time

The carrier shall deliver the goods within the time limit agreed in the contract of carriage or, if no time limit has been agreed, within the time limit which could reasonably be required of a diligent carrier, taking into account the circumstances of the voyage and unhindered navigation.

Article 6 Obligations of the shipper

1 The shipper shall be required to pay the amounts due under the contract of carriage.
2 The shipper shall furnish the carrier in writing, before the goods are handed over, with the following particulars concerning the goods to be carried:

(a) dimensions, number or weight and stowage factor of the goods;
(b) marks necessary for identification of the goods;
(c) nature, characteristics and properties of the goods;
(d) instructions concerning the Customs or administrative regulations applying to the goods;
(e) other necessary particulars to be entered in the transport document.

The shipper shall also hand over to the carrier, when the goods are handed over, all the required accompanying documents.

3 If the nature of the goods so requires, the shipper shall, bearing in mind the agreed transport operation, pack the goods in such a way as to prevent their loss or damage between the time they are taken over by the carrier and their delivery and so as to ensure that they do not cause damage to the vessel or to other goods. According to what has been agreed with a view to carriage, the shipper shall also make provision for appropriate marking in conformity with the applicable international or national regulations or, in the absence of such regulations, in accordance with rules and practices generally recognized in inland navigation.
4 Subject to the obligations to be borne by the carrier, the shipper shall load and stow the goods and secure them in accordance with inland navigation practice unless the contract of carriage specifies otherwise.

Article 7 Dangerous and polluting goods

1 If dangerous or polluting goods are to be carried, the shipper shall, before handing over the goods, and in addition to the particulars referred to in article 6, paragraph 2, inform the carrier clearly and in writing of the danger and the risks of pollution inherent in the goods and of the precautions to be taken.
2 Where the carriage of the dangerous or polluting goods requires an authorization, the shipper shall hand over the necessary documents at the latest when handing over the goods.
3 Where the continuation of the carriage, the discharge or the delivery of the dangerous or polluting goods are rendered impossible owing to the absence of an administrative authorization, the shipper shall bear the costs for the return of the goods to the port of loading or a nearer place, where they may be discharged and delivered or disposed of.
4 In the event of immediate danger to life, property or the environment, the carrier shall be entitled to unload the goods, to render them innocuous or, provided that such a measure is not disproportionate to the danger they represent, to destroy them, even if, before they were taken over, he was informed or was apprised by other means of the nature of the danger or the risks of pollution inherent in the goods.
5 Where the carrier is entitled to take the measures referred to in paragraphs 3 or 4 above, he may claim compensation for damages.

Article 8 Liability of the shipper

1 The shipper shall, even if no fault can be attributed to him, be liable for all the damages and costs incurred by the carrier or the actual carrier by reason of the fact that:

(a) the particulars or information referred to in articles 6, paragraph 2, or 7, paragraph 1, are missing, inaccurate or incomplete;
(b) the dangerous or polluting goods are not marked or labelled in accordance with the applicable international or national regulations or, if no such regulations exist, in accordance with rules and practices generally recognized in inland navigation;
(c) the necessary accompanying documents are missing, inaccurate or incomplete.

The carrier may not avail himself of the liability of the shipper if it is proven that the fault is attributable to the carrier himself, his servants or agents. The same applies to the actual carrier.

2 The shipper shall be responsible for the acts and omissions of persons of whose services he takes use to perform the tasks and meet the obligations referred to in articles 6 and 7, when such persons are acting within the scope of their employment, as if such acts or omissions were his own.

Article 9 Termination of the contract of carriage by the carrier

1 The carrier may terminate the contract of carriage if the shipper has failed to perform the obligations set out in article 6, paragraph 2, or article 7, paragraphs 1 and 2.
2 If the carrier makes use of his right of termination, he may unload the goods at the shipper's expense and claim optionally the payment of any of the following amounts:

(a) one third of the agreed freight; or
(b) in addition to any demurrage charge, a compensation equal to the amount of costs incurred and the loss caused, as well as, should the voyage have already begun, a proportional freight for the part of the voyage already performed.

Article 10 Delivery of the goods

1 Notwithstanding the obligation of the shipper under article 6, paragraph 1, the consignee who, following the arrival of the goods at the place of delivery, requests their delivery, shall, in accordance with the contract of carriage, be liable for the freight and other charges due on the goods, as well as for his contribution to any general average. In the absence of a transport document,

or if such document has not been presented, the consignee shall be liable for the freight agreed with the shipper if it corresponds to market practice.

2 The placing of the goods at the disposal of the consignee in accordance with the contract of carriage or with the usage of the particular trade or with the statutory regulations applicable at the port of discharge shall be considered a delivery. The imposed handing over of the goods to an authority or a third party shall also be considered a delivery.

Article 11 Nature and content

1 For each carriage of goods governed by this Convention the carrier shall issue a transport document; he shall issue a bill of lading only if the shipper so requests and if it has been so agreed before the goods were loaded or before they were taken over for carriage. The lack of a transport document or the fact that it is incomplete shall not affect the validity of the contract of carriage.

2 The original of the transport document must be signed by the carrier, the master of the vessel or a person authorized by the carrier. The carrier may require the shipper to countersign the original or a copy. The signature may be in handwriting, printed in facsimile, perforated, stamped, in symbols or made by any other mechanical or electronic means, if this is not prohibited by the law of the State where the transport document was issued.

3 The transport document shall be prima facie evidence, save proof to the contrary, of the conclusion and content of the contract of carriage and of the taking over of the goods by the carrier. In particular, it shall provide a basis for the presumption that the goods have been taken over for carriage as they are described in the transport document.

4 When the transport document is a bill of lading, it alone shall determine the relations between the carrier and the consignee. The conditions of the contract of carriage shall continue to determine the relations between carrier and shipper.

5 The transport document, in addition to its denomination, contains the following particulars:

(a) the name, domicile, registered office or place of residence of the carrier and of the shipper;
(b) the consignee of the goods;
(c) the name or number of the vessel, where the goods have been taken en board, or particulars in the transport document stating that the goods have been taken over by the carrier but not yet loaded on the vessel;
(d) the port of loading or the place where the goods were taken over and the port of discharge or the place of delivery;
(e) the usual name of the type of goods and their method of packaging and, for dangerous or polluting goods, their name according to the requirements in force or, if there is no such name, their general name;

(f) the dimensions, number or weight as well as the identification marks of the goods taken on board or taken over for the purpose of carriage;
(g) the statement, if applicable, that the goods shall or may be carried on deck or on board open vessels;
(h) the agreed provisions concerning freight;
(i) in the case of a consignment note, the specification as to whether it is an original or a copy; in the case of a bill of lading, the number of originals;
(j) the place and date of issue.

The legal character of a transport document in the sense of article 1, paragraph 6, of this Convention is not affected by the absence of one or more of the particulars referred to in this paragraph.

Article 12 Reservations in transport documents

1 The carrier is entitled to include in the transport document reservations concerning:

(a) The dimensions, number or weight of the goods, if he has grounds to suspect that the particulars supplied by the shipper are inaccurate or if he had no reasonable means of checking such particulars, especially because the goods have not been counted, measured or weighed in his presence or because, without explicit agreement, the dimensions or weights have been determined by draught measurement;
(b) Identification marks which are not clearly and durably affixed on the goods themselves or, if the goods are packed, on the receptacles or packagings;
(c) The apparent condition of the goods.

2 If the carrier fails to note the apparent condition of the goods or does not enter reservations in that respect, he is deemed to have noted in the transport document that the goods were in apparent good condition.
3 If, in accordance with the particulars set out in the transport document, the goods are placed in a container or in the holds of the vessel and sealed by other persons than the carrier, his servants or his agents, and if neither the container nor the seals are damaged or broken when they reach the port of discharge or the place of delivery, it shall be presumed that the loss or damage to the goods did not occur during carriage.

Article 13 Bill of lading

1 The originals of a bill of lading shall be documents of title issued in the name of the consignee, to order or to bearer.
2 At the place of destination, the goods shall be delivered only in exchange for the original of the bill of lading submitted initially; thereafter, further delivery cannot be claimed against other originals.

3 When the goods are taken over by the carrier, handing over the bill of lading to a person entitled thereby to receive the goods has the same effects as the handing over of the goods as far as the acquisition of rights to the goods is concerned.

4 If the bill of lading has been transferred to a third party, including the consignee, who has acted in good faith in reliance on the description of the goods therein, proof to the contrary of the presumption set out in article 11, paragraph 3, and article 12, paragraph 2, shall not be admissible.

Article 14 Holder of the right of disposal

1 The shipper shall be authorized to dispose of the goods; in particular, he may require the carrier to discontinue the carriage of the goods, to change the place of delivery or to deliver the goods to a consignee other than the consignee indicated in the transport document.

2 The shipper's right of disposal shall cease to exist once the consignee, following the arrival of the goods at the scheduled place of delivery, has requested delivery of the goods and,

(a) where carriage is under a consignment note, once the original has been handed over to the consignee;
(b) where carriage is under a bill of lading, once the shipper has relinquished all the originals in his possession by handing them over to another person.

3 By an appropriate entry in the consignment note, the shipper may, when the consignment note is issued, waive his right of disposal to the consignee.

Article 15 Conditions for the exercise of the right of disposal

The shipper or, in the case of article 14, paragraphs 2 and 3, the consignee, must, if he wishes to exercise his right of disposal:

(a) where a bill of lading is used, submit all originals prior to the arrival of the goods at the scheduled place of delivery;
(b) where a transport document other than a bill of lading is used, submit this document, which shall include the new instructions given to the carrier;
(c) compensate the carrier for all costs and damage incurred in carrying out instructions;
(d) pay all the agreed freight in the event of the discharge of the goods before arrival at the scheduled place of delivery, unless the contract of carriage provides otherwise.

Article 16 Liability for loss

1 The carrier shall be liable for loss resulting from loss or damage to the goods caused between the time when he took them over for carriage and the time

of their delivery, or resulting from delay in delivery, unless he can show that the loss was due to circumstances which a diligent carrier could not have prevented and the consequences of which he could not have averted.

2 The carrier's liability for loss resulting from loss or damage to the goods caused during the time before the goods are loaded on the vessel or the time after they have been discharged from the vessel shall be governed by the law of the State applicable to the contract of carriage.

Article 17 Servants and agents

1 The carrier shall be responsible for the acts and omissions of his servants and agents of whose services he makes use during the performance of the contract of carriage, when such persons are acting within the scope of their employment, as if such acts or omissions were his own.

2 When the carriage is performed by an actual carrier in accordance with article 4, the carrier is also responsible for the acts and omissions of the actual carrier and of the servants and agents of the actual carrier acting within the scope of their employment.

3 If an action is brought against the servants and agents of the carrier or the actual carrier, such persons, if they prove that they acted within the scope of their employment, are entitled to avail themselves of the exonerations and limits of liability which the carrier or the actual carrier is entitled to invoke under this Convention.

4 A pilot designated by an authority and who cannot be freely selected shall not be considered to be a servant or agent within the meaning of paragraph 1.

Article 18 Special exonerations from liability

1 The carrier and the actual carrier shall be exonerated from their liability when the loss, damage or delay are the result of one of the circumstances or risks listed below:

(a) acts or omissions of the shipper, the consignee or the person entitled to dispose of the goods;

(b) handling, loading, stowage or discharge of the goods by the shipper, the consignee or third parties acting on behalf of the shipper or the consignee;

(c) carriage of the goods on deck or in open vessels, where such carriage has been agreed with the shipper or is in accordance with the practice of the particular trade, or if it is required by the regulations in force;

(d) nature of the goods which exposes them to total or partial loss or damage, especially through breakage, rust, decay, desiccation, leakage, normal wastage (in volume or weight), or the action of vermin or rodents;

(e) lack of or defective condition of packaging in the case of goods which, by their nature, are exposed to loss or damage when not packed or when the packaging is defective;

(f) insufficiency or inadequacy of marks identifying the goods;
(g) rescue or salvage operations or attempted rescue or salvage operations on inland waterways;
(h) carriage of live animals, unless the carrier has not taken the measures or observed the instructions agreed upon in the contract of carriage.

2 When, in the circumstances of the case, damage could be attributed to one or more of the circumstances or risks listed in paragraph 1 of the present article, it is presumed to have been caused by such a circumstance or risk. This presumption does not apply if the injured party proves that the loss suffered does not result, or does not result exclusively, from one of the circumstances or risks listed in paragraph 1 of this article.

Article 19 Calculation of compensation

1 Where the carrier is liable for total loss of goods, the compensation payable by him shall be equal to the value of the goods at the place and on the day of delivery according to the contract of carriage. Delivery to a person other than the person entitled is deemed to be a loss.
2 In the event of partial loss or damage to goods, the carrier shall be liable only to the extent of the loss in value.
3 The value of the goods shall be fixed according to the commodity exchange price or, if there is no such price, according to their market price or, if there is no commodity exchange price or market price, by reference to the normal value of goods of the same kind and quality at the place of delivery.
4 In respect of goods which by reason of their nature are exposed to wastage during carriage, the carrier shall be held liable, whatever the length of the carriage, only for that part of the wastage which exceeds normal wastage (in volume or weight) as determined by the parties to the contract of carriage or, if not, by the regulations or established practice at the place of destination.
5 The provisions of this article shall not affect the carrier's right concerning the freight as provided by the contract of carriage or, in the absence of special agreements in this regard, by the applicable national regulations or practices.

Article 20 Maximum limits of liability

1 Subject to article 21 and paragraph 4 of the present article, and regardless of the action brought against him, the carrier shall under no circumstances be liable for amounts exceeding 666.67 units of account per package or other shipping unit, or 2 units of account per kilogram of weight, specified in the transport document, of the goods lost or damaged, whichever is the higher. If the package or other shipping unit is a container and if there is no mention in the transport document of any package or shipping unit consolidated in the container, the amount of 666.67 units of account shall be replaced by the amount of 1,500 units of account for the container without the goods

it contains and, in addition, the amount of 25,000 units of account for the goods which are in the container.

2 Where a container, pallet or similar article of transport is used to consolidate goods, the packages or other shipping units enumerated in the transport document as packed in or on such article of transport are deemed packages or shipping units. Except as aforesaid, the goods in or on such article of transport are deemed one shipping unit. In cases where the article of transport itself has been lost or damaged, that article of transport, if not owned or otherwise supplied by the carrier, is considered one separate shipping unit.

3 In the event of loss due to delay in delivery, the carrier's liability shall not exceed the amount of the freight. However, the aggregate liability under paragraph 1 and the first sentence of the present paragraph shall not exceed the limitation which would be established under paragraph 1 for total loss of the goods with respect to which such liability was incurred.

4 The maximum limits of liability mentioned in paragraph 1 do not apply:

(a) where the nature and higher value of the goods or articles of transport have been expressly specified in the transport document and the carrier has not refuted those specifications, or

(b) where the parties have expressly agreed to higher maximum limits of liability.

5 The aggregate of the amounts of compensation recoverable from the carrier, the actual carrier and their servants and agents for the same loss shall not exceed overall the limits of liability provided for in this article.

Article 21 Loss of right to limit liability

1 The carrier or the actual carrier is not entitled to the exonerations and limits of liability provided for in this Convention or in the contract of carriage if it is proved that he himself caused the damage by an act or omission, either with the intent to cause such damage, or recklessly and with the knowledge that such damage would probably result.

2 Similarly, the servants and agents acting on behalf of the carrier or the actual carrier are not entitled to the exonerations and limits of liability provided for in this Convention or in the contract of carriage, if it is proved that they caused the damage in the manner described in paragraph 1.

Article 22 Application of the exonerations and limits of liability

The exonerations and limits of liability provided for in this Convention or in the contract of carriage apply in any action in respect of loss or damage to or delay in delivery of the goods covered by the contract of carriage, whether the action is founded in contract, in tort or on some other legal ground.

Article 23 Notice of damage

1 The acceptance without reservation of the goods by the consignee is prima facie evidence of the delivery by the carrier of the goods in the same condition and quantity as when they were handed over to him for carriage.

2 The carrier and the consignee may require an inspection of the condition and quantity of the goods on delivery in the presence of the two parties.

3 Where the loss or damage to the goods is apparent, any reservation on the part of the consignee must be formulated in writing specifying the general nature of the damage, no later than the time of delivery, unless the consignee and the carrier have jointly checked the condition of the goods.

4 Where the loss or damage to the goods is not apparent, any reservation on the part of the consignee must be notified in writing specifying the general nature of the damage, no later than 7 consecutive days from the time of delivery; in such case, the injured party shall show that the damage was caused while the goods were in the charge of the carrier.

5 No compensation shall be payable for damage resulting from delay in delivery except when the consignee can prove that he gave notice of the delay to the carrier within 21 consecutive days following delivery of the goods and that this notice reached the carrier.

Article 24 Limitation of actions

1 All actions arising out of a contract governed by this Convention shall be time-barred after one year commencing from the day when the goods were, or should have been, delivered to the consignee. The day on which the limitation period commences is not included in the period.

2 The person against whom an action is instituted may at any time during the limitation period extend that period by a declaration in writing to the injured party. This period may be further extended by one or more further declarations.

3 The suspension and interruption of the limitation period are governed by the law of the State applicable to the contract of carriage. The filing of a claim in proceedings to apportion limited liability for all claims arising from an event having led to damage shall interrupt the limitation.

4 Any action for indemnity by a person held liable under this Convention may be instituted even after the expiry of the limitation period provided for in paragraphs 1 and 2 of the present article, if proceedings are instituted within a period of 90 days commencing from the day on which the person instituting the action has settled the claim or has been served with process, or if proceedings are instituted within a longer period as provided by the law of the State where proceedings are instituted.

5 A right of action which has become barred by lapse of time may not be exercised by way of counter-claim or set-off.

Article 25 Nullity of contractual stipulations

1 Any contractual stipulation intended to exclude or to limit or, subject to the provisions of article 20, paragraph 4, to increase the liability, within the meaning of this Convention, of the carrier, the actual carrier or their servants or agents, to shift the burden of proof or to reduce the periods for claims or limitations referred to in articles 23 and 24 shall be null and void. Any stipulation assigning a benefit of insurance of the goods in favour of the carrier is also null and void.

2 Notwithstanding the provisions of paragraph 1 of the present article and without prejudice to article 21, contractual stipulations shall be authorized specifying that the carrier or the actual carrier is not liable for losses arising from:

(a) an act or omission by the master of the vessel, the pilot or any other person in the service of the vessel, pusher or tower during navigation or in the formation or dissolution of a pushed or towed convoy, provided that the carrier complied with the obligations set out for the crew in article 3, paragraph 3, unless the act or omission results from an intention to cause damage or from reckless conduct with the knowledge that such damage would probably result;

(b) fire or an explosion on board the vessel, where it is not possible to prove that the fire or explosion resulted from a fault of the carrier or the actual carrier or their servants or agents or a defect of the vessel;

(c) the defects existing prior to the voyage of his vessel or of a rented or chartered vessel if he can prove that such defects could not have been detected prior to the start of the voyage despite due diligence.

Article 26 General average

Nothing in this Convention shall prevent the application of provisions in the contract of carriage or national law regarding the calculation of the amount of damages and contributions payable in the event of general average.

Article 27 Other applicable provisions and nuclear damage

1 This Convention does not modify the rights or duties of the carrier provided for in international conventions or national law relating to the limitation of liability of owners of inland navigation or maritime vessels.

2 The carrier shall be relieved of liability under this Convention for damage caused by a nuclear incident if the operator of a nuclear installation or other authorized person is liable for such damage pursuant to the laws and regulations of a State governing liability in the field of nuclear energy.

Article 28 Unit of account

The unit of account referred to in article 20 of this Convention is the Special Drawing Right as defined by the International Monetary Fund. The amounts mentioned in article 20 are to be converted into the national currency of a State according to the value of such currency at the date of judgment or the date agreed upon by the parties. The value, in terms of the Special Drawing Rights, of a national currency of a Contracting State is to be calculated in accordance with the method of evaluation applied by the International Monetary Fund in effect at the date in question for its operations and transactions.

Article 29 Additional national provisions

1 In cases not provided for in this Convention, the contract of carriage is governed by the law of the State agreed by the Parties.

2 In the absence of such agreement, the law of the State with which the contract of carriage is most closely connected is to be applied.

3 It is to be presumed that the contract of carriage is most closely connected with the State in which the principal place of business of the carrier is located at the time when the contract was concluded, if the port of loading or the place where the goods are taken over, or the port of discharge or the place of delivery or the shipper's principal place of business is also located in that State. Where the carrier has no place of business on land and concludes the contract of carriage on board his vessel, it is to be presumed that the contract is most closely connected with the State in which the vessel is registered or whose flag it flies, if the port of loading or the place where the goods are taken over, or the port of discharge or the place of delivery or the shipper's principal place of business is also located in that State.

4 The law of the State where the goods are located governs the real guarantee granted to the carrier for claims set out in article 10, paragraph 1.

Article 30 Carriage by way of specific inland waterways

1 Each State may, at the lime of signing this Convention or of ratification, acceptance, approval or accession, declare that it will not apply this Convention to contracts relating to carriage by way of specific inland waterways situated on its territory and to which international rules of navigation do not apply and which do not constitute a link between such international waterways. However, such a declaration may not mention all main waterways of that State.

2 Where the purpose of the contract of carriage is the carriage of goods without transshipment both on waterways not mentioned in the declaration referred to in paragraph 1 of this article and on waterways mentioned in this declaration, this Convention equally applies to this contract, unless the distance to be travelled on the latter waterways is the longer.

3 When a declaration has been made according to paragraph 1, any other Contracting State may declare that it will not apply either the provisions of this Convention to the contracts referred to in this declaration. The declaration made in accordance with the present paragraph shall take effect at the time of entry into force of the Convention for the State which has made a

declaration according to paragraph 1, but at the earliest at the time of entry into force of the Convention for the State which has made a declaration according to the present paragraph.

4 The declarations referred to in paragraphs 1 and 3 of this article may be withdrawn in whole or in part, at any time, by notification to the depositary to that effect, indicating the date on which they shall cease to have effect. The withdrawal of these declarations shall not have any effect on contracts already concluded.

Article 31 National transport or transport free of charge

Each State may, at the time of the signature of this Convention, of its ratification, its approval, its acceptance, its accession thereto or at any time thereafter, declare that it will also apply this Convention:

(a) to contracts of carriage according to which the port of loading or the place of taking over and the port of discharge or the place of delivery are located in its own territory;
(b) by derogation from article 1, paragraph 1, to carriage free of charge.

Article 32 Regional provisions concerning liability

1 Each State may, at the time of signature of this Convention, or of its ratification, its approval, its acceptance, its accession thereto or at any time thereafter, declare that in respect of the carriage of goods between ports of loading or places where goods are taken over and ports of discharge or places of delivery, of which either both are situated on its own territory or one is situated on its own territory and the other on the territory of a State which has made the same declaration, the carrier shall not be liable for damage caused by an act or omission by the master of the vessel, pilot or any other person in the service of the vessel, pusher or tower during navigation or during the formation of a pushed or towed convoy, provided that the carrier complied with the obligations set out for the crew in article 3, paragraph 3, unless the act or omission results from an intention to cause damage or from reckless conduct with the knowledge that such damage would probably result.

2 The provision concerning liability referred to in paragraph 1 shall enter into force between two Contracting States when this Convention enters into force in the second State which has made the same declaration. If a State has made this declaration following the entry into force of the Convention for that State, the provision concerning liability referred to in paragraph 1 shall enter into force on the first day of the month following a period of three months as from the notification of the declaration to the depositary. The provision concerning liability shall be applicable only to contracts of carriage signed after its entry into force.

3 A declaration made in accordance with paragraph 1 may be withdrawn at any time by notification to the depositary. In the event of withdrawal, the

provisions concerning liability referred to in paragraph 1 shall cease to have effect on the first day of the month following the notification or at a subsequent time indicated in the notification. The withdrawal shall not apply to contracts of carriage signed before the provisions concerning liability have ceased to have effect.

Article 33 Signature, ratification, acceptance, approval, accession

1 This Convention shall be open for signature by all States for one year at the headquarters of the depositary. The period for signature shall start on the day when the depositary states that all authentic texts of this Convention are available.

2 States may become Parties to this Convention:

(a) by signature without reservation as to ratification, acceptance or approval;
(b) by signature subject to ratification, acceptance or approval, followed by ratification, acceptance or approval;
(c) by accession after the deadline set for signature.

3 Instruments of ratification, acceptance, approval or accession shall be deposited with the depositary.

Article 34 Entry into force

1 This Convention shall enter into force on the first day of the month following the expiration of a period of three months as from the date on which five States have signed this Convention without any reservation as to ratification, acceptance or approval or have deposited their instruments of ratification, acceptance, approval or accession with the depositary.

2 For each State which signs this Convention without any reservation as to ratification, acceptance or approval, or deposits the instruments of ratification, acceptance, approval or accession with the depositary after the entry into force of this Convention, the same shall enter into force on the first day of the month following the expiration of a period of three months as from the date of signing without any reservation as to ratification, acceptance or approval, or the deposit of the instruments of ratification, acceptance, approval or accession with the depositary.

Article 35 Denunciation

1 This Convention may be denounced by a State Party on the expiration of a period of one year following the date on which it entered into force for that State.

2 Notification of denunciation shall be deposited with the depositary.

3 The denunciation shall take effect on the first day of the month following the expiration of a period of one year as from the date of deposit of the notification of denunciation or after a longer period referred to in the notification of denunciation.

Article 36 Review and amendment

At the request of not less than one third of the Contracting States to this Convention, the depositary shall convene a conference of the Contracting States for revising or amending it.

Article 37 Revision of the amounts for limitation of liability and unit of account

1 Notwithstanding the provisions of article 36, when a revision of the amount specified in article 20, paragraph 1, or the substitution of the unit defined in article 28 by another unit is proposed, the depositary shall, when not less than one fourth of the States Parties to this Convention so request, submit the proposal to all members of the United Nations Economic Commission for Europe, the Central Commission for the Navigation of the Rhine and the Danube Commission and to all Contracting States and shall convene a conference for the sole purpose of altering the amount specified in article 20, paragraph 1, or of substituting the unit defined in article 28 by another unit.

2 The conference shall be convened at the earliest six months after the day on which the proposal was transmitted.

3 All Contracting States to this Convention are entitled to participate in the conference, whether or not they are members of the organizations referred to in paragraph 1.

4 The amendments shall be adopted by a majority of two thirds of the Contracting States to the Convention represented at the conference and taking part in the vote, provided that not less than one half of the Contracting States to this Convention are represented when the vote is taken.

5 During the consultation concerning the amendment of the amount specified in article 20, paragraph 1, the conference shall take account of the lessons drawn from the events having led to damage and in particular the amount of damage resulting therefrom, changes in monetary values and the effect of the proposed amendment on the cost of insurance.

6 (a) The amendment of the amount in accordance with this article may take effect at the earliest five years after the day on which this Convention was opened for signature and at the earliest five years after the day on which an amendment made previously in accordance with this article entered into force.

(b) An amount may not be so increased as to exceed the amount of the maximum limits of liability specified by this Convention, increased by six per cent per annum, calculated according to the principle of compound interest as from the day on which this Convention was opened for signature.

(c) An amount may not be so increased as to exceed the triple of the maximum limits of liability specified by this Convention.

7 The depositary shall notify all Contracting States of any amendment adopted in accordance with paragraph 4. The amendment is deemed to have been accepted after a period of eighteen months following the day of notification, unless during such period not less than one fourth of the States which were Contracting States at the time of the decision concerning the amendment have informed the depositary that they will not accept that amendment; in such case, the amendment is rejected and does not enter into force.

8 An amendment which is deemed to have been accepted in accordance with paragraph 7 shall enter into force eighteen months after its acceptance.

9 All Contracting States are bound by the amendment unless they denounce this Convention in accordance with article 35 not later than six months before the amendment enters into force. The denunciation takes effect when the amendment enters into force.

10 When an amendment has been adopted but the scheduled eighteen-month period for acceptance has not elapsed, a State which becomes a Contracting State during that period is bound by the amendment if it enters into force. A State which becomes a Contracting State after that period is bound by an amendment accepted in accordance with paragraph 7. In the cases cited in the present paragraph, a State is bound by an amendment as soon as it enters into force or as soon as this Convention enters into force for that State if this takes place subsequently.

Article 38 Depositary

1 This Convention shall be deposited with the Government of the Republic of Hungary.

2 The depositary shall:

(a) communicate to all States which participated in the Diplomatic Conference for the Adoption of the Budapest Convention on the Contract for the Carriage of Goods by Inland Waterway, for checking, the present Convention in the official language version which was not available at the time of the Conference;

(b) inform all States referred to under subparagraph (a) above of any proposal for the amendment of the text communicated in accordance with subparagraph (a) above;

(c) establish the date on which all official language versions of this Convention have been brought into conformity with each other and are to be considered authentic;

(d) communicate to all States referred to in subparagraph (a) above the date established in accordance with subparagraph (c) above;

(e) communicate to all States which were invited to the Diplomatic Conference for the Adoption of the Budapest Convention on the Contract for the Carriage of Goods by Inland Waterway and to those which have signed this Convention or acceded thereto, certified true copies of this Convention;

(f) inform all States which have signed this Convention or acceded to it:

   (i) of any new signature, notification or declaration made, indicating the date of the signature, notification or declaration;
   (ii) of the date of entry into force of this Convention;
   (iii) of any denunciation of this Convention and of the date on which such denunciation is to take effect;
   (iv) of any amendment adopted in accordance with articles 36 and 37 of this Convention and of the date of entry into force of such amendment;
   (v) of any communication required under a provision of this Convention.

3 After the entry into force of this Convention, the depositary shall transmit to the Secretariat of the United Nations a certified true copy of this Convention for registration and publication, in accordance with Article 102 of the Charter of the United Nations.

Index